The Ecclesiology of Thomas F. Torrance

Praise for *The Ecclesiology of Thomas F. Torrance: Koinōnia and the Church*

"As appreciation of the work of Thomas F. Torrance continues to grow, so too will the value of careful and thorough studies of the broad scope and impressive coherence of his theological vision. Kate Tyler here provides such a study. She explores Torrance's understanding of the church, a community called into being by the Triune God and commissioned to participate in the loving service to the world offered by Jesus Christ. Readers will find here a rich account of the church's true nature and calling."—**Murray Rae, University of Otago**

"Kate Tyler engages partly in a theological autobiography of Thomas Torrance, one of the twentieth century's most important theologians, but more importantly she seeks to demonstrate Torrance's unique trinitarian approach to ecclesiology and how Torrance can be a resource for renewing the concept of communion, ecumenism, and ecclesial life today. Well-written, insightful, and useful for anyone interested in Torrancian theology or current issues in ecclesiology today."—**Michael F. Bird, Ridley College**

"This excellent new addition to Torrance scholarship from Kate Tyler complements the work of Lee, Habets, Maclean, Eugenio, Ziegler, and others by examining the theology of Torrance from yet another angle. Where other theologians might stand accused of reading their preferred ecclesiology into the doctrine of the Trinity, Tyler demonstrates the rigor with which Torrance endeavors to work from the doctrine of the Trinity to ecclesiology. This is then extended into the implications for the life and mission of the Church today. This scholarly assessment of Torrance's work is an important one not only to students of Torrance but for ecclesiology and mission studies today."—**Thomas A. Noble, president, T. F. Torrance Theological Fellowship**

The Ecclesiology of Thomas F. Torrance

Koinōnia *and the Church*

Kate Tyler

LEXINGTON BOOKS/FORTRESS ACADEMIC
Lanham • Boulder • New York • London

Published by Lexington Books/Fortress Academic
Lexington Books is an imprint of The Rowman & Littlefield Publishing Group, Inc.
4501 Forbes Boulevard, Suite 200, Lanham, Maryland 20706
www.rowman.com

6 Tinworth Street, London SE11 5AL

British Library Cataloguing in Publication Information Available

Library of Congress Cataloging-in-Publication Data Available

ISBN 978-1-9787-0165-6 (cloth : alk. paper)
ISBN 978-1-9787-0166-3 (electronic)

∞™ The paper used in this publication meets the minimum requirements of American National Standard for Information Sciences Permanence of Paper for Printed Library Materials, ANSI/NISO Z39.48-1992.

Contents

Permissions

Quotations from Thomas F. Torrance, *Royal Priesthood* (1955); Thomas F. Torrance, *The Trinitarian Faith* (1993); and Thomas F. Torrance, *The Christian Doctrine of God* (1996) are used with permission of T & T Clark.

Quotations from Thomas F. Torrance, *Atonement* (2009) are used with permission of InterVarsity Press and Paternoster Press.

Quotations from Thomas F. Torrance, *Theology in Reconciliation* (1996); Thomas F. Torrance, *Theology in Reconstruction* (1996); Thomas F. Torrance, *Conflict and Agreement in the Church* (1996); Thomas F. Torrance, *Reality and Evangelical Theology* (2003); and Thomas F. Torrance, *Gospel, Church and Ministry* (2012) are used with permission of Wipf and Stock.

Quotations from documents in boxes 10, 20, 22, 29, and 96 of the Thomas F. Torrance Manuscript Collection are used with permission of Princeton Theological Seminary.

Introduction

The study of ecclesiology involves a wide range of questions, and yet the most central question, "What is the Church?" can only be answered on the basis of prior assumptions. For Thomas F. Torrance, the starting point of all ecclesiology is the doctrine of God—ecclesiology done from above rather than below. Instead of focusing on the Church as institution wherein attention is naturally more drawn to institutional aspects such as form, organization, and "how things are done," Torrance emphasizes that the Church must be understood as an empirical community in space and time that is ultimately shaped by the Triune God who is a *perichoretic* communion of the three divine persons. The Church is far more than a mere human institution for it is a divine gift that gathers humanity into union and communion with the living God. Even though the Church has an empirical existence, its historical actuality is subordinate to its relation to the divine being of Father, Son, and Holy Spirit.

ECCLESIOLOGICAL TRAJECTORIES

In the twentieth century, ecclesiology emerged as a key topic of theological dialogue. This theological renewal was pragmatically oriented, occasioned by a growing awareness of the Church's calling to participate in God's mission in ways appropriate to its context and faithful to divine revelation. Diverse approaches to ecclesiology resulted, along with different types of categorization. Alister McGrath's analysis divides Christocentric ecclesial understandings into three streams: the sacramental presence of Christ, the presence of Christ through the Word, and the presence of Christ through the Spirit. Alternatively, McGrath highlights three other categories of twentieth-century ecclesiology: the Church as communion, the Church as the people of God, and the Church as a charismatic community.[1]

In another categorical vein, Cheryl Peterson identifies the three ecclesiological paradigms of the twentieth century as word-event, communion, and *missio dei*. Her premise is that the Church should not begin by asking "What shall the Church do?" but rather "Who is the Church?" Peterson argues that before the Church can properly face the challenges of ecclesial life in the twenty-first century, especially declining numbers in mainline denominations, it must first come to terms with its theological identity crisis, which it can only do by returning to the narrative theology of the Book of Acts.[2] Bryan Stone approaches the issue of theological identity in terms of the Church's external relations, suggesting that in the twentieth century the Church found itself "needing to radically re-negotiate its relationship to nations, culture, and empires in an increasingly post-Christendom world."[3] On one hand, there was a significant rise in missionary and ecumenical concerns, while, on the other, globalization forced the Church to reevaluate both its internal and external relationships.[4] These different pressures all forced the Church to confront its state of division and to engage in significant theological reflection. This is demonstrated by McGrath's identification of the ecumenical movement and Vatican II as the two major ecclesiological forces of the twentieth century.[5]

These examples, while far from exhaustive, represent significant diversity in theological and ecclesiological dialogue. However, the centrality of the doctrine of the Trinity for ecclesiology across all major movements in the twentieth century is well documented; as Ralph Del Colle notes, "the explicit thematization of the church in a trinitarian register would await the significant ecumenical developments of the twentieth century, a century that has resulted in a near consensus that the nature of church life and order is a matter of *communio* or *koinonia*."[6] The extremes of this are noted by Grenz and Olson, who suggest that theology in the twentieth century can be viewed as a seesaw between God's transcendence and God's immanence; when we find the correct balance, we realize that "the God who addresses us from beyond—from the then-and-there—is the God who is with us in the present—in the here-and-now."[7]

The recentralization of the doctrine of the Trinity and the call for a more theological approach to ecclesiology are the background to the material presented in our exploration of Torrance's work. His ecclesiology is proclaimed in this "trinitarian register." Although Torrance's trinitarian approach to ecclesiology is not unique, an in-depth exploration of his work still has much to offer.

METHODOLOGY

The challenge of studying Thomas F. Torrance is well noted given that he never published a systematic theology. Colyer suggests that the density and lack of systemization of Torrance's theology means that to grasp Torrance's integrative thought, or "architectonic structure," one needs to work their way through the majority of his published corpus.[8] This is a formidable task that one cannot go over, under, or around but must go through. Familiarity with Torrance's wider corpus allows the reader to grasp the interconnections between the various aspects of his work and to draw conclusions that are faithful to Torrance's intentions.

The methodology is one of constructive analysis involving a critical appreciation of Torrance's work and then exploring how further dialogue with Torrance's work can be fruitfully undertaken. Shaped by Torrance's conviction that the direction of ecclesiological inquiry must proceed from above rather than below, this project advances an understanding that the doctrine of the Church is not primarily derived from observable historical phenomena or interpersonal relationships but has the doctrine of the Holy Trinity as its ultimate reference. It is notable that no one has explored the constitutive relationship between these two foci of Torrance's work, particularly given how explicit he is about this relationship. As he explains the correlation,

> The doctrine of the Trinity belongs to the very heart of saving faith where it constitutes the inner shape of Christian worship and the dynamic grammar of Christian theology: it expresses the essential and distinctively Christian understanding of God by which we live, and which is of crucial significance for the evangelical mission of the Church as well.[9]

OVERVIEW OF CONTENT

This book is structured in two sections. In the first section, we will develop the theological relationship between the Trinity and the Church, focusing on the theological foundations of Torrance's ecclesiology and emphasizing that the doctrine of the Trinity has precedence over ecclesiology—or if described from the other direction, ecclesiology requires a "backward reference" to the Trinity. While the doctrine of the Church is the immediate object of our consideration, we cannot begin by considering the Church in itself as a spatiotemporal institution but rather must look "through the Church" to find its dimension of depth, which is found in the Holy Trinity.[10] Beginning with some biographical and contextual material, we will pay attention to the Trinity, to Torrance's vision of a diachronic ecclesiology, and to the integration of the doctrine of the Trinity and the doctrine of the Church through the motif of *koinōnia*.[11]

In the second section, we will explore the implications of this trinitarian approach to ecclesiology for Torrance's understanding of Church order, the notes of the Church, and the ministry of the Word and sacraments in the Church. The doctrine of reconciliation will be clearly tied to the Church's understanding of missions and ecumenism in the time between Christ's two advents. This study of Torrance's ecclesiology will be situated in a wider theological dialogue by comparing his work with that of Kathryn Tanner, Jürgen Moltmann, and John Zizioulas.

LITERARY CONTEXT

During any close engagement with Torrance's work, almost every major doctrine will need to be considered given the interwoven complexity of theological themes throughout his work. Although secondary literature on Torrance has dealt with his approach to the doctrine of the Trinity and the doctrine of the Church, usually in a single chapter as part of a broader discussion, there has not yet been a comprehensive, full-length engagement with the relationship between Trinity and ecclesiology in Torrance's thought.

Torrance's theological output can largely be divided into two streams, and although there is inevitably some overlap between the two, secondary works can be loosely categorized into those that focus on his scientific-epistemological work or those that focus on his dogmatic content. We will not engage Torrance's scientific-epistemological work in and of itself except to consider how Torrance's scientific approach to theology is shaped by and in return shapes his doctrine of the Holy Trinity.

We may familiarize ourselves with the general contours of the landscape by briefly mentioning five works in the dogmatic stream that contain material complementary to our consideration of Torrance's trinitarian ecclesiology.

Kye Won Lee's work *Living in Union with Christ: The Practical Theology of Thomas F. Torrance* is a systematic analysis in which Won Lee argues that "union with Christ" is the unifying theme of Torrance's work. He focuses on how Torrance's theology can be defined according to the Christological pattern, paying particular attention to ecclesiology and sacramentology.[12] Won Lee explores Torrance's thought under the three categories of epistemological union, ontological union, and sacramental or eschatological union. The third category is comprised of three chapters—"Union with Christ," "The Relation Between the Church and Christ," and "The Church as the Sphere of Union with Christ"—in which Won Lee discusses many aspects of Torrance's ecclesiology. However, Won Lee approaches ecclesiology through the primary framework of union with Christ rather than the doctrine of the Trinity. His thesis demonstrates that Torrance draws upon both Christology and the doctrine of the Trinity to develop his ecclesiology but argues for the preeminence of the doctrine of the Trinity when considering the order of doctrines.

Myk Habets's work *Theosis in the Theology of Thomas Torrance* must also be considered. Habets contends that the patristic concept of *theosis* is determinative for Torrance's theology—even more so than the theme of union with Christ.[13] It is proposed that the doctrine of *theosis* illuminates Torrance's incarnational theory of the atonement, enabling him to embrace his own Reformed tradition while building bridges to both Eastern and Western theology.[14] Of particular interest is Habets's chapter on Torrance's "pneumatological-ecclesiology" in which Habets argues that it is primarily through pneumatology undergirded by Christology and the Trinity that the Church is formed as the individual believer participates in Christ. Habets's material includes reflections on the nature of *koinōnia* and the sacraments but is once again a much briefer overview than this study will offer.

Another work is Stanley MacLean's *Resurrection, Apocalypse and the Kingdom of Christ: The Eschatology of Thomas F. Torrance*. Maclean outlines the "eschatological orientation" of Torrance's early theology, drawing on sermons delivered at Alyth and Beechgrove and on Torrance's involvement in the World Council of Churches Faith and Order Commission between 1948 and 1963.[15] MacLean shows how Torrance's emphasis on the centrality of eschatology for ecclesiology is unique for his day, focusing on Torrance's argument that an eschatological orientation prevents the Church from conforming to the "old and crumbling" age because through union with Christ it participates in the new age.[16] MacLean's work offers some helpful insights in regard to Torrance's doctrine of the Church "between the times"; however, his exclusive focus on Torrance's early work results in a lack of engagement with Torrance's trinitarian theology—no mention is made at all of *The Trinitarian Faith* or *The Christian Doctrine of God*. MacLean therefore argues that Torrance's eschatology is "christologically over-determined," which results in such a literal understanding of the Church as the body of Christ that Torrance neglects the Holy Spirit.[17] This results in a thesis that is excellent in what it sets out to accomplish but that falls short of developing a comprehensive account of Torrance's mature ecclesiology.

Another complementary work is Dick Eugenio's *Communion with the Triune God: The Trinitarian Soteriology of T. F. Torrance*. Eugenio makes excellent use of Torrance's unpublished sermons to connect Torrance's soteriological doctrine of the Trinity and trinitarian soteriology,[18] arguing that the *telos* of salvation is humanity's participation in the triune life. Eugenio devotes a chapter to the distinct-but-perichoretic agency of each of the triune persons, which are then integrated in a final chapter where he considers the relations of God *in se* and how humanity shares in "the primordial community of love."[19] Eugenio's work develops the theme of triune communion and the Church's "enabled *perichoretic participation* in the triune life, love and communion"[20] in a way that is similar to the theological foundations we will begin to unpack shortly. However, Eugenio does not consider the structure or forms that comprise the temporal existence of the Church in between the two advents of Christ in much detail.

Finally, Geordie Ziegler's *Trinitarian Grace and Participation: An Entry into the Theological Thought of Thomas F. Torrance* contains a chapter considering Torrance's ecclesiology in relation to his doctrine of grace. Ziegler attends to Torrance's preference for the language of the body of Christ; the nature of order in the Church as constituted by its ontological relation to Christ; the Church as "place"; and the relationship between the ministry of the Church and the ministry of Christ. He concludes by focusing on the Word and sacrament in their relation to a doctrine of grace.[21]

It is worth observing that the amount of secondary literature on T. F. Torrance has burgeoned to a point where one could almost begin significant comparative analysis of the secondary material in its own right. This is not the intent of this study; Torrance's work will be the primary source from which we draw, and secondary material will be used to deepen understanding or to acknowledge a difference of interpretive opinion. It is also worth noting the relative lack of engagement with Torrance's ecclesiology in volumes that survey both trinitarian theology and ecclesiology of the twentieth century. It is hoped that this work will generate productive conversations, showing that T. F. Torrance's work has great potential for ongoing ecclesiological dialogue.

STYLISTIC NOTES

Readers will note that Torrance's use of gendered terms has been retained in direct quotations reflecting his intention to use "man" or "men" as they were used "in the Bible, without any intention of excluding or being derogatory of the feminine sex."[22] In the same way, masculine pronouns are used with reference to the Triune God, keeping with Torrance's own stylistic preference, while simultaneously acknowledging the importance of his insistence that "gender belongs only to the creaturely world and may not be read back into God."[23] In reference to the Church, feminine pronouns have been used when directly quoting Torrance but otherwise neutral pronouns are used.

Where unpublished sources have been used from the T. F. Torrance Special Collection, typos occasionally appear in typewritten material. These have been silently corrected for clarity. Most mistakes in the originals were simple typographical errors, but where there is any uncertainty, the editing has been noted. There is also inconsistency within Torrance's published material in the capitalization of theological terms. In this book these terms have generally not been capitalized except in direct quotes. One notable exception is the capitalization of "Church" to refer to the one Church that is grounded in the Holy Trinity for the theological reason that there is only one Church of which Christ is the head. A final inconsistency exists in Torrance's use of Greek and Hebrew words or their transliteration. In the discussion that follows, these words have been all been transliterated.

During the course of my research, I was very appreciative of the approach taken by Tapio Luoma, another Torrance scholar, who comments upon the difference between scholarly criticism that affirms "I know better!" and appreciative criticism that concedes "I wish I knew better!"[24] It is in the spirit of the latter that this work is offered in the hope that it will be of service to the Church of the Triune God.

NOTES

1. Alister McGrath, *Christian Theology: An Introduction* (Oxford: Wiley-Blackwell, 2011), 385–90.

2. Cheryl M. Peterson, *Who Is the Church? Ecclesiology for the 21st Century* (Minneapolis, MN: Fortress Press, 2013), 4.

3. Bryan P. Stone, *A Reader in Ecclesiology* (Surrey, UK: Ashgate, 2012), 145.

4. Ibid., 145–46.

5. McGrath, *Christian Theology*, 385. It can be argued that Vatican II is really part of the ecumenical movement, however it was only after Vatican II that the Roman Catholic Church found that many of the barriers that had inhibited its participation in ecumenical dialogue had been removed.

6. Ralph Del Colle, "The Church," in *The Oxford Handbook of Systematic Theology*, ed. Kathryn Tanner, John Webster, and Iain Torrance, 253 (New York: Oxford University Press, 2007).

7. Stanley J. Grenz and Roger E. Olson, *20th-Century Theology: God & the World in a Transitional Age* (Downers Grove, IL: InterVarsity Press, 1992), 315.

8. Elmer M. Colyer, *How to Read T. F. Torrance: Understanding His Trinitarian & Scientific Theology* (Downers Grove, IL: InterVarsity Press, 2001), 16.

9. Thomas F. Torrance, *The Christian Doctrine of God: One Being Three Persons* (Edinburgh: T&T Clark, 1996), 10.

10. Thomas F. Torrance, *Preaching Christ Today: The Gospel and Scientific Thinking* (Grand Rapids, MI: Eerdmans, 1994), 57.

11. For consistency, original transliteration has been left within quotes, but where transliteration is provided, it follows *koinōnia* rather than *koinonia.*

12. Kye Won Lee, *Living in Union with Christ: The Practical Theology of Thomas F. Torrance* (New York: Peter Lang, 2003), 8.

13. Myk Habets, *Theosis in the Theology of Thomas Torrance* (Surrey, UK: Ashgate, 2009), 1.

14. Ibid., 168, 97.

15. Stanley S. MacLean, *Resurrection, Apocalypse, and the Kingdom of Christ*, Princeton Theological Monograph Series (Eugene, OR: Pickwick Publications, 2012), 190.

16. Ibid., 192.

17. Ibid., 199.

18. Dick O. Eugenio, *Communion with the Triune God: The Trinitarian Soteriology of T. F. Torrance* (Eugene, OR: Pickwick Publications, 2014), xx.

19. Ibid., 156.

20. Ibid., 204.

21. Geordie Ziegler, *Trinitarian Grace and Participation: An Entry into the Theological Thought of Thomas F. Torrance* (Minneapolis, MN: Fortress Press, 2017) , 185–239.

22. Thomas F. Torrance, *The Doctrine of Jesus Christ* (Eugene, OR: Wipf & Stock, 2002), iii.

23. Torrance, *Christian Doctrine of God*, xii.

24. Tapio Luoma, *Incarnation and Physics: Natural Science in the Theology of Thomas F. Torrance* (Oxford: Oxford University Press, 2002), 13.

Chapter One

Torrance's Approach to Theology

An introduction to the theology of Thomas Torrance should begin with a biographical introduction to his life. Our purpose is to understand how his upbringing strongly shaped his sense of a theological career as a missionary calling. This will lead us to assessing Torrance's theological contribution, which will be further aided by referencing two key methodologies that run through everything he writes: his scientific approach to the theological task and the inseparability of Christology and the doctrine of the Trinity. Both the biographical background and these methodological considerations will aid us in reading Torrance's work.

A BRIEF BIOGRAPHICAL SUMMARY

Recognized as one of the most significant English-language theologians of the twentieth century by his biographers,[1] Thomas Forsyth Torrance was both pastor and professor, exemplified by Colyer's description of him as "a scholar's scholar, a true theological heavy-weight"[2] and yet "a humble and godly disciple of Jesus Christ, deeply committed to the gospel and the church, and deserving of the appellation *evangelical*."[3] Behind Torrance's prodigious number of publications lies a deep commitment to the Triune God and to God's people, a commitment highlighted in this chapter through use of Torrance's unpublished autobiographical material.[4]

FAMILY INFLUENCE

Thomas Torrance was born in the mission field in China, where he remained until he was fourteen. When the Torrance family was forced to return to

Scotland in 1928 because of severe persecution of missionaries, Torrance experienced the cost of proclaiming the Gospel early in his life. He remained with his siblings and his mother in Scotland to continue his education while his father returned to China for a further seven years. Torrance considered his mother "the predominant theological force in our home," whose "imprint upon my spiritual and theological development was incisive, profound and indelible."[5] The formative influence of these early years on his later evangelistic and ecumenical activity is seen in Torrance's autobiographical reflection:

> I was deeply conscious of the task to which my parents had been called by God to preach the Gospel to heathen people and win them for Christ. This orientation to mission was built into the fabric of my mind, and has never faded—by its essential nature Christian theology has always had for me an evangelistic thrust. My father was a Presbyterian and my mother an Anglican, which imparted to my thinking a deeply ingrained blend of conviction that has always remained.[6]

Torrance also attributes his strong personal faith to the influence of his parents, saying, "My belief in God was very vivid and strong, and always has been, due, I know, to the way in which we were brought up by our parents, and the sense of Christian mission that pervaded their lives and our home."[7] He further remarks,

> Belief in God was so natural that I could no more doubt the existence of God than the existence of my parents or the world around me. I cannot remember ever having had any doubts about God. Moreover, as long as I can recall my religious outlook was essentially biblical and evangelical, and indeed evangelistic.[8]

Education

Torrance completed a bachelor of arts in classics at the University of Edinburgh before commencing theological studies at New College—also part of the University of Edinburgh—with the intent of preparing for missionary service in Tibet.[9] As one of the leading Scottish programs in theology, New College focused on not just academic success but on developing well-rounded ministers who understood the demands of the call to preach Christ. Torrance reflects on how this was driven home to him at the start of his time at New College:

> One of the first things I had to do was to write a short essay on "My Call to the Ministry" prescribed to us by the Principal, the Very Rev. Professor Alexander Martin, who was to retire the following year. Each of us had a searching interview with him in which he discussed with us what we had written. He

> made it clear to us that as the centre of divine Revelation Christ must be the centre of all our theological studies, and the centre of Christian life which, in the words of Irenaeus and John Calvin, he spoke of as "union and communion" with Christ.[10]

The theme of participating in the union and communion of the Triune God became a preeminent theme in Torrance's work. Although Torrance did not end up as a foreign missionary—he did return to visit China later in his life—these years at Edinburgh laid solid foundations for his pastoral and theological career.

Among his professors, Hugh Ross Mackintosh warrants particular mention. Torrance often quotes Mackintosh's statement that "a theology which failed to sustain and encourage a missionary or evangelistic attitude was not a theology worthy of the name"[11] in connection with his realization that an academic career as a theologian could allow him to serve God in as full a way as if he had served in foreign missions. Mackintosh was unrelenting in his insistence that all theology had to be applicable, and he taught his students to test doctrine by asking, "Will it preach?" in order to consider how it would be received in the mission field.[12] Mackintosh died shortly before Torrance's final year at New College began, and Torrance was greatly disappointed not to hear his expository lectures on Karl Barth.[13] Torrance reflects at length on the way he was influenced by Mackintosh, and Mackintosh's prescient sense about what the future held for Torrance:

> I made a point of reading all Mackintosh's books and all those of Karl Barth that were then available, and found myself becoming more and more deeply involved in the tide of theological renewal. It had always been my intention to be a missionary, but as I sat at the feet of Mackintosh the calling to engage in a theological ministry in the service of the Gospel began to force itself upon me—little did I realise then what this would lead to. Years later after I had become Moderator of the General Assembly of the Church of Scotland, Dr. Douglas Johnston, who had long been the General Secretary of the Inter-Varsity Fellowship of Christian Unions, wrote to tell me of a conversation between Mackintosh and Robert Wilder at the missionary conference held at New College in 1936. When Wilder spoke to Professor Mackintosh of my devotion to overseas missions, Mackintosh replied that while he was glad I had "all this missionary enthusiasm," he was sure that "I was destined to be a theological professor in this or a similar College, and one day be Moderator of the Church of Scotland"! When I read that I found it to be very humbling, but also very reassuring in view of the fact that I had not been disobedient to God's call in staying at home instead of going overseas. However, even as a professor of theology I have always tried to be a missionary.[14]

These personal reflections highlight an important aspect of Torrance's sense of vocation that should be grasped in order to understand the missional and ecclesiological nature of his theological vision. Torrance viewed his theological work as a distinct calling to serve the mission of the Church[15] and recalls that he "was never able to separate lecturing in my Christian Dogmatics class in New College from showing something of the personal and pastoral thrust and power of the truths of the gospel."[16]

At New College Torrance had become increasingly interested in the theology of Karl Barth despite the opposition of professors like John and Donald Baillie.[17] Upon completion of his studies at New College, Torrance commenced doctoral studies in Basel under Karl Barth. He was chosen to participate in Barth's *Sozietät*, an advanced study group of 12–15 students chosen by examination. Although letters from the time show that Torrance was critical of elements of Barth's teaching, feeling that it lacked a missionary and evangelical emphasis, Torrance would later affirm that Barth's work had a much stronger missionary note than he had originally recognized. He refers to hearing Barth preach a sermon series to the prisoners in Basel Jail in which he laid such an emphasis on the saving love of God that Torrance had to conclude, "Barth was certainly very missionary minded."[18]

After a year in Germany, Torrance spent a year teaching at Auburn Theological Seminary in the United States. Although he would subsequently spend almost a decade in parish and chaplain ministry before returning to New College, this initial year as a faculty member was invaluable for Torrance for as he reflects,

> I myself benefited theologically and spiritually from that year in Auburn, for in having to prepare courses on the whole body of systematic theology, I was forced to think out my own theological convictions very carefully, and find the best way of expressing biblical and theological truth to people living in the modern world. I also came to realise how difficult it is for people, who had not been brought up like myself, really to grasp the significance and face the challenge of the Gospel. I learned an immense amount about people that year. It was with that deepening understanding of the cost of faith and discipleship that I learned something of how to be a theological teacher.[19]

It appears that Torrance developed early in his career as a theologian the "philosophical and theological judgements and attitudes which would stay with him for the rest of his career," working out his theological convictions and not wavering from them.[20] Even though Torrance did not publish his major trinitarian works until late in his career, there is an incipient form of his trinitarian theology consistent with these later publications demonstrated throughout his early publications. The inner consistency of Torrance's work is what allows us to undertake a systematic exploration of his work without needing to engage in a chronological description of the development of his trinitarian thought. This kind of study could make a helpful contribution, as exemplified by Stanley MacLean, but would not make a significant contribution to the exploration of Torrance's trinitarian ecclesiology.[21]

Parish Ministry

After his time at Auburn, Torrance rejected an invitation to teach theology at Princeton University because of the impending war. On his return to Scotland, Torrance wished to enlist as an army chaplain but was unable to do so until he had been ordained for two years. He entered pastoral ministry "in order to bring a serious and solid dose of reality to his academic reflection."[22] Inducted into his first parish at Alyth in early 1940, on the day of his ordination Torrance wrote the words of Jesus in the front of his Bible, "Ye have not chosen me, but I have chosen you, and ordained you, that you should go and bring forth fruit, and that your fruit should remain: that whatsoever you shall ask of the Father in my name, he may give it to you" (John 15:16). He later reflected that these words had remained a "great source of strength" throughout his ministry.[23]

In addition to his preaching twice every Sunday, Torrance's ministerial responsibilities were demanding. He prioritized house-to-house visitation of every member of his parish in Alyth and reckoned this to be the most fruitful aspect of his ministry because this was when the deep significance of the Gospel to meet people's needs became real for him.[24]

The early stages of Torrance's parish ministry reveal a deep conviction that the Church should always be on the move, always reaching outward to gather more people into the community as befits those who have themselves been gathered into union with Jesus Christ. It was at Alyth that Torrance gave an address titled "The Place and Function of the Church in the World."[25] A summary of this from his autobiographical reflection on his parish ministry reveals the fundamental way in which the Church's missionary calling gave impetus to his ministerial calling and his commitment to theological renewal:

> If the Church does recover the New Testament vision, she will see that the great task of the Church is the redemption of the world and not a comfortable life in little, religious churches and communities. The Church simply cannot keep alive unless her eyes are upon the farthest horizons of the world, unless she keeps herself in line with the master-passion and the world outlook of Christ who was the propitiation not for our sins only but for the sins of the world. It is for that reason that mission work does not arise from arrogance in the Christian Church—mission is its cause and its life.[26]

After the requisite two years in ordained ministry,[27] during which time war was never far from his mind,[28] Torrance enlisted as a Church of Scotland "Huts and Canteens" chaplain. His work, which included the running and maintenance of a canteen for the soldiers, allowed him to become much more familiar with the soldiers in his care than normal regimental chaplains could, although Torrance "made a point of never pressing the need for Christian commitment on the troops, for I found that kind of thing was always best if it happened spontaneously."[29] As a chaplain, Torrance remained with the soldiers through warfare so overwhelming that later on there was much that he could not recall with accuracy. However, he notes that "throughout those harrowing days, I found that the influence of a Christian life on the soldiers in the midst of all that terror and carnage was very telling."[30]

It was during his army service that Torrance had the seminal experience that he often relates concerning the identity of being between the Father and the Son.

> When daylight filtered through, I came across a young soldier (Private Philips), scarcely twenty years old, lying mortally wounded on the ground, who clearly had not long to live. As I knelt down and bent over him, he said: "Padre, is God really like Jesus?" I assured him that he was—the only God that there is, the God who had come to us in Jesus, shown his face to us, and poured out his love to us as our Saviour. As I prayed and commended him to the Lord Jesus, he passed away.[31]

Torrance would later reflect, "I found that the fundamental theological questions were the very stuff of the deepest anxieties of the human heart, questions such as 'Is God really like Jesus?'"[32] This experience profoundly shaped Torrance's theology and his recurring insistence that the God we meet in Jesus Christ is no different *in se* than *ad alios*—God is identical in his own triune being to how he meets us in Christ and the Spirit. Although Torrance would go on to write extensive theological treatises on the relationship between the theological and the economic Trinity, this simple anecdote profoundly demonstrates the evangelical significance of the Trinity. It was this type of deeply theological and yet immediately practical thought that strengthened Torrance's sense of his vocation "to be a theologian who could support the missionary and evangelistic work of the church."[33]

Upon his return to Alyth after the war, Torrance resumed normal ministerial duties, completed his doctoral examination in Basel, and married. He was called to Beechgrove Church in Aberdeen in 1947. The transition from a rural to city environment took some adjustment, but Beechgrove offered new opportunities for ministry such as running a Youth Fellowship for students and young professionals.[34] House-to-house visitation remained important, and Torrance found the adage "The spiritual level of the Church outside the home cannot rise above the level of the Church in the home"[35] to be as true in Beechgrove as it was in Alyth. In both parishes, Torrance was especially surprised by the strong reaction of his congregants to the message of justification by faith in which Christ deals not only with our sin but also removes any meritorious basis on which we think we deserve to be saved. This distressed Torrance greatly but also emphasized that one of the greatest challenges to receiving the immense grace of salvation is any individual's deeply ingrained notion of merit based on moral goodness.[36]

An Academic Calling

During his time at Beechgrove, Torrance started the *Scottish Journal of Theology* as a vehicle for the dissemination of Karl Barth's work in the English-speaking world. He maintained an active editorial role. He was also heavily involved with the English-language reception of Barth, translating into English and editing Barth's *Church Dogmatics* alongside Geoffrey W. Bromiley.[37] While there is some debate over whether Torrance should be called a Barthian, we can observe that while Torrance appreciated Barth's theology, he did not hesitate to challenge Barth's theology when he felt it necessary.[38]

In 1950, Torrance left Beechgrove to accept his first academic position at New College as the chair of ecclesiastical history. He held this position for two years until he was appointed to the chair of Christian dogmatics despite opposition from the principal, John Baillie, because of Torrance's pro-Barth tendencies. McGrath reflects, "The outcome of this transfer would prove decisive in terms of Edinburgh's theological profile worldwide. If Baillie determined that profile in the 1940s, Torrance would determine it throughout the 1960s and 1970s."[39] While he was at Edinburgh, Torrance's teaching responsibilities included Christology, soteriology, and the related area of Church, ministry, and sacraments.[40] Due to the bifurcated faculty structure of New College, the doctrine of God fell within the teaching responsibilities of the chair of divinity so that Torrance was unable to teach or write at length on the doctrine of God until after his retirement from New College in 1979. It is a misnomer to suggest that Torrance "retired" in any real sense for he remained very active in theological scholarship and ecclesial dialogue. His two major trinitarian publications, *The Christian Doctrine of God: One Being Three Persons* and *The Trinitarian Faith*, were both published after he left his position at New College.

The Ecumenical Movement

The final noteworthy aspect of Torrance's career was his involvement in the ecumenical movement, which began while he was at New College and continued after his formal retirement.[41] During the 1950s and 1960s, Torrance participated in the dialogue between the Church of England and the Church of Scotland, served on the Faith and Order Commission, and attended various World Council of Church meetings. Despite this flurry of attendance,

McGrath argues that Torrance's most important ecumenical activity began after his retirement from Edinburgh for it was during these later years that he was instrumental in a dialogue between the Reformed and Greek Orthodox Churches, mirroring his theological focus at the time on trinitarian theology.[42]

HOW TO READ T. F. TORRANCE: A SCIENTIFIC APPROACH TO THEOLOGY

As previously noted, Torrance's work can be loosely divided into two streams: his dogmatic work, and his work relating to theology and science. While distinct, these streams inform each other.[43] Awareness of Torrance's scientific approach to the theological task will help us be confident that our reading of particular aspects of Torrance's work is consistent with his work as a whole. Nevertheless our concern is not with the outcome of Torrance's work in the area of science and theology but rather with Molnar's observation that "even his dogmatic theology shows signs of his commitment to the scientific method."[44]

Torrance considered himself a dogmatic theologian, an older style today referred to as a systematic theologian. "Dogmatic" is more apt than "systematic," however, since Torrance was not concerned with constructing a logical or systematic structure for theological knowledge. Instead, he considered his scientific approach to theology to stand in the same tradition as the movement that emerged about two centuries before the birth of Christ when *dogmatikoi* philosophers asked "the kind of questions that do yield positive answers and thus contribute to the advancement of knowledge"[45] rather than questions that could not be answered. Torrance argues that dogmatic, or positive, theology was the way that early Christians responded to the spread of Christianity in Graeco-Roman culture. Because the incarnation was incompatible with Graeco-Roman philosophical dualisms and could not be assimilated into the existing paradigms of belief, early Christian theologians were required to develop a distinctly Christian account of reality on the basis of God's self-revelation in Jesus Christ so that dogmatic theology

> must proceed to lay bare the essential interrelation of all the doctrines of the faith, and their integration within the one Body of Christ, within the whole structure of obedience to Christ. This is the *interior logic* of dogmatic theology . . . which can be studied and used as a norm or criterion for helping to shape the true form of each doctrine, for testing and proving the different doctrines to see whether they really fit into the essential structure of the whole.[46]

"Dogmatic theology" thus refers to a theology "that is forced upon us by the actual interaction of God with the universe he has made and by his intelligible self-revelation within that interaction."[47] It is theology on the basis of what we can know from God's revelation. It does not have the negative connotation of someone who is dogmatic, as in someone who refuses to waver from beliefs that are based on received tradition or teaching and have not been subject to critical judgment.[48]

Torrance's interest in the relationship between science and theology began early in his studies, influenced by Daniel Lamont, another New College professor who was attempting to think out the relationship between evangelical truth and modern science in his own research.[49] When Torrance first began studying with Barth, he had hoped to complete a thesis on "a scientific account of Christian dogmatics from its Christological and soteriological centre and in the light of its constitutive Trinitarian structure."[50] Barth dissuaded him from such a mammoth task, and Torrance instead produced his thesis, "The Doctrine of Grace in the Apostolic Fathers."[51] He went on to spend much of his career developing a "scientific theology" or "theological science." The idea of a scientific theology is best illustrated by a story related in McGrath's biography. At the end of his year lecturing at Auburn Theological Seminary, Torrance was invited to teach theology at Princeton University. The hiring board insisted that the content would need to be taught in a dispassionate way and not on a confessional or evangelistic basis. Torrance responded that he would like to teach theology as a science but could not guarantee that there would be no conversions! He believed that the rigorous questioning and examining of the natural universe through the natural sciences could be profitably applied to Christian theology. He was offered the position but returned to Scotland because of the pending war.[52]

The weight that Torrance gave to the scientific undertakings of his work is reflected by the fact that he regarded *Theological Science* as one of his most important works alongside *The Trinitarian Faith* and *The Christian Doctrine of God.*[53] Furthermore, wider recognition of the significance of Torrance's work on the relationship of science and theology saw him awarded the Templeton Prize in 1978.[54] For our purposes, three primary characteristics of Torrance's scientific approach to theology will be useful: the kataphysic method, the rejection of dualism, and the importance of personal knowledge. These three characteristics are intrinsic to his approach to dogmatic theology.

The Kataphysic Method

Daniel Hardy observes that for Torrance "the *means to understanding* must be in accordance with the *substance of what is sought*; epistemology must follow ontology, just as form and being are inseparable in what is known."[55]

How we know and what we know is to be dictated by the object of our enquiry. The purpose of scientific inquiry is "to discover the relations of things and events at different levels of complexity, and to develop our understanding and expression of them in such a way that their real nature becomes progressively disclosed to us."[56] In order for this to happen, Torrance turns to the kataphysic method in which each object of inquiry is studied *kata physin*, or according to its own nature.[57] Hence each discipline develops an appropriate methodology in accordance with the object of its study.[58] It is not that there is a generic method of scientific inquiry that can be applied to any field of knowledge but rather that the object being studied determines the specific questions that need to be asked of it—thus Hardy's observation that epistemology is derived from ontology. The kataphysic method opens up true scientific objectivity; disciplining one's subjectivities, one enters into active engagement with the object, "prepared and ready for whatever it may reveal in the give-and-take of investigation."[59]

Torrance is fond of describing humans as "priests of creation" designed to explore and discover the created rationality of the universe. The exploration of natural science is part of our obedience as created beings and has a redemptive pattern.[60] Torrance suggests that the rational unity of the universe is the correlate to the doctrine of one Creator while the contingent rationality of the universe points to the uncreated rationality of the Creator. The created universe has a genuinely open-ended yet limited contingent freedom that derives from God's unlimited freedom.[61] However, although theology and the natural sciences are both rationally comprehensible, the correlation between them is limited for "while theological science shares with other sciences a generally recognised scientific procedure based on the principle of objectivity, theology has its own particular scientific requirements determined by the unique nature of its own particular object."[62]

Theological study should therefore be "a positive and progressive inquiry into the knowledge of God proceeding under the determination of his self-revelation but within the limits of our creaturely rationality."[63] It involves a commitment to "act toward things in ways appropriate to their natures, to understand them through letting them shine in their own light, and to reduce our thinking of them into orderly forms on the presumption of their inherent intelligibility."[64] This is Torrance's epistemological realism, or critical realism.[65]

The need to know God genuinely while reckoning with the limitations of our humanity shapes Torrance's argument that while God stands in a "transcendent and creative, not a spatial or temporal"[66] relationship to the world, the incarnation is the actual coming of God into the "determinations, conditions and conceptualities of our world."[67] This unique event involves God "appropriating to himself perceptibility and conceptuality, together with linguistic communicability"[68] as the unique locus of God's self-disclosure shapes the method of theological inquiry.[69] Jesus comes "breaking into the continuity of our human knowledge as an utterly distinctive and unique fact,"[70] as both a historical and eternal event that can only be interpreted on its own basis.[71]

In scientific theology, the object—God—is *actively* making himself known unlike in natural science where nature is *passive* in the process of inquiry. Consequently, theological knowledge is given—received, and not discovered.[72] We genuinely know God but only because he enables us to do so. As Torrance explains,

> We are never allowed to impose ourselves with our notions upon Him, but we are freed and lifted up as rational subjects in communion with God, and summoned to decisions and acts of volition in that communion, so that knowledge of Him arises and increases out of obedient conformity to Him and the way He takes with us in revealing Himself to us.[73]

Rejection of Dualism

Because scientific theology means knowing God in accordance with the way that God has revealed himself, this entails the rejection of both epistemological and cosmological dualism.[74] These dualistic tendencies developed within Hellenistic philosophy where "Greek thought identified the real with what is necessarily and timelessly true, and discounted the sensible or material as deficient in rationality or merely contingent and accidental."[75] Despite the robust efforts of the Nicene Fathers to promote a more interactionist view of God in relation to the world, the same dualistic tendencies, but with an insidious theological slant, reemerged in the work of Augustine[76] and came to influence modern scientific thought through the foundational work of figures like Galileo and Descartes. This led to the idea of an inertial system, or the extremes of process theology, and caused a divorce between the "One God" and the "Triune God."[77] It was not until the later work of Clerk Maxwell and Einstein and their focus on the unification of geometry and experience, or epistemology and ontology, that Torrance believes a more unitary outlook was once again predominant in scientific method.[78]

The history of scientific thought shows that as developments in science have required the adaptation of the paradigms within which knowledge of the natural world is sought and interpreted, the framework within which the world is understood has correspondingly changed. Torrance views the incarnation as the same kind of paradigmatic shift, asserting that God has really come into the world and can really be known by humanity. It is "an invasion of God among men and women in time, bringing and working out a salvation not only understandable by them in their own historical and human life and existence, but historically and concretely accessible to them on earth and in time, in the midst of their frailty, contingency, relativity and sin."[79] As we will explore in a later chapter, while the early Church viewed itself in continuity with the redemptive history of Israel, the incarnation signaled a revolution in the knowledge of God and the existence of God's people.

This is where we see what it means to describe Torrance as a dogmatic theologian in the best sense of the word: he is committed to the positive content of theology, which has at its heart the coming of God into creation, nullifying any dualistic view of the relationship between God and creation. Such dualism is inconsistent with the biblical witness and denies the reality of the incarnation as was seen in the Gnostic sects of the early Church whose separation of creation and redemption "made mythological nonsense of the Incarnation."[80] When such dualism is prevalent it results in a "doctrine of the immutability and impassibility of God," which leads to "a deistic disjunction between God and the universe."[81] Against this view, Torrance promotes a unified cosmology and argues for an interactionist, relational view of the universe where God interacts with the world of nature and history yet remains transcendent to it.[82] Consequently, "while the Incarnation does not mean that God is limited by space and time, it asserts the reality of space and time for God in the actuality of his relations with us, and at the same time binds us to space and time in all our relations with him."[83] This is a key point in Torrance's trinitarian ecclesiology for the Church is the empirical body of Christ that exists in history and must be able to relate to the Triune God within space and time.

Torrance concludes that although theology has had to wrestle with recontextualization at points in history when there has been significant upheaval in the prevailing scientific or cosmological perspective, the real issue is not the change in science or cosmology but the assumption that there is a radical disjunction between God and the world.[84] In this light, we can understand why Torrance considered his goal of unification (that is, the rejection of dualism) in both science and theology as a missionary scheme with significant implications for the ecumenical movement as well.[85]

Torrance explains that epistemological or cosmological dualism leads to a projected image of God that is not actually grounded in who God is. Both cosmological and epistemological dualism result in humankind's attempts to "close the gap between the world and God," which lead to the various approaches categorized under the title of natural theology.[86] Natural theology is a result of dualistic ways of thinking; it flourishes whenever dualist modes of thought prevail.[87] The problem is that since "nature by itself speaks only ambiguously of God,"[88] natural theology can only point us to an abstract concept of a god rather than the Triune God who has revealed himself to us in Jesus Christ and through the Holy Spirit.[89] This is why Torrance follows Barth in rejecting natural theology as an independent conceptual system that can reveal God to humanity. Unlike Barth, Torrance seeks to make use of select aspects of the tradition by *reformulating* natural theology, suggesting that it can function within the sphere of, and as a subsidiary to divine revelation.[90] We must not only look at or through creation but *beyond* creation for "if we are to recover the meaning of the universe, and meaning of the universe as a whole, we must learn again to look beyond the universe, or look through the universe, to its transcendent ground in the uncreated Rationality of God."[91] Colyer helpfully comments that Torrance's reformulated approach diverges from natural theology at his insistence that natural theology must "give up its *independent* status and find its place *within* revealed theology."[92] Here we see once again Torrance's absolute commitment to the uniqueness of God's triune self-revelation. This shapes his insistence that all proper theological science is a posteriori, or operating from the given knowledge of God's self-revelation, rather than a priori, or operating from what we observe in the world.[93]

Personal Knowledge

The final point that Torrance makes is that the human knower has a vital place in the knowledge of God. Alongside the kataphysic method in which prior frameworks of understanding are consistently revised in light of a deeper understanding of the object in question and the rejection of any dualistic separation of God and creation, theological knowledge must be personal. While this was applied to the natural sciences through the work of Michael Polanyi,[94] Torrance takes Polanyi's insights further by arguing that theological knowledge is personal knowledge precisely because God reveals himself to us as a personal being, as the perichoretic communion of the three divine persons. Since in theology the objective reality with which we are concerned is the Holy Trinity revealed to us in Jesus Christ and the Spirit, "the mode of assent and the nature of the conviction aroused is appropriately personal and not impersonal."[95]

It is significant that theology is not primarily about humanity's knowing of God but rather the fact that we are first known by God. Our sinful human nature is estranged from God. It is alienated and unable to grasp the truth because of the dehumanizing and corrupting consequences of sin on our rational mind. This is the consequence of sin for humans are so turned in on themselves that "double vision results, in which human knowers are unable to trace the thought of God back to its proper ground in His reality."[96] This is why Torrance is so emphatic that revelation and reconciliation must be considered together for "men and women need to be reconciled with the truth if they are to know the truth, and they cannot really know it without becoming at-one with the truth, which cannot but involve radical self-denial and conversion on our part."[97] Sin prevents us from discovering God by ourselves for we are unable to know God except through his act of grace in simultaneously revealing himself to us and reconciling us to himself. As humans are invited to participate in fellowship with God, "the subject is given freedom and place before God and yet in which the subject is summoned into such communion with Him that he can only engage in it with self-criticism and repentance."[98] Torrance elaborates,

> If we are really to know God in accordance with his nature as he discloses himself to us, we require to be adapted in our knowing and personal relations toward him . . . Knowledge and vision of God involve cognitive union with him in accordance with his nature as holy love, in which reconciliation and communion with God through Christ and under the purifying impact of the Holy Spirit are progressively actualised in the renewal and transformation of human patterns of life and thought.[99]

Finally, we must acknowledge that personal knowledge is not subjective or individualistic. One of the problems of modern theology is that personal knowledge is not sufficiently related to the analogy of faith so that the human assumes primacy in the God-human theological relationship.[100] Torrance follows Polanyi again in his perspective that all belief has two poles: the subjective knower, and the objective reality which is independent of the knower. Objective knowledge arises as one looks away from oneself and toward the other object[101] so that personal belief is not a subjective notion of faith or belief that emerges from the human mind as it tries to make sense of the world but is "a basic act of recognition in which our minds respond to a pattern or structure inherent in the world around us which imprints itself upon them."[102] As Torrance explains,

> personal being is . . . the prime bearer of objectivity, for that kind of relation is the relation in which persons as persons are. What we mean by personal being is precisely that kind of being which by its nature is oriented beyond itself, in the other, in God ultimately, and in other human beings relatively, that is, in other personal beings. Hence the person cannot be defined through exclusive reference to itself but through its relation to other persons, i.e. objectively.[103]

While we will return to this sense of needing to define persons in relation to other persons in future chapters, we may conclude our discussion of personal knowledge in theology by observing that the role of the knower in theology goes beyond the "truism that knowledge of an object is knowledge by a subject, for the subject has always had a logical place in knowledge."[104] This is because "when we think of the object as the living God who enters into living and personal communion with man through revelation and reconciliation then the place of the human subject in knowledge of God can no longer be excluded from the full content of that knowledge."[105] For Torrance, the personal element of theological knowledge is appropriate according to the kataphysic method and also is in keeping with his non-dualistic view of the God-world-humanity relation.

THE ECCLESIOLOGICAL TASK: WHY A TRINITARIAN THEOLOGY?

The final section of this chapter will offer some clarification of the research approach that has been taken in focusing on the doctrine of the Trinity since in some places Torrance argues that the doctrine of the Trinity has primacy while in others he argues that all doctrines must be expressed with Christology at their heart.[106] This is not demonstrative of inconsistency in Torrance's thought but has to do with his insistence that "the doctrine of Christ and the doctrine of the Holy Trinity belong intrinsically and inseparably together, and are to be coordinated in any faithful account of them."[107] There is no clear-cut division between these two doctrines for they are incomplete without the other: the Trinity is constitutive for Christology, and Christology is always a corollary of the economic Trinity. Because Christ is both fully human and fully divine, Christ's divinity cannot be understood except in relation to the Father and the Spirit.[108] This is a matter that will occupy our attention throughout this book, but in order to briefly "clear the ground," we shall consider the way in which Torrance gives doctrinal primacy to the Trinity while still incorporating a robust Christology.

Torrance suggests that the doctrine of the Church arose in the light of two major veins of Scriptural teaching. The first of these was St. Paul's teaching on the Church as the body of Christ, and the second was the baptismal tradition, proclaimed in the name of the Father, Son, and Spirit.[109] These traditions are held together for "we cannot teach a doctrine of God and then add on to that a doctrine of Christ."[110] The same pattern applies to ecclesiology: we cannot develop a doctrine of the Church and then consider it in its relation to the doctrine of God. Any attempt to explicate the doctrine of the Church solely based on its current forms or on the doctrinal formulations that have been produced by theologians throughout the ages will ultimately fail to get at the heart of the being and mission of the Church. This is because the primary basis for ecclesiology is not the empirical Church itself but rather God's self-revelation. As Torrance concludes,

> the objective pole of the Church's faith is the truth of God which has seized hold of it in Christ and His Gospel and will not let it go, truth over which it has no control but truth which makes it free and establishes it in the love of God. Hence the Church cannot but confess its faith in God, before God, with an unreserved endorsement of belief in the truth of Christ and his Gospel, as the truth with which its very existence is bound up as the Church, the one Body of

> Christ, and as the saving grace of God which constitutes the very essence of its message and mission.[111]

The nature of the Church as the servant and body of Christ requires it to look to Jesus, the head of the body.[112] In knowing Christ, the Church knows the Triune God. This is why the incarnation is such a central doctrine in Torrance's theological oeuvre and also why he insists that "faithful theological inquiry operates with concrete positive reference to Jesus."[113] While the eternal nature of God is triune, the incarnation is the way in which God has chosen to reveal himself to humankind and is the unique place where knowledge of God is actualized within space and time and made accessible to humanity. Torrance explains the relationship between Christology and the Trinity in a precise way when he states that

> to speak about who Jesus Christ was and is, to speak in ontological terms of his being and his work, means to speak of Jesus Christ as Son of God the Lord, and as son of David; but to speak of Jesus as Son of God means, in the same breath, speech about the Father and the Holy Spirit. No doctrine of the person of Christ in his divine and human being is possible, except in that eternal mystery and in that trinitarian context.[114]

In the theological movement where we begin with the doctrine of God and move from that to consider the doctrine of the Church, we are incorporating Torrance's scientific theological method and especially the three characteristics that we have explored. We are using the kataphysic method where the Church is to be known according to its true source, the Triune God who calls it into being. We are rejecting dualism in holding that the Church continues to be sustained by the active and ongoing work of God within space and time. Finally, we are emphasizing the role of the personal knower in theological knowledge by affirming that our knowledge of the Triune God is shaped as we participate in the life of the Church. By holding all these elements together, we understand the Church to be the empirical body of Christ, viewed both in the light of God's economic work through the Son and Spirit and in the light of who the eternal God is in his own being. Our ecclesiology is prevented from becoming inappropriately subjective because it retains its objective ground in the way that Jesus Christ reveals the transcendent God to us as the one who "belongs both to the eternal world of divine reality and to the historical world of contingent realities."[115] This is why we have chosen to consider the preeminence of the doctrine of the Trinity for Torrance's ecclesiology, which then properly incorporates Christology and pneumatology. This explicates the core assumption that the doctrine of the Holy Trinity is foundational for Torrance's approach to the theological task. It is also worth noting that many of Torrance's ecumenical works were published before he released his major trinitarian publications, which could be why sometimes Christocentric language appears more dominant than trinitarian language.

CONCLUSION

In this chapter we have offered a brief biographical overview of Torrance's life and ministry, highlighting his sense of a theological career as a personal vocation. Important features of Torrance's theology have been introduced that must shape our understanding of his theology and are thus key to the continuing development of our argument. Finally, we have offered some introductory comments on how Torrance develops his theological account of the Trinity-Church relationship in such a way that we, as the human recipients of the Gospel, are made able to participate in the *koinōnia* of the Trinity and, on this basis, to live out our common life in such a way that others are also embraced within the Church as the human correlate to the fellowship of the Holy Trinity.

NOTES

1. Alister E. McGrath, *T. F. Torrance: An Intellectual Biography* (Edinburgh: T&T Clark, 1999), xi; Paul D. Molnar, *Thomas F. Torrance: Theologian of the Trinity* (Farnham, UK: Ashgate, 2009), 1; and Elmer M. Colyer, *How to Read T. F. Torrance: Understanding His Trinitarian & Scientific Theology* (Downers Grove, IL: InterVarsity Press, 2001), 15.
2. Colyer, *How to Read T. F. Torrance*, 11.
3. Ibid.
4. I was given the privilege of spending a semester accessing this material in 2014 thanks to a generous scholarship from Princeton Theological Seminary as part of their Doctoral Research Scholars Program. Use of the archival material was limited so I have restricted my citations to places where the material adds additional support or a slightly different angle to the material that is found in Torrance's published material.
5. Thomas F. Torrance, "Itinerarium Mentis in Deum" (Box 10: Itinerarium Mentis in Deum, Thomas F. Torrance Manuscript Collection, Princeton Theological Seminary), 3.
6. Ibid., 1. Partly cited in McGrath, *T. F. Torrance*, 9. Torrance repeats the latter sentiment on page 3 of the same autobiographical document, specifically acknowledging that his mother's Anglican background shaped his own ecumenical outlook. Torrance also dedicated one of his earliest books to his parents, describing them as "my first and best teachers in theology." See the first-page dedication in Thomas F. Torrance, *Calvin's Doctrine of Man* (London: Lutterworth Press, 1949).
7. Thomas F. Torrance, "My Boyhood in China, 1913–1927" (Box 10: My Boyhood in China, Thomas F. Torrance Manuscript Collection, Princeton Theological Seminary), 10.
8. Torrance, "Itinerarium Mentis in Deum," 1.
9. Thomas F. Torrance, "Student Years—Edinburgh to Basel, 1934–1938" (Box 10: Student Years—Edinburgh to Basel, Thomas F. Torrance Manuscript Collection, Princeton Theological Seminary), 1.
10. Torrance, "Itinerarium Mentis in Deum," 9.
11. McGrath, *T. F. Torrance*, 30–31.
12. Torrance, "Itinerarium Mentis in Deum," 25. See also Torrance's reflection on Mackintosh's ministry in Thomas F. Torrance, "Hugh Ross Mackintosh: Theologian of the Cross," *Scottish Bulletin of Evangelical Theology* 5, no. 2 (Autumn 1987): 160–73.

13. McGrath, *T. F. Torrance*, 32–33.
14. Torrance, “Itinerarium Mentis in Deum,” 19–20.
15. We can see the influence of Karl Barth clearly here for as Torrance notes, one of the developments throughout Barth’s theological career is the progression from pursuing theological studies in separation from the life and mission of the Church toward the insistence that theology and the Church require each other. The latter position is the one that Torrance came to hold. See Thomas F. Torrance, *Karl Barth: An Introduction to His Early Theology, 1910–1931* (London: SCM Press, 1962), 201–4.
16. Thomas F. Torrance, *Gospel, Church and Ministry*, in *Thomas F. Torrance Collected Studies*, ed. Jock Stein, 1:35 (Eugene, OR: Pickwick Publications, 2012). This was recognized by others: see David W. Torrance, “Introduction: Discovering the Incarnate Saviour of the World,” in *An Introduction to Torrance Theology: Discovering the Incarnate Saviour*, ed. Gerrit Scott Dawson, 1–2 (London: T&T Clark, 2007).
17. McGrath, *T. F. Torrance*, 36–39.
18. Torrance, “Student Years—Edinburgh to Basel, 1934–1938,” 14.
19. Thomas F. Torrance, “Auburn” (Box 10: Auburn, Thomas F. Torrance Manuscript Collection, Princeton Theological Seminary), 6. These lectures are published as Thomas F. Torrance, *The Doctrine of Jesus Christ* (Eugene, OR: Wipf and Stock, 2002).
20. John Webster, *Thomas Forsyth Torrance, 1913–2007*, in *Biographical Memoirs of Fellows of the British Academy*, vol. 8 (London: British Academy, 2014), 418. This perspective on the stability of Torrance’s theological position was reiterated in a conversation I had with John Webster in St. Andrews, Scotland, on October 15, 2015.
21. As was noted in the introduction, Stanley S. MacLean, *Resurrection, Apocalypse, and the Kingdom of Christ*, Princeton Theological Monograph Series (Eugene, OR: Pickwick Publications, 2012) deals excellently with the period of Torrance’s early work but fails to present a comprehensive view of Torrance’s ecclesiology due to its lack of engagement with his later trinitarian publications.
22. McGrath, *T. F. Torrance*, 60.
23. Torrance, *Gospel, Church and Ministry*, 30.
24. Ibid., 46. In a reflection published decades later in 1977, Torrance noted that if he were to start parish ministry again as a young minister, he would engage in Christ-centered ministry, focusing on prayer and worship in, through, and with Christ; give himself “more than ever to study and contemplation and . . . avoid committees like the plague”; make pastoral visitation central; and continue to seek understanding of scientific advances in order to be able to understand the universe that God had created. See Thomas F. Torrance, “If I Were Starting Again,” *New Pulpit Digest* (March/April 1997): 64
25. Published as “The Church in the World” in Torrance, *Gospel, Church and Ministry*, 74–84.
26. Ibid., 43.
27. During this time, Torrance published his first piece, “Theology and the Common Man.” See Thomas F. Torrance, *Life and Work: The Record of the Church of Scotland* (1940): 177–178.
28. One such example of war-related ruminations is an article published in *British Weekly* in which Torrance argues that we must be careful not to point the finger at Germany, or any totalitarian state, without also being willing to deal with the same problems in their different manifestations at home. See Thomas F. Torrance, “The Importance of Fences in Religion,” *British Weekly*, January 30, 1941.
29. Thomas F. Torrance, “War Service” (Box 10: War Service, Thomas F. Torrance Manuscript Collection, Princeton Theological Seminary), 14.
30. Ibid., 53–54.
31. Ibid., 49. Quoted in McGrath, *T. F. Torrance*, 73–74. During my research I have had a number of conversations with students who although unfamiliar with Torrance’s theological distinctives can identify him as “the one who tells that story about the soldier and Jesus being like God.”
32. McGrath, *T. F. Torrance*, 84. While this is a theological relationship that appears throughout the whole corpus of T. F. Torrance, the best summary is found in Thomas F.

Torrance, *The Mediation of Christ* (Edinburgh: T&T Clark, 1992), 56–67. Torrance also reflected later that he did not regret his decade of parish ministry precisely because it was there that he learned that the fundamental theological questions had to do with these deep human anxieties about the identity between God and Jesus. See Michael Bauman, *Roundtable Conversations with European Theologians* (Grand Rapids, MI: Baker Book House, 1990), 111–18.

33. McGrath, *T. F. Torrance*, 83.

34. Thomas F. Torrance, "Aberdeen" (Box 10: Aberdeen, Thomas F. Torrance Manuscript Collection, Princeton Theological Seminary), 2.

35. Ibid., 5.

36. Ibid., 7; Torrance, *Gospel, Church and Ministry*, 40–41.

37. McGrath, *T. F. Torrance*, 118–33.

38. Habets notes that while Torrance rejected the "Barthian" title, he remained an "appreciative critic of Barth." See Myk Habets, *Theology in Transposition: A Constructive Appraisal of T. F. Torrance* (Minneapolis, MN: Fortress Press, 2013), 12. Douglas Farrow highlights that "Protestants can learn from Torrance something that Barth cannot teach them: a degree for respect for liturgy and sacraments and even for episcopal ministry. They can learn something else as well—something Torrance tried to teach Barth—namely, to find a place for natural theology and metaphysics within an evangelical framework." See Douglas Farrow, "T. F. Torrance and the Latin Heresy," *First Things* 238 (December 2013): 28.

39. McGrath, *T. F. Torrance*, 90.

40. Torrance's lecture material was edited for readability and publication by Robert T. Walker, resulting in his two most-readable volumes, Thomas F. Torrance, *Incarnation: The Person and Life of Christ*, ed. Robert T. Walker (Downers Grove, IL: InterVarsity Press, 2008); and Thomas F. Torrance, *Atonement: The Person and Work of Christ*, ed. Robert T. Walker (Downers Grove, IL: InterVarsity Press, 2009).

41. The start of the modern ecumenical movement is usually dated to the Edinburgh Missionary Conference in 1910, which as an interesting sidenote was attended by Torrance's father. It was after World War II, with the 1948 formation of the World Council of Churches, that the steady ecumenical momentum of the 1950s and 1960s began to develop. See later chapters for a fuller description of Torrance's ecumenical involvement.

42. McGrath, *T. F. Torrance*, 94–102.

43. Readers are directed to primary works such as Thomas F. Torrance, *Theological and Natural Science* (Eugene, OR: Wipf and Stock, 2002); Thomas F. Torrance, *The Christian Frame of Mind* (Eugene, OR: Wipf and Stock, 1989); and Thomas F. Torrance, *Theological Science* (Edinburgh: T&T Clark, 1996), 337–52.

44. Molnar, *Thomas F. Torrance*, 2.

45. Thomas F. Torrance, *Transformation and Convergence in the Frame of Knowledge: Explorations in the Interrelations of Scientific and Theological Enterprise* (Eugene, OR: Wipf and Stock, 1998), 267. The post-Platonic New Academy had philosophers known as skeptics (*skeptikoi*) whose tactic was to ask lots of purely academic questions without requiring concrete answers. In response to this, from about 200 BC a contrasting philosophical movement developed to ask questions about the actual world, the answers to these questions being determined by the real nature of things. These philosophers were known as dogmatics (*dogmatikoi*).

46. Thomas F. Torrance, *Theology in Reconstruction* (Grand Rapids, MI: Eerdmans, 1965), 148–49.

47. Thomas F. Torrance, *The Ground and Grammar of Theology* (Charlottesville: University Press of Virginia, 1980), 50. "Forced upon us" does not have negative connotations here but rather reflects that if God does not authentically communicate himself to us through his Word, then "we are thrown back upon ourselves to authenticate His existence and to make Him talk by putting our own words into His mouth and by clothing Him with our own ideas." See Torrance, *Theological Science*, 31.

48. For Torrance's reasoning and the positive, scientific sense in which he qualifies dogmatic theology rather than the negative sense of one who refuses to budge from received teaching and tradition, see Thomas F. Torrance, "Reformed Dogmatics Not Dogmaticism," *Theology* 70 (1967): 152–56. Torrance also deals with the topic "dogmatic theology" as a positive science in Thomas F. Torrance, "Science, Theology, Unity," *Theology Today* 21 (1964): 149–54.

49. McGrath, *T. F. Torrance*, 34.

50. Thomas F. Torrance, "My Interaction with Karl Barth," in *How Karl Barth Changed My Mind*, ed. Donald K. McKim, 54 (Grand Rapids, MI: Wm. B. Eerdmans, 1986). This article is not so much a theological summary of Barth's work as it is a discussion of the theological and personal interaction between Torrance and Barth.

51. Published as Thomas F. Torrance, *The Doctrine of Grace in the Apostolic Fathers* (Eugene, OR: Wipf and Stock, 1996).

52. McGrath, *T. F. Torrance*, 57–58.

53. Ibid., 107. See also Habets, *Theology in Transposition*, 39–93.

54. http://www.templetonprize.org/previouswinner.html.

55. Daniel W. Hardy, "T. F. Torrance," in *The Modern Theologians*, ed. David Ford, 167 (Malden, MA: Blackwell, 2005).

56. Torrance, *Transformation and Convergence in the Frame of Knowledge*, 265.

57. From the Greek *kata physin*: *kata*, "according to" and *physin*, "nature." See Thomas F. Torrance, *The Trinitarian Faith* (Edinburgh: T&T Clark, 1993), 51. See also McGrath, *T. F. Torrance*, 141.

58. Torrance, *Theology in Reconstruction*, 13–17.

59. Thomas F. Torrance, *God and Rationality* (Oxford: Oxford University Press, 2000), 9. Torrance also notes (9–11) the difference between scientific *objectivity* and *objectification*.

60. Torrance, *The Ground and Grammar of Theology*, 5; Thomas F. Torrance, *Divine and Contingent Order* (Edinburgh: T&T Clark, 1998), 128–39.

61. Torrance, *Christian Frame of Mind*, 50–65.

62. Torrance, *Theological Science*, 112–13.

63. Thomas F. Torrance, *Reality and Scientific Theology*, 2nd ed. (Eugene, OR: Wipf and Stock, 2001), xiv.

64. Torrance, *Theological Science*, 107.

65. An accessible chapter centered on the *homoousion* is Thomas F. Torrance, "Theological Realism," in *The Philosophical Frontiers of Christian Theology, Essays Presented to D. M. MacKinnon*, eds. B. Hebbelethwaite and S. Sutherland (Cambridge: Cambridge University Press, 1982), 169–96. For secondary comment, see Habets, *Theology in Transposition: A Constructive Appraisal of T. F. Torrance*, 95–121; and Douglas F. Kelly, "The Realist Epistemology of Thomas F. Torrance," in *An Introduction to Torrance Theology: Discovering the Incarnate Saviour*, ed. Gerrit Scott Dawson, 75–102 (London: T&T Clark, 2007).

66. Thomas F. Torrance, *Space, Time and Incarnation* (Edinburgh: T&T Clark, 1997), 60.

67. Ibid., 61.

68. Ibid., 80.

69. Torrance, *Theological Science*, 97.

70. Torrance, *Incarnation*, 1.

71. Torrance, *Theology in Reconstruction*, 26. Commenting on this further, see Jason Hing-Kau Yeung, *Being and Knowing: An Examination of T. F. Torrance's Christological Science* (Hong Kong: Alliance Bible Seminary, 1996), 90.

72. Thomas F. Torrance, *Christian Theology and Scientific Culture* (Eugene, OR: Wipf and Stock, 1998), 116–18.

73. Torrance, *Theological Science*, 97.

74. A concise discussion of Torrance's rejection of dualism can be found in Alan G. Marley, *T. F. Torrance in a Nutshell* (Edinburgh: Handsel Press, 1992).

75. Thomas F. Torrance, "Immortality and Light," *Religious Studies* 17, no. 2 (1981): 149.

76. Thomas F. Torrance, "A New Reformation?" *London Holborn and Quarterly Review* 189 (1964): 277. However, see Radcliff's interaction with Torrance's take on the "Latin heresy" in Jason Radcliff, "T. F. Torrance and Reformed-Orthodox Dialogue," in *T. F. Torrance and Eastern Orthodoxy: Theology in Reconciliation*, ed. Matthew Baker (Eugene, OR: Wipf and Stock, 2013).

77. Torrance, *The Ground and Grammar of Theology*, 146.

78. Torrance, *Christian Theology and Scientific Culture*, 23–25. The fight against dualism is an important and repeated note in Torrance's historical view of theology. He argues that the train was derailed, as it were, by the consequences of dualistic thought.

79. Torrance, *Incarnation*, 8.

80. Torrance, *The Mediation of Christ*, 62–63.

81. Torrance, *The Ground and Grammar of Theology*, 146; Thomas F. Torrance, *Trinitarian Perspectives: Toward Doctrinal Agreement* (Edinburgh: T&T Clark, 1994), [illegible]–4.

82. Thomas F. Torrance, "The Problem of Natural Theology in the Thought of Karl Barth," *Religious Studies* 6, no. 2 (Fall 1970): 121.

83. Torrance, *Space, Time and Incarnation*, 67.

84. Torrance, "A New Reformation?" 276.

85. Thomas F. Torrance, "A New Vision of Wholeness: An Interview of Thomas F. Torrance, Given to Mary Doyle Morgan," *Presbyterian Survey* (December 1980): 21–23.

86. Torrance, *The Ground and Grammar of Theology*, 80.

87. Ibid., 75.

88. Torrance, *Space, Time and Incarnation*, 59.

89. Torrance, *The Ground and Grammar of Theology*, 89.

90. Ibid., 87–98.

91. Torrance, *Reality and Scientific Theology*, 34.

92. Colyer, *How to Read T. F. Torrance*, 199 offers a summary of Torrance, *The Ground and Grammar of Theology*, 76–78. For further comments see Paul D. Molnar, "Natural Theology Revisited: A Comparison of T. F. Torrance and Karl Barth," *Zeitschrift für dialektische Theologie* 21 (2005): 55–83; and W. Travis McMaken, "The Impossibility of Natural Knowledge of God in T. F. Torrance's Reformulated Natural Theology," *International Journal of Systematic Theology* 12, no. 3 (July 2010): 319–40.

93. Torrance, *Theological Science*, 32–34. Torrance suggests we must distinguish between genuine-theology and "mere paper theology," the latter involving genuine argumentation but being "palpably unreal" because it does not derive from divine revelation.

94. Thomas F. Torrance, "Michael Polanyi and the Christian Faith—A Personal Report," *Tradition & Discovery* 27, no. 2 (2000–2001). Polanyi did not publicly identify himself as a Christian in his writing, but in this personal reflection, Torrance makes it clear that he knew Michael and Magda Polanyi to have a deep commitment to Christian faith. The same point is explicitly made in Thomas F. Torrance, "Answer to Prosch on Polanyi's Convictions about God, Letter to the Editor," *Tradition and Discovery: The Polanyi Society Periodical* 14, no. 1 (1986–1987): 30. For one of the clearest examples of Torrance's appreciation for Michael Polanyi, see Thomas F. Torrance, *Belief in Science and in Christian Life: The Relevance of Michael Polanyi's Thought for Christian Faith and Life* (Eugene, OR: Wipf and Stock, 1998), 1–27. For a further discussion of the contribution of Polanyi and Einstein along with others to Torrance's understanding of the importance of personal belief, see Torrance, *Christian Theology and Scientific Culture*, 41–73.

95. Torrance, *Belief in Science and in Christian Life*, 12. Torrance also cites Kierkegaard as an influence on his stance that because truth has been embodied in Jesus, we cannot know truth without a personal encounter with Christ that calls from us a faithful and obedient response. See Torrance, *Incarnation*, 25–27.

96. Torrance, *Theological Science*, x.

97. Torrance, *Reality and Scientific Theology*, 150. For further reading on Torrance's view of the knowledge of God and the self-knowledge of humanity, see Torrance, *Calvin's Doctrine of Man*, 13–22; and Thomas F. Torrance, "The Word of God and the Nature of Man," in *Reformation Old and New: Festschrift for Karl Barth*, ed. F. W. Camfield, 121–41 (London: Lutterworth Press, 1947).

98. Torrance, *Theological Science*, 98.

99. Torrance, *The Mediation of Christ*, 25–26.

100. Torrance, *Theological Science*, xiv. The analogy of faith, or *analogia fidei*, is a principle introduced by Calvin that is "a movement of thought in which we test the fidelity of our knowledge by tracing our thought back to its ground in the reality known, in which we refer everything to God and not to ourselves."

101. Torrance, *Belief in Science and in Christian Life*, 10–12.

102. Ibid., 12.

103. Torrance, *Reality and Scientific Theology*, 110.

104. Torrance, *Theological Science*, 85.
105. Ibid.
106. As an example, in one of his articles from 1958, Torrance says much more about the Christological reorientation needed within Anglicanism rather than referring to the Trinity. See Thomas F. Torrance, "The Mission of Anglicanism," in *Anglican Self-Criticism*, ed. D. M. Paton, 199 (London: SCM Press, 1958).
107. Thomas F. Torrance, *The Christian Doctrine of God: One Being Three Persons* (Edinburgh: T&T Clark, 1996), 1–2.
108. Torrance, *Incarnation*, 174–75. One of the leading influences of this aspect of Torrance's thought was Athanasius. While we will refer to several sources that have to do with Athanasius, see in particular Thomas F. Torrance, *Theology in Reconciliation* (Eugene, OR: Wipf and Stock, 1996), 250–57 where Torrance explores the inseparability of Christocentric and theocentric emphases within Athanasius's theology.
109. Torrance, *The Trinitarian Faith*, 253.
110. Thomas F. Torrance, *The School of Faith* (London: James Clarke and Co., 1959), xxi.
111. Torrance, *The Trinitarian Faith*, 23.
112. Thomas F. Torrance, *Conflict and Agreement in the Church: Order and Disorder* (Eugene, OR: Wipf and Stock, 1996), 16.
113. Torrance, *Theological Science*, 144.
114. Torrance, *Incarnation*, 164.
115. Torrance, *The Ground and Grammar of Theology*, 39. Torrance suggests that theology divorced from its objective ground in God "inevitably degenerates into anthropology" (37).

Chapter Two

The Trinity

A Theological Foundation

As we proceed in our enquiry into Torrance's trinitarian ecclesiology, we need to explore the detailed contours of Torrance's trinitarian convictions. Torrance's doctrine of the Trinity is neatly encapsulated by the phrases "one being, three persons" and "three persons, one being." His confidence that we cannot speak of the one without thinking of the three, or of the three without thinking of the one, demonstrates just how central the doctrine of the Trinity is to Torrance's approach to the whole theological task and particularly ecclesiology. Reflecting on the rich *koinōnia* of the Father, Son, and Spirit will enable us to deepen our understanding of God's "being for others" and the way in which the Church is formed as a creaturely counterpart to the divine fullness of communion.

THE SHAPING OF T. F. TORRANCE'S DOCTRINE OF THE HOLY TRINITY

Torrance's doctrine of the Trinity is drawn primarily from the implicit witness of Scripture, the explicit doctrinal development of the Fathers, and, to a lesser extent, the theologians of the Reformation. In this next section we will briefly trace his interaction with these sources.

Scripture

The primary place that Torrance draws his doctrine of the Trinity from is Scripture. As he comments, "the Church must always turn to the Holy Scriptures as the immediate source and norm of all revealed knowledge of God and of his saving purpose in Jesus Christ."[1] Torrance appropriates the patristic axiom that "God can only be known through God" and allows it to function as a theological aphorism in his own view of revelation. Since "God alone can name himself and bear witness to himself," interpretation of Scripture cannot be reduced to deconstructing biblical texts but must primarily be about hearing the Word of God.[2]

This is a key element of Torrance's understanding of revelation. As Webster surmises, Torrance "is concerned only secondarily with scripture as literary-historical text and primarily with scripture as sign—that is, with scripture's ostensive functions rather than with its literary surface or the historical processes of its production."[3] Torrance is more interested in what the text refers to rather than the actual text itself. By describing Scripture as a sign, Torrance is insisting that we must not turn the written Word of God into an idol—instead, "biblical statements are to be treated, not as containing or embodying the Truth of God in themselves, but as pointing, under the leading of the Spirit of Truth, to Jesus Christ himself who is the Truth."[4] Because in Christ word and deed are inseparable, Torrance describes the "union of uncreated Word and created Word"[5] in Jesus Christ as "the real text of God's self-revelation to mankind."[6] We are to look "through" the New Testament, which is a signifying text, to the basic text of Jesus Christ's obedient humanity[7] and through Christ to the Triune God.

Consequently, although the New Testament does not give us a formal doctrine of the Trinity, "it exhibits a coherent witness to God's trinitarian self-revelation imprinted upon its theological content in an implicit conceptual form evident in a whole complex of implicit references and indications."[8] Although the Scriptures do not outline "dogmatic propositions" about the Trinity, "they do present us with definite witness to the oneness and differentiation between the Father, the Son and the Holy Spirit."[9] This means that

> the meaning and truth of divine revelation conveyed to us through the Scriptures cannot be read off the linguistic patterns apparent in them or be deduced from the statements of the biblical authors as if they contained the truth in themselves, but may be discerned only by following through the semantic reference of biblical statements to the divine realities upon which they rest, and by thinking them out theologically within the whole organic frame of God's revealing and saving activity as Father, Son and Holy Spirit.[10]

Torrance views the whole of Scripture as witnessing to the Triune God for it was written under the "creative impact of divine revelation."[11] The Gospels, with their written description of Christ's life, ministry, and teaching, show us the historic manifestation of God as Father, Son, and Spirit particularly in their account of Jesus' baptism.[12] The Fourth Gospel reveals the mutuality between Father, Son, and Spirit through Jesus' "I am" sayings,[13] as well as through his discourse about the Holy Spirit on the night before the crucifixion. Throughout the Epistles there are various references to the triune persons and various forms of triadic expression, of which Torrance comments that although they "do not give us an explicit *doctrine* of the Holy Trinity, they do more than pave the way for it."[14] Torrance usually utilizes the order of the triune persons that is provided in the baptismal formula (Matt 28:19), Father, Son, and Holy Spirit,[15] and ascribes "primary importance" to this order.[16] Occasionally he uses the alternative order given in the doxological benediction of 2 Corinthians 13:14, of Son, Father, and Holy Spirit for it is in this order that we come to know the persons of the Trinity.[17] The different orders in which Scripture refers to the triune persons show that they are "distinguished by position and not status, by form and not being, by sequence and not power, for they are fully and perfectly equal."[18] There is no ontological hierarchy within the Trinity for Torrance.

Some issues with Torrance's approach to Scripture are identified by Webster, who notes the way Torrance demonstrates a "curious lack of attention to the *use* of scripture in the pre-modern Christian tradition, and to its commentarial modes of theology."[19] There is an obvious interplay between Scripture and tradition in Torrance's work and at points it seems that his interpretation of the tradition influenced his reading of Scripture rather than the other way around. Webster insists that Torrance's "distance from inquiries into the pragmatics of scripture and Christian literary culture"[20] and consequent lack of interest in "portraying textual culture: how texts are produced, disseminated and appropriated" is a significant problem.[21] Attention to the text itself tends to fall by the wayside because Torrance is so committed to focusing on what the text refers to: the reality behind the words.

Patristic Influences

Drawing on Scripture and the apostolic tradition, Torrance attributes the formalization of the doctrine of the Trinity to the Fathers. *The Trinitarian Faith* offers a detailed examination of Nicene, post-Nicene, and Constantinopolitan Fathers, and their varying perspectives on the Trinity.[22] Of the many Fathers quoted, Irenaeus and Athanasius emerge as two dominant figures. Athanasius was certainly the most influential for Torrance in terms of trinitarian theology, particularly in his role in the Church's reconstruction of epistemology and philosophy that cleared the philosophical ground that made way for the formulation of the Nicene Creed.[23] Athanasius also provided the first formal statement on the relationship between Christology and the doctrine of the Spirit, which was a precursor of acknowledging the *homoousion* of the Spirit at Constantinople.[24] Torrance cites Irenaeus as an example of how early confessions of faith and doctrine were not reached through logical deduction but instead were understood to be "statements that are ordered and integrated from beyond themselves by their common ground in the apostolic deposit of Faith."[25]

The Council of Nicea gathered in 325 AD to counter the Arian teaching that the Son was a creature and therefore not eternally coexistent with the Father. The deity of the Son was affirmed in the original Nicene Creed, but only later did the importance of affirming the deity of the Spirit become apparent. It was at the Council of Constantinople in 381 AD that the adapted creed affirmed that both the Son and Spirit are *homoousios*—of the same being—as the Father,[26] an event that Torrance considers "of definitive and irreversible significance" for the Church.[27] It is in this light that Torrance views the Nicene-Constantinopolitan Creed as the "supreme Ecumenical Creed of Christendom."[28] It does not contain any new truth and is not equal to revelation but functions as an elucidatory doctrinal statement.

Although Torrance seeks to be a faithful reader of the Fathers, Radcliff observes that Torrance's "imaginative reconstruction" of the Fathers is not that of a patrologist but rather of a theologian who "uses them as theological conversation partners at the great ecumenical and historical table of Christianity."[29] Torrance's reading of the Fathers has significant potential as an example for those who want to re-appropriate the Fathers but remain faithful to their own tradition despite the fact that Torrance can be criticized for the way that he sometimes goes too far in amalgamating modern and patristic theology.[30] One must be aware of the elements of Torrance's reading of the Fathers that come from his own context, since he "reads the Fathers from a theological and Reformed evangelical perspective."[31]

Reformation and Modern Influences

Torrance does not have much to say about the development of the doctrine of the Trinity during the medieval period, and when he does it is usually to highlight the contrast between Reformation theology and Latin theology. Torrance views Latin theology as following Aquinas, beginning with a philosophical ontology and then "adding on" the biblical idea of God.[32] However, Torrance views the Reformation as the other pivotal moment alongside Nicea of doctrinal development for the doctrine of the Holy Trinity. The Reformation emphasized God's being in his acts and his acts in his being, returning to the biblical conception of the God who meets us in Jesus Christ.[33] This is illustrated through considering Calvin's influence on Torrance.[34] His influence on Torrance's doctrine of the Trinity is seen in Torrance's summary of Calvin's "guiding principles," which sets the tone at the start of *The Christian Doctrine of God.* Torrance notes that (1) Calvin had a profoundly reverent attitude of mind, considering the being of God as "more to be worshipped than investigated." It is not difficult to see the similarity with Torrance's oft-used phrase "The Trinity is more to be adored than expressed."[35] (2) Calvin rejects abstract questions about what God is and instead asks, "Who is God?" considering the concrete way in which God has revealed himself to humanity. Torrance also argues that we must focus on what God *has* done not what he *could have* done, thereby rejecting any knowledge of God that does not derive from his manifestations in space and time.[36] (3) Calvin maintains that since God alone knows himself, God can only be known through God so we cannot know the Triune God except through Jesus Christ and the Holy Spirit. Torrance also follows this approach, although he tends to cite Irenaeus as the originating source of this idea. (4) Calvin insists that to speak of God as triune is to describe the very being of God and is not just a way of thinking about God.[37] Echoing this, Torrance argues that we are required to speak of God as triune since this is in accordance with how God has revealed himself as Father, Son, and Holy Spirit.

Regrettably, despite the significant shift that took place in the doctrine of God at the Reformation, later Reformed theology tended to drift back toward the abstract nature of scholasticism, developing its doctrine of God in abstraction from the work of Christ and resulting in an impersonal and distant concept of God.[38] This same tendency is present in the contemporary tendency to separate the "one God" from the "Triune God," a move that Torrance also traces back to medieval theology.

In the contemporary context, Torrance attributes the re-centralization of the doctrine of the Trinity to "the epoch-making work of Karl Barth."[39] In Torrance's reading of historical theology, Barth's emphasis upon the evangelical significance of the Trinity was vital because it set Christian theology back upon a soteriological basis.[40] Torrance mentions other theologians who followed Barth in his re-centralization of the Trinity, including H. R. Mackintosh—who we saw in the last chapter was a key figure in Torrance's theological formation—and Karl Rahner, a Roman Catholic theologian who shared Barth's rejection of any division between the "one God" and the "Triune God."[41] Torrance suggests that individuals such as these, rejecting the inherent dualism that such a division entails, have done much to recover the classical doctrine of the Holy Trinity.[42] Torrance also derived great ecumenical hope from the fact that despite their divergent denominational backgrounds, Barth and Rahner reached very similar conclusions in their doctrine of the Trinity.[43]

THE REVEALING OF THE DOCTRINE OF GOD

Torrance views the doctrine of the Trinity as theology proper: "the innermost heart of the Christian Faith, the central dogma of classical theology, the fundamental grammar of our knowledge of God."[44] The doctrine of the Trinity signals one of the most startling mysteries and distinctive aspects of the

Christian faith: God wants to be known by those whom he has created. Humanity was created to be in relationship with their Creator so the doctrine of the Trinity is of redemptive significance. Since all that God does in love for humanity flows from his eternal being, the transcendent doctrine of the Holy Trinity has to do with the "lofty yet down-to-earth truth of the Gospel."[45] Torrance writes in awe,

> God is not some immutable, impassible deity locked up in his self-isolation who cannot be touched with our human feelings, pains and hurts, but on the contrary is the kind of God who freely acts and passionately interacts with us in this world, for in his own eternal Being he is the ever living, loving and acting God who will not be without us but who in his grace freely determines himself for us as our God and Saviour.[46]

For Torrance it is the person of Jesus Christ who is the interpretative key to the Trinity and for all ensuing theological endeavors. "It is certainly the incarnation of the eternal Word of God made flesh in Jesus Christ which prescribes for us in Christian theology both its proper matter and form."[47] At the same time, Torrance is emphatic that we must understand Jesus both in the matrix of his divine relations and the historical human context he was born into. This section will continue by briefly considering the partial knowledge of God revealed in the Old Testament and its preparation for Christ before turning to what must be said about God in light of his full revelation as Father, Son, and Spirit.

The Trinitarian Work of Creation

While God has made himself known since the beginning of the world, creation by itself does not give rise to the personal knowledge of God that we receive through the Son and in the Spirit.[48] Since there is no direct correlation of identity between God and what he has made, we cannot extrapolate what God *must* be like on the basis of what the world is like. Doing this creates a concept of a god who is not identical to the God who has revealed himself to us in Jesus Christ.

A helpful dictum for thinking about the work of God in creation is Athanasius's statement "God was always Father, he was not always Creator or Maker."[49] The first identifier is an ontological and uncreated relation of identity; the second is a contingent, created relation.[50] The fatherhood of God is intrinsic to his being—God has *always* been Father, Son, and Holy Spirit—but creating the world out of nothing was something *new*. God's fatherhood is not constituted by his relationship to creation. Again quoting Torrance, "While God was always Father and was Father independently of what he has created, as Creator he acted in a way that he had not done before, in bringing about absolutely new events—this means that the creation of the world out of nothing is something *new even for God*. God was always Father, but he *became* Creator."[51] Although we may name God "Father" as the unbegotten source and creator of all that exists, this is quite a different sense from the way in which we must think of God as the unique Father of the Lord Jesus Christ, a distinct triune *hypostasis*. Torrance takes his cue in this from another Athanasian quote, "It would be more godly and true to signify God from the Son and call him Father, than to name God from his works alone and call him Unoriginate."[52]

Creation is a trinitarian work and to argue otherwise results in a curtailed understanding of the scope of God's redemptive work.[53] Even though creation is a "new" act for God, Torrance considers it proper to God's being for it was not something that God was forced to undertake but an act of divine freedom and love. Both creation and incarnation reveal God's freedom to do new things outside his own being without compromising his transcendence. The paradoxical way in which God is distinct from creation yet has freely chosen to be present within it is developed by Torrance's focus on the strong connection between creation and covenant. Torrance remarks that it is unsurprising that "the creation and its history should bear the imprint of the Trinity upon it."[54]

When we view the divine act of creation through the lens of the incarnation and see God's free outpouring of love manifest in Jesus Christ, we find the basis on which we may reverently speak of a *reason* for creation. We only understand the Creator-creation relation in the light of the incarnation: the universe's existence is upheld on the basis of God's being as love.[55] Because the divine love revealed in the incarnation lies at the very heart of God's being, creation itself is to be understood by that very love.[56] As Torrance summarizes, "creation is proleptically conditioned by redemption."[57] Creation involves human beings made in the image of God. The re-creation involves God taking on the image of humanity, involving incarnation and substitution so that humanity may be re-made.[58] Creation is the work of the whole Trinity, for, as Torrance concludes,

> The whole *raison d'être* of the universe lies in the fact that God will not be alone, that he will not be without us, but has freely and purposely created the universe and bound it to himself as the sphere where he may ungrudgingly pour out his love, and where we may enjoy communion with him.[59]

Israel's Role in Anticipating the Triune God

Having seen that creation is a triune work, even though the internal relations of God's being are not revealed in the Old Testament, we must next consider how the doctrine of the Trinity is anticipated by God's interaction with the people of Israel. Israel was chosen to fulfill a purpose that transcended their own national existence—they were to be the primary conduit of God's self-revelation. The image of Israel being "molded" is frequently used by Torrance, drawing on the metaphor of a potter who continues to mold the clay on his pottery wheel until he is happy with the finished creation. In the same way God continued to mold Israel throughout the centuries in such a way that their communal existence prepared the way for the incarnation to take place. Torrance explains what he draws from this metaphor, stating that God "selected one small race out of the whole mass of humanity, and subjected it to intensive interaction and dialogue with himself in such a way that he might mould and shape this people in the service of his self-revelation."[60]

Israel's primary knowledge of God was drawn from the covenantal context. God was known to Israel both as their Creator and Redeemer, but knowledge of God *as he was in his own being* was restricted by the demarcation that existed between God and the people. The mediatorial office of the priesthood was a visible sign of this separation, based on God's declaration to Moses that no one may see God's face and live (Exod. 33:20).[61] Late Judaism also veered away from the positive knowledge of God revealed in his acts, instead holding God "to be so utterly transcendent that he is ineffable and unnameable, quite unknowable in the undifferentiated oneness of his being, so that any claim to know him in himself was rejected with horror as impiety."[62] This was a divergence between Judaism and the early Church because, while Judaism increasingly viewed God as far off, the Christian Church acknowledged that God was no longer knowable only according to his external works for through Christ and the Spirit God's internally differentiated being is revealed.[63]

We noted the trinitarian significance of Jesus' using "I am" language in the Gospel of John in our previous discussion of the way Torrance draws on Scripture to develop a doctrine of the Trinity. Continuing in this vein, Torrance notes the clear link between God's self-naming to Israel as Yahweh—"I am"—and Jesus' adoption of this language as revealing the identity of being between the Father and the Son. In the Old Testament, this self-naming is in the context of God's covenantal redemption of Israel where God is known through his actions to redeem Israel, but it was not until the Son's incarnation that God could be known "familiarly and personally."[64] This is again strengthened by Jesus' own use of "I am." In him we meet God personally, and when Jesus Christ speaks, it is God who we hear speaking.[65] There is no conflict between the monotheism that was vital to Israel's faith and the unfolding trinitarian revelation of the New Testament so Torrance can insist, "Nowhere is there any suggestion either that this new revelation of God as Father, through Jesus Christ his Son and the Communion of the Holy Spirit, is given or received apart from God's revelation of himself through the medium of Israel. Jesus himself was a Jew, and insisted that salvation is from the Jews, and that Jews know whom they worship while Gentiles do not."[66]

The Incarnation and the Revelation of the Triune God

On this basis it is fitting to return to the centrality of the incarnation for our knowledge of God. There is no knowledge of God available to humanity unless God reveals himself to us. Irenaeus describes Jesus as the "bridge" between God and humanity. Christ is both fully God and fully human, and it is uniquely in him that there exists no gap between human knowledge of God and God's self-knowledge. Jesus is fully human, and yet his divine nature is "grounded in, derived from and is continuously upheld by what is called the 'consubstantial communion' within the Holy Trinity."[67] It is thus that Torrance terms the self-revelation of God through Jesus Christ as the "greatest revolution in our knowledge of God."[68] God is no longer far off and unknowable but comes to us in Christ, condescending to be with us without losing his transcendence, drawing us into communion. The following quote summarizes the doctrine of the incarnation well.

> By the Incarnation Christian theology means that at a definite point in space and time the Son of God became man, born at Bethlehem of Mary, a virgin espoused to a man called Joseph, a Jew of the tribe and lineage of David, and towards the end of the reign of Herod the Great in Judaea. Given the name of Jesus, He fulfilled His mission from the Father, living out the span of earthly life allotted to Him until He was crucified under Pontius Pilate, but when after three days He rose again from the dead the eyes of Jesus' disciples were opened to what it all meant: they knew Him to be God's Son, declared with power and installed in Messianic Office, and so they went out to proclaim Him to all nations as the Lord and Saviour of the World. Thus it is the faith and understanding of the Christian Church that in Jesus Christ God Himself in His own Being has come into our world and is actively present as personal Agent within our physical and historical existence. As both God of God and Man of man Jesus Christ is the actual Mediator between God and man and man and God in all things, even in regard to space-time relations. He constitutes in Himself the rational and personal Medium in whom God meets man in his creaturely reality and brings man without, having to leave his creaturely reality, into communion with Himself.[69]

Jesus Christ is the complete and true revelation of the eternal God within time and space. It is through Jesus Christ's unique relationship to the Father that we are able to know God as our Father and are invited into the communion of the Trinity. Conversely, it is in the light of the Father's love revealed through the Son that we know God as the Creator who has freely chosen to be "for others" and is acting to reconcile and redeem his creation. Since Torrance argues that theological inquiry should know God in accordance with the way that his internal relations are disclosed to us through the incarnation,[70] we must begin with the fact that

> it is only in Christ in whom God's self-revelation is identical with himself that we may rightly apprehend it and really know God as he is in himself, in the oneness and differentiation of God within his own eternal Being as Father, Son and Holy Spirit, for what God is toward us in his historical self-manifestation in the Gospel as Father, Son and Holy Spirit, he is revealed to be inherently and eternally in himself.[71]

This is the deep truth that Torrance refers to when he reminds us that there is no God behind the back of Jesus, demonstrating the evangelical significance of the doctrine of the Holy Trinity. If there were, we could not help but live anxiously lest the God whom we will meet at the end of the age is different from the God who meets us in Jesus Christ.[72] Familiarity with the concept of the *homoousion* will be of great help in understanding this further. The *homoousion* affirms the absolute identity of being between the Father, Son, and Spirit. It operates as an "exegetical and clarificatory expression" but also as an "interpretative instrument of thought."[73] Torrance states that the *homoousion* stands for the Church's assertion that Jesus Christ is

> not a mere symbol, some representation of God detached from God, but God in his own Being and Act come among us, expressing in our human form the Word which he is eternally in himself, so that in our relations with Jesus Christ we have to do directly with the ultimate Reality of God. As the epitomized expression of that fact, the *homoousion* is the ontological and epistemological linchpin of Christian theology. With it, everything hangs together; without it, everything ultimately falls apart.[74]

Sometimes when Torrance refers to the *homoousion* he does so only with reference to the oneness of the Father and Son, with no mention of the Spirit. This is because the Council of Nicea initially applied the *homoousion* only to the Son, which is why Torrance sometimes focuses on how everything rests on the mutual relation between the Father and Son. It is not that the Spirit does not come into this but rather that in terms of God's economy, the Son reveals the Father to us first.[75] Although the *homoousion* of the Son was affirmed at Nicea, it was not until Constantinople in 381 AD that the *homoousion* of the Spirit was affirmed. It was between these two major councils that the Council of Alexandria agreed to the statement "one being, three persons" in 362 AD. The recognition of the Spirit as *homoousios* with the Father and Son is vital, for the Word and Spirit are not "ephemeral modes of God's presence" or "transient media external to himself" but are "the objective ontological personal forms of his self-giving and self-imparting."[76] The Spirit is not an impersonal force emanating from God but is fully and equally God with the Father and the Son.

To conclude this section, we need to look to the different roles of the Son and Spirit. While God is known "as he makes himself known to us through the revealing and saving agency of his Word and Spirit,"[77] the Son becomes incarnate but the Spirit does not. The mutual mediation of the Son and Spirit is a vital part of Torrance's doctrine of the Trinity. The incarnate Son is God veiled in human flesh. In comparison, the Spirit meets us in his direct objectivity as God so that our interaction with the Spirit within space and time is notably different from that with the Son. Jesus Christ was born of the Spirit, received the Spirit, and offered himself to the Father through the Spirit. He now mediates the Spirit to us so that humanity may enter into communion with God.[78] In the incarnate Son "the eternal Spirit of the living God has composed himself, as it were, to dwell with human nature, and human nature has been adapted and become accustomed to receive and bear the same Holy Spirit."[79]

Developing this further, Torrance observes that the Spirit is a "transparent and translucent hypostasis"[80] who rather than being directly known in his own person "hides himself, as it were, behind Christ."[81] The Spirit is the invisible light who lights up the face of God in Jesus Christ. Without this light being "thrown upon" Christ, we are unable to grasp the oneness of being and act between the Father and the Son—this must be "reinforced and deepened by the indwelling illumination of the Holy Spirit."[82] This is where we find the "critical edge" of the *homoousion*. It means that we can't project "creaturely, corporeal or sexist" elements of Jesus' humanity into the divine being of God.[83] Human knowledge of God only takes place as the Spirit enables us to participate in the union and communion of the Trinity through sustaining and upholding our finite, creaturely selves and bringing us to our true *telos* of participation in the triune life of God while simultaneously preventing us from creating any form of anthropomorphic theology.[84] We are enabled to know the Triune God in the movement from the Father through the Son and in the Spirit, and we are enabled to respond to God in the Spirit, through the Son, to the Father.[85]

To conclude this brief consideration of the *homoousion* we may cite Torrance:

> The doctrine of the *homoousion* was as decisive as it was revolutionary: it expressed the evangelical truth that what God is toward us and has freely done for us in his love and grace, and continues to do in the midst of us through his Word and Spirit, he really is *in himself*, and that he really is *in the internal relations and personal properties* of his transcendent Being as the Holy Trinity the very same Father, Son, and Holy Spirit, that he is in his revealing and saving activity in time and space toward mankind, and ever will be.[86]

A COMMUNION OF FULLNESS—ONE BEING, THREE PERSONS

The rest of this chapter will explore the theological vocabulary that Torrance uses to explain the doctrine of the Trinity—including *hypostasis*, *ousia*, and *perichoresis*—and then offer a thorough survey of the relationship between the ontological Trinity and the economic Trinity in order to unpack the idea of *koinōnia*, or "communion," the motif that is central not only to Torrance's doctrine of the Trinity but to understanding how the Trinity shapes his ecclesiology. Our exposition of the doctrine of the Holy Trinity will consequently be "intentionally circular" as we shift between thinking about God in himself (*in se*) and God for us (*ad alios*). When we think of the whole Trinity, we are "subsidiarily aware" of the persons, and when we think of a particular person, we are implicitly aware of the whole Trinity.[87] This is in keeping with Torrance's observation that "understanding of the whole is not built up from a prior grasp of its constituent parts, but in which the whole while understood out of itself is nevertheless understood with subsidiary attention to its parts, and the parts are properly understood in the light of the whole."[88]

Torrance never considers the one *ousia* (being) of God apart from the three *hypostases* (persons) or the three persons apart from the one being. God is only known as a whole "in a circle of reciprocal relations,"[89] and all three persons are worshipped together. The language of "whole" and "part" is only used reluctantly because Father, Son, and Spirit are each wholly God. We never think of God's being as an undifferentiated wholeness but always of the three-in-one, God's fullness of personal being.[90] Offering a faithful account of the Trinity thus requires us to move between God's Trinity and God's Unity, not giving either precedence.[91]

In order to determine the specific way in which we are to think of God, we need to comprehend the meaning of *ousia* (being) and *hypostasis* (person). These were originally used as cognate terms in the original text of the Nicene Creed where they both referred to "being." However, there was potential ambiguity in their interpretation: referring to the three persons as three divine beings inadvertently promoted tritheism. Their usage was then more carefully defined so that *ousia* began to refer to the being of God while *hypostasis* signified the distinctions of the three persons. Expressed in another way, *ousia* refers to being in respect of internal reality and so has a primarily inward reference, while *hypostasis* has to do with the outward reference of being and thus with the *onto*-relations that constitute the three hypostases.[92] While *ousia* has to do with God's "internal relations" and *hypostasis* is "being as otherness," both *ousia* and *hypostasis* have to do with God's being.[93] In our technical usage here, following Torrance, *ousia* refers to the "one being" while *hypostasis* refers to the "three persons."

A brief comment here on the use of theological terms will help as we proceed. Because of the significant clashes between Jewish belief, its development into Christian doctrine, and its articulation in the Graeco-Roman world, new concepts and terminology were required.[94] Hellenistic vocabulary, such as *homoousion*, was reinterpreted in accordance with Scripture and the apostolic tradition and given a distinctly theological slant.[95] Torrance thus notes,

> Technical terms are a kind of theological shorthand which helps us to give careful expression to basic truths and their conceptual interconnections . . . in the passage of theological clarification from one level of understanding to another and back again. However, in the last resort they are no more than empty abstract propositions apart from their real content in the specific self-communication of God to us in his revealing and saving acts in history in which he has made himself known to us as Father, Son and Holy Spirit.[96]

Theological statements require "an interior and dynamic logic that enables them to correspond faithfully to and therefore set forth adequately the economic pattern of God's saving acts in Jesus Christ."[97] They must derive from truly hearing the Word of God rather than being "speculative constructs out of the Church's creative spirituality."[98]

Ousia

Ousia is a key example of a theologically reinterpreted word. Torrance insists we should not understand God's *ousia* in any metaphysical and static sense or according to philosophical categories. Although we can speak of God's being as that "which is and subsists by itself,"[99] the theological usage of this term derives from God's creative, revelatory, and redemptive actions.[100] Torrance follows Athanasius who noted that *ousia* was derived from *einai* (to be) and then linked it to the divine statement *ego eimi* (I am). Using the definitive text of Exodus 3:14, Athanasius concluded that just as Yahweh's redemptive acts for Israel revealed the dynamic nature of the Father, Jesus appropriates this saying to himself in order to reveal his shared *ousia* and redemptive mission with the Father.[101] *Ousia* came to refer to the shared internal reality of the Triune God, with a particular emphasis on God's "fullness of being" expressed in the identity of being between the Father, Son, and Spirit.[102]

This focus on *ousia* as dynamic being is why we find relatively little in Torrance's work that is concerned with the perfections, or the divine attributes. These derive more from Hellenistic philosophy than from God's active work in the world, which is also why Torrance rejects the idea of essences, substances, and energies.[103] When Torrance does mention the divine perfections, he is careful to ground them in God's economic actions. Among these we may include omnipotence, which Torrance defines by what God has done in humbling himself in becoming incarnate—"omnipotence clothed in littleness"[104]—rather than by what God could potentially do; impassibility, which is defined in the light of the crucifixion for it is as one who is both fully God and fully human that Christ dies and therefore God's ability to suffer is demonstrated in this historical event;[105] and immutability, which is not a static concept but rather God's "living immutability"[106] as one "who is and always will be one and the same in his eternal faithfulness."[107]

Hypostasis

In contrast to *ousia*, *hypostasis* was developed by the Church as they tried to work out how to speak of the distinctions within the Godhead of the Father, Son, and Spirit. The original use of *hypostasis* is from Hebrews 1:3, which refers to the Son as the image of God's being. Its theological meaning was then filled out in association with the other biblical references to *onoma* (name), *autos* (oneself), and *prosōpon* (face).[108] Torrance defines the divine *hypostasis* as "self-subsistent self-identifying subject-being in objective relations with others."[109] We cannot think of any of the divine persons independently. Since they have their being in one another, neither Father, Son, nor Spirit may be known apart from the other two persons of the Trinity.[110]

This is where Torrance's description of the triune onto-relations comes into play, without which we cannot properly understand the trinitarian *hypostases*. The three persons of the Trinity are what they are only in relation to each other. Since they share the same *ousia*, each distinct person is simultaneously part of a whole so that "the relations between the divine Persons belong to what they are as Persons—they are constitutive onto-relations."[111] The relationships between the three persons are therefore ontological relations and have to do with the very being of God. The triune persons are persons-in-relation and not three individual persons, for Father, Son, and Spirit share their "absolute identity of being."[112]

Perichoresis

So that we may understand these onto-relations better, we must also define the term *perichoresis*, which has to do with the coinherence, or the mutual indwelling, of the three triune persons.[113] *Perichoresis* was first used as a verb to refer to the two natures of Christ and then later as a noun to refer to how the triune persons contain each other without commingling. The key point is that they dwell *in* and *with* each other,[114] for "the three divine Persons mutually dwell in one another and coinhere or inexist in one another while nevertheless remaining other than one another and distinct from one another."[115] *Perichoresis* is therefore primarily a concept that deals with the inner relations of the Triune God.

> "Father," "Son" and "Holy Spirit" are found to refer not just to three interrelated forms in which divine revelation functions, but to three distinctly hypostatic or personal Realities, or objective self-identifying Subsistences of God's Being and Activity. They are more than modes, aspects, faces, names or relations in God's manifestation of himself to us, for they are inseparable from the hypostatic Realities of which they are the distinctive self-presentations of divine Being—the three divine Hypostases or Persons, Father, Son and Holy Spirit who in their differentiation from one another and in their communion with one another *are* the one eternal God.[116]

A STRATIFIED STRUCTURE OF REALITY

When we hold together *ousia* and *hypostasis*, we think correctly of God as a "fullness of Personal Being" and a "transcendent Communion of Persons."[117] Neither one undifferentiated reality nor three independent persons, the three persons who are in eternal communion with each other are the eternal God and undertake the same redemptive work. God is the Father who gave his Son in atoning sacrifice, the Son who loves and gave himself for us, and the Spirit who brings us into the Triune communion.[118] This way of thinking of God is central for Torrance and as such it offers a helpful example of how his scientific theology interacts with his trinitarian theology.

In developing a structure of theological knowledge, Torrance draws on the process that takes place in natural science—when the scientist intuitively discerns patterns that reveal an intrinsic order in the natural world, investigates them rigorously, and seeks to refine the concepts—and applies this to the structure of our knowledge of God, particularly in relation to the doctrine of the Holy Trinity.[119] This leads to a "stratified structure comprising several coordinate levels concerned with God as he is in himself, with the incarnation of his self-revelation in Jesus Christ, and with our receiving and articulating of that revelation."[120] Such a structure helps us reckon with the way that in the incarnation God reveals himself in space and time without becoming "netted within the spatial-temporal processes of our world."[121]

Torrance identifies three primary levels of reality that are constantly cross-referenced with each other. There are theoretically an indefinite number of levels, but he considers three sufficient for a structure of theological reality.[122] Benjamin Myers describes these three levels as the levels of "tacit theology," "formalised theology," and "the meta-theological."[123]

The primary level is the "basic level," also referred to as the "evangelical and doxological level" or that of "incipient theology." It has to do with our intuitive apprehension of knowledge through experience.[124] In theological terms, knowledge of God is found in the ongoing experience of the Church's worship, communion, and fellowship. This involves the proclamation of Christ as witnessed in the New Testament as well as our personal encounter with Christ in space and time. We only know God through sharing in his fellowship and participating in the fellowship of the Church. "We learn far more about God as Father, Son and Holy Spirit, into whose Name we have been baptised, within the family and fellowship and living tradition of the Church than we can ever say."[125] This is why the split between academic theology and the lived experience of the Christian life is so devastating.[126]

The secondary level is theological, where the intuitive knowledge of the first level is organized and expressed with a focus on simplicity of expression. Concepts at this secondary level must both clarify the reality of the first level and be testable by that prior intuitive knowledge.[127] The theologian must form

> appropriate intellectual instruments with which to lay bare the underlying epistemological patterns of thought, and by tracing the chains of connection throughout the coherent body of theological truths, they feel their way forward to a deeper and more precise knowledge of what God has revealed of himself.[128]

At the secondary level, the inchoate or implicit knowledge of God as triune, which is known from redemptive history and experience, is given explicit formulation as the doctrine of the Trinity. There is a strong focus on the acts of God just as it was the focus of the patristic writers on God's self-communication to us through the incarnation, in time and space and without ceasing to be God, that formed their understanding of God's economic activity. This level has a strong soteriological bent.[129] The *homoousion* is a core principle because it distills all that the New Testament has to say on the oneness of the Father, Son, and Spirit,[130] guides the movement from a preconceptual to conceptual understanding of the Holy Trinity,[131] and allows our thought to pass from the economic to the ontological Trinity.[132]

The *homoousion* and hypostatic union function in tandem, allowing us to advance first from the level of intuitive knowing to the second level where we are concerned with the economic Trinity, enabling us then to refine our grasp of the doctrine of the Trinity as we move from considering the economic Trinity to considering the ontological Trinity at the tertiary level.[133] In moving between these three levels, a radical theological revolution takes place in how we think; rejecting epistemological dualism, we learn that "Jesus Christ the incarnate Son is one in Being and Act with God the Father. What Jesus Christ does for us and to us, and what the Holy Spirit does in us, is what God himself does for us, to us and in us."[134]

At the tertiary level, or the "higher theological level," the theory of the secondary level is deepened, simplified, and formalized in "ultimate theoretic structures characterised by logical economy and simplicity."[135] The fewer concepts that exist at this level, the wider their applicability, so one seeks to refine principles and patterns to be as simple as possible.[136] In theological terms, we move from what has been revealed through God's economic actions into the "Trinitarian relations immanent in God himself which lie behind, and are the sustaining ground of, the relations of the economic Trinity."[137] There is a strong focus on the epistemological and ontological structure of our knowledge of the eternal being of God.[138] At this level we become even more aware of the finiteness of our capacity to know God and to express what we know about God. The key theological concept that Torrance draws on at the level of the ontological Trinity is *perichoresis*, which we have already defined as the mutual coinherence of the three divine persons.

The three levels of this stratified structure of knowledge are governed from the higher levels to the lower levels. Although the truth-content is derived "from below"—for this is how God reveals himself to us in space and time—the truth content is "ontologically constituted" from above in accordance with revelation.[139] This is because "in the hierarchy of theological truths it is the living God himself who is the supreme Truth who retains his own authority over all our inquiry and understanding."[140] Another way of expressing this is demonstrated by Habets, who describes the movement from the first to third level as an epistemic movement that has to do with our knowing and the movement from the third to first level as a theological movement that has to do with the being of God.[141]

The Critical and Constructive Contributions of This Model

God has genuinely revealed himself to humanity, but while we can truly apprehend God, we are incapable of fully comprehending God. God is not contained by our knowledge of him. Consequently, this stratified model is not a "picturing model" or a "theoretic model" but a "disclosure model."[142] It does not derive from what we observe of God or our ideas about what God must be like. Because "not the representative, but the referential element is primary,"[143] this model allows divine reality to disclose itself to us. Rather than the doctrine of the Trinity being molded according to human thought categories, we instead think of the Trinity in accordance with its objective reality. Such theological constructs must remain open to constructive revision in the light of God's self-revelation, but this stratified structure gives us confidence that humankind's reception of revelation genuinely corresponds to the reality of God so that God is known according to his nature (*physin*), and according to his truth (*aletheia*).[144]

The first contribution of this stratified model is that it directs the way in which we think of the relationship between the economic and ontological Trinity, reminding us that the way in which God is revealed by his actions in space and time is also who God is in himself eternally. When Jesus came among us as a human he lived a real human life, but through his human life he showed us who God was.[145] Torrance argues that "while everything pivots upon the downright act of God himself in Christ, that act of God takes the concrete form of the actual historical man Jesus."[146] This structure of knowledge lies behind our earlier discussion of the centrality of the incarnation to revelation.

The second contribution of this model is that it reminds us that temporal ideas and concepts cannot be read back into the eternal life of God.[147] This helps to prevent anthropomorphism and highlights the importance of critical awareness in all our speech about God. Because the Son *and* the Spirit are both *homoousios* with the Father—and each other—we encounter the incarnate Son within space and time as a human and the Holy Spirit in his "direct objectivity" as God. The joint activity of the Son and the Spirit stops us reading material images back into God's eternal being.[148]

The third, and most significant, contribution of this model is for the life of the Church. Ecclesiology is "worked out" in space and time on the basic level, is heavily shaped by the secondary level, and is controlled by the tertiary level so that this is a way of correlating the life and experience of the Church with the being of God.

UNION AND COMMUNION WITH THE TRIUNE GOD

The final element of Torrance's trinitarian theology that needs to be highlighted is the idea of participation—the way in which humanity is enabled to share in the union and communion of the Triune God. Our focus at this juncture will not be on our participation in the triune *koinōnia* but rather on the nature of God's being that enables this participation. What needs to be made clear is the way in which the communion that humanity has with God derives from the fullness of communion that God is in his own being.

We have seen that God's being is not to be thought of in static terms, as in the Greek philosophical sense of "essence" or "substance," and that Torrance instead argues that our knowledge of God is based on the incarnation of Jesus Christ. We have also discussed how creation and incarnation are both new events for God—not new in the sense of an external factor added into God but new as historical events that required a definite act. They are events that take place so that God can share his own life and love with us. This invites us to think of movement within the life of God, which Torrance describes as the *direction* of God's eternal life.[149] God's life has its own time—an eternal time that is different from created time in that it lacks the distinction of past, present, and future but that nonetheless has movement and constancy.

Pentecost also correlates to creation and the incarnation in the sense that it marks a shift in how God is present to us in the world. As Torrance comments, "taken together these new decisive acts of God in creation, incarnation, and the coming of the Spirit, have breath-taking implications for our understanding of the unlimited *freedom* of God."[150] Together these events demonstrate "the movement and activity of God towards the fulfilment of his eternal purpose of love" and reveal that his "eternal Being is also a divine Becoming"[151] or that "His Becoming is his Being in movement."[152] On the other hand, we must not doubt that God remains "who he is in the undeviating self-determination of his own Life and Activity."[153] God's economic actions flow from his eternal and unchanging life.

In discussing terms such as *ousia*, *hypostasis*, and *perichoresis* alongside the triune onto-relations, we have emphasized that God's being is neither an undifferentiated oneness nor three individual persons. Instead God's being is a communion of love and is "essentially personal, dynamic and relational Being."[154] The three divine persons only have their being in each other, which is why we think of their relations to each other as constitutive onto-relations—the Father is not the Father without the Son and the Spirit, the Son is not the Son without the Father and the Spirit, and the Spirit is not the Spirit without the Father and the Son. The three triune persons share complete identity of being, revealing God's *ousia* as "an ever-living ever-loving Being, the *Being for Others*, which the three divine Persons have in common."[155] The triune onto-relations are not selfish but selfless love: they are relations of freely given reciprocal love.[156]

The other aspect that must be considered alongside the perichoretic onto-relations of the Trinity is the equality of the triune persons. Torrance attributes the issue of subordinationism, or a form of hierarchy within the Trinity, to the Cappadocian Fathers. He argues that by downplaying the personal sense of *ousia*, Cappadocian teaching led to tritheistic tendencies and a weakened form of Athanasius's statement that whatever we say of the Father, we may say of the Son and Spirit except "Father." This led to the idea that the *hypostasis* of the Father alone is the *archē*, the "Principle, Origin, or Source" of the Trinity, which consequently means that the Son and Spirit derive their deity from the Father, denying their full equality.[157] Torrance views subordinationism as a heresy alongside Arianism and Sabellianism[158] and strongly reacts against this aspect of the Cappadocian teaching,[159] bringing the doctrine of *perichoresis* to bear on the idea of the divine monarchy in order to insist that the *monarchia* speaks of the whole Godhead rather than the Father only.[160] Eugenio rightly notes that "although Torrance accepts a trinitarian economic subordination, he repudiates any talk about priority or superiority that is read back into the Trinity *in se*."[161] This is also the subject of a chapter in Molnar's work *Faith, Freedom and the Spirit* in which he explains why he thinks that Torrance's reasoning is more consistent than Barth's on the issue of relating Christ's economic obedience to the perichoretic equality of the three triune persons.[162]

Torrance's conclusion is that for the triune God, "Being and Communion are one and the same."[163] Since God is revealed to be a communion in himself, this is the basis for the communion that he establishes with us.

> The real meaning of the Being or *I am* of God becomes clear in the two-way fellowship he freely establishes with his people as their Lord and Saviour, for it has to do with the saving will or self-determination of God in his love and grace to be with them as their God as well as his determination of them to be with him as his redeemed children. The Being of God is to be understood, therefore, as living and dynamic Being, fellowship-creating or communion-constituting Being, but if it is communion-constituting Being toward us it is surely to be understood also as ever-living, ever-dynamic Communion (*koinōnia*) in the Godhead. By his very Nature he is a Communion in himself, which is the ground in the Being of God for his communion with his people.

Consequently, because "being for others" is who God is *in himself*, this is also how we understand God's being in relation to humanity. God is not constituted by, or dependent on, his relationship to others, for the free outflow of his love toward us is determined by his being *ad intra*.[164] God is a communion of love in himself, and it is on this basis that he seeks and establishes a communion of love between himself and us. God's being is fellowship-creating and communion-constituting but only because this is who God has always been in his own eternal life. Since God's being and acts are inseparable, we come to understand that

> the Love that God is, is not that of solitary inactive or static love, whatever that may be, but the active movement of reciprocal loving within the Being of God which is the one ultimate Source of all love. That God is Love means that he is the eternally loving One in himself who loves through himself, whose Love moves unceasingly within his eternal Life as God, so that in loving us in the gift of his dear Son and the mission of his Spirit he loves us with the very Love which he is.[165]

Continuing to think in this same way, we see that the incarnation and the ascension are two corresponding moments. In the incarnation, the eternal triune love moves into history, most fully revealed at the Cross. In the ascension, the love revealed in the incarnation is shown to be grounded in the trinitarian *koinōnia* itself. Thus *theologia* and *economia* are once more intertwined; God's being and acts are inseparable, seen in the trinitarian love that gives itself to us.[166] The condescension of God to share in our humanity, and the lifting up of humanity through his Spirit to participate in the fellowship of the Trinity, gives a "triune grammar" to our knowledge of God.[167]

CONCLUSION

All that God is revealed to be in his actions toward humanity is entirely consistent with who God is in his triune self as the three persons who "dwell in one another, love one another, give themselves to one another and receive from one another in the Communion of the Holy Trinity."[168] The *koinōnia* of the Holy Trinity, and God's nature as "being for others" are key to keep in mind as we continue to unpack Torrance's trinitarian ecclesiology.

NOTES

1. Thomas F. Torrance, *Divine Meaning: Studies in Patristic Hermeneutics* (Edinburgh: T&T Clark, 1995), 5.
2. Thomas F. Torrance, *Reality and Evangelical Theology: The Realism of Christian Revelation* (Eugene, OR: Wipf and Stock, 2003), 119.
3. John Webster, "T. F. Torrance on Scripture," *Scottish Journal of Theology* 65, no. 1 (2012): 37–38.
4. Torrance, *Reality and Evangelical Theology*, 119.
5. Ibid., 91.
6. Ibid., 89.
7. Torrance, *Divine Meaning*, 7–10; Thomas F. Torrance, *Atonement: The Person and Work of Christ*, ed. Robert T. Walker, 340 (Downers Grove, IL: InterVarsity Academic Press, 2009).
8. Thomas F. Torrance, *The Christian Doctrine of God: One Being Three Persons* (Edinburgh: T&T Clark, 1996), 49.
9. Ibid., ix. For further information, see Myk Habets, "Theological Interpretation of Scripture in Sermonic Mode: The Case of T. F. Torrance," in *Ears That Hear: Explorations in Theological Interpretation of the Bible*, ed. Joel B. Green and Tim Meadowcroft, 43–69 (Sheffield, UK: Sheffield Phoenix Press, 2013).
10. Ibid., 43.
11. Ibid., 35.
12. Ibid., 43.
13. Ibid., 48, 58, 71, 164, 95.
14. Ibid., 71.
15. This is the order taken in Torrance, *The Christian Doctrine of God*, 13[illegible]–67.
16. Ibid., 137. Torrance also makes note of 2 Cor. 13:14, 1 Cor. 12:4–6, Gal. 4:4–6, and Eph. 4:4–6. These are all explicit triadic formulations, but notably, the persons are mentioned in different orders so that there is no sense of a hierarchical trinitarian formula being developed.
17. Thomas F. Torrance, "A Sermon on the Trinity," *Biblical Theology* 6, no. 2 (1956) serves as an example, as does Torrance, *The Christian Doctrine of God*, 32–[illegible]2. These different orders demonstrate the difference between the *ordo cognoscendi* (order of knowing) and *ordo essendi* (order of being.)
18. Torrance, *The Christian Doctrine of God*, 176.
19. Webster, "T. F. Torrance on Scripture," 59.
20. Ibid., 60.
21. Ibid. See also Darren Sarisky, "T. F. Torrance on Biblical Interpretation," *International Journal of Systematic Theology* 11, no. 3 (July 2009): 345 in which Sarisky acknowledges the challenges of Torrance's a priori approach to Scripture. See also Bryan J. Gray, "Towards Better Ways of Reading the Bible," *Scottish Journal of Theology* 33, no. 4 (1980): 301–15.
22. Thomas F. Torrance, *The Trinitarian Faith* (Edinburgh: T&T Clark, 1993), 2. Torrance claims that he tried to let the Fathers speak for themselves, however we should note that his

selection of quotations definitely highlights the congruence between the Fathers and his own theology.

23. Thomas F. Torrance, *Incarnation: The Person and Life of Christ*, ed. Robert T. Walker, 198 (Downers Grove, IL: InterVarsity Press, 2008); Thomas F. Torrance, *Trinitarian Perspectives: Toward Doctrinal Agreement* (Edinburgh: T&T Clark, 1994), 7–20; Thomas F. Torrance, *Theology in Reconciliation* (Eugene, OR: Wipf and Stock, 1996), 215–66; and Thomas F. Torrance, "Athanasius: A Reassessment of His Theology," *Abba Salama* 5 (1974): 186.

24. Thomas F. Torrance, "Review of C. R. B. Shapland (trans.), *The Letters of St. Athanasius: Concerning the Holy Spirit*," *Scottish Journal of Theology* 5, no. 2 (June 1952): 205–6.

25. Torrance, *The Christian Doctrine of God*, 76. For a fuller sample of Torrance's engagement with Irenaeus's teaching, take note of Thomas F. Torrance, "The Deposit of Faith," *Scottish Journal of Theology* 36, no. 1 (1983): 128; and Thomas F. Torrance, "Kerygmatic Proclamation of the Gospel: The Demonstration of Apostolic Preaching of Irenaios of Lyons," *Greek Orthodox Theological Review* 37, nos. 1–2 (1992): 105–21.

26. Torrance, *The Trinitarian Faith*, 2–3.

27. Torrance, *The Christian Doctrine of God*, ix–x.

28. Torrance, *The Trinitarian Faith*, 17.

29. Jason Robert Radcliff, *Thomas F. Torrance and the Church Fathers: A Reformed, Evangelical, and Ecumenical Reconstruction of the Patristic Tradition* (Eugene, OR: Pickwick Publications, 2014), 55–56.

30. Ibid., 23, 193.

31. Jason Radcliff, "T. F. Torrance and the Patristic Consensus on the Doctrine of the Trinity," in *The Holy Trinity Revisited: Essays in Response to Stephen R. Holmes*, ed. Thomas A. Noble and Jason S. Sexton, 78 (Milton Keynes, UK: Paternoster, 2015).

32. Thomas F. Torrance, *The School of Faith* (London: James Clarke, 1959), lxxi.

33. Ibid., lxxii–lxxiii.

34. Torrance is appreciative of Calvin but distances himself from federal Calvinism, noting that Calvinism sometimes "obscures the flexibility as well as the range and profundity of [Calvin's] thought. Thomas F. Torrance, *Calvin's Doctrine of Man* (London: Lutterworth Press, 1949), 7.

35. Torrance, *The Christian Doctrine of God*, 81, 93, 151. Torrance also illustrates the mystery of God's being with his frequent use of an Athanasian quote, "Thus far human knowledge goes. Here the cherubim spread the covering of their wings."

36. Ibid., 204. See also Thomas F. Torrance, "Predestination in Christ," *Evangelical Quarterly* 13 (1941): 114 where Torrance attributes this point to H. R. Mackintosh.

37. Torrance, *The Christian Doctrine of God*, 10–13. See also Torrance, *Trinitarian Perspectives*, 41–76.

38. Torrance, *The School of Faith*, lxx–lxxix.

39. Torrance, *The Christian Doctrine of God*, 9. See also Thomas F. Torrance, *The Mediation of Christ* (Edinburgh: T&T Clark, 1992), 99–101. To separate the "one God" and the "Triune God" so isolates the doctrine of the Holy Trinity that it ends up divorced from salvation history.

40. Ibid. It is worth noting that Torrance is careful in his own work to avoid the reduction of the doctrine of the Trinity to soteriology in order to avoid any blurring of the distinction between God's transcendent self and God's relationship to the world.

41. Ibid., 9–10. For Torrance's evaluation of Rahner's contribution on the doctrine of the Trinity, see Torrance, *Trinitarian Perspectives*, 77–102.

42. Torrance, *Trinitarian Perspectives*, 4. Torrance also highlights that Barth tended to orient himself toward the Greek rather than the Latin Patristics. See Thomas F. Torrance, "Karl Barth and Patristic Theology," in *Theology beyond Christendom: Essays on the Centenary of the Birth of Karl Barth*, edited by John Thomson, 219 (Allison Park, PA: Pickwick Publications, 1986).

43. Torrance, *Theology in Reconciliation*, 286.

44. Torrance, *Trinitarian Perspectives*, 1.

45. Torrance, *The Christian Doctrine of God*, 8.

46. Ibid., 4. A development that is (loosely) based on Torrance's theology and is quite helpful here is a comparison of "Holiness as Separation" and "Holiness as a Communion of Love" in T. A. Noble, *Holy Trinity: Holy People* (Eugene, OR: Cascade Books, 2013), 209–24. Noble explores the implications of these two models, noting that the Fathers rarely associate "love" with the doctrine of the Holy Trinity.

47. Ibid., 1.

48. Ibid., 25.

49. Torrance, *The Trinitarian Faith*, 87.

50. Torrance, *The Christian Doctrine of God*, 207.

51. Ibid., 208.

52. Ibid., 49. Molnar makes some helpful observations about the significance of this quote for the theology of both Barth and Torrance in Paul Molnar, *Faith, Freedom and the Spirit* (Downers Grove, IL: InterVarsity Press, 2015), 92–94.

53. Ibid., 8.

54. Ibid., 219.

55. Thomas F. Torrance, *Space, Time and Incarnation* (Edinburgh: T&T Clark, 1997), 14.

56. Torrance, *The Christian Doctrine of God*, 209–10.

57. Ibid., 210. See also Myk Habets, "How Creation Is Proleptically Conditioned by Redemption," *Colloquium* 41 (2009): 3–21, which is supplemented by the discussion in Myk Habets, *Theology in Transposition: A Constructive Appraisal of T. F. Torrance* (Minneapolis, MN: Fortress Press, 2013), 145–61.

58. Torrance, *Incarnation*, 39–40.

59. Torrance, *The Trinitarian Faith*, 94–95.

60. Torrance, *The Mediation of Christ*, 7.

61. Torrance, *The Trinitarian Faith*, 67.

62. Ibid., 66.

63. Ibid., 66–67.

64. Torrance, *The Christian Doctrine of God*, 14.

65. Ibid., 120.

66. Ibid., 67.

67. Torrance, *The Mediation of Christ*, 65.

68. Torrance, *The Christian Doctrine of God*, 3.

69. Torrance, *Space, Time and Incarnation*, 52.

70. Thomas F. Torrance, *The Ground and Grammar of Theology* (Charlottesville: University Press of Virginia, 1980), 151.

71. Torrance, *The Christian Doctrine of God*, 1.

72. Thomas F. Torrance, "Introduction," in *The Incarnation: Ecumenical Studies in the Nicene-Constantinopolitan Creed*, ed. Thomas F. Torrance, xvi (Edinburgh: Handsel Press, 1981).

73. Ibid., xi–xxii; and Torrance, *The Christian Doctrine of God*, 80. Torrance likens the *homoousion* to a jigsaw puzzle because once we have seen the assembled picture, we can never "unsee" it.

74. Torrance, *The Ground and Grammar of Theology*, 160–61.

75. Torrance, *The Mediation of Christ*, 55. "Knowledge of God the Father and knowledge of Jesus Christ the incarnate Son of the Father arise in us together, not one without the other."

76. Torrance, *The Christian Doctrine of God*, 3.

77. Ibid., 13. Torrance draws heavily on the work of Irenaeus, Hilary of Poitiers, and John Calvin to develop this point.

78. Torrance, *The Trinitarian Faith*, 61.

79. Thomas F. Torrance, *Theology in Reconstruction* (Grand Rapids, MI: Eerdmans, 1965), 246; and also cited in Elmer M. Colyer, "Thomas F. Torrance on the Holy Spirit," *Word & World* 23, no. 2 (Spring 2003): 162.

80. Torrance, *The Christian Doctrine of God*, 151.

81. Thomas F. Torrance, "The Christ Who Loves Us," in *A Passion for Christ: The Vision That Ignites Ministry*, ed. Gerrit Dawson and Jock Stein, 18 (Eugene, OR: Wipf and Stock, 2010).

82. Ibid., 19. Further reflection on the analogy of light, or the theology of light, can be found in Thomas F. Torrance, *Christian Theology and Scientific Culture* (Eugene, OR: Wipf and Stock, 1998), 75–108; and Thomas F. Torrance, "The Light of the World: A Sermon," *Reformed Journal* 38, no. 12 (December 1988): 9–12.
83. Torrance, *The Christian Doctrine of God*, 158.
84. Torrance, *The Trinitarian Faith*, 229.
85. Torrance, *The Christian Doctrine of God*, 147.
86. Ibid., 130.
87. Ibid., 34.
88. Ibid., xi.
89. Ibid., 174.
90. Ibid., 24, 28.
91. Ibid., 27–28. Torrance's use of the idea of moving from whole to parts, rather than from parts to whole, is linked to his understanding of Clerk Maxwell's method in science—see Torrance, *Christian Theology and Scientific Culture*, 51–53.
92. Ibid., 128–33.
93. Ibid., 131.
94. Torrance, *The Trinitarian Faith,* 48.
95. Torrance, *The Christian Doctrine of God*, 128.
96. Ibid., 203.
97. Torrance, *Theology in Reconstruction*, 52.
98. Torrance, *Divine Meaning*, 6.
99. Torrance, *The Christian Doctrine of God*, 116.
100. Ibid., 4–5.
101. Ibid., 118–25.
102. Ibid., 116–17.
103. Ibid., 123, 187–88; Torrance, *Trinitarian Perspectives*, 37–39.
104. Torrance, *The Christian Doctrine of God*, 204, 15.
105. Ibid., 246–54. Torrance affirms that "the whole Trinity is involved in the sacrifice of Christ on the Cross" (247) and that "the whole undivided Trinity is involved in our salvation, and thus in the central atoning passion of Christ, God the Father and God the Spirit, as well as God the Son, in their different but coordinated ways." (252). It is not that suffering is part of God *in se* but rather that through God's condescension in becoming a human, he experiences suffering. This suffering cannot be attributed only to the humanity of Jesus without detaching the humanity of Jesus from his divinity, which would call the fullness of the *hypostatic* union into question, so we must begin any question of whether God can suffer from the doctrine of the incarnation.
106. Ibid., 244.
107. Ibid., 236.
108. Ibid., 156–58.
109. Ibid., 156.
110. Ibid., 174. See also the discussion of *in solidum* in Torrance, *Trinitarian Perspectives*, 36.
111. Ibid., 157.
112. Ibid., 125. This is why Torrance comments that we are not to think of the relationship between *ousia* and *hypostasis* as the general to the particular.
113. Ibid., 168–70.
114. Ibid., 172. The earlier use is first attributed to Gregory Nazianzen and the later use to Pseudo-Cyril and John of Damascus. Torrance elsewhere attributes the terminology of *perichoresis* to Gregory Nazianzen. See Torrance, *Trinitarian Perspectives*, 32–33.
115. Ibid., 102.
116. Ibid., 92.
117. Ibid., 104.
118. Ibid., 132.
119. Alister McGrath, *T. F. Torrance: An Intellectual Biography* (Edinburgh: T&T Clark, 1999), 168–74.

120. Torrance, *The Christian Doctrine of God*, 83–84. Torrance takes the stratified idea from Einstein and Polanyi.

121. Ibid., 82.

122. Ibid., 84.

123. Benjamin Myers, "The Stratification of Knowledge in the Thought of T. F. Torrance," *Scottish Journal of Theology* 61, no. 1 (2008): 1.

124. Torrance, *The Ground and Grammar of Theology*, 156–57.

125. Torrance, *The Christian Doctrine of God*, 89.

126. Thomas F. Torrance, *God and Rationality* (Oxford: Oxford University Press, 2000), 4.

127. Torrance, *The Christian Doctrine of God*, 84.

128. Ibid., 91.

129. Torrance, *The Ground and Grammar of Theology*, 157.

130. Torrance, *The Christian Doctrine of God*, 94.

131. Ibid., 98.

132. Torrance, *The Incarnation: Ecumenical Studies in the Nicene-Constantinopolitan Creed*, xx.

133. Torrance, *The Christian Doctrine of God*, 94.

134. Ibid., 95.

135. Ibid., 85.

136. Thomas F. Torrance, *Reality and Scientific Theology*, 2nd ed (Eugene, OR: Wipf and Stock, 2001), 156.

137. Torrance, *The Christian Doctrine of God*, 99.

138. Torrance, *The Ground and Grammar of Theology*, 157–58.

139. Torrance, *The Christian Doctrine of God*, 87.

140. Ibid.

141. Habets, *Theology in Transposition*, 38.

142. Torrance, *The Ground and Grammar of Theology*, 124–27.

143. Ibid., 126; Torrance, *God and Rationality*, 16–26.

144. Torrance, *Theology in Reconstruction*, 48.

145. Torrance, *The Christian Doctrine of God*, 55.

146. Torrance, *The Trinitarian Faith*, 148.

147. Torrance, *The Christian Doctrine of God*, 97.

148. Torrance, *The Ground and Grammar of Theology*, 165–67. See also Torrance, *Christian Theology and Scientific Culture*, 8.

149. Torrance, *The Christian Doctrine of God*, 241. On this, see Molnar, *Faith, Freedom and the Spirit*, 187–224 where Molnar explores Torrance's refusal to read elements of God's economic actions back into the ontological Trinity in any way that would suggest an eternal subordination or hierarchy within the Godhead, focusing on the work of the Trinity in terms of election.

150. Ibid., 208.

151. Ibid., 242.

152. Ibid.

153. Ibid., 235.

154. Ibid., 124.

155. Ibid., 133.

156. Ibid., 165–66.

157. Ibid., 181. See also Torrance's evaluation of Athanasius, Gregory Nazianzen, and John Calvin on this in Torrance, *Trinitarian Perspectives*, 14–20, 28–32.

158. Ibid., 115.

159. Ibid., 127. Torrance does highlight that Gregory Nazianzen disassociates himself from the description used by the other Cappadocians of the "modes of being" of the Trinity and from the way they viewed the Father as the "principle" or "cause" (*archē*) of the Son and Spirit's deity. There is also some question around Torrance's reading of the Fathers here, and we will examine this in our dialogue with Zizioulas toward the end of this book.

160. Ibid., 179. Also helpful is Molnar's discussion of the difference between Barth and Torrance in regard to subordinationism. See Molnar, *Faith, Freedom and the Spirit*, 313–54.

Torrance's critique of Barth on subordinationism can be found in Thomas F. Torrance, *How Karl Barth Changed My Mind*, ed. Donald K. McKim, 60–61 (Grand Rapids, MI: Wm. B. Eerdmans, 1986).

161. Dick O. Eugenio, *Communion with the Triune God: The Trinitarian Soteriology of T. F. Torrance* (Eugene, OR: Pickwick Publications, 2014), 27.

162. Molnar, *Faith, Freedom and the Spirit*, 313–54. Molnar draws on Torrance throughout the book, but this chapter is the clearest comparison of Torrance and Barth offered.

163. Torrance, *The Christian Doctrine of God*, 104.

164. Ibid., 132.

165. Ibid., 5.

166. Ibid., 164–65.

167. Torrance, *The Ground and Grammar of Theology*, 154–55.

168. Torrance, *The Christian Doctrine of God*, 163.

Chapter Three

A Diachronic Ecclesiology

Having explored Torrance's doctrine of the Trinity, we are well positioned to grasp the inner coherence of his ecclesiology. Adopting the approach of biblical theology, Torrance holds together the Old and New Testament. Viewing history from the perspective of God's creative relationship to space and time, with God neither contained nor constrained by creation, Torrance argues that the one Church has three historical stages. There is significant continuity and discontinuity between Israel, the Church, and the age yet to come, nevertheless, God is constantly at work shaping a people to be his own. In the story of Israel we see God preparing the way for their Messiah while the events of the New Testament confirm that the Church is the fulfillment of God's promise to bless the nations through Abraham's descendants.

ONE CHURCH, THREE STAGES

The history of God's interaction with Israel recorded in the Old Testament and what God is doing through the Church of the New Testament are not two different redemptive actions. They are one unified undertaking, linked through the incarnation, which the Old Testament stretches forward to in expectation and the New Testament fulfills and explains. Because of this, the Church cannot be considered a recently created institution or as having its beginning at the incarnation or Pentecost. There is one Church that God sustains comprised of all who have received or will receive salvation in the past, present, or future. It has a continuity that runs through the whole of God's diachronic interaction with humanity.

This view of salvation history is evident in some of the patristic authors, who saw an intrinsic continuity between the Old Testament Scriptures and the revelation of Jesus Christ.[1] It is also in keeping with the Reformed view of salvation history as one continuous historical movement of redemption with its center in the incarnation.[2] However, Torrance divides the Church's one life into three distinct historical stages.

> While there is only one people and Church of God throughout all ages from the beginning of creation to the end, there are three stages or phases of its life. It took a *preparatory form* before the Incarnation as in the covenant mercies of the Father one people was called and separated out as the instrument through which all peoples were to be blessed; it was given a *new form in Jesus Christ* who gathered up and reconstructed the one people of God in himself, and poured out his Spirit upon broken and divided humanity that through his atoning life and death and resurrection all men might be reconciled to God and to one another, sharing equally in the life and love of the Father as the new undivided race; but it is yet to take on its *final and eternal form* when Christ comes again to judge and renew his creation, for then, the Church which now lives in the condition of humiliation and in the ambiguous forms of this age, will be manifested as the new creation without spot or wrinkle, eternally serving and sharing in the glory of God.[3]

These three stages are separated by the transitional moments of the two advents of Christ on earth. Christ's first advent marked the transition between the preparatory form of the Church in Israel and the new form of the Church as believers are gathered into union with Christ by the Spirit. Christ's second advent will mark the transition from the Church as an anticipatory sign of the *telos* of God's redemptive and reconciliatory plan in the midst of a world tangled up with the effects of sin and the full actualization of that *telos* in the new creation.

In all of this, Torrance's relational understanding of God to the world comes into play, offering a "specifically theological understanding of the relation of God to the world of space and time"[4] without undermining the importance of creation because space is the "place of meeting and activity in the interaction between God and the world."[5] Rejecting both cosmological and epistemological dualism, Torrance instead asserts with Nicene theology that while there is an absolute distinction between God and what he has made, we must reckon with the tangible presence of Jesus Christ in space and time. Since God is the Creator of everything, including space and time, he "stands in a creative, not a spatial or a temporal relation, to it."[6] Rather than focusing on Hellenistic concepts of space as a container and the problems this posed for the relation of God to the world,[7] Torrance highlights the importance of Jesus as the *topos*, the true place where two dimensions—the vertical and the horizontal—meet.[8] On the basis of the incarnation, space must be considered "essentially open-ended, for it is defined in accordance with the interaction between God and man, eternal and contingent happening. It is treated as a sort of coordinate system (to use a later expression) between two horizontal dimensions, space and time, and one vertical dimension, relation to God."[9] This is all rather technical, but it highlights that the ongoing interaction of God with the world is of profound importance for Torrance's doctrine of the Church.

This relational understanding of God's interaction with the world is the only way to grasp the supernatural nature of events like the incarnation, the crucifixion, and the resurrection. These are events that involve the "breaking in" of God to natural history, requiring us to discard any sense of a transcendent God who does not intervene in human affairs. They point to God's reordering of human history so that it is directed toward its *telos* of humanity's participation in union and communion with God.[10] While Jesus Christ is the one person in whom the horizontal and vertical dimensions meet, the Church also exists in a way appropriate to its creaturely status at the intersection of the vertical dimension and the horizontal dimension.

THE ANTICIPATORY EXISTENCE OF ISRAEL AS THE CHURCH IN THE OLD TESTAMENT

We initially turn to the first stage of the existence of the people of God. There are two sub-stages that we must consider: first, the "prelude to salvation history"—this includes the act of creation and the promise of future redemption from the effects of sin[11]—and, second, the beginning of salvation history with the calling of Abraham and the people of Israel.

Creation

Although the biblical narrative begins with an account of God creating the heavens and earth, the Church "did not come into being automatically with the creation of the world or all at once with the establishment in the world of a human society."[12] Male and female were created to have perfect fellowship with God, to have perfect fellowship with each other, and to live in harmony with their environment. That which makes us human is the bond between God and human,[13] and yet it is only with others that humans can fully exist "in the image of God," reflecting his glory.[14] Adam and Eve were created to live in unbroken communion with God, but when they sinned as individuals, all humanity experienced the consequences with them.[15] Sin hinders divine-human communion and therefore "entails a rupture within each between what a person *is* and what the person *ought* to be."[16] When this divine-human bond is broken, we are separated from each other since communion is hindered not only between God and humanity but also between humans.[17]

The Scriptural narrative tells the story of human brokenness and of our failed attempts to mend these broken relationships. "On one side it is the story of the atomisation of mankind, for the internal rupture results in individualisation and conflict. On the other it is the story of human attempts at re-socialisation, great attempts to mend the broken relations, to heal the internal rupture, to bind divided humanity together again, as at Babel."[18] These efforts come to nothing for humanity cannot heal itself. Nevertheless, despite the separation caused by sin, God does not abandon his creation and give it over to destruction nor does he turn away and leave humanity to fend for themselves. Instead God maintains a covenant of grace with all people and nations with the teleological goal of restoring all to communion with God.[19] God's redemptive intentions are clearly visible even if the method of their accomplishment has not yet been made plain. God created humans so that they might participate in the overflow of his eternal triune life, the communion of love that God essentially is, and this purpose will not be thwarted. Viewing the initial act of creation through the lens of the incarnation points us to the ultimate *telos* of the redeemed creation.

Abraham, Israel, and the Exodus

Despite the sins of the first parents, Torrance insists that the Fall did not involve the failure of the Church as a divine institution.[20] The incipient form of the Church exists anywhere that God enters into a particular redemptive relationship with humankind and so it is among the people of Israel that we see God initiate his redemptive actions. This is why Torrance describes the people of Israel as the *preparatory form* of the Church. God calls Abraham and his descendants into a unique divine-human relationship. The faithfulness of God to Abraham, Isaac, and Jacob, and the preservation of their descendants through Joseph's wisdom in Egypt, testifies to the providence of God and yet it is not until four hundred years of slavery have passed that God initiates the historical events that will forge Israel into a distinct nation shaped by a unique, covenantal relationship to the self-revealing and self-naming God, *Yahweh*, "I am." God reveals himself to Israel in the context of freeing them from slavery and on this basis claims them as his own. Israel's covenantal identity as the people of God is shaped by the Exodus; this liberating redemptive event is far more significant for Israel's knowledge of God than the act of creation since it is through God's salvation and redemption of Israel that he is known as their Saviour and Redeemer, which is the basis for the covenant formed at Sinai.[21]

The Old Testament describes the community, or gathering, of Israel as both *'edhah* and *qahal*. While the translation is not straightforward, since both are translated into the Greek terms *synagōgē* and *ekklēsia*, Torrance notes that *qahal* in particular emerges from the same root as *qol* (voice), which "suggests that the Old Testament *qahal* was the community summoned by the Divine Voice, by the Word of God."[22] Torrance further expounds on the nature of Israel's covenantal relation to God by noting that the doctrine of grace in the Old Testament involves both *ḥesed* (love) and *tsedeq* (righteousness). Although there is no single word used for grace in the Old Testament, this concept is defined by the unsolicited, sovereign, and gracious love God shows toward Israel.[23] The existence of the covenant depended on Yahweh's gracious and free choice to choose Israel as his own

Torrance describes Israel's history as "the prehistory of the incarnation."[24] Divine revelation was given expression in a form that humanity could comprehend, and human understanding and language were shaped to articulate this divine revelation.[25] There are two elements to this. The first is the suffering that was entailed in Israel's calling, and the second is the way this is related to Israel's formation as the medium of revelation and reconciliation.

Israel's Suffering as a Medium of Reconciliation

Throughout its history, Israel's communal life has been shaped in a way that lays the conceptual foundations for the coming of Christ. Although Israel was called to be the people of God, significant tension existed between Israel's desire to be *ethnos* (a nation like those surrounding them) and God's claim on them as *laos* (the people of God, a community formed by the divine Word).[26] We see the conflict of their history related in Scripture: Israel repeatedly turns to idolatry, and God refuses to let them do so Israel was not elected as God's people for their own sake or on their own merit but were elected to serve the fulfillment of God's revealing and redemptive purposes.[27] The covenant relationship meant that Israel "had to suffer, for it shattered itself on the unswerving persistence of the divine purpose of love. Israel suffered inevitably from God, for God would not let His people go."[28]

God would not let Israel go because they were to be the vehicle through which divine revelation was proclaimed and manifested.[29] As divine revelation penetrated deeper and deeper into the very being of Israel, they found themselves unwillingly suffering, dying, and being made alive again,[30] for they were

> a people invaded by divine revelation and progressively subjected to its molding and informing power in such a way that the responses which divine revelation provoked from it, whether of obedience or disobedience, enlightenment or blindness, were made instruments for its deepening penetration into its existence and understanding until there were forged structures of thought and speech in terms of which it became understandable and communicable. And so throughout Israel's tradition the Word of God kept pressing for articulation within the corporate medium of covenant reciprocity, creating formal and empirical correlates of its own self-utterance through which it extended its activity in space and time, progressively taking verbal and even written form through the shared understanding and shared response that developed in this

> people. Thus Israel became in a unique way the bearer of the oracles of God, a church as much as a people charged with priestly and prophetic significance for all mankind and divinely destined for the universalization of its revelatory mission in the advent of God himself in space and time.[31]

God keeps drawing closer to Israel through their rebellion and rejection. Their sinfulness is made to serve his purposes. This pattern is demonstrated throughout the Old Testament. Torrance maintains that Israel's continual rejection of God's love and repetitive disobedience to the covenant was something that "in a profound sense it *had* to do so in our place and for our sakes,"[32] or to put it more plainly, "Israel was elected also to reject the Messiah."[33] It was not that Israel did not recognize Jesus as the Son of God but rather, Torrance insists, that "in the very act of perceiving the truth they insisted that it should not apply to them for they could not bear the Gospel."[34]

Although from an external historical point of view Jesus was crucified for political and religious reasons, Torrance suggests that the theological reality is that Christ assumes the very depths of humanity's estrangement from God and is rejected on our behalf. It is there that he forges "a bond of union and communion between man and God in himself."[35] If the climax of human sinfulness is seen in Israel's greatest rejection of God's love and grace toward us—at the Cross—then how astounding it is that this same moment is taken and transformed into the mechanism by which humanity receives their greatest healing. It was in love and mercy that God refused to let Israel go despite their constant attempts to reject him. This is how Israel's rejection of God became the means through which God lovingly actualized reconciliation.[36]

Israel as the Medium of Revelation

In the history of Israel, divine revelation is communicated *through* the community's life and speech. Torrance explains,

> In order to be heard and understood, and to be communicable as Word, divine revelation penetrates into the speaker-hearer relationship within the interpersonal structure of humanity and becomes speech to man by becoming speech of man to man, spoken and heard through the intelligible medium of a people's language. Thus the reciprocity formed by the movement of divine revelation takes the form of a community of reciprocity between God and man established in human society, which then under the continuing impact of divine revelation becomes the appropriate medium of its continuing communication to man.[37]

Israel is a "community of reciprocity" formed by revelation in order to mediate revelation and reconciliation.[38] Illustrating this, Torrance highlights the biblical theme of "the one and the many." Israel was a servant people called to a mediatory role on behalf of the nations, one on behalf of many. Yet within the many individuals of this one people, one specific person was called the "Servant of the Lord" who "would fulfil in his own body and soul the covenant-will of God for his people, and fulfil the covenanted obedience of the people to God's will."[39] Israel was drawn into covenantal relationship with God in order to provide a place for the Word to become flesh, and so it is in Jesus Christ, the Suffering Servant, that we most clearly encounter "the mystery of the One and the Many."[40] Through the one person of Christ and his redeeming work, all are welcomed into the kingdom of God. In Israel we see "the election of one for the salvation of all," while in Jesus "the election of one for all becomes salvation for all in the rejection of one for all."[41]

The redemptive and reconciliatory existence of Israel is related to the wider patterns of redemption in the Old Testament.[42] Torrance identifies three primary terms for redemption—each of which has its own cognate terms. The first is *padah*, which focuses on "the cost of redemption and the nature of the redeeming act rather than upon the nature of the redeemer"[43] and speaks of Israel's redemption out of slavery in Egypt. It evokes freedom from the power of guilt, sin, and judgment and redemption into victory and freedom. The second is *kipper*, which has to do with "redemption as the actual wiping out of sin and guilt, and so of effecting propitiation between man and God."[44] It has to do with the covering-over of sin, particularly by shed blood. Finally, we have *gaal*, or *goel*, which is the idea of "redemption out of bankruptcy, or bondage or forfeited rights, undertaken by the advocacy of a kinsman who is bound to the person in need not only by blood ties, but by a community in property."[45] The emphasis falls upon the relational aspect of the one who redeems—such as we see in the story of Ruth, with Boaz as her kinsman-redeemer. God himself is clearly described as Israel's kinsman-redeemer in the Old Testament. On the basis of the covenantal relation that he has established with Israel in initially redeeming them from slavery, he repeatedly redeems them from sin and delivers them from their enemies.[46]

These three strands of redemption are all present throughout the Old Testament but converge most closely in the places where they are "associated with the new exodus and the work of the servant of the Lord,"[47] which Torrance reads as anticipating the life and work of Christ. These three redemptive strands may also be correlated with the threefold anointed offices of the prophet, the priest, and the king. Torrance argues that the Sinai covenant rested upon the double foundation of Moses, the prophet, and Aaron, the high priest, and that this covenant prepared the way for the kingdom, which was made manifest in Jerusalem under the Davidic dynasty.[48] Together "prophet, priest, and king were made to point forward to the Messiah, the archetypal Prophet, Priest, and King."[49] This is an excellent example of how Yahweh's redemptive relationship with Israel generated appropriate concepts and forms so that as a people their communal life became a "womb for the Incarnation."[50] Torrance produces a list of examples:

> Let me refer to the Word and Name of God, to revelation, mercy, truth, holiness, to messiah, saviour, to prophet, priest and king, father, son, servant, to covenant, sacrifice, forgiveness, reconciliation, redemption, atonement, and those basic patterns of worship which we find set out in the ancient liturgy or in the Psalms.[51]

Ultimately, Israel's historical witness to Yahweh was gathered up and fulfilled in Christ. For the Jewish people, the idea of God's kingdom was closely tied to their identity as the people of God, as a kingdom that would be realized at the coming of the Messiah and would transcend Israel's geographic and ethnic boundaries to encompass every nation. There was no early sense of divergence from Judaism for Messianic Jews since Jewish people who came to believe in Jesus as their Messiah saw themselves as standing in continuity with all that God had done historically in their midst. The eventual distinction that emerged is suggested by the use of different linguistic terms. We have already discussed Israel's sense of being a community called through the divine Word when Yahweh spoke to them at Mount Sinai.[52] Old Testament authors used the term *qahal* to refer to the assembly of the people, rendered in Greek by *ekklēsia*, while Judaism itself came to prefer the Greek term *synagōgē*.[53] Torrance thus suggests that "when the Christian Church came to refer to itself as the *ekklēsia* rather than *synagōgē* (with one or two exceptions), it was clearly claiming to be the 'Israel of God' in distinction from the Synagogue,"[54] a development that appears to signal an emerging awareness of the distinctions between Judaism and Christianity. There is also the element here that *ekklēsia* does not refer to "any sociological or political sense of assembly."[55] However, the actual schism between Jews and Gentiles is seen by Torrance as having its roots in the crucifixion and as being exacerbated by the Roman overthrow of Jerusalem in 70 AD. It was the persecution of the Jewish people that solidified the discrepancy between Jewish believers and those who identified as Christians, a schism that has damaged our understanding of the atonement.[56]

Torrance concludes that the historical contribution of Israel in preparing the world to receive the Gospel cannot be ignored. As he states, "it is still through the story of Israel, through the Jewish soul shaped by the hand of God, through the Jewish scriptures of the Old Testament and the Jewish scriptures of the New Testament church, that the gospel comes to us and Jesus Christ is set before us face to face as Lord and savior."[57]

THE CHURCH IN THE TIME BETWEEN

The Relation of the Church to Christ in the Time Between

Jesus was born as a Jew and so "Christ cannot be understood without the Old Testament."[58] Torrance highlights that "from the very beginning the Christian Church thought of itself as Israel in the new phase of its election marked by the Incarnation."[59] He holds that "Christian religion is an essential development of the inner history and experience of Israel. By its very nature Christianity cannot cease to be Hebraic or Jewish."[60] It follows that the Day of Pentecost does not signal the "birth" of the Church; instead the Church transitions into a new form as Gentiles are freely grafted into the covenant people of Israel who recognize Jesus as their Messiah.[61]

Jesus threw the whole history of Israel into "critical reorientation,"[62] notwithstanding the further challenges that this posited to Graeco-Roman dualism. Events such as the incarnation and resurrection forced themselves upon the first believers "*in sharp antithesis* to what they had believed about God and *in genuine conflict* with the framework of secular thought."[63] The incarnation signaled a decisive shift in the mode of reconciliation and revelation from the *preparatory form* of the Church in Israel, to its *new form in Jesus Christ*. Israel was longing for a Messiah, an anointed king whose presence would signal the arrival of the eschatological kingdom. Jesus was this Messiah but he fulfilled this role in a radically different way than had previously been conceptualized by the people of Israel. "The Old Testament speaks of the Coming One, and the coming Kingdom; the New Testament speaks of the One who has come, and of the Kingdom as having arrived in Jesus Christ Himself."[64]

Torrance doesn't like to talk of the second coming of Christ as if it were an event separate from his first coming. He notes that the term *parousia* only appears in the singular form in the New Testament, and the apostolic witness only speaks of one advent (*parousia*) and one kingdom (*basileia*) of Christ. From this he derives that while Christ has two advents, he remains continuously present. As Torrance observes, "the term *parousia* was used in the New Testament to speak of all three: the coming, arrival, and presence of Christ; and thus not only the presence of one who has come but of the presence of one who is to come again. His presence is an advent, and his advent is a presence."[65] Torrance thinks of this in connection with Einstein's "relativity of simultaneity" where "it is possible for one event in the physical world to have two different 'real times.'"[66] The time of the Church is not a time of Christ's absence but a time when Christ is present in a different way. Torrance titles this an eschatological pause, "an interval in the heart of the *parousia* which makes it possible for us to speak of a first advent and a second or final advent of Christ."[67] By no longer being present bodily in history, Christ holds his two advents apart. While his first coming saw him come in humility, he will come in glory at his final advent.[68]

The ascension is the correlate to Christ's condescension in which he took on human flesh. It declares the divine endorsement and efficacy of all that took place in his life and on the Cross.[69] During this eschatological pause Christ is outside time but we cannot explain this in physical terms[70] except to use the language provided by Scripture, where we are told that Christ is at the right hand of the Father in heavenly places, which suggests a position of power and authority.[71] This is to be "functionally not metaphysically interpreted."[72] Jesus is "historically absent and actually present,"[73] absent in his incarnate body but present to us through his Spirit.[74]

An important point here is the eternally enduring reality of Christ's humanity, which we have already discussed. Since the incarnation is not something temporal or limited—"the involvement of the Son of God in our human and creaturely being, even after His resurrection, ascension, and *parousia* must be maintained without reserve"[75]—we learn that there is an *ontological relation* formed between Christ and the Church, not simply an external relationship.[76] This is "a relation of mutual indwelling between Christ and the Church which derives from and is grounded in the mutual indwelling of the Father, the Son and the Holy Spirit."[77]

Two outcomes of this are highlighted by Torrance's description of Jesus as the humanizing man and the personalizing person. As the humanizing man, or the humanizing human, Christ redeems and reinstates our humanity, setting us in proper relation to God. As the personalizing person, Jesus frees us from self-centered individualism and restores us to the personal relations that are constitutive of who we are as human beings, although they are not constitutive in the way that the triune relations are constitutive of the divine being.[78] Together these two outcomes show that Jesus restores us to proper relationship with God and to proper relationship with others. The Church is therefore not to be understood as merely another human gathering or society.

> It is apparent that the Church of Christ was not just the holy society founded to perpetuate his memory, or to observe his teachings, or to proclaim his Gospel, but that it inhered in his being as the Incarnate Son, was rooted in his humanity as the historical Jesus, and grew out of the fulfilment of his ministry in the flesh. The Church of the new covenant arose out of the indivisible union of the Messiah and the people of God he came to redeem and raise up; it grew out of the concrete way in which he lived his divine life within their human existence thereby transforming their whole way of life; it took shape and form in every act that he performed, and derived its essential structure from the way in which he fulfilled his ministry on their behalf.[79]

The existence and mission of the Church is intimately bound up with the person of Jesus Christ, for "it was the kind of person Jesus was and the kind of mission he undertook which determined and gave form and structure to the messianic kingdom and messianic people."[80] He remains the head of the Church that is his body, which is why Torrance appropriates Barth's description of the Church as the "earthly-historical form of Christ's existence"[81] or the "earthly-historical form of his own existence."[82] We do not refer to the Church as the body of the Spirit because it was not the Spirit but Christ who became incarnate. It is Christ's incarnate presence—or absence—that frames the time of the Church. "There is but one Christ who is both the Head and the Body, so that the Body cannot exist apart from Christ, or be divided without dividing Christ. Thus the Church has no independent existence."[83]

The Life of the Church in the Time Between

How then are we to think of the Church's existence in this time between? On one hand, through Christ's death and resurrection the new creation has "already interpenetrated the age in which we live so that this is already the fullness of time."[84] This means that "here and now in the ongoing life of the Church we live in the midst of the advent-presence of Christ, already partake of the great regeneration (*paliggenesia*) of the future, and share in its blessings with one another."[85] On the other hand, the Church humbly lives "in the ambiguous forms of this age,"[86] in an "age of faith and trust . . . where there is no sight but where there is faith."[87] The Church's existence is one of tension. As Molnar summarizes, Torrance believes that "the church is not yet what it will be until Christ actually returns to complete the redemption of the world."[88] Nevertheless, this tension is temporary because Christ will complete what he has started.[89]

Torrance proposes that the nature of the time between Christ's two advents is illuminated by thinking about the way that Jesus often held apart his word and action in order to give people time to respond. Jesus never manifested himself in such a way that his majesty overwhelmed humanity's ability to freely respond, for "in Him the *eschaton* had broken into the present, but if men had been confronted openly with the *eschaton* in the Word and Presence of Jesus they would have been faced with the final judgment."[90] Torrance invites us to think of Jesus' parable of a king who goes into a far country and spends time there before returning to his servants. Alternatively, consider the Markan account of the healing of the paralytic—where there is a gap between the pronouncement of forgiveness and the miracle of healing—when Christ "deliberately held apart His *Word* of forgiveness and His *Act* of healing."[91] Torrance suggests that "it was precisely that lapse of time or eschatological reserve between the Word of the Kingdom and its power that Jesus was concerned to preserve in His *kerygma*."[92] In Jesus the consummation of all things has already taken place but the Church does not yet experience this fully for it "lives between the penultimate and the ultimate acts of the *Heilsgeschichte*."[93] As Torrance explains, living between these two moments shapes the "time between" or the "overlap of the ages" as an age of grace, a time when the kingdom is already realized but not yet fully manifest. He writes,

> The Church is redeemed not in Word only but also in power, and yet it waits for the redemption of the body. The new age has already overtaken it and through the Spirit it stands on the resurrection side of the Cross, and yet it still waits for the day when the form and fashion of this world will be torn aside and the new creation will be revealed. The Church lives between those two moments, between the Cross and the *parousia*, between the Word of forgiveness and the final act of healing, between Pentecost and the resurrection of the body. In the mercy of God the Word of the Gospel and the final deed of God are partially held apart in eschatological reserve until the *parousia*. This is the age of grace, the age of *kerygma*, in which the Gospel is proclaimed to all, in which time and space are given for repentance and decision. But this is the age, too, when by the Holy Spirit, who inhabits the Church and energizes its kerygmatic ministry, all who believe in Jesus Christ may taste the powers of the age to come through sacramental incorporation into the new creation.[94]

The eschatological pause gives humans room to make "personal relations in decision and faith and repentance, and so for the growth of personal communion in union and love."[95] Jesus has made room—*chorein*—for the Church, "freedom to believe, freedom to decide, and freedom to be obedient,"[96] showing that "God takes seriously the relations of time such as human reactions, choices and decisions."[97] God has given time for Gospel proclamation and for repentance and faith.[98] As Ziegler also observes, this is the time in which Christian formation stretches forward to the *telos* of union and communion with the Triune God but takes the shape of a movement toward our re-personalization, and our re-humanization.[99]

We must not identify the historical existence of the Church as the sum total of salvation history or as the full expression of the kingdom of God for salvation is bound up with the person of Christ and not with the historical institution of the Church. Nor should we think of the Church's existence in any way that "carries with it the notion of sinless perfection or deification."[100] This would lead us into ecclesiological docetism and the idea of the "mystical Church" that has greater similarity to Platonic thought than to the biblical witness. As Torrance notes, "failure to believe the biblical witness that the Church is at once sinful and redeemed, until the redemption and resurrection of body, leads on one hand to the Catholic deification of the Institution, and on the other hand to the Novatianism of the sects."[101] The language more commonly used here is of the visibility and invisibility of the Church. Torrance is adamant that in using these terms, the Reformers viewed the Church as "an ontological and eschatological reality" because as the

Nicene Creed states, *credo sanctam ecclesiam* not *video sanctam ecclesiam*. The Church is seen by faith.[102]

THE CHURCH AS THE NEW CREATION

Christ's Second Advent as a Transition and the Consummation of Time

The final stage in the Church's life is an unrealized future reality. The event that will precipitate eternity will be the second advent of Christ but it will not signal a new world completely discontinuous from the current one, just as the incarnate Son does not cease to be incarnate, so the union of his humanity and divinity is an eternal reality. This also means that there is no change in the message proclaimed by Jesus in his earthly ministry and that of the *eschaton*. Rather, the last things will signal the consummation of all that has thus far been limited and imperfect. Christ's second advent will herald the final consummation of history "in a great act of crisis in which all time will be gathered up and be changed."[103] Space and time will be redeemed from the consequences of sin and death and renewed as the new creation.[104]

This future period of the Church's life is best characterized by the idea of "fulfillment" understood from both an eschatological and a teleological perspective. The final judgment will not bring out new responses to God; rather, it will force both individuals and churches to own up to the way that they have lived. Churches will be revealed either as places of reconciliation and love or as places of division and bitterness.[105] This applies to the individual as well. Torrance suggests that an individual's experience in relation to God at the close of the present historical age will not be unexpected; rather, "it will mean the consummation of their experience and relations with God."[106] In Christ, "the voice of divine forgiveness and the voice of divine judgment are one and the same. This unity belongs to the very heart of salvation mediated through Jesus."[107] However, the outcomes will be quite different for "whether a man believes or not, the creative Word continues activity . . . Some eat and drink salvation; others out of the same cup and the same plate eat and drink damnation."[108]

For believers, the return of Christ is when we will no longer need faith that trusts in the unseen for we will see Christ face to face. The final judgment for believers will mean the actualization of God's victory over sin and guilt. In the present age, although our sins are forgiven in Christ, we remain subject to the consequences of fallen human nature. At the final judgment, the believer will be fully reconciled to God. Union with Christ "necessarily carries with it sharing with him in the resurrection of the dead and the life of the world to come . . . Christ has set us upon an entirely different basis in relation to God in which there is no longer any place for corruption and death."[109]

Those who have resisted God during their earthly lives will also find themselves standing before the judgment of God. Torrance notes that rarely do humans actually reject the Cross but rather keep on evading it, which in the end leads to the same result.[110] They will encounter the holiness of God that will manifest itself as the wrath of God "that is the resistance of God which his Holiness as Holiness cannot but take against unrepentant sinners."[111] Torrance does not write lightly of this, describing the rejection of God's love as an absurd mystery.[112] Even in judgment Torrance still sees God's mercy at work, noting that even though the Word of God always elicits a yes or a no from us, in the event of unbelief, "Jesus intends that the judgment shall fall with a delayed action still leaving room and time for decision and faith."[113]

Torrance suggests that when the final judgment comes, God's judgments may very well take us by surprise because they will not be based on our works but on the overflowing abundance of God's atoning love. He applies this not so much to individuals but to the corporate Church, suggesting that it is better to be a Church that is aware of how desperately poor and needy it is and willing to throw itself on the mercy and judgment of Christ than it is to be one that proudly justifies itself by its own self and righteousness and lives in disagreement with God's love or in contradiction to the reconciliation that is worked out through the person of Christ.[114]

One of the other issues that we must consider here is the relationship between election and predestination. Torrance suggests that election refers to the "eternal decision which is nothing less than the Love that God himself is, in action,"[115] or expressed another way, election has to do with God's "being for others." Again, "divine election is the free sovereign decision and utterly contingent act of God's love . . . It is neither arbitrary nor necessary, for it flows freely from an ultimate reason or purpose in the invariant Love of God."[116] This eternal decision takes on a specific historicity with the incarnation as the fullest actualization of that love.[117] The doctrine of predestination is intrinsically connected to the doctrine of election for Torrance and relates to the point that we have made about the *eschaton* as the actualization of one's prior decision in relation to God. Since election and predestination are both grounded in the eternal decree of God and also in our election in and through Jesus Christ, they must be thought of together.

In pairing predestination and election, Torrance is responding to the unhelpful way in which determinist frameworks of thought have influenced the doctrine of election, particularly as inherited from Calvin. Viewing predestination "as an absolute-temporal and absolute-causal *prius*, gave rise to very grave problems."[118] Torrance rejects these errors, whether irresistible grace or the idea that humans possess a completely independent and neutral free-will, and develops his own take on election on the basis that "union with Christ" rather than predestination is the central theme in Calvin's theology.[119] Election cannot be thought of as some impersonal divine determinism but rather as the way that when an individual encounters Christ, they are for the first time made free to make a decision in relation to God. In encountering Christ, we are for the first time given freedom to say yes or no to God and thus must think of this decision as intrinsically linked to the divine decision already made on our behalf in Christ.[120] Without Christ, human free will is not neutral but held in bondage to sin.

Although the incarnation happens at a specific moment in time, we know that what takes place in Jesus' incarnate life is grounded in the eternal being of God. Election is therefore grounded outside space and time in the eternal life and personal relations of the Father, the Son, and the Holy Spirit. It is in the same vein that Torrance explicitly rejects the doctrine of universalism, noting that it must remain only a possibility rather than a logical necessity and commenting that "the fallacy of every universalist argument lies not in proving the love of God to be universal and omnipotent but in laying down the impossibility of ultimate damnation."[121]

Israel

Torrance also believes that Israel has a continuing role in God's redemptive plan that is not replaced by the Church. It is his opinion that the Jews still have a role of testimony; they bear witness to God's faithfulness in both judgment and mercy, they bear witness to the roots of the Christian faith, and they bear witness to the inherent antagonism of humanity toward God.[122] Torrance posits that "Israel constitutes God's sign-post in the history of world-events, pointing ahead to a culmination in his saving interaction with mankind in space and time"[123] but states that its role "will become fully manifest only in the consummation of his Kingdom at the end-time."[124] Writing in 1950, Torrance highlighted the Holocaust and the establishment of an independent Jewish state as signs of the times, signs that tell us that God is about to act in history, although Torrance is careful to note that we can't know *what* God is about to do but only that he is about to act.[125] For Torrance, the establishment of Israel as a nation brought to the fore once again their ongoing struggle between *laos* and *ethnos*. They exist as a political nation-state but also identify as a holy people. Torrance argues that this ongoing tension will be used by God to ready Israel for all that must happen in order for eschatological and teleological fulfillment to take place.[126] This signals some sort of eschatological imminence for

> the Christian Church and the Jewish Church are now harnessed together in the mysterious judgements of God for witness, service and mission in the acceler-

> ating rush of world-events toward the end-time, when Christ himself will come to take up his reign and make all things new.[127]

Having described the Jewish-Gentile split as the greatest schism in the Church, Torrance goes on to argue that the reconciliation of Jew and Gentile is vital for the wider mission of the Church. Much of Torrance's perspective on Israel is polemical, particularly in a twenty-first-century context and its increasing distance from the horrors of the Holocaust.[128] What can be widely appreciated about Torrance's perspective on Israel, however, is his adoption of a Christological lens to view their historical existence and future eschatological role. Torrance's insistence that since Jesus was a Jew we cannot understand him outside this historical matrix is useful and so is his insistence that there must be reconciliation between Jew and Gentile—but only ever in and through Christ and not independent of the recognition of Jesus as Messiah.

Eschatology as a Divine Act

Torrance rejects any sense that the *eschaton* involves God acting in a way that terminates time, instead arguing that God's eschatological acts "gather up time in the fulfilling of the divine purpose."[129] God's acts are both present and future, fully realized but not yet fully unveiled. Whereas the Old Testament understood the kingdom of God to be a future event that would be realized apocalyptically, the New Testament transfers the emphasis from being solely in the future to being realized in the present, emphasizing that the kingdom of God is already breaking into time. The *eschaton* is not so much an event as it is a person: Christ, the first and the last, in whom redemption has already been accomplished and who pours out his Spirit so that redemption is subjectively realized in each of us. In the person of Jesus Christ, God and human are united through the Holy Spirit in such a way that eternity and time are united, "and though that union is inserted into our history with its limitations and relativities it is a union that is carried through the contradiction of sin and death itself into the resurrection."[130] Fallen time is already invaded by the completed redemptive work of Jesus Christ, but it is veiled behind the "forms and fashions [of history], so that we are unable to see it directly."[131] New time can be glimpsed through the Spirit but cannot be simply read from human history for as Torrance puts it, new time is concealed by old time, which is only visible to faith.

Torrance is careful to emphasize that the *eschaton*, or the full consummation of the kingdom, is not something that can be inaugurated by human effort; the primacy of the act belongs to God alone. Writing shortly before he took up army chaplaincy, Torrance reflected on the great danger of assimilating Church and society,

> One of the greatest tragedies that ever happened in the religious and social history of this country was during and after the last war, when the Church deluded the people into thinking that the Kingdom of God would gradually develop upon the earth, produced out of the kingdoms of the world by the efforts of the world plus divine aid, and that there would come a time when the Church would be at home in this world, identified with a better order. People were thoroughly disillusioned, and they have left the kirk by the tens of thousands. The Church herself is largely to blame, because she did not have a right understanding of her place and function in the world; because she failed to grasp the supernatural nature of her New Testament faith and vision.[132]

There is an inherent danger of this in any eschatology that overemphasizes human agency in "causing" the *eschaton*. The Church must continually return to the fact that its calling in the time between is to point to the work of Christ in anticipation of its full consummation and not to achieve the work of Christ on his behalf.

The Apocalypse Today

To conclude this chapter, we will engage in a brief consideration of Torrance's eschatology. He reflects on the differences between Jewish and Christian apocalyptic. Jewish apocalyptic had a predominantly negative view of the new age breaking in as judgment on the old age, while Christian apocalyptic positively emphasizes the restoration heralded by the resurrection and the overlap of the two ages.[133] Christian eschatology is also intrinsically related to Christology since Jesus Christ himself is the *Eschatos*: "the last things have already overtaken the Church for in Christ all is fulfilled."[134]

This Christocentric eschatology is elucidated in Torrance's published sermon series *The Apocalypse Today*, which contains sermons preached at Alyth and Aberdeen on the Book of Revelation. Torrance observes that the incarnation is the model for our understanding of how God continues to be at work in history. Just as God was fully present among us but veiled in Christ, so the kingdom of God has already broken into history and is present but veiled. He explains further,

> Apocalypse or Revelation is the unveiling of history already invaded and conquered by the Lamb of God. Apocalypse means the tearing aside of the veil of sense and time to reveal the decisive conquest of organic evil by the incarnate Son of God. Apocalypse means the unveiling of the new creation as yet hidden from our eyes behind the ugly shape of sinful history . . . No doubt we are unable by mere outward inspection to trace the lineaments of the Kingdom of God in history, but it is nevertheless a fact that even now God governs and orders the course of the world.[135]

For Torrance, Revelation is full of symbolic language that demonstrates the difference between our view of history and God's view of history.[136] We "no longer look past history to its consummation, but look behind the process of history into its divine secrets."[137] This is metaphorical language that lets us glance behind the black clouds of history and acknowledge that all history is ultimately governed by Christ.[138] Revelation 21 and 22 describe the fulfillment of the kingdom and the consummation of God's original intention to have fellowship with humankind, for

> the Garden of Eden meant that God has made man to have communion with Him in a perfect environment, and that true human life is essentially life in such a perfect environment . . . The Christian hope is fulfilled only in a new heaven and a new earth peopled with human beings living in holy and loving fellowship with God, with one another, and in harmony with the fullness of creation.[139]

The breaking in of the kingdom heralds "the time of life abundant, of fulfilment, the time of the end that is also the beginning, the time that gathers up in itself all things visible and invisible in the perfection of communion with the living God."[140] However, there is a very real evil power that stands against God and the Church, pictured throughout Revelation as a dragon, a beast, or a false prophet. Torrance describes it as a "demonic trinity."[141] The world order that is created in opposition to God and in defiance of sin is named Babylon, an "imitation Kingdom of God."[142] Yet despite this challenge to God's authority, Torrance is emphatic that God is in control of history and is keen to ensure that the Church knows that it is not impotent within history, arguing that "the real cause of the world-disturbance is the prayer of the Church and the fire of God . . . All history moves at the impulse of prayer."[143] Even though it appears as if the rulers of the earth are free to do whatever they want, the Apocalypse prompts us to look past the chaos of this world to see that God is on his throne. It is in the midst of this conflict that the Church is called to bear witness, a task that will require much patience and will cost the Church everything. Christ's victory was won through the incarnation, through his entering into weakness, humility, and death, and in the same way, it is only through its patient endurance of suffering that the Church will overcome evil. God allows this for the testing of the Church because "it is only in the testing of tribulation, in the trial of suffering that we can tell who are sealed with the blood of Christ and marked out as belonging to Him in heart and faith."[144]

CONCLUSION

We have explored Torrance's view of salvation history, noting the diachronic connection that endures through each of the three stages of the Church because the Church is the people that God has drawn into relationship with himself. Torrance consequently reads the Old and New Testament as complementary parts of one redemptive story in which God is bringing people into true fellowship with himself and each other.

NOTES

1. Thomas F. Torrance, *The Trinitarian Faith* (Edinburgh: T&T Clark, 1993), 279–80.
2. Thomas F. Torrance, *The School of Faith* (London: James Clarke, 1959), lxv.
3. Thomas F. Torrance, *Theology in Reconstruction* (Grand Rapids, MI: Eerdmans, 1965), 193. Emphasis mine.
4. Thomas F. Torrance, *Space, Time and Incarnation* (Edinburgh: T&T Clark, 1997), vi.
5. Ibid., 24.
6. Ibid., 3.
7. Ibid., 39. The idea of space as a receptacle or container is what led to the idea of the *extra Calvinisticum*. See Thomas F. Torrance, *Incarnation: The Person and Life of Christ*, ed. Robert T. Walker, 213–28 (Downers Grove, IL: InterVarsity Press, 2008).
8. Ibid., 15.
9. Ibid., 18.
10. Thomas F. Torrance, *Theological Science* (Edinburgh: T&T Clark, 1996), 334–37.
11. Torrance, *Incarnation*, 38–40.
12. Torrance, *Theology in Reconstruction*, 192.
13. Torrance, *Incarnation*, 39.
14. Ibid., 38.
15. Torrance, *Theology in Reconstruction*, 193–94.
16. Torrance, *Incarnation*, 39.
17. See Thomas F. Torrance, "The Goodness and Dignity of Man in the Christian Tradition," *Modern Theology* 4, no. 4 (July 1988): 311–14.
18. Torrance, *Incarnation*, 39.
19. Thomas F. Torrance, *Conflict and Agreement in the Church: Order and Disorder* (Eugene, OR: Wipf and Stock, 1996), 287.
20. Thomas F. Torrance, *Atonement: The Person and Work of Christ*, ed. Robert T. Walker, 343 (Downers Grove, IL: InterVarsity Academic Press, 2009).
21. Thomas F. Torrance, *The Christian Doctrine of God: One Being Three Persons* (Edinburgh: T&T Clark, 1996), 120.
22. Torrance, *Conflict and Agreement in the Church: Order and Disorder*, 286.
23. Thomas F. Torrance, "The Doctrine of Grace in the Old Testament," *Scottish Journal of Theology* 1 (1948): 55–65.
24. Torrance, *Incarnation*, 41.
25. Thomas F. Torrance, *The Mediation of Christ* (Edinburgh: T&T Clark, 1992), 7–9.
26. Torrance, *Atonement*, 346; Torrance, *The Mediation of Christ*, 12–1[illegible]; Thomas F. Torrance, "Israel: People of God—God, Destiny and Suffering," *Theological Renewal* 13 (October 1979): 4.
27. Torrance, *Theology in Reconstruction*, 195.
28. Torrance, *Conflict and Agreement in the Church: Order and Disorder*, 289.
29. Torrance, *Theology in Reconstruction*, 196.
30. Torrance, *The Mediation of Christ*, 10–12.

31. Thomas F. Torrance, *Reality and Evangelical Theology: The Realism of Christian Revelation* (Eugene, OR: Wipf and Stock, 2003), 87. Make note of the phrase "a church as much as a people," once again showing us the correlation of the people of God with the Church.

32. Thomas F. Torrance, "The Divine Vocation and Destiny of Israel in World History," in *The Witness of the Jews to God*, ed. David W. Torrance, 89 (Edinburgh: Handsel Press, 1982).

33. Torrance, *The Mediation of Christ*, 34.

34. Thomas F. Torrance, *Conflict and Agreement in the Church: The Ministry and Sacraments of the Gospel* (Eugene, OR: Wipf and Stock, 1996), 65. Torrance notes that Paul describes this as Israel's "holding down the truth in unrighteousness" so that God allows them to be blinded.

35. Torrance, *The Mediation of Christ*, 30.

36. Ibid., 32–33.

37. Torrance, *Reality and Evangelical Theology*, 86. See also Torrance, *The Mediation of Christ*, 12–15.

38. *The Mediation of Christ* is Torrance's most accessible work on the preparatory role of Israel for the incarnation, particularly the first two chapters.

39. Torrance, *Theology in Reconstruction*, 196.

40. Torrance, *Conflict and Agreement in the Church: Order and Disorder*, 266.

41. Torrance, *Incarnation*, 52.

42. See Torrance, *Atonement*, 25–60. See also Torrance, *The School of Faith*, lxxxvii–xcv for a discussion of the threefold office of Christ in the specific context of Reformed theology and Torrance, *The School of Faith*, ciii–cvi for the work of the Spirit in relation to the threefold office.

43. Torrance, *Atonement*, 27. Cognates given are *pidyon*, *lutrousthai*, and *lutron*.

44. Ibid., 33. Cognates given are *kopher* and the Greek terms *lutrousthai* and *lutron*.

45. Ibid., 44.

46. Ibid., 44–48. For a helpful overview of these three strands and some further comment on the way Torrance views atonement, see Thomas F. Torrance, "Atonement: Thomas F. Torrance on the Atonement as Ransom, Priestly Atonement, Justification, Reconciliation and Redemption," in Andrew Purves, *Exploring Christology and Atonement: Conversations with John McLeod Campbell, H. R. Mackintosh and T. F. Torrance* (Downers Grove, IL: InterVarsity Press, 2015), 199–240.

47. Torrance, *Atonement*, 51.

48. Torrance, *Conflict and Agreement in the Church: Order and Disorder*, 288–89.

49. Ibid., 289.

50. Torrance, *Incarnation*, 43. See also Kevin Chiarot, *The Unassumed Is the Unhealed* (Eugene, OR: Pickwidk, 2013), 23–29.

51. Torrance, *The Mediation of Christ*, 18.

52. Torrance, *Conflict and Agreement in the Church: Order and Disorder*, 286–87.

53. Ibid., 286. The New Testament use of *ekklēsia* to refer to the gathered people of God derives from the use of this term in the Septuagint where it "refers to the congregation regarded collectively as a people and as a whole, rather than to the actual assembly or meeting of the people."

54. Ibid., 285.

55. Ibid., 286.

56. Torrance, *The Mediation of Christ*, 37–38, 99–126.

57. Torrance, *Incarnation*, 43–44.

58. Thomas F. Torrance, *The Doctrine of Jesus Christ* (Eugene, OR: Wipf and Stock, 2002), 5.

59. Torrance, *Conflict and Agreement in the Church: Order and Disorder*, 285.

60. Thomas F. Torrance, *Theology in Reconciliation* (Eugene, OR: Wipf and Stock, 1996), 28. For a wider discussion of the way that the Jewish-Gentile schism hindered the development of the Church, see Torrance, *Theology in Reconciliation*, 24–31.

61. Torrance, *The School of Faith*, cxix–cxii.

62. Torrance, *Incarnation*, 38.

63. Thomas F. Torrance, *Space, Time and Resurrection* (Edinburgh: Handsel Press, 1976), 17.

64. Torrance, *Conflict and Agreement in the Church: Order and Disorder*, 287.

65. Torrance, *The Trinitarian Faith*, 300.

66. Thomas F. Torrance, *Preaching Christ Today: The Gospel and Scientific Thinking* (Grand Rapids, MI: Eerdmans, 1994), 70.

67. Torrance, *Atonement*, 303.

68. Ibid.

69. Torrance, *The Doctrine of Jesus Christ*, 192–96.

70. Torrance, *Atonement*, 290.

71. Ibid., 287.

72. Torrance, *The Doctrine of Jesus Christ*, 192.

73. Torrance, *Atonement*, 293.

74. Thomas F. Torrance, *Royal Priesthood* (Edinburgh: Oliver and Boyd, 1955), 45; and Thomas F. Torrance, "The Christ Who Loves Us," in *A Passion for Christ: The Vision That Ignites Ministry*, ed. Gerrit Dawson and Jock Stein, 18 (Eugene, OR: Wipf and Stock, 2010).

75. Torrance, *Space, Time and Incarnation*, 4.

76. Torrance, *The Mediation of Christ*, 40–41.

77. Ibid., 67.

78. Ibid., 67–70.

79. Torrance, *Theology in Reconstruction*, 201.

80. Torrance, *Atonement*, 350.

81. Torrance, *The Christian Doctrine of God*, 233.

82. Ibid., 34, 163, 229. Torrance footnotes this reference to Karl Barth, *Church Dogmatics* IV/2, trans. G. W. Bromiley, ed. G. W. Bromiley and T. F. Torrance, 614ff (Edinburgh: T&T Clark, 1956).

83. Torrance, *Theology in Reconstruction*, 205.

84. Torrance, *Conflict and Agreement in the Church: The Ministry and Sacraments of the Gospel*, 160.

85. Torrance, *The Trinitarian Faith*, 300.

86. Torrance, *Atonement*, 342.

87. Torrance, *The Doctrine of Jesus Christ*, 191.

88. Paul Molnar, *Thomas F. Torrance: Theologian of the Trinity* (Farnham, UK: Ashgate, 2009), 269.

89. Torrance, *The School of Faith*, cxxv.

90. Torrance, *Conflict and Agreement in the Church: The Ministry and Sacraments of the Gospel*, 159.

91. Ibid., 146. Emphasis original.

92. Ibid., 159. See also 66–68.

93. Torrance, *Conflict and Agreement in the Church: Order and Disorder*, 17.

94. Torrance, *Conflict and Agreement in the Church: The Ministry and Sacraments of the Gospel*, 159–60.

95. Ibid., 146.

96. Thomas F. Torrance, *Gospel, Church and Ministry*, ed. Jock Stein, 1:102 (Eugene, OR: Pickwick Publications, 2012).

97. Thomas F. Torrance, "Predestination in Christ," *Evangelical Quarterly* 13 (1941): 120.

98. Torrance, *Gospel, Church and Ministry*, 102.

99. Geordie Ziegler, *Trinitarian Grace and Participation: An Entry into the Theological Thought of Thomas F. Torrance* (Minneapolis, MN: Fortress Press, 2017), 241–92.

100. Thomas F. Torrance, "Review of *The Realm of Redemption: Studies in the Doctrine of the Nature of the Church in Contemporary Protestant Theology* by J. Robert Nelson," *Scottish Journal of Theology* 6, no. 3 (September 1953): 322.

101. Ibid., 322.

102. Ibid., 323.

103. Torrance, *The Doctrine of Jesus Christ*, 197.

104. Ibid., 192; Torrance, *Gospel, Church and Ministry*, 85.

105. Thomas F. Torrance, "What Is the Church?" *Ecumenical Review* 11, no. 1 (October 1958): 21.

106. Torrance, *The Doctrine of Jesus Christ*, 197.

107. Thomas F. Torrance, "The Christ Who Loves Us," in Dawson and Stein, *A Passion for Christ*, 15.

108. Torrance, *Conflict and Agreement in the Church: The Ministry and Sacraments of the Gospel*, 72–73.

109. Torrance, *The Trinitarian Faith*, 299.

110. Torrance, "Predestination in Christ," 126.

111. Torrance, *The Doctrine of Jesus Christ*, 199.

112. Torrance attributes the "surd-like quality of sin" to H. R. Mackintosh in Torrance, "Predestination in Christ," 122–27. He makes the point that evil cannot be explained rationally in Torrance, *The Mediation of Christ*, xiii.

113. Torrance, *Conflict and Agreement in the Church: The Ministry and Sacraments of the Gospel*, 65.

114. Torrance, "What Is the Church?" 21.

115. Thomas F. Torrance, *Christian Theology and Scientific Culture* (Eugene, OR: Wipf and Stock, 1998), 132.

116. Ibid., 131.

117. Torrance, *The Christian Doctrine of God*, 5.

118. Torrance, *Christian Theology and Scientific Culture*, 134.

119. Thomas F. Torrance "Our Witness through Doctrine," in *Proceedings of the 17th General Council of the Alliance of Reformed Churches Throughout the World Holding the Presbyterian Order*, 134 (Geneva: World Presbyterian Alliance, 1954).

120. For a full account of Torrance's doctrine of predestination, see Torrance, "Predestination in Christ," 108–41. It is clear that Torrance rejects any idea that God saves some and rejects some, repeatedly insisting that Christ died for all. A useful secondary article is Myk Habets, "The Doctrine of Election in Evangelical Calvinism: T. F. Torrance as a Case Study," *Irish Theological Quarterly* 73 (2008): 334 –54.

121. Thomas F. Torrance, "Universalism or Election?" *Scottish Journal of Theology* 2, no. 3 (September 1949): 312. See also Torrance, *The Mediation of Christ*, xiii. See also Stephen D. Morrison, *T. F. Torrance in Plain English* (Columbus, OH: Beloved Publishing, 2017), 85–90; and Habets, "The Doctrine of Election."

122. Thomas F. Torrance, "Salvation Is of the Jews," *Evangelical Quarterly* 22 (1950): 167–71. See also David W. Torrance, "The Mission of Christians and Jews," in Dawson and Stein, *A Passion for Christ.*

123. Thomas F. Torrance, "The Divine Vocation and Destiny of Israel in World History," in *The Witness of the Jews to God*, ed. David W. Torrance, 104 (Edinburgh: Handsel Press, 1982).

124. Ibid., 85.

125. Torrance, "Salvation Is of the Jews," 172.

126. Torrance, "The Divine Vocation and Destiny of Israel in World History," 94–96; and Torrance, *The Mediation of Christ*, 13.

127. Torrance, "The Divine Vocation and Destiny of Israel in World History," 96.

128. Torrance, "Israel: People of God," 2–14. Evidence of the polemical response provoked by Torrance's view on Israel that we have discussed here can be found in various published letters. See Colin Morton and Chris Wigglesworth, "Response to 'Mission to the Jews,'" *Life and Work* (June 1989): 7; and Torrance's later response, Thomas F. Torrance, "Tom Torrance's Reply on Israel," *Life and Work* (July 1989): 33–34.

129. Torrance, *Space, Time and Resurrection*, 151.

130. Torrance, *Conflict and Agreement in the Church: The Ministry and Sacraments of the Gospel*, 162.

131. Torrance, *Atonement*, 411.

132. Torrance, *Gospel, Church and Ministry*, 82.

133. Thomas F. Torrance, "Liturgy and Apocalypse," *Church Service Society Annual* 24 (1953): 4.

134. Thomas F. Torrance, "Review of *The Prophetic Faith of Our Fathers: The Historical Development of Prophetic Interpretation*, by Leroy Edwin Froom, vols. I–III," *Scottish Journal of Theology* 6 (1953): 209.

135. Thomas F. Torrance, *The Apocalypse Today* (London: James Clarke, 1960), 12–13.

136. Ibid., 163.

137. Ibid., 41.

138. Ibid., 166.

139. Ibid., 177.

140. Ibid., 164.

141. Ibid., 138.

142. Ibid., 140.

143. Ibid., 73–74.

144. Ibid., 65.

Chapter Four

The Church of the Triune God

Having discussed the doctrine of the Trinity and Torrance's historical view of the Church, we now bring the Trinity and ecclesiology together in a more decisive fashion. For Torrance, ecclesiology functions as a subsidiary of the doctrine of God. Holding that ecclesiology is "essentially evangelical doctrine, inseparably bound up with faith in the holy Trinity and with the saving operation of Christ through the Holy Spirit,"[1] Torrance negates any possibility of ecclesiology without reference to the Triune God. In what follows, we will explore Torrance's use of the motif of *koinōnia* in order to reflect on the ways in which the community of the Church is shaped by the communion of Father, Son, and Spirit.

INTRODUCING THE TRINITY-CHURCH RELATION

Walker appropriately observes that the unity of Torrance's work does not arise from his logical development of doctrine but rather "in the object to which his theology points, the incarnate Christ in the heart of the Trinity."[2] While the doctrine of the Church is the immediate object of our consideration, we cannot consider the Church in itself as a historical object or interpersonal set of human relationships but rather must look through the historical appearance of the Church to view it in its "dimension of depth," which comes into focus only as we give due precedence to the doctrine of the Holy Trinity. This foundational move is required for us to understand the true being, nature, and mission of the Church. Torrance succinctly states: "The Church does not exist by and for itself, and therefore cannot be known or interpreted out of itself."[3] For the Church to really be understood as "the Body of Christ, as the sphere in which the risen Lord is present through his Spirit and mightily active through his Word,"[4] the doctrine of the Church must include not only historical elements but must reckon with the transcendence and eternality of God, therefore including apocalyptic and eschatological elements.[5]

For Torrance, the Christian doctrine of God is grounded in the truth that, in the incarnate Son, "the eternal God 'defines' and identifies himself for us as he really is."[6] Jesus "is both God and man in the fullest and proper sense" so that the incarnation is "a real becoming on the part of God, in which God comes *as man* and acts *as man*, all for our sake."[7]

This is helpfully summarized by referring again to the *homoousion*, the hypostatic union, and *perichoresis*. The doctrine of the *homoousion* signals that Jesus is fully God, eternally coinherent with the Father and Son, and that Jesus is fully human, having assumed our fallen humanity. The hypostatic union describes how these two natures, divine and human, are unified in the one person of Jesus Christ without confusion, change, division, or separation. Through the dynamic union of these two natures throughout his life, Jesus restores and heals our fallen humanity and makes us able to participate in his new humanity.[8] Finally, *perichoresis* affirms the unity and triunity of God and that there is only ever one divine activity, "that of God the Father through the Son and in the Holy Spirit."[9] Father, Son, and Spirit are perichoretically *homoousios* with each other, deepening the Church's understanding of the trinitarian onto-relations within the Godhead. God makes himself known in a whole and not in parts so that we can never think of one of the persons without the others or of God as an undifferentiated whole.

This is all in keeping with Torrance's stance that while the "Christological pattern" appears throughout "the whole body of Christian dogmatics," every doctrine needs to correspond to the full revelation of the Trinity, "the ultimate ground upon which our knowledge of Jesus Christ himself and of God's self-revelation through Christ rests becomes disclosed as trinitarian."[10] It belongs to the essential faith of the Church that God is not far off and unknowable but has really communicated himself to us and given us access to participate in his own divine life through the Word and Spirit.[11]

Consequently, appropriate theological method holds together the economic reality of God revealed through his actions in space and time (God *ad alios*) on one hand, with his eternal being (God *in se*) on the other.[12] In this way we avoid "mythological thinking," which is projected from humanity onto our doctrine of God, and instead demonstrate "theological thinking," which is centered in God's self-revelation.[13] Here we see the epistemological centrality of the incarnation, for our understanding of God is formed "under the compulsion of his self-revelation in Jesus Christ."[14] The doctrine of the Trinity is thus seen by Torrance as enshrining "the essentially Christian concept of God."[15]

PRE-NICENE ECCLESIOLOGY AS PRESENTED BY TORRANCE

Torrance follows the Fathers—particularly those of the Eastern tradition—in the move of looking back to the Trinity in order to see the Church in its "dimension of depth."[16] The Fathers paid more attention to the salvific content of the Gospel and the nature of the Triune God than to the Church as an institution or social grouping. This is an approach that is mirrored in Torrance's insistence that ecclesiology must be derived from the doctrine of the Triune God who has revealed himself to us in Christ and the Spirit.

In both Eastern and Western pre-Nicene theology, the doctrine of the Church was only mentioned incidentally. In the East, Athanasius and the Cappadocians emphasized union to Christ through the Spirit as the means that created union with other members of the body, while Basil stressed the indwelling of the Spirit in each individual and accordingly in the Church as a whole. The Church was defined by its triune worship and participation in the triune *koinōnia* so that Basil could state that, through the Spirit, "the worshipping Church is, so to speak, the doxological correlate of the triunity of God."[17] Torrance argues that Eastern theology subordinated issues that had to do with the life of the Church—such as organization and jurisdiction—to the doctrine of God so that an incipient Eastern ecclesiology developed "within an essentially trinitarian understanding of the Church in which Church authority and government were construed in terms of *koinōnia* rather than in terms of hierarchical structure."[18] Returning to his favorite early theologian, Torrance notes that even though Athanasius mentioned the Church in his writings, "it was always the objective reality of the self-revealing and self-giving of the Father through the Son and in the Holy Spirit that occupied the centre of his vision."[19]

In contrast to the Eastern church, Torrance suggests that Hilary of Poitiers best exemplifies the development of the Western doctrine of the Church. Influenced by the Eastern theologians he met during his exile, Hilary had a strong sense of the Church as constituted and unified in Christ but also distinguished between the Church as an empirical fellowship and as a mystical body. This was a more Western tendency.[20] While the Western Church initially resisted the re-incursion of dualistic thought, it retained a latent tendency from Hellenistic philosophy to think in dualistic terms. Torrance identifies Clement and Origen's acceptance of the Platonic split between the physical and sensible, or the spiritual and eternal, as leading to the teaching that the same gnostic split existed within the Gospel and, accordingly, within the Church. This is why Clement and Origin argued that the temporal, visible, and earthly Church was simply a "passing similitude of the real thing," the invisible, spiritual, and eternal Church.[21] When this was integrated with Hilary's distinction between the empirical and mystical Church, it laid the foundation for the dualisms that emerged in the Western doctrine of the Church.

Nicene-Constantinopolitan Theology

Torrance maintains that Nicene-Constantinopolitan ecclesiology was non-dualistic, as seen in its assertion "that through the sanctifying and renewing presence of the Holy Spirit, *the empirical Church is the Body of Christ*."[22] There was no sense of only the spiritual Church being the true Church or of any separation between the visible and invisible Church. Nicene theology operated "with an internal ontological relation between the Person and work of Christ, and thus with an internal relation between the Church and Christ of a dynamic and ontological kind established through the reconciling and incorporating activity of the incarnate Son and the communion of the Holy Spirit."[23] There is a real, dynamic relation between the Triune God and the Church that is formed in history and that cannot be separated into divergent aspects that are either temporal or eternal, or alternatively physical or spiritual. This trinitarian approach may be contrasted with non-trinitarian theologies such as Arianism for when Christ only has a moral or external relation to the Father, the real ontological relation between God and the Church is lacking so that the Church is merely "a community formed through the voluntary association of like-minded people."[24] In contrast,

> it was made abundantly clear that in accordance with its apostolic and catholic faith the Church regarded itself as wholly centred in the Lordship of Christ, and his reign as the enthroned and exalted *Kurios Christos*, who was and is and ever will be coequal and coeternal with the Father and the Holy Spirit in the supreme sovereignty and power of the Holy Trinity. In the life and mission of the empirical Church on earth it was the kingdom of Christ that was predominant, for all power in heaven and earth had been given to him, and things visible and invisible, earthly and heavenly, were subject to him. They had in any case been created by him as the Word of God. What gave concrete shape and structure to the faith of the Catholic Church was the incarnation, the economic condescension of God in Jesus Christ to be one with us in the concrete realities of our human and social life, and his saving activity within the structures of our creaturely existence in space and time.[25]

The primary challenge that faced the Fathers was how to communicate the Gospel in the context of the Graeco-Roman world. It is helpful to remember that the patristic writers were not theologians in the professional sense in which we use the term today. They were not employed by universities as full-time teachers of theology. The majority were pastors or bishops whose primary concern was for the people of God and the wider life and mission of the Church. This is why trinitarian doctrine was thought out in a context of faith and godliness for it was a matter of worship and not just intellectual assent.[26]

It was rare in Nicene theology for the organization, or structure, of the Church to be considered an essential matter of faith.[27]

As the "pattern and order of God's Triune Life" imposed itself upon the Church, resulting in trinitarian ways of thinking, something took place that was "of immense significance for the whole life, worship and mission of the Church."[28] Torrance maintains that the Nicene-Constantinopolitan Creed has "a fundamental orientation and theological structure of a conceptually irreversible nature."[29] Even though the doctrine of the Church was not included in the original text of the Creed at Nicea—it was merely mentioned in a list of appended heresies—Torrance notes that when the Council of Constantinople amended the creed to explicitly affirm the *homoousion* of the Spirit,[30] thus bringing the doctrine of the Trinity to full expression, the time was also right for the Church to be included among the articles of saving faith. This was a development that was in keeping with the Church's early trinitarian baptismal tradition so that the inclusion of the Church in the creed was a result of "the Church's matured convictions about the Holy Spirit and the Holy Trinity."[31] Torrance therefore maintains that within the Nicene-Constantinopolitan Creed,

> the clauses on the Church do not constitute an independent set of beliefs, but follow from belief in the Holy Spirit, for *holy* Church is the fruit of the *Holy* Spirit, the result of his sanctifying activity in mankind, and as such is, as it were, the empirical correlate of the *parousia* of the Spirit in our midst. If we believe in the Holy Spirit, we also believe in the existence of one Church in the one Spirit. Belief in "one, holy, catholic and apostolic Church" is thus regarded in the Creed as a function of belief in the Spirit, or rather of belief in the Father, Son and Holy Spirit.[32]

THE TRIUNE CHURCH

Torrance holds strong convictions about how the doctrine of the Trinity "expresses the essential and distinctively Christian understanding of God by which we live, and which is of crucial significance for the evangelical mission of the Church as well."[33] An ecclesiology based on order, ministry, practices, or varying doctrinal formulations—in short, on anything temporal—fails to get at the theological underpinnings of the Church's being and nature, for the primary basis on which an understanding of the Church is to be sought is not in the Church as an institution but in God's triune being. One must begin with the doctrine of the Trinity and from that point move to engage with ecclesiology. The term "trinitarian" is an absolute term for our knowledge of God for

> if God is triune in his nature, then to really know God means that we must know him in accordance with his triune nature from the start . . . That means

> we must know him as the Triune God who within himself has relations between Father, Son and Holy Spirit; so that for us to know that God, we must know him in a mode of understanding on our part appropriate to the Trinity of Persons in God. There must be a "trinitarian" character in our knowing of God, corresponding to the trinity of relations in God himself.[34]

We may clarify here what Torrance means by this trinitarian "mode of understanding" by expanding on our earlier discussion of the "stratified structure of reality" with its three cross-referenced levels that explicate the multi-leveled way in which Torrance views the theological task. When we apply this stratified model to ecclesiology, we see that ecclesiology is worked out in space and time on the basic level, is heavily shaped by the secondary level, and is controlled by the tertiary level. "Controlled" suggests that the ultimate reference point for ecclesiology is the ontological being of God, which is the content of the tertiary level. However, the Triune God is not known to us without the person of Jesus Christ, through whom God reveals himself in space and time, which is the concern of the secondary level. Epistemic primacy is given to the tertiary level, but since this trinitarian framework of theological knowledge is never divorced from the incarnation, there is a dynamic interplay between the doctrine of the Trinity at the tertiary level and Christology at the second level, which together influence the doctrine of the Church at the basic level.

Exploring this from the other direction, since the basic level is concerned with the intuitive grasp of reality that we gain as personal knowers in the community of faith, then the secondary level is of a more theological nature where the intuitive knowledge of the first level is organized and expressed in systematic propositions. Although the Gospel means we begin at the basic level of our experience, the three levels of this stratified structure of knowledge are ultimately governed from the higher levels to the lower levels.[35]

The relationships between the three levels may be illustrated by Torrance's preference for the biblical metaphor of the Church as the body of Christ. The experience of the Church is on the basic level, but the doctrine of the Church itself is a secondary-level concept. Christ is God incarnate within space and time, and through its relation to him, the Church exists in space and time but works out its ontological relationship to Christ on the secondary level. Nevertheless, because Jesus Christ may only be understood in the light of the eternal Trinity, the body-of-Christ analogy ultimately derives from the ontological being of God at the tertiary level. Consequently, it is in the light of the tertiary level that we must judge our statements about God and experience of God in order to be as faithful as possible in how we speak about God within the Church.[36]

The Motif of *Koinōnia*

We now turn our attention to the concept of *koinōnia*, which is the central motif in Torrance's trinitarian ecclesiology. Torrance's use of *koinōnia* must be put alongside his use of the New Testament terms *mystērion* and *prothesis* to show how Scripture situates Christ's incarnation, life and ministry, death, resurrection, and ascension within God's eternal purpose.[37] Each term has a primary and a secondary usage in Scripture. Torrance argues that *mystērion* refers primarily to the union of God and humanity in the incarnation of Jesus Christ and secondarily to the union of Christ and his Church through the Spirit. This mystery is related to *prothesis*, God's eternal purpose. The primary sense of *prothesis* is the eternal purpose of God that is set forth in Jesus Christ and then reaches out to its fulfillment and consummation in the Church, so the secondary sense of *prothesis* is the way that the Church sets forth the mystery of Christ in the time between, particularly through Word and Sacrament.[38] Finally, the term *koinōnia* has the primary sense of humanity's participation in Jesus Christ's completed work of atonement and the secondary sense of the fellowship or communion that exists between members of Christ's body. Together, these terms summarize the teaching of Ephesians 1 and 2: through Christ and in one Spirit we have access to the Father.[39] Torrance suggests that *mystērion* relates primarily to the Son, *prothesis* primarily to the Father, and *koinōnia* primarily to the Spirit.[40]

In Torrance's attributing *koinōnia* to the Spirit, *koinōnia* also becomes the overarching theme that he uses in relating the Church to the Trinity. Instead of a relation of likeness as seen in social trinity models, Torrance prefers the concept of participation: humans are really drawn through the Son and in the Spirit into the union and communion of the eternal Trinity. It is through an actual relation to Christ that humanity is able to participate through the Holy Spirit in the union and communion of the Holy Trinity. As he observes, "It is the incarnate Son who naturally constitutes the real focus for the doctrine of the Trinity, and the regulative centre with reference to which all the worship, faith and mission of the Church take their shape . . . it is correspondingly the New Testament teaching about the Church as the Body of Christ incarnate, crucified and risen, that provides the immediate focus and controlling centre of reference for a doctrine of the Church founded and rooted in the self-communication of the Holy Trinity."[41]

To unfold Torrance's use of *koinōnia*, we will explore the parallel models of a "threefold communion" and the "two dimensions of *koinōnia*." He starts with the language of a "threefold communion" through which humanity can participate in the fellowship, or communion, of the Triune God. Although Torrance uses fellowship and communion interchangeably, he appreciates the Orthodox perspective that "fellowship" is a superficial translation of *koinōnia* and observes their preference for "communion."[42] The concept of a threefold communion is the primary structural undergirding of Torrance's trinitarian ecclesiology and shows how he maps out the connections between the Triune God and the Church as a community that God calls into being within space and time. We will then unpack the two complementary dimensions of *koinōnia*. These are the vertical dimension, which is concerned with humanity's relation to God, and the horizontal dimension, which has to do with humanity's relation to each other.

The Threefold Communion

Torrance explains his concept of a threefold communion by beginning with a description of the consubstantial communion of God *in se*, Father, Son, and Spirit, who form an eternal perichoretic communion of love. The eternal love of the Godhead—the love that *is* the triune Godhead—takes on human embodiment in the person of Jesus Christ. This happens through the hypostatic union because in Jesus Christ, divine and human nature are united throughout the whole atoning work of his life, death, and resurrection. Christ has healed our humanity and made it possible for humans to participate in the communion of the Spirit. The same Holy Spirit that is the bond of love within the Trinity pours out the love of God within the Church so that through the communion of the Spirit, the Church is made able to participate in the eternal love of God. The Church is formed as a community of love on earth as it participates through Christ and the Spirit in the communion of the Trinity.[43]

The theological basis for this threefold model is that through Christ's incarnational atonement, believers are united to God so that they "organically cohere with and in him as one Body in one Spirit."[44] This is the realist view of union with Christ that Torrance shares with Irenaeus, who is also adamant that communion with God takes place in "the most realist sense," for in Christ there is "a soteriological and ontological unification of people in whose midst God himself dwells through the presence of his Spirit."[45] Jesus Christ is fully God and fully human. In him the eternal relations of the triune Godhead assume an economic form yet remain immanent, "thus opening out history to the transcendence of God while actualising the self-giving of God within it."[46] In a corresponding way, through the Spirit, God unites us to Christ "in such a way that his human agency in vicarious response to the Father overlaps with our response, gathers it up in its embrace, sanctifying, affirming and upholding it in himself, so that it is established in spite of all our frailty as our free and faithful response to the Father in him."[47] This understanding is supported by Hunsinger, who acknowledges that for Torrance, Christ's vicarious humanity is how we are joined to Christ and therefore able to share in the triune communion.[48]

The relationship of being that exists between Father, Son, and Holy Spirit is eternal but has become embodied in our humanity through the incarnation.

Because of the vicarious nature of Jesus' life and work, our human nature is united with his so that through Jesus' assumption of human nature, God "has once and for all assumed human nature into that mutuality and opened his divine being for human participation."[49] Torrance consequently views it as being directly through the life of the incarnate Son that the Holy Spirit has "accustomed himself" to dwell with humanity and "adapted human nature to receive him and be possessed by him."[50]

This threefold communion model incorporates both trinitarian and Christological foci and shapes our thinking about the unequivocal way in which "the Church is the work of the three divine persons."[51] It is not simply that all humanity is part of the Church. Torrance is clear that the Church is composed of those who have been baptized in the name of the Trinity and more decisively, those who "live in faith and obedience to him."[52] As individual believers are incorporated into the living body of Christ through the Holy Spirit, this creates a new dynamic, divine dimension in the world.[53] To fill this understanding of *koinōnia* out further, Torrance describes the Church as the "universal family of God," adopted as God's children. The Church is the "community of the reconciled," who are united to Christ and through him find redemption, and the "communion of the saints," who are filled with the Spirit in such a way that they are sent out in power to proclaim and bear witness to the redemptive work of God.[54]

The Two Dimensions of Koinōnia

Torrance also talks of two dimensions of *koinōnia*—vertical and horizontal. The vertical dimension is simply the threefold communion model, which is how Torrance views humanity as participating in the eternal *koinōnia* of God through Christ and the Spirit. This vertical dimension has a corresponding horizontal dimension, which is the communion formed among humanity that is correlative to their participation in the communion of the Trinity. As God communicates himself to humanity in a movement of love, this creates a circle of loving and knowing, which in turn generates a reciprocal community of love, the Church.[55] These two dimensions are inseparable from each other for as Torrance clarifies,

> it is only through vertical participation in Christ that the Church is horizontally a communion of love, a fellowship of reconciliation, a community of the redeemed. Both these belong together in the fullness of Christ. It is only as we share in Christ Himself that we share in the life of the Church, but it is only as we share with all saints in their relation to Christ that we participate deeply in the love and knowledge of God.[56]

When Torrance says "in Christ" here, he is referring to the work of atonement through which we are given to participate in the fellowship of the

Trinity rather than the work of Christ in distinction from the other two persons of the Trinity. Although it was the Son who became incarnate, the Father and Spirit were still at work and present throughout his whole incarnate life, even unto his death.[57] Torrance further suggests that we should think of love being the Church's "participation in the humanity of Jesus Christ for he is the love of God poured out for mankind. In him it is rooted and grounded in love, and in him it becomes itself a communion of love through which the life of God flows out in love toward every human being."[58]

Although Torrance rejects directly applying the perichoretic onto-relations of the Trinity to humanity's relationships, the Christian concept of the person is still shaped by the idea that to be a person is to be in community.[59] Torrance explains,

> Here there arises again the distinctively Christian concept of the person, deriving from the community of love in God and defined in onto-relational terms in which the inveterate ego-centricity of the self-determining personality is overcome, which demands and gives shape to a new and open concept of human society.[60]

These two dimensions of *koinōnia* further support Torrance's perspective that the Church "represents that area within humanity where the love of God is poured out by the Holy Spirit and where men and women are given to share together in their life on earth, and within the social cohesions of humanity, in the overflow of the divine Life and Love."[61] This sense of the Church as the place where the love of God overflows is yet again demonstrative of Torrance's ecclesiology because it exemplifies the backward reference that is necessary to understand the true nature of the Church as that which does not exist independently of the Triune God. The Church reposes upon God's *ousia* as "being for others" for "if he were not Love in his innermost Being, his love toward us in Christ and the Holy Spirit would be ontologically groundless."[62] However, since God is not dependent upon, nor is his essential nature changed by, his relationship with humanity, his choice to be the God who creates and loves is "sheer gratuitous grace . . . the transcendent freedom of his self-determination in love for us."[63] This makes it all the more startling that God was not *required* to create but still freely *chose* to create. His being is *being for others*.

God is a *koinōnia*, a rich and full communion of love within himself, but a love that freely overflows for God's being as love is being for others. The Church is thus created as a creaturely community that is formed and sustained through the love of God, which is manifested through Christ and the Spirit. The Church has a creaturely form of *koinōnia* that reflects the divine *koinōnia*. It is only as we participate in this creaturely *koinōnia* that we are given to know God in the depths of his divine *koinōnia*. Christ became one with us in order to claim us "so that as Church we find our essential being and life not in ourselves but in Him alone."[64]

THE PERSONS OF THE TRINITY AND ECCLESIOLOGY

We now move to a more nuanced investigation of the distinctive economic work of each of the three persons. While there is only one divine activity that Father, Son, and Holy Spirit all partake in, there are distinctions within the inherent oneness of the Triune God that are possible to explore in regard to the economic activity of the Trinity. Although this approach may seem somewhat partitive, it will provide a more in-depth understanding of *how* the Church is the work of the three divine persons. Therefore, although we speak of differing acts of the Triune God, these are not independent acts but acts-in-relation just as the persons are never independent persons but persons-in-relation. We may cite here Gunton's observation that Torrance has comparatively little interest in how each person of the Trinity is "distinctly themselves,"[65] which means that "all the questions which should be asked of this consistent, creative, and important doctrine of God center in some way on the relation between the one and the many."[66]

Of further help is Torrance's understanding of the traditional doctrine of appropriation or attribution, described elsewhere as a "theological procedure in which a feature belonging to the nature of God, common to all three persons, is specially ascribed to one of the divine persons."[67] Although Torrance rejects the way that in Latin theology, qualities or acts of the Trinity as a whole became constitutive of a particular triune person, he does not dismiss the doctrine of appropriation completely.[68] Instead, he follows Barth in partnering the doctrine of appropriation with the doctrine of *perichoresis*. McIntosh observes that for Barth these are the "two hermeneutical principles of the concept of triunity," which complement each other. When Barth speaks of the "*Trinity* in unity," he relates this to the doctrine of appropriation, and when he speaks of its complement, the "*unity* in Trinity," he relates this to the *perichoresis* of the Trinity.[69] This is why even though Barth speaks of the threeness of God as "God the Creator, God the Reconciler and God the Redeemer,"[70] he also argues that "no attribute, no act of God is not in the same way that attribute or act of the Father, the Son and the Spirit."[71] Barth establishes three key principles in regard to the tri-unity of God: first, "the appropriation must not be arbitrary"—not every triad, or grouping of three, may be related to the Trinity; second, "the appropriation must not be exclusive" so that where a quality or act is appropriated to one of the triune modes of being, it does not become uniquely constitutive of either Father, Son, or Spirit; and finally, "appropriations must not be invented freely. They are authentic when they are taken literally or materially from Holy Scripture."[72] We see the same principles reflected in Torrance's insistence that in any act, "each Person who is himself whole God acts without any surrender of his distinctive hypostatic properties."[73] However, while Barth primarily speaks of the redemptive acts of creation, reconciliation, and redemption, Torrance primarily speaks of the grace of the Lord Jesus Christ, the love of the Father, and the communion of the Holy Spirit.

The Grace of the Lord Jesus Christ

Salvation is attained through the person and work of Christ. The true content of grace is the decisive act of Jesus Christ. Jesus' obedience was the undoing of the first Adam's disobedience, and through the union of his humanity with his divinity, sinful and broken humanity was both judged and healed.[74] Jesus is both the one who elects and the elected one, the God who chooses and the human who is chosen, the spoken word of God and the one who offers a perfected human response to God's word. He lived not just *as* man but as *a* man in such a way that he converted humankind from its rebellion against God to "glad surrender."[75] This is the primary sense of *mystērion*, the union of God and humanity in Jesus Christ that is necessary for humanity's union with Christ to be enacted. It is only through Jesus that humankind is restored to being sons and daughters of God and made able to be God's image-bearers.[76] Christ does not just proclaim salvation but *is* our salvation so that

> the message of Christ must be regarded as more than a message of who he was and what he has done for us, for it is so integrated with him that it is itself the saving Word and power of God constantly at work among his people precisely as Word, and effectively operative in the faith of the Church, anchoring it and giving it substance in the Person of Christ as Saviour and Lord.[77]

This view of atoning reconciliation through Christ's vicarious humanity is the central tenet of Torrance's Christology. He finds its pattern in the Old Testament covenantal pattern of two unequal parties. Israel could not independently fulfill the requirements of the covenant,[78] so God provided a means of covenantal response for them, exemplified on an individual level by the provision of a ram to replace Isaac (Gen. 23:1–19) and at a corporate level by the establishment of the Israelite priesthood. This pattern is fulfilled in the new covenant where the "third dimension" is the vicarious humanity of Jesus Christ in whom God has provided a means of response that not only deals with the external requirements of the covenant but heals and renews our very humanity. Jesus Christ is both God and human, not only mediating God to us but also serving as the mediator of our response toward God.[79] Furthermore, Christ assumes our whole humanity, including our minds, for as Gregory Nazianzen argues, if he had not done so we would be alienated from God in our mind, alienated from God and unable to think aright of him.[80] The whole human had to be assumed by God in order for the whole human to be saved. Torrance frequently notes, and Nazianzen also states, "That which is unassumed is unhealed, or unredeemed."[81]

The doctrine of *anhypostasia* and *enhypostasia* is relevant at this juncture. Complementing each other, this pairing insists that Christ's human nature does not exist independently of its union with God but is a full and genuine human mind, will, and body. Jesus' human nature is not assumed into his divine nature but rather into his *person*, the hypostatic union of his divinity and humanity.[82] However, while Jesus assumes a specific, individual humanity, he assumes this humanity in ontological solidarity with humanity. He shared with us a "solidarity in terms of the interaction of persons within our human and social life, in personal relations of love, commitment, responsibility, decision, etc."[83] This is why we may think of salvation as to do not only with our reconciliation to God but also with our reconciliation to each other.

This discussion may appear to be more in the realm of soteriology rather than ecclesiology, however the Church only exists because of the ontological relationship that is formed between Christ and the Church through Christ's assumption of humanity, bringing us once more to the biblical concept of the Church as the body of Christ. Humans are drawn into union with God and therefore into union with each other—into "personal union and corporate communion"[84]—which provides the basis for Torrance's assertion that describing the Church as the "body of Christ" is the most appropriate analogy of all those that Scripture uses. This image is informed by other analogies for the Church but "holds most of them together within itself."[85]

Torrance views the body of Christ as the fullest Scriptural image because "it is the most deeply Christological of them all, and refers us directly to Christ Himself, the Head and Saviour of the Body."[86] Such language, referring to the Church as a "body," is analogical: we speak of the Church as the body of Christ without inappropriately projecting a human understanding of embodiment onto the being of the Church. Torrance explains further what it means to say that this is an analogical relationship, noting that the relationship between Christ and the Church is

> not a metaphorical relationship, though it does partake of metaphor and figure, but a *real relation* established in Grace, whereby the Church in all its unlikeness is given to be like Christ through sharing in His image, and in all its utter difference yet to be one with Christ through participation in His Spirit. This relation of likeness and unlikeness, of difference and yet of some kind of identification, which is not just figurative but reality, is a true analogical relation.[87]

This analogy expresses the doctrine of the Church in terms of its internal relation to Christ "for it is in Christ and his inherent relation to the Father and to the Holy Spirit that the essential nature of the Church is to be found."[88] Jesus' assumption of our humanity is key to a trinitarian ecclesiology because it emphasizes that believers are incorporated into Christ on the basis of his death and resurrection, are given to share and participate in his risen humanity, and through him are enabled to participate in the fellowship of the Trinity. The Church is the body of Christ precisely because of Christ's assumption of humanity,[89] so this analogy is "no mere figure of speech but describes an ontological reality, [the Church is] enhypostatic in Christ and wholly dependent on him."[90] To phrase this another way, the Church is constituted of "all who are reconciled to God in one body through the Cross and are made one in Christ, united with his humanity in such a way that he now comprises both in himself, their humanity and his own, as 'one new man,' for he is in them as they are in him."[91] Torrance relates this to Jesus' prayer in John 17 where Christ asks that the oneness that he has with the Father might be extended to include believers, albeit in a way appropriate to our created status.[92] It is through Christ's vicarious life that the Church comes into being; he is the "ontological ground and the unifying core of the Church which he appropriated to himself as his own peculiar possession."[93]

The union of divine nature and human nature in Jesus Christ signals that "it is not due to some external relation in moral resemblance to Christ that the Church is his Body, but due to a real participation in him who is consubstantial with God the Father."[94] However, as we have repeatedly emphasized, this is not just participation in Christ but participation in the fellowship of the Triune God, for "through the communion of the Holy Spirit the Church is united to Christ and grounded in the hypostatic union of God and man embodied in him, and through Christ and in the Spirit it is anchored in the consubstantial union and communion of the Father, Son and Holy Spirit in the Holy Trinity."[95] Furthermore, although the relationship between Christ and the Church is modeled on the hypostatic union of the two natures in Christ, it is important to note that this union with Christ "is not one of nature but one of adoption and grace effected through the gift of the Spirit who comes to dwell in us as he dwells in God."[96] It is a relation of difference rather than of direct identity so we must think of the identification between Christ and the Church as "the amazing identity of grace."[97] Nevertheless, despite this difference, this analogous relationship helps us to further "think out" the form of the Church. It is made up of many creaturely persons who are formed into "one body" by the Spirit yet remain "differentiated in their individuality."[98]

Finally, the emphasis upon Christ, rather than the Church, remains paramount. When we describe the Church as the body of Christ, we must emphasize "of Christ" rather than "body of." Torrance comments,

> The advantage of this expression is that it does not focus our attention upon the Church as a sociological or anthropological magnitude, nor upon the Church as an institution or a process, but upon the Church as the immediate property of Christ which He has made His very own and gathered into the most intimate relation with Himself; and it reminds us that it is only the Body of which He is the Head, and is therefore to be subject to Him in everything.[99]

As a way of elaborating more fully on the relationship between Christ and the Church, Torrance identifies four aspects of the Church's relation to Christ that help to fill out our understanding of this relation. First, the church relates to Christ crucified, who makes "expiation for our sin and guilt by bearing it all vicariously in the sacrifice of Himself, He the just for the unjust, that we might be made righteous in Him."[100] The Church continues to be a body of sinners who are justified in Christ but remain subject to fallen time and sinful nature. Second, the church relates to the risen Christ for just as Christ died on the Church's behalf, he also rose on the Church's behalf. "The Church which is His Body will surely and certainly follow Him in the resurrection."[101] As the body of the risen Christ, the Church already shares in his resurrection while still awaiting its own. The Church that has grasped the reality of the resurrection is called to live anticipating its own resurrection. Although the Church should live free from its sinful past and tradition, it often "lives as though it were still bound hand and foot by the grave-clothes of the past,"[102] "crusted over with secularism and [going] about in the shabby second-hand clothing of a transient age."[103]

Third is the relationship of the Church to Christ ascended, hidden from sight. This has three points of significance. The ascension declares the distinction between Christ and the Church and the distinction between their ministries. The ascension reveals Christ's refusal to be separated from his Church for the ascended Christ has poured out his Spirit on his Church, anointing it as his "servant in history." Finally, the ascension also causes the Church to look backward to the historical Christ so that we do not encounter Christ apart from his incarnate life, death, and resurrection and only in this light look forward to the day when Christ will return in power and glory.[104]

Finally, the Church is related to the advent Christ and so must "look beyond all history to find the fullness of its life in the coming Lord and in the unveiling of the new creation."[105] As the Church of the advent Christ, the Church knows that "although it is already one Body with Christ through the Spirit, it has yet to be made one Body with Him in the consummation of His Kingdom."[106] The Church that lives in the time between the ascension and the *eschaton* is to be characterized by its joyful expectation of Christ's return to make all things new and its commitment to bear witness to that anticipation.

The Love of the Father

Eugenio notes that Torrance's soteriology is unusual in referring to the salvific work specific to the person of the Father,[107] which can be extended to also suggest that the Father has a specific role in relation to ecclesiology. However, the specific work of the Father is less visible than the economic work of the Son and the Spirit. Torrance reminds us that although God is the Source of all being, he "directs us in our knowledge of him not to some superessential realm beyond the space-time universe which he has brought into being out of nothing but to his unceasing interaction with us in the midst of our creaturely and historical existence where in his loving purpose he makes himself known to us as our God and Father."[108] We must certainly speak of the Father alongside the Son and Spirit, but we are limited in what we may say of the Father's economic work.

While God is described in the Old Testament as Israel's father and binds himself to them in covenant as their God, it is only through God's self-giving and self-revealing in his Son that God's fatherhood is fully defined. We do not know the Father except through the Son for it is the love of the Father and the Son for each other that reveals to us the love of God.[109] This love is not a self-contained and selfish love but a fullness of love that overflows, a generous love that "reveals that he loves us to the uttermost with an eternal Fatherly love."[110] The love of the Father is given its fullest content in the crucifixion of the Son "for it is in that personal sacrifice of the Father to which everything in the Gospel goes back."[111]

It is the love of the Father who gives us all things that lies behind the Father's *prothesis*, the eternal purpose that is set forth through the Father's sending of the Son and the Spirit to enable humanity's participation in God's own triune life, which then leads to the formation and existence of the Church. In the incarnation, the Father does not send the Son as a gift to humankind, as something external to the divine being, but rather, "the fact that Jesus Christ is the incarnation within our alienated human being and perishing existence of the eternal Son of the eternal Father means that the message of reconciliation, salvation and redemption does indeed have divine content and eternal validity."[112] The historic mission of the Son is an event that flows from the eternal triune being of God. In Christ, "God turns towards men and women and wills to be one with them, and in him they are turned wholly towards God to be one with God."[113] These are not two different movements but one integrated movement of electing love. God freely decides to give himself in love but in love that demands a response from humanity.[114] The love of the Father is therefore "the steadfastness of love and grace even in judgment, of electing love even in condemning sin."[115] This means that everything we see revealed in the grace of Jesus Christ is identical with the love of the Father.[116]

The Communion of the Holy Spirit

We come now to the work of the third person of the Trinity, the Holy Spirit, which has historically been among the weakest doctrines in the Church.[117] However, what is clear is that for Torrance the work of the Spirit is inseparable from that of the Son; union with Christ is correlative to the communion of the Spirit.[118] Without the Holy Spirit this is not actualized in us as individuals, and we are unable to participate in the fellowship of the Holy Trinity. Torrance observes,

> The mission of the Spirit sent from the Father in the name of the Son as the Spirit of truth is to convict people of the truth as it is in Jesus, in judgment and mercy, to enlighten, inform and strengthen the Church through serving the centrality of Christ and deepening its understanding of his teaching and person as the incarnate Son of the Father, the one Lord and Saviour of humanity.[119]

We can express the distinctiveness of the Spirit in another way by recalling that even though the Son is the Word made flesh, humankind can only hear that Word as we share in the Spirit through whom the Word became flesh.[120] The Son's incarnation reveals God to us, but this is "a knowledge mediated through the Son which we may have only through the activity of the Holy Spirit and as in the Spirit we participate in the Son and through him in God."[121]

To speak of the Triune God as Spirit describes his personal being (*ousia*) for God is Spirit "in utter differentiation from all created nature."[122] The Hebraic understanding of "holy" evokes a sense of something transcendent, unapproachable, and wholly "other than," but since it is paired by Scripture with the term *ruach*, which has a distinctly "active and concrete sense,"[123] the Scriptures reveal that the Holy Spirit is not an impersonal force acting upon humanity but rather God "personally and objectively present meeting and speaking with his people."[124] "Spirit" is not simply a reference to God's agency, revealing an impersonal way in which the Father interacts with humankind. Instead it is through the Spirit that God creates our relation to him, "by the presence of his Spirit within us as a relation of himself to himself."[125]

The person of the Holy Spirit "no less than the Son is the *self-giving* of God: in him the Gift and Giver are identical."[126] It is through the Holy Spirit that "God makes himself open to our knowing" as a reciprocal action to the fact that, through Jesus Christ, humanity has been made open to the possibility of true and genuine knowledge of God.[127] The Spirit "marvellously gives us access to the intrinsic intelligibility of God, while nevertheless preserving inviolate the ultimate mystery and ineffability of his divine being."[128] Torrance elaborates,

> The Spirit is not just something divine or something akin to God emanating from him, not some sort of action at a distance or some kind of gift detachable from himself, for in the Holy Spirit God acts directly upon us himself, and in giving us his Holy Spirit God gives us nothing less than himself.[129]

Furthermore, belief in the Church is the correlate of belief in the Holy Spirit for "the doctrine of the Church is a function of the doctrine of the Spirit who proceeds from the Father through the Son."[130] Consequently, the Church is considered by Torrance to be "the manifestation in humanity correlative to the gift of the Spirit, the sphere described by God's people where God's Spirit is at work" so that "no doctrine of the Church can neglect the doctrine of the Spirit."[131] Our understanding of this is deepened by thinking once again of the incarnation and Pentecost as complementary events. Pentecost was not the beginning of the Church—given that Torrance views the people of Israel as part of the Church—but rather the moment of its transformation into the body of the risen Christ through the Spirit.[132] Once the people and structure had been prepared, the Spirit was poured out on the Church as the "effective counterpart in us of his self-offering to the Father through the eternal Spirit. In other words, Pentecost must be regarded, not as something added on to atonement, but as the actualisation within the life of the Church of the atoning life, death and resurrection of the Saviour."[133]

Through the outpouring of the Spirit, God causes the Church to "participate in his own divine life and love,"[134] which constitutes it as "the unique 'place' where access to the Father through the Son was grounded in space and time among the nations of mankind."[135] It is the sanctifying presence and activity of the Spirit that forms the Church, joining us to Christ and giving us access to the Father.[136] It is through the communion of the Holy Spirit that "the Church shares in the incarnate mystery of Christ, and through his power and operation within it that the Church as the Body of Christ is progressively actualised among the people of God."[137] Humanity is brought into the union and communion of the Trinity—the vertical dimension that we have discussed—which has as its parallel the creation of unity among believers, or the horizontal dimension of *koinōnia*. Torrance explains,

> We have communion or *koinōnia* in the mystery of Christ, and are made members of his Body. The personalising incorporating activity of the Spirit creates, not only reciprocity between Christ and ourselves, but a community of reciprocity among humankind, which through the Spirit is rooted in and reflects the Trinitarian relations in God himself. It is thus that the Church comes into being and is constantly maintained in its union with Christ as his Body. This is the Church of the triune God, embodying under the power of the Spirit, the Lord and Giver of Life, the divine *koinonia* within the conditions of human and temporal existence.[138]

The work of the Spirit is to bring creatures to their true *telos* of participation in the *koinōnia* of the Triune God.[139] Just as Christ received the Spirit in his humanity, we are made able to receive the Spirit, and "to have the Spirit dwelling in us is to be made partakers of God beyond ourselves."[140] It is important to note that even though Torrance suggests that "our 'deification' in Christ, through the Spirit, is the obverse of his 'inhomination,'"[141] he is careful to quantify "deification," translated from the Greek *theosis* or *theopoiesis*. It is not that humans are made divine or become gods, for *theosis* is the way in which God "gives *himself* to us and *adopts us* into the communion of his divine life and love through Jesus Christ and in his one Spirit, yet in such a way that we are not made divine but are preserved in our humanity."[142] The presence of God sustains, rather than overwhelms, creaturely being.[143] As Torrance also states, "*all of grace means all of man*, for the fullness of grace creatively includes the fullness and completeness of our human response."[144] Through the active presence of the Holy Spirit, our focus is lifted beyond ourselves as we are enabled to be "partakers of God beyond ourselves" and "even share in the inwardness of God himself"[145] but not in any way that transgresses the bounds of our humble and creaturely status. We must retain the absolute distinction between the Holy Spirit and the human spirit.

The Church's Relation to the Son and Spirit in the Time between Christ's Two Advents

Our discussion of each of the three persons has filled out our understanding of the whole Trinity. This section will conclude with some reflection on the "mutual mediation" of the Son and Spirit since it is through this mutual mediation that the Church is made the place within space and time where humankind can meet with God.[146] The activity of the Son and Spirit are inseparable but distinguishable from each other and "constitute the two-fold way in which the one incomprehensible God communicates himself to us, grounded in and issuing from the transcendent and undivided reality of the three divine Persons."[147]

This mutual mediation takes place as Christ comes to us and the Spirit outworks in us the capacity to receive what Christ has done on our behalf; our *objective* union with Christ on the basis of the incarnation is *subjectively* actualized in us by the Spirit's indwelling.[148] Thus, redemption takes place

> *in Christ*, for it is in hypostatic union that the self-giving of God really breaks through to man, when God becomes himself what man is and assumes man into a binding relation with his own being; and *in the Spirit*, for then the self-giving of God actualises itself in us as the Holy Spirit creates in us the capacity to receive it and lifts us up to participate in the union and communion of the incarnate Son with the heavenly Father.[149]

Although the Church is primarily described as the body of Christ for "it was not, after all, the Spirit but the Son who became incarnate and gave Himself for the Church and affianced it to Himself as His very own,"[150] Christ imparts the Spirit to the Church in order to unite it to himself as his body "but in such an interior ontological and soteriological way that Christ himself is both the Head and the Body in one."[151] This takes place in the eschatological pause, the time between Christ's two advents when "the realm of grace is not yet dissolved by the realm of glory."[152] The kingdom of God has not yet fully been unveiled so the Church must truly walk by faith, not sight. This eschatological pause determines the Church's mission in history and its relation to Jesus Christ; while the Church is "rooted in the incarnation" through the Son's incarnate assumption of our humanity, the Church is "maintained through the operation of the Spirit."[153] It is through Christ's concrete historic works that we are saved and brought into union with God,[154] and yet this only ever takes place as the Spirit renews afresh our union to Christ. Torrance describes the Spirit as Christ's *Alter Ego*—their being and activity are inseparable so that the Spirit glorifies Christ and acts in his place.[155] Torrance also cites Athanasius's statement that "while Christ is the only *Eidos* or 'Form' or 'Image' of Godhead, the Spirit is the *Eidos* or 'Image' of the Son."[156] Through the Spirit who unites us to God and to each other the Church is made more open to God and "is thus more and more universalised or 'catholicised' as the one Body of him whose fullness fills all in all."[157]

The Filioque Controversy

In all our speech about the Trinity we must reckon with the difficulty of using finite language to describe infinite realities—and that which comes into focus when we consider the trinitarian relations—which we have no other frame of reference for except revelation. There are three basic relations within the Trinity, "referred to by the Church Fathers as 'fatherhood' or 'unbegottenness,' 'sonship' or 'begottenness,' and 'procession' or 'spiration.'"[158] These terms are unexplainable using human logic or comparison for they

> denote ineffable relations and refer to ineffable realities . . . But what do "breathing" and "pouring" or "proceeding" mean beyond indicating divine actions which in their nature are quite incomprehensible to us? As Karl Barth pointed out, we can no more offer an account of the "how" of these divine relations and actions than we can define the Father, the Son and the Holy Spirit and delimit them from one another.[159]

We must recognize that the processions within the Trinity are "incomprehensible mysteries which are not explicable through recourse to human modes of thought"[160] and so we must think of them in imageless ways—for example, to say that the Son is begotten cannot be understood using the metaphor of human birth.[161] Thus we affirm that there are real relations within the Trinity such as "begetting" and "proceeding" but we maintain apophatic reserve in our speech about God and do not seek to explain *how* these relationships function.[162]

This leads us into a discussion of the historical controversy over the *filioque* that arose when the Western church un-ecumenically inserted a clause into the Nicene Creed affirming the Holy Spirit proceeds from the Father and the Son.[163] This created an issue around whether the Spirit proceeds from the Father alone or from the Father and the Son. Western theologians felt that if the Spirit did not proceed from the Father and Son, then this suggested the subordination of the Son to the Father, although Torrance notes that they followed St. Augustine, holding this view "in a modified form according to which the Spirit is understood to proceed from the Father principally."[164] In response to this, Eastern theologians held that if the Spirit proceeds from both the Father and Son, this "appeared to posit two ultimate Principles or *archai*"[165] in the Godhead, and so they worked from the perspective that the Spirit proceeds from the Father only, basing this upon the difference between the "eternal procession of the Spirit from the Father, and the historical mission of the Spirit from the Son."[166] This all led to great division within the Church and was one of the causes of the schism between East and West.

Torrance argues that there is a solution that would have allowed the Church to avoid the historical East-West schism. The key is that the Son and Spirit both proceed from the *ousia* of the Father, referring to the shared being of the whole Godhead, rather than from the *hypostasis* of the Father, the specific person.[167] In Torrance's opinion, this is much more faithful to the Athanasian doctrine of coinherence for "since the Holy Spirit like the Son is of the Being of God, and belongs to the Son, since he is in the Being of the Father and in the Being of the Son, he could not but proceed from or out of the Being of God inseparably from and through the Son."[168] The following quote offers a full explanation of Torrance's solution to the *filioque* controversy.

> It is when we apply the concept of *perichoresis* rigorously to this doctrine of the Holy Trinity together with the concept of the triune *Monarchia* that it becomes possible for us to think through and restate the doctrine of the procession of the Holy Spirit from the Father in a way that cuts behind and sets aside the problems that divided the Church over the *filioque*. If we take seriously the understanding of the Trinity in Unity and the Unity in Trinity in which each Person is perfectly and wholly God, and in which all three Persons perichoretically penetrate and contain one another, then we cannot but think of the procession of Holy Spirit from the Father through the Son, for the Son belongs to the Being of the Father, and the Spirit belongs to and is inseparable from the Being of the Father and of the Son. In proceeding from the Being of the Father,

> however, the Holy Spirit proceeds from the One Being which belongs to the Son and to the Spirit as well as to the Father, and which belongs to all of them together as well as to each one of them, for each one considered in himself is true God without any qualification . . . Thus the procession of the Spirit cannot be thought of in any partitive way, but only in a holistic way as "whole from whole."[169]

This reading of history means that it is theologically correct to use the expression "from the Father and the Son" but also to use "from the Father through the Son." This only applies if we hold that the Spirit proceeds from the whole Godhead and not only the person of the Father, emphasizing the full perichoretic equality of the deity of the three persons. Torrance thus contends that returning to the Nicene doctrine of God provides the "ground for deep doctrinal agreement that cuts beneath and behind the historical divisions in the Church between East and West, Catholic and Evangelical, and [points] the way forward for firmly based ecumenical agreement in other areas of traditional disagreement."[170]

THE CHURCH AS A "COMMUNITY OF RECIPROCITY"

For Torrance everything depends on the reality that God actually interacts with his creation. Giving us access to his inner fellowship means there is genuine reciprocity between God and humans, which creates reciprocity between human and human. Another way of summarizing this exchange is to say that "through personal interaction with us, God creates reciprocity between us";[171] however, God's interaction with us never falls under human control and thus "retains its incomprehensibility and mystery as *grace*."[172]

Israel was formed as a covenant community of reciprocity. The vertical covenant bond of love that God established between himself and Israel became manifest in Israel as a "brotherly covenant" among the Israelites.[173] However, the covenant of Israel is fulfilled and transcended by the Word of God in Christ.[174] As humanity is drawn into the twofold movement of divine revelation where God speaks to humanity and humanity is enabled to hear and receive and respond to divine revelation, the resultant reciprocity between God and humanity results in a community that itself "under the continuing impact of divine revelation becomes the appropriate medium of its continuing communication to man."[175] God has "ordained that we receive His Word through the historical communication of other men, so that the communication of the Word and the growth of the Church as historical community are correlative."[176] Each new generation of the Church stands in a great tradition that stretches all the way back to the New Testament writers and their understanding of the Old Testament,[177] so the proclamation of the

Word is always "conditioned by the hearing and understanding of all the generations that have gone before."[178]

It is this sense of the Church as a social and historical community through which the Word is communicated that causes Torrance to describe it as the social coefficient of theological knowledge. This fits with his stance on the corporate dimension of theology, for a "society or community provides the semantic frame within which meaning emerges and is sustained."[179] By this Torrance means that the Church is the "cultural milieu within which our understanding is nourished, and within which new thoughts and fresh glimpses of reality are born."[180] It is through participation in the community of the Church, and through taking part in the horizontal dimension of *koinōnia*, that we learn how to relate experience, patterns of meaning, and acts of identification to each other. Torrance draws on Polanyi again, stating that within the shared experience of the Church an individual may move beyond subjective knowledge and experience to that which is objective because the really objective is that which is shareable.[181] This is objective kataphysic knowledge because the object of theology remains the subject. Torrance further observes, when writing about the nature of catechetical instruction, that "Christian instruction requires the community of others. It does not properly take place in isolation, but only in the midst of the Church, that is in the whole fellowship of life and mission and preaching and worship, for it is only in the essential integration of the Truth with being and action that it can be either received or communicated."[182]

This also draws on Torrance's insistence that theological knowledge is personal knowledge. Since God's being is *personal* being, then the nature of the Truth is personal and relational. Revelation was embodied in human form in Jesus Christ and must be communicated in a way appropriate to the nature of the knower as a human being. Revelation's proclamation takes place in space and time through the communication of other people who also exist in space and time, although—as we will see in our discussion of *kerygma* in coming chapters—the Church's proclamation is filled with Christ's presence through the Holy Spirit so that it is actually Christ who "communicates Himself personally in and through the historical Church where the Word is historically communicated to us by others, and where through them He comes Himself immediately in direct and personal address."[183]

In the following quote, participation in the space-time structure of the Church and participation in the eternal communion of the Trinity interact with each other to deepen our understanding of the role of the Church in the way that we are made able to think properly of God.

> It is within the communion of the Spirit we learn obedience to God's self-giving in Jesus Christ, and instead of being conformed to the cultural patterns of this world are inwardly transformed through a radical change of our mind,

> that we are able to discern the will of God and acquire the basic insights we need if we are really to develop our knowledge of him in a clear, articulate way. That is to say, within the interpersonal life of the church as the body of Christ and its actualization of corporate reciprocity with God in the space and time of this world, we find not only that we ourselves are personally assimilated into the onto-relational structures that arise, but that our minds become disposed to apprehend God through profoundly intelligible, although non-formalizable (or at least not completely formalizable) relations and structures of thought. We are spiritually and intellectually implicated in patterns of order that are beyond our powers to articulate in explicit terms, but we are aware of being apprehended by divine Truth which steadily presses for increasing realization in our understanding.[184]

Humans are incapable of persuading one other about the existence of God, which is why the Church is the place of dialogical theology, where God declares himself to humanity while enabling us to respond to him and to each other.[185] However, our conversations about God must never be detached from conversation with God or else dialogical theology becomes dialectical, "more concerned with a consistent system of ideas than with real conversation with the living God."[186] Theological knowledge arises from its embodiment in the Church and must be "joint-thinking, thinking-in-fellowship"[187] so that our thinking is informed by our interaction with each other. However, our thinking is also shaped by the many other social, historical, and cultural environments that we live and participate in,[188] so the Church needs to consistently bring "its teaching and preaching and worship to the criticism of God's word in order that through repentant self-denial it may be conformed in mind and understanding to the mind of Christ."[189]

CONCLUSION

This chapter has explored the theological Trinity-Church relationship, seeking to demonstrate that for Thomas F. Torrance, speech about the Church is always subsidiary to speech about the Holy Trinity. This is succinctly summarized when he writes that the Church is "the empirical community of men, women and children called into being through the proclamation of the Gospel, indwelt by the Holy Spirit in whom it is united to Christ and through him joined to God. Far from being a human institution it was founded by the Lord himself and rooted in the Holy Trinity."[190] Through exploring the motif of *koinōnia* as well as delving further into the doctrine of the Trinity and how it relates to ecclesiology, we have shown that the Church is Church in the most theological sense "when it looks away from itself to its objective source and ground in the Godhead, and dwells in the Holy Trinity, for it is in the Father, Son and Holy Spirit that the Church and its faith are rooted and grounded."[191]

NOTES

1. Thomas F. Torrance, *Atonement: The Person and Work of Christ*, ed. Robert T. Walker, 358 (Downers Grove, IL: InterVarsity Academic Press, 2009).

2. Robert T. Walker, "Introduction," in Thomas F. Torrance, *Incarnation: The Person and Life of Christ*, ed. Robert T. Walker, xxx (Downers Grove, IL: InterVarsity Press, 2008).

3. Thomas F. Torrance, *Theology in Reconstruction* (Grand Rapids, MI: Eerdmans, 1965), 192.

4. Ibid., 25.

5. Ibid.

6. Thomas F. Torrance, *The Christian Doctrine of God: One Being Three Persons* (Edinburgh: T&T Clark, 1996), 1.

7. Thomas F. Torrance, *The Trinitarian Faith* (Edinburgh: T&T Clark, 1993), 150.

8. Thomas F. Torrance, *Incarnation: The Person and Life of Christ*, ed. Robert T. Walker (Downers Grove, IL: InterVarsity Press, 2008); see also Myk Habets, *Theology in Transposition: A Constructive Appraisal of T. F. Torrance* (Minneapolis, MN: Fortress Press, 2013), 163–95.

9. Torrance, *The Trinitarian Faith*, 233–34.

10. Torrance, *The Christian Doctrine of God*, 1.

11. Ibid., 3.

12. Thomas F. Torrance, *The Ground and Grammar of Theology* (Charlottesville: University Press of Virginia, 1980), 96–98.

13. Torrance, *Theology in Reconstruction*, 48–49; Thomas F. Torrance, *Preaching Christ Today: The Gospel and Scientific Thinking* (Grand Rapids, MI: Eerdmans, 1994), 52. For further comment see Alan Torrance, *Persons in Communion: Trinitarian Description and Human Participation* (Edinburgh: T&T Clark, 1996), 191–94.

14. Ibid., 49. A marked contrast to this Christocentric trinitarianism is found in the work of Katherine Sonderegger who focuses on the "One God" rather than the Trinity, focuses on the importance of Christ's deity over his humanity, and insists that in theology, not everything can be reduced to Christology. See Sonderegger, *Systematic Theology: Volume 1, The Doctrine of God* (Minneapolis, MN: Fortress Press, 2015), xi–xxi. Another useful article on this topic is Thomas F. Torrance, "The Eclipse of God," *Baptist Quarterly* 22 (October 1967): 194–214.

15. Torrance, *The Christian Doctrine of God*, 2.

16. Jason Radcliff, *Thomas F. Torrance and the Church Fathers: A Reformed, Evangelical, and Ecumenical Reconstruction of the Patristic Tradition* (Eugene, OR: Pickwick Publications, 2014), 54–158.

17. Torrance, *The Trinitarian Faith*, 269n58. Torrance is paraphrasing Basil the Great from a number of sources.

18. Ibid., 272.

19. Ibid., 268.

20. Ibid., 270.

21. Ibid., 276.

22. Ibid.

23. Ibid., 278.

24. Ibid., 277.

25. Ibid., 273–74.

26. Ibid., 13–46.

27. Ibid., 270–71.

28. Torrance, *The Christian Doctrine of God*, ix.

29. Ibid., xi.

30. Torrance, *The Trinitarian Faith*, 191–97.

31. Ibid., 264.

32. Ibid., 252.

33. Torrance, *The Christian Doctrine of God*, 10.

34. Torrance, *The Ground and Grammar of Theology*, 148.

35. Torrance, *The Christian Doctrine of God*, 87.

36. Thomas F. Torrance, *Christian Theology and Scientific Culture* (Eugene, OR: Wipf and Stock, 1998), 37–39.

37. Torrance, *Incarnation*, 161–62.

38. Ibid., 168–70.

39. Torrance, *The Christian Doctrine of God*, 2.

40. Torrance, *Incarnation*, 174. We will be cautious around the use of a doctrine of appropriation in order not to suggest that the persons ever work in isolation from each other.

41. Torrance, *The Trinitarian Faith*, 263.

42. Thomas F. Torrance, "Trinity Sunday Sermon on Acts 2:41–47," *Ekklesiastikos Pharos* 52 (1970): 194.

43. Torrance, *Atonement*, 360. A more imaginative analogy of the threefold communion model is offered by Kye Won Lee, who likens Torrance to Ben Hur as the champion of the Trinity and who has *perichoresis*, the hypostatic union, and *koinōnia* as the three wheels of his chariot. See Kye Won Lee, *Living in Union with Christ: The Practical Theology of Thomas F. Torrance* (New York: Peter Lang, 2003), 317.

44. Torrance, *The Trinitarian Faith*, 254.

45. Ibid.

46. Thomas F. Torrance, *Theology in Reconciliation* (Eugene, OR: Wipf and Stock, 1996), 101.

47. Ibid., 103.

48. George Hunsinger, "The Dimension of Depth: Thomas F. Torrance on the Sacraments of Baptism and the Lord's Supper," *Scottish Journal of Theology* 54, no. 2 (May 2001): 166.

49. Torrance, *Theology in Reconciliation*, 101.

50. Ibid., 102.

51. Torrance, *Atonement*, 360.

52. Ibid., 362.

53. Torrance, *The Trinitarian Faith*, 254.

54. Torrance, *Atonement*, 362.

55. Thomas F. Torrance, *Reality and Scientific Theology*, 2nd ed. (Eugene, OR: Wipf and Stock, 2001), 178–85.

56. Thomas F. Torrance, "What Is the Church?" *Ecumenical Review* 11, no. 1 (October 1958): 9–10.

57. Torrance, *The Christian Doctrine of God*, 252–53.

58. Torrance, *Atonement*, 374–75.

59. Torrance, *Christian Theology and Scientific Culture*, 50–51. Torrance relates this to Clerk Maxwell's scientific insistence that "the relations between things, whether so-called objects or events, belong to what things really are." The alternative to an understanding of "person" shaped by the doctrine of the Trinity is that which was "logically derived from the notions of individuality and rational substance and not derived ontologically from the Trinity." See Torrance, *Theology in Reconciliation*, 285.

60. Torrance, *Theology in Reconciliation*, 287.

61. Torrance, "What Is the Church?" 16.

62. Torrance, *The Christian Doctrine of God*, 5.

63. Ibid.

64. Torrance, "What Is the Church?" 9.

65. Colin Gunton, "Being and Person: T. F. Torrance's Doctrine of God," in *The Promise of Trinitarian Theology: Theologians in Dialogue with T. F. Torrance*, ed. Elmer M. Colyer, 127 (Lanham, MD: Rowman & Littlefield, 2001).

66. Ibid., 129.

67. Gilles Emery, *The Trinitarian Theology of Saint Thomas Aquinas* (Oxford: Oxford University Press, 2010), 312.

68. Torrance, *The Christian Doctrine of God*, 200; Dick O. Eugenio, *Communion with the Triune God: The Trinitarian Soteriology of T. F. Torrance* (Eugene, OR: Pickwick Publications, 2014), 26, notes that although Torrance is negative toward the doctrine of appropriation in this specific citation, "his trinitarian theology in general and his trinitarian soteriology in

particular indubitably employs the doctrine as a hermeneutical principle, most especially in that he follows Barth's procedure."

69. Adam McIntosh, "The Contribution of Karl Barth's Doctrine of Appropriation to a Trinitarian Ecclesiology," *Trinitarian Theology after Barth*, ed. Myk Habets and Phillip Tolliday, 222–23 (Eugene, OR: Pickwick Publications, 2011).

70. Karl Barth, *Church Dogmatics* I/1, *The Doctrine of the Word of God*, 2nd ed, trans. G. W. Bromiley, ed. G. W. Bromiley and T. F. Torrance, 362 (Edinburgh: T&T Clark, 1956).

71. Barth, *Church Dogmatics* I/1, 362.

72. Ibid., 374.

73. Torrance, *The Christian Doctrine of God*, 200.

74. Torrance, *Incarnation*, 72–82. See discussion on the dynamic hypostatic union.

75. Ibid., 113–15.

76. Ibid., 115.

77. Torrance, *The Trinitarian Faith*, 260.

78. Thomas F. Torrance, *The Mediation of Christ* (Edinburgh: T&T Clark, 1992), 73–81.

79. Ibid.

80. Thomas F. Torrance, *The Christian Frame of Mind* (Eugene, OR: Wipf and Stock, 1989), 6–11. See also Torrance, *The Trinitarian Faith*, 184–88.

81. Torrance, *The Mediation of Christ*, 39; and Torrance, *The Christian Doctrine of God*, 250. The question of Jesus' humanity is significant for our understanding of the atonement, and while the vicarious humanity of Christ is drawn into our discussion in various places, other scholars have already done an admirable job exploring Torrance's view of Christ assuming our fallen nature. In addition to Colyer, McGrath, and Molnar's commentaries, see Daniel J. Cameron, *Flesh and Blood: A Dogmatic Sketch Concerning the Fallen Nature View of Christ's Human Nature* (Eugene, OR: Wipf & Stock, 2016), particularly chapter 2. See also Christian D. Kettler, *The Vicarious Humanity of Christ and the Reality of Salvation* (Eugene, OR: Wipf & Stock, 2011).

82. Torrance, *Incarnation*, 84–85, 228–33.

83. Ibid., 231.

84. Torrance, *The Trinitarian Faith*, 9.

85. Torrance, "What Is the Church?" 6.

86. Ibid.

87. Thomas F. Torrance, "Ecclesiology Lecture 1: The Being and Nature of the Church" (Box 29: The Being and Nature of the Church, Thomas F. Torrance Special Collection, Princeton Theological Seminary), 5.

88. Torrance, *The Trinitarian Faith*, 264.

89. Thomas F. Torrance, *Conflict and Agreement in the Church: Order and Disorder* (Eugene, OR: Wipf and Stock, 1996), 231.

90. Ibid., 248. See also Thomas F. Torrance, *Royal Priesthood* (Edinburgh: Oliver and Boyd, 1955), 29–35.

91. Torrance, *The Trinitarian Faith*, 267.

92. Ibid., 265n38, 265n9.

93. Ibid., 290–91.

94. Ibid., 265.

95. Ibid., 278.

96. Ibid., 265.

97. Torrance, "Ecclesiology Lecture 1," 5.

98. Torrance, *Atonement*, 370. For further discussion of the hypostatic union in relation to the union of Christ and the Church, see Torrance, *Theology in Reconstruction*, 184–86.

99. Torrance, "What Is the Church?" 7.

100. Ibid., 13.

101. Ibid., 14.

102. Ibid.

103. Torrance, *Conflict and Agreement in the Church: Order and Disorder*, 224.

104. Torrance, "What Is the Church?" 14–15.

105. Ibid., 15.

106. Ibid.
107. Eugenio, *Communion with the Triune God*, 83.
108. Torrance, *The Christian Doctrine of God*, 138.
109. Ibid., 59.
110. Ibid., 55.
111. Ibid., 2.
112. Ibid., 142.
113. Torrance, *Incarnation*, 109.
114. Ibid.
115. Ibid., 113.
116. Thomas F. Torrance, "A Sermon on the Trinity," *Biblical Theology* 6, no. 2 (1956): 42.
117. Thomas F. Torrance, *The School of Faith* (London: James Clarke, 1959), xcv. Torrance himself is sometimes accused of having an underdeveloped pneumatology due to the emphasis that he places on Christ for our knowledge of God, but when one integrates all the different trinitarian material that is contained throughout his corpus, this accusation is seen to be unfounded. See a discussion of this charge in Gary W. Deddo, "The Holy Spirit in T. F. Torrance's Theology," in Colyer, *The Promise of Trinitarian Theology*, 81–114. This is followed by Torrance's response (311–14).
118. Torrance, *The School of Faith*, cvi–cxviii.
119. Thomas F. Torrance, "The Christ Who Loves Us," in *A Passion for Christ: The Vision That Ignites Ministry*, ed. Gerrit Dawson and Jock Stein, 19 (Eugene, OR: Wipf and Stock, 2010).
120. Torrance, *The Trinitarian Faith*, 61–62.
121. Ibid., 64.
122. Ibid., 207.
123. Ibid., 192.
124. Ibid., 103.
125. Torrance, *The Christian Doctrine of God*, 60.
126. Torrance, *The Trinitarian Faith*, 201.
127. Ibid., 214. See Thomas F. Torrance, *God and Rationality* (Oxford: Oxford University Press, 2000), 165–92.
128. Ibid., 215.
129. Ibid., 191.
130. Ibid., 9.
131. Torrance, *Conflict and Agreement in the Church: Order and Disorder*, 16.
132. Torrance, *Atonement*, 353.
133. Torrance, *The Trinitarian Faith*, 190.
134. Ibid., 254.
135. Ibid., 278.
136. Ibid., 257.
137. Ibid., 291.
138. Ibid., 251.
139. Ibid., 229.
140. Ibid., 189.
141. Ibid.
142. Torrance, *The Mediation of Christ*, 64.
143. Torrance, *The Trinitarian Faith*, 227.
144. Torrance, *The Mediation of Christ*, xii.
145. Torrance, *The Trinitarian Faith*, 208.
146. Thomas F. Torrance, *Gospel, Church and Ministry*, ed. Jock Stein, 1:108 (Eugene, OR: Pickwick Publications, 2012).
147. Torrance, *Theology in Reconciliation*, 101.
148. Torrance, *The Mediation of Christ*, 67.
149. Torrance, *Theology in Reconciliation*, 100.
150. Torrance, *Conflict and Agreement in the Church: Order and Disorder*, 17.
151. Torrance, *The Trinitarian Faith*, 277.

152. Torrance, *Royal Priesthood*, 59.
153. Torrance, *Atonement*, 359.
154. Torrance does not agree with the observational and phenomenal perspective on the "historical Jesus," and in contrast, he refers to the incarnate Son and his life, ministry, death, and resurrection. See Torrance, *The Mediation of Christ*, 51. See also the way Torrance relates the "search for the historical Jesus" to the phenomenalist approach of modern science in Torrance, *Theology in Reconciliation*, 278–82.
155. Torrance, *The Trinitarian Faith*, 249.
156. Ibid., 194. See 194n10.
157. Ibid., 292.
158. Torrance, *The Christian Doctrine of God*, 193.
159. Ibid.
160. Ibid., 157.
161. Ibid., 158.
162. Ibid.
163. Ibid., 186; Torrance, *The School of Faith*, xcvii–xcix.
164. Torrance, *The Christian Doctrine of God*, 186.
165. Ibid.
166. Ibid.
167. Ibid., 179. Elsewhere Torrance comments on how the Athanasian doctrine of coinherence helps to undercut the *filioque* issue for "there is no suggestion, then, either that there is more than one Source of Deity or that somehow the Son is less than the Father if the Spirit does not proceed from the Father as one who is proper to the Being of the Son." See Thomas F. Torrance, *Trinitarian Perspectives: Toward Doctrinal Agreement* (Edinburgh: T&T Clark, 1994), 20.
168. Torrance, *The Christian Doctrine of God*, 188.
169. Ibid., 190.
170. Torrance, *Trinitarian Perspectives*, 5.
171. Torrance, *Reality and Scientific Theology*, 179.
172. Torrance, *Theology in Reconciliation*, 101.
173. Torrance, *The Mediation of Christ*, 13.
174. Thomas F. Torrance, *Reality and Evangelical Theology: The Realism of Christian Revelation* (Eugene, OR: Wipf and Stock, 2003), 93.
175. Ibid., 86.
176. Torrance, *Royal Priesthood*, 70.
177. Torrance, *The School of Faith*, lxvii.
178. Ibid.
179. Torrance, *Reality and Scientific Theology*, 103. For a wider exploration of Torrance's thought about social coefficients of knowledge, see Eric G. Flett, *Persons, Powers, and Pluralities: Toward a Trinitarian Theology of Culture* (Cambridge: James Clarke, 2012), 139–216.
180. Torrance, *Reality and Scientific Theology*, 102.
181. Ibid., 104–12.
182. Torrance, *The School of Faith*, xxxi.
183. Ibid., xxixiv.
184. Torrance, *Reality and Evangelical Theology*, 49.
185. Torrance, *The School of Faith*, xlvii.
186. Ibid., xlix.
187. Torrance, *Atonement*, 377.
188. Torrance, *Reality and Scientific Theology*, 119.
189. Torrance, *Atonement*, 377. For further consideration of the interaction between doctrine and community in Torrance's material, see Elmer M. Colyer, *The Nature of Doctrine in T. F. Torrance's Theology* (Eugene, OR: Wipf and Stock, 2001), 93–128.
190. Torrance, *The Trinitarian Faith*, 253.
191. Ibid., 268.

Chapter Five

Church Order in the Time Between

Building on the rich trinitarian and ecclesiological material that has been discussed, this chapter considers the visible life of the Church in the time between the two advents of Christ. The next step in our exploration of Torrance's ecclesiology is to think theologically and practically about Church order. A range of historical views are surveyed in order to situate Torrance's perspective that all Church order is to be shaped by participation in the life and love of the Triune God. Grounding a discussion of Church structures in the doctrine of the Trinity enables us to reflect with Torrance on the vital differences between the ministry of Christ and the ministry of the Church and to ask how these differences shape the mission of the Church between Christ's two advents.

THE DEVELOPMENT OF DOCTRINE AND THE FORMALIZATION OF CHURCH STRUCTURES

What Is "Order"?

Even though God's creative intentions were revealed in the original act of creation, sin meant that disorder entered the created order. However, God does not let the world disintegrate into non-being but continues to sustain it in mercy and faithfulness. Torrance defines order as everything that stands opposed to *anomia*, to sin, lawlessness, and disorder.[1] Torrance explains,

> When God made the world He made it in order and everything was set in its due proportion. But through the lawlessness of sin the world fell out of proportion, out of order, and was threatened with sheer chaos. Were it not for the persistent fact of God's purpose of love the world would destroy itself; but in His Covenant mercy God holds the world together in spite of its chaos.[2]

In the Old Testament, order is primarily understood in its negative sense as judgment upon disorder. Nevertheless, the Mosaic law points beyond itself to the new economy that is revealed with the incarnation of Jesus Christ.[3] It is the presence of Christ through the Spirit that causes creation to become rightly ordered. To use our earlier language of the two dimensions, order is bestowed upon the horizontal by its interaction with the vertical. This is not to say that the horizontal is subordinated to the vertical but rather that Torrance is "placing the horizontal plane in a relationship where it may serve the purpose for which it exists and by doing so arrive at its true *telos*."[4]

How then are we to consider the issue of order in relation to the Church? Although it is Christ who is the "controlling center of the church's life, thought, and mission in the world today,"[5] the Church requires certain temporal structures that give form to its spatiotemporal existence. There are therefore two aspects of order: "the aspect that derives from the *nomos*-form of historical succession on the stage of this world, and the aspect that derives from the new being of the Church in the risen Lord."[6] While there is a true order that has to do with the Church's ontological relation to Christ, the Church has a temporal order that Torrance describes with an metaphor of scaffolding. The Church lives and works in the disorder of the current time and thus requires scaffolding that "frames the shape" of its teleological participation in the *koinōnia* of the Triune God.[7] This scaffolding will be torn down when the building is complete and Christ returns to fully establish the new order of the new creation.[8] The temporary order has no divine validity; rather, the "purpose of this order is to make room in the midst for the presence of the risen Christ so that the Church's fellowship becomes the sphere where the resurrection of Christ is effectively operative here and now."[9] Without looking forward to the *eschaton*, "order is dead for it does not serve the resurrection, and does not manifest either the love of Christ or His coming again to reign."[10] However, in what follows our concern will primarily be with the temporal ordering of the Church in the time between and not with the eschatological order that will be realized at the end of the "eschatological pause" with the return of Christ. For further comment on this, readers are encouraged to make use of Flett's exploration of Torrance's relational and redeemed concept of order.[11]

Oikonomia speaks of the "ordering of a household," and when we consider the incarnation as God's way of coming into our world, then we see that order is something that is enacted from within not without. The physicality of the incarnation also reminds us that the Church cannot be reduced to something that is only spiritual without ignoring its "stark actuality and corporeality" for "the continuity of the Church is a *somatic* continuity, and its order within that continuity is of a *somatic* kind."[12] This is why when we speak of this temporal order, we are able to refer to the structures and formalized approaches that characterize the life of the Church without reducing the life of the Church to these structures. Because the Church is an empirical body that has a real relation to Christ in space and time and through him participates in the fellowship of the Holy Trinity, the Church must submit all it is and does to the Triune God.[13] In this way, order in the Church is the "co-ordinating of the life of the Church in its fellowship, worship, and mission in the service of the glory of God."[14]

There is much more to be said about Torrance's view of order in the Church and how it is shaped by his view of the Church as a community constituted by its participation in the fellowship of Father, Son, and Holy Spirit. It will be useful to contrast this with a brief survey of Torrance's perspective on several key moments in the historical development of Church order: the apostolic period, the Patristic-Nicene period, and the Reformation. According to Torrance, it was not until after the Nicene period that the Church began to focus on external ecclesial structures as a matter of primacy, and even though this had damaging effects in both the Eastern and Western Church, the Reformation saw the Church regain a sense of the centrality of Christ and the doctrine of God. It is worth noting that in what follows, Torrance's Presbyterian lens results in a rather biased—although not altogether unfair—view of ecclesial history.

Apostolic Foundations

"Church order" is not well defined in relation to the apostolic period. We may think of the apostles as formulating an embryonic trinitarian ecclesiology, for although doctrine was not yet formally explicated, their way of life embodied the values and teaching of the community formed around Jesus Christ. The motif of *koinōnia* that is so central to Torrance's ecclesiology leads to his comment that the apostolate is "the nucleus of the *koinōnia*, the *communio sanctorum*, the communion of the saints. It is the *koinōnia* of those who all together have *koinōnia* in the mystery of Christ."[15]

However, the first apostles did have a unique role in the formation of the Christian community. It is clear that Jesus chose to establish a community with a structure and ministry shaped after his own. While all Jesus' followers were summoned to the task of witness, these leaders were given "special responsibilities and a special commission of pastoral care over his flock, endowed with an authoritative office to act in his name."[16]

Just as the Father sent the Son and anointed him with the Holy Spirit, Jesus breathed upon the disciples and commissioned them "as apostles to act in his name, thereby linking their subordinate mission with his own supreme mission."[17] Jesus is Apostle "in the absolute sense," while the apostles are empowered and sent out as his witnesses. This is the "peculiar function of the apostles, to be the link between Christ and the Church, the hinge on which the incarnational revelation objectively given in Christ was grounded and realised within the continuing membership of the Church."[18] While the Church is related *supernaturally* to Christ in the Spirit, it has its *historical* relation to Christ through the apostolic witness.[19]

By examining the role of the apostles, we see that the Church is "constituted by Christ to be the receptacle of the Gospel proclaimed and handed on by the apostles";[20] there is an "essential and fundamental translation"[21] between Jesus' self-witness and the witness of the Church. Torrance outlines the disciples' growth from being ordinary fishermen and tax collectors to those appointed to be the "hinge" between God's revelation in Christ and the human transmission of that revelation. First, Christ appoints twelve disciples from among his wider group of followers and teaches them what it means to live according to the values of the kingdom of God. Eventually there comes a crisis point when the disciples must either deny themselves and follow Christ fully or cease following altogether. Their decision to follow Jesus means that he begins to explain his divine identity to them, although they do not fully comprehend what he says. These twelve apostles, chosen to represent the twelve tribes of Israel, lived and traveled with Jesus, were given to share in the messianic secret, and were sent out even before his crucifixion to participate in Jesus' ministry. However, there came a time when even the disciples abandoned Jesus. They could not journey with Christ to the Cross for he alone could stand forth as the representative and substitute for all humanity. Nevertheless, even in the disciples' denial of Christ, God is at work for after Christ's resurrection, the disciples remember what Jesus had said to them at the Last Supper and realize that despite their abandonment of Jesus in the hour of his greatest suffering, they have been atoned for through Christ's sacrifice.[22] Through his death and resurrection, sin has been destroyed and humanity redeemed from the power of death.[23] Just as it was only in the light of the resurrection that the apostles understood who Jesus truly was, their written accounts only fully disclose the messianic identity of Christ in the light of his death and resurrection.[24]

Thus, although Jesus had many followers, it was the twelve apostles who formed the nucleus of the Church "within which his own self-witness was integrated with inspired witness to him and translated into the appropriate form (i.e., the New Testament scriptures) for its communication in history."[25] The apostles are thus commissioned as the "recipients of revelation and as ambassadors of reconciliation"[26] and as "plenipotentiaries of Christ, specially trained in order to be authoritative transmitters of his own *kerygma*, so that whoever hears them, hears Christ himself."[27]

The twelve apostles who were at the Last Supper and entered into the new covenant with Christ uniquely represent the transition between the twelve tribes of Israel and the new kingdom of God. "The longed-for age of salvation had come when the tribes would no longer be scattered but be gathered into one."[28] The theme of "the one and the many" is again prevalent for the twelve disciples were twelve living stones who had been called to follow Christ. They were anticipatorily united to him, so the Last Supper may be thought of as an incipient gathering of the Church,[29] anticipating a new way of salvation that would be objectively realized through Jesus' crucifixion and resurrection and subjectively actualized when the Spirit was poured out at Pentecost upon those gathered to pray in the Upper Room.

Torrance is insistent that a key facet of the apostolic role is that they were *eyewitnesses* of the incarnate life of Jesus so their testimony is controlled by "the actual history of Jesus, who he actually was and what he actually did."[30] It is on this basis that they were given unique authority to be Christ's representatives; just as the Son was sent by the Father, the apostles were sent by Christ to the world.[31] Through their personal experience of walking with Jesus and hearing the words of God from the incarnate Word of God, the apostles are equipped by the Spirit to translate Christ's words into their own words about Christ. Their ministry had no validity on its own; rather Christ was present through the Spirit, authenticating himself in their ongoing ministry.[32] This is how the apostles serve as the hinge between Jesus' self-witness and the witness given to the Church in Scripture and tradition. In describing their role as a "hinge," Torrance is observing that the apostolic witness is where the vertical reference and the horizontal reference meet. The apostolic witness has a vertical reference, which is the apostles' direct personal relation to Christ, and a horizontal reference, the communication through which they convey the truth of Christ to others. The apostles are the first to fulfill the Church's *kerygmatic* function, for the self-revelation of Jesus Christ is articulated through the apostles and passed on to us in the medium of the New Testament.[33] The apostles have a unique and unrepeatable role in the transmission of revelation,[34] for through them, the Holy Scriptures came to constitute "the divinely provided and inspired linguistic medium which remains of authoritative and critical significance for the whole history of the Church of Jesus Christ."[35]

Finally, here we should also observe that although the apostles had a unique role in the translation and transmission of revelation, Torrance notes that they also acted as presbyters who ministered the Word and sacraments as well as having pastoral oversight. These elements of their role were passed on, but "when separated from the apostles' unique ministry, they inevitably assumed another and subordinate character."[36] The tasks that were passed on came to include the roles of presbyters, bishops, prophets, teachers, shepherds, and leaders, and while none of these roles retain apostolic authority in the sense of the Twelve, they take place "within the sphere of the apostolic commission, and under apostolic authorization."[37]

The Early Patristic Period

We continue our brief survey of order by turning to the patristic period after the first generation of believers but before the formulation of the Nicene Creed. The early development of Christianity was marked by the strong commitment of the Church Fathers to speak as faithfully as possible of God's self-revelation and relatively little concern with developing a formal ecclesiastical structure. Torrance thinks it noteworthy that there are very few writings on the nature and function of the Church from the early centuries. This is significant because it shows a situation where Christ and the Spirit occupied the unqualified center of Christian faith and life empirically as well as spiritually.[38] During this period, the development of the doctrine of God was paramount in terms of theological focus.

Although there was no formal set of doctrinal propositions taught by the early Church, there was a body of material, the "deposit of faith," that was recognized and taught as authoritative before the creeds were formulated. This was not a systematic theology but rather the amassed knowledge of those who had walked with Christ, heard his teaching, and passed it on to the next generations of believers. It was not regarded as something different from the self-revelation of God in the incarnation but as the continuing way in which God gave a concrete, unchanging form to His self-revelation that became the historical foundation for the Church. This was the process of

> the living and dynamic *Word* which was at work in the foundation and growth of the Church (Acts 6.7, 12.24, 19.20; cf. Col. 1:5–6) communicating himself through the Spirit in the witness and preaching of the Apostles, letting his self-revelation take definitive shape in the Apostolic mind and embody itself in the Apostolic mission, in such a constituting way that the identity and continuity of the Church and its teaching in history became inseparably bound up with it (cf. Rom. 6.17).[39]

The New Testament witness, alongside the wider apostolic tradition, was the content of this deposit of faith, "the unrepeatable foundation on which the Church was built, and to which the Church was committed ever afterwards to refer as its authoritative norm for the understanding and interpretation of the Gospel."[40] This apostolic tradition allowed the Church to interpret Scripture "in accordance with their objective intention in God's self-revelation and thereby to discern how each expression of the Gospel taken from the Scriptures fits into the coherent pattern of its essential message."[41] Irenaeus in particular thought of the apostolic tradition as a "continuously rejuvenating force";[42] describing it as a "coherent body of informal truth"[43] that had an "intrinsic order or structure reflecting the economic design of God's redemptive action in Jesus Christ and the essential pattern of the self-revelation of

God the Father through the Son and in the Holy Spirit."[44] As the source that shaped the life of the Church, it was trinitarian in nature.

On one level the content of the deposit of faith was simply the Gospel. On another level it had to do with the reception of that Gospel through the apostolic tradition. It was the embryonic understanding of what came to be formalized in creedal statements. We have noted that the pre-Nicene tradition was "characterised by a deep intertwining of faith and godliness, understanding and worship" that gave rise to the evangelical convictions held by the Church in response to the revelation of God through the Son and in the Spirit.[45] Consequently the deposit of faith was inseparable from the living substance of the Gospel and was given to the Church for the purpose of "informing, structuring and quickening its life and faith and mission as the Body of Christ in the world."[46] The Fathers believed that only within the living tradition of the Church could the saving event of Christ be appropriated and mediated through the Spirit to the world.[47] Torrance continues this theme by teaching that theological truth is "not given in an abstract or detached form but in a concrete embodied form in the Church."[48] This is because "it is to the Church that God has entrusted the deposit of faith, to the Church that he has given his Holy Spirit, and in the Church that he has provided us with the ministry of the Gospel and all the other means through which the Spirit works."[49]

The deposit of faith developed in connection with the full life and experience of the Church. As a body of teaching it was not separated from the ongoing *koinōnia* of the Church so Church order in the patristic period primarily had to do with proper belief in Jesus Christ. Torrance summarizes,

> While the deposit of faith was replete with the truth as it is in Jesus, embodying kerygmatic, didactic and theological content, by its very nature it could not be resolved into a system of truths or a set of normative doctrines and formulated beliefs, for the truths and doctrines and beliefs entailed could not be abstracted from the embodied form which they were given in Christ and the apostolic foundation of the Church without loss of their real substance.[50]

The Nicene Creed

The apostolic tradition served as the impetus for the emergence of the earliest creedal formulations, but it was the need to universally define orthodox belief in response to various heresies like Arianism that gave rise to the Nicene Creed. We have already pointed out Torrance's view that the Nicene Creed was not a set of systematic propositions imposed upon the Gospel but rather arose "in compulsive response to the objective self-revelation of God."[51] Torrance makes a determined effort to justify his view that the Nicene Creed was not an intellectual construct or a human initiative to give some clarification to doctrine. Instead, he insists that the explicit formalization of the "whole body of belief implicit in the apostolic tradition" arose under the compulsion of divine revelation.[52] This is why time and time again Torrance insists that the creed expresses what the Fathers felt they *had* to say about God. Consequently, the Nicene Creed represents a distillation of Christian beliefs and a form of order that is trinitarian in nature.

Torrance joins a number of the later patristic writers in considering the formulation of the Nicene Creed as second in significance only to the apostolic tradition of the Church.[53] The important thing that we need to incorporate here is his analysis that the real content of the Nicene Creed was not found in "analytical theological statements, but in a doxological declaration of embodied truth and embodied doctrine."[54] Because the creed developed under the constraint of divine revelation, Torrance notes that the "integration of the basic convictions on which the Church had always relied in its worship and mission into a coherent pattern gave sharpness and precision to the Church's interpretation of the NT Gospel."[55] Nothing new was added; instead, the basic convictions of the Church about the Gospel, and the God who is at work in and through the Church, were clarified. The Nicene Fathers saw their theology as faithful to their reception of God's self-revelation since long before the creeds were formalized, the early Church was aware of God's triune nature. Thus, Torrance suggests that the "doctrinal formalisation of the faith was recognised as relying on what the Catholic Church had always believed and intuitively known to be true."[56] Since the early Church tradition, before being given formal conceptualization at Nicaea, was trinitarian in nature, Torrance states that "Trinitarian worship and Trinitarian faith thus provided the implicit controlling ground both for a faithful restructuring of the life of the Church and for a godly renewing of its understanding in the Mind of Christ."[57]

The period between the Councils of Nicea and Constantinople is described by Torrance as "theologically turbulent."[58] The Fathers sought to further clarify the Gospel and to "provide the Church with a structural framework within which its members could meditate upon the Holy Scriptures; worship the Holy Trinity; proclaim the Gospel of forgiveness, reconciliation, and sanctification; and so fulfil its mission in obedience to the command of Christ."[59] At every point, those assembled for these councils sought to demonstrate fidelity to Scripture and the apostolic tradition. The Fathers wrestled "with the Holy Scriptures to express what they were *compelled* to think and hold within the context of the apostolic tradition under the impact of God's self-revelation through the Word and Spirit of Christ, and on that basis alone, to confess their faith in the Father, the Son and the Holy Spirit."[60]

The Nicene Creed formalizes the doctrine of the Trinity as the foundation of the Church—Torrance argues that it acts as a regulatory tool by which the being, life, and mission of the Church can be evaluated for faithfulness to their divine foundation. While there was always the risk that the truth presented in the Nicene Creed could be detached from its embodied form in the Church and turned into an independent conceptual system[61]—as happened with Tertullian, who viewed the deposit of faith as a "fixed formula of truth for belief"[62]—this did not take place. Furthermore, while it is clear that Torrance holds the patristic authors in high regard and views the Nicene Creed as normative for Christian belief, he is careful to subjugate the creed to divine revelation. The Nicene Creed as a theological statement was never considered equal to the apostolic *kerygma*,[63] but these early councils were important as the first ecumenical gatherings of Church leaders with an explicit focus on clarifying doctrine. They gathered in a context where faith, godliness, and worship informed doctrine and praxis, and their concern was to develop right theology, focusing on who God was rather than the specifics of church order in and of itself.

Medieval Theology

Although the Church remained largely focused on the doctrine of the Trinity, it must also be noted that Torrance believes that the positive trinitarian advances of the Nicene-Constantinopolitan period were complicated by the lingering effects of dualism that "remained latent in the social and legal structures of organised life in East and West" and increasingly affected the life of the Church.[64] As the differences between East and West solidified, Eastern theology became more mystical, "theocentric and contemplative in nature," while Western theology "became more anthropocentric and pragmatic, and indeed more juridical."[65] The doctrine of the Trinity and disagreement over the *filioque* is considered by Torrance the "crucial issue, which aggravated every other."[66]

Both Roman Catholic and Orthodox allowed the introduction of secular categories, whether juridical, sociological, or political, "into the constitution and life of the Church in such a way as to overlay the essential and intrinsic nature of the Church with non-evangelical and non-theological elements."[67] Torrance traces this back to the initial rift of the Church from Judaism, and thus its disconnection from the wider story of God's redemptive actions, so that Christians "adapted themselves more readily, and too easily, to the socio-legal framework of empire centred in Rome or Byzantium."[68] Rather than changing the structures of civil and legal life as it had done with Hellenistic philosophy in the Nicene period, the Church wrongly assimilated them into its own life.[69] Because the Church was thought to embody divine truth in its physical and institutional structures, the Church itself came to represent theological authority, "for the expression of the mind of the Church in its dogmatic definitions was held to be the expression of the nature of the Truth."[70] Torrance also suggests that the medieval tension between temporal and spiritual power resulted in a "system of hierarchical structures and constitutional authorities."[71] Consequently the Church began to emphasize its double nature as both "mystical body" and "juridical institution," enshrining this view in canon law[72] rather than viewing itself as a community constituted by its participation in the *koinōnia* of the Holy Trinity.

In this context where the institutionality of the Church was overemphasized, "the traditional Faith tended to be codified in the rational structures of the Church and Grace tended to be institutionalized in canonical forms for its easy ministration to the multitudes."[73] The Roman Catholic Church particularly saw itself as "an organised and juridically structured society endowed with ecumenical authority and supreme jurisdiction," losing the universal sense of the *koinōnia* of the Church.[74] Theological treatises focused on ecclesiastical and papal power, and scholarly emphasis fell on canon law rather than theology proper so that theological consideration of the relation between the doctrine of God and the doctrine of the Church was lacking. In light of this, Torrance finds it unsurprising that the Roman Catholic Church gave rise to Christendom by insisting on its own primacy at the expense of its relationship with the Orthodox Church and, later on, with the Reformation Churches.[75] In contrast, Torrance commends the Greek Orthodox Church for retaining a sense of *koinōnia* in its historical existence and being able to do so because it finds "its life and light beyond itself in Christ and in the Holy Trinity."[76]

Torrance observes that even though the beginnings of the modern scientific approach to theology can be traced as far back as Anselm, medieval theology generally did not follow his emphasis on the conformity of reason and Truth,[77] operating instead with the basic assumption of a "sacramental universe" within which the particular form of the Church "as sacramental institution . . . was related as redemptive microcosm to the microcosm of the whole universe."[78] The outcome of this was that by the end of the Middle Ages, Latin theology frequently denied that what God is toward us as the incarnate Word, as communicated to us by Scripture, is who God is in God's own being[79]—a split that Torrance identifies as incredibly damaging. Roman theology became dialectical rather than dialogical, and theology was "subordinated to a philosophical ontology."[80] This dualistic theology is what allowed a dualistic view of the universe and for the Church to be seen as a sacramental institution that bridged the gaps within that universe instead of giving Christ his rightful preeminence as the one mediator between God and humanity. Medieval theologians believed that the pattern of the kingdom of God could be read from the historical consciousness of the Church just as the eternal pattern of nature could be read from the physical world through the natural sciences. This static medieval view of history was radically revolutionized with the Reformation affirmation that the living God of the Bible is actively at work in history.[81]

Reformation Theology

It is apparent that Torrance views the doctrine of the Church as being revolutionized in the same way as the doctrine of God in the Reformation. Although the Roman Catholic Church had begun to attempt internal reform, it was so enclosed by "the ramparts of papal authority and canon law" that this was nearly impossible.[82] The temporal order of the Church was believed to be inseparable from divine order, so the Church was obviously the harbinger of the kingdom. The Reformation was a reaction against the immovable structures of Roman Catholicism, involving a genuine search for the Church's renewal as the body of Christ.[83] It moved away from defining ecclesiology according to secular power structures and moved toward an "understanding of the Church through primary reference to Christ as its authoritative King and Head even in its visible constitutional life, and therefore through reference to the Church as the community of believers following Christ and looking to him for salvation."[84] This was not a shift from one static position to another but rather the call for the Church to be ever-reforming, *ecclesia semper reformanda.*[85]

Despite the immovable structures of Roman Catholicism, Reformation theology embraced the understanding of "the Church as the Body of Christ, the earthly-historical form of his real presence indwelling the community of the faithful."[86] The centrality of the incarnation also lent itself to this, highlighting that since the Word of God became incarnate and shattered our frame of historical continuity, the Church cannot embrace a view of history as the "irreversible unfolding of certain eternal forms . . . through the institution of the Church on earth."[87]

The nature of this shift in the view of the Church may be illustrated through a brief discussion of the idea of the "means of grace." This is not an insignificant issue for as Torrance notes, the historical debate over the means of grace is one of the issues where Church "conflict is most acute and agreement is most difficult."[88] In the medieval period, grace was not understood as the self-communication and self-giving of God to humanity but rather as "the communication of healing power which indirectly makes us participate in God,"[89] a substance or gift controlled by the Church and administered to the congregants by the priesthood. Grace was therefore an "intermediary reality between God and man which holds God himself apart from us."[90]

The Reformers reacted against this notion of grace as a substance subject to the institutional Church's hierarchy and structure. In place of "the systematic conception of a sacramental universe with its doctrine of an inherent relation between the structure of Being and the immanent forms of the rational understanding drawn from philosophy, Reformed theology substituted the doctrine of the Covenant of Grace drawn from the Biblical Revelation."[91] Embracing this relational and covenantal theology, with the systemic principle of the fulfillment of one covenant of grace in Jesus Christ—a covenant always subordinate to Christology so that it can't become an overarching principle—the Reformers' theology stood in stark contrast to the Roman concept of a sacramental universe.[92]

In covenantal theology and its rejection of dualisms, the correspondence between God and creation "is construed in historical and dynamic terms" for the Triune God really interacts and intervenes in human history.[93] Consequently, because "the gift and the Giver are one,"[94] grace is not a quality detachable from God but rather "properly understood grace is Christ so that to be saved by grace alone is to be saved by Christ alone."[95] Torrance claims that "Christ Himself is the objective ground and content of *charis* in every instance of its special Christian use."[96] This insistence on the nature of grace as God himself rather than a mediated substance was part of a wider theological move that stressed the self-revelation of God.[97] In this way, grace is not just about receiving salvation but about being enabled to participate in the very fellowship of the Triune God. This relates to earlier comments about the Church as a community of reciprocity, for the covenant of grace is relationship-establishing by nature and thus marks out the way that dialogue between God and humanity can take place.[98]

Reformed theologians understood that grace is not the Creator-creation relation "construed in terms of efficient causality" but the very self-giving of God that takes place through the incarnation for "it is such a self-communicating of God to man that man is given access to, and knowledge of God in his own inner life and being as Father, Son and Holy Spirit."[99] The Reformation returned to the Christological emphasis of the early councils, but rather than faltering where the early councils had—in not carrying through "the results of its work in Christology into the whole round of the Church's thought and life"—the Reformers applied this Christological correction especially to soteriology, the Church, and mission, which resulted in rethinking salvation, sanctification, and the sacraments.[100] Reformation theology consequently demonstrates a shift back toward understanding the true nature of the Church as related to the Trinity rather than as a merely historical institution for "the doctrine of the Church as the community of believers livingly united to [Christ] as His Body through the Spirit received its first great formulation since patristic times."[101] This was the replacement of Roman canon law by "the ancient patristic and conciliar concept of ministry and authority through communion or *koinonia* which took an essentially corporate form,"[102] signaling a much more trinitarian understanding of Church order.

The other thing that the Reformation contributed to an understanding of ecclesiology was the doctrine of justification. Torrance prefers to emphasize justification by Christ alone rather than justification by faith. This places the emphasis solely on the work of Christ instead of involving any of our acts—or of faith as something that we must feel or create within ourselves.[103]

Justification through Christ alone involves a further distinction between objective justification and subjective justification. Objective justification is what has taken place in Christ through his assumption and sanctification of our humanity, through his active and passive obedience. Subjective justification is the translation of God's mighty act into human life, which takes place through humankind's union with Christ.[104] In soteriological terms, justification does away not only with our sins but also with our natural goodness and our natural knowledge. We cannot justify ourselves on the basis of our assumed goodness. In ecclesiological terms, justification does away with all tradition by forcing it to conform to Christ and thus forces all systems and orders to be examined by the same criterion since Jesus Christ alone has primacy.[105]

Torrance views Reformation theology as a reaction against the elevation of human traditions over the freedom of the Word and Spirit, particularly emphasizing God's redemptive intervention in history. Seeking to be faithful to Scripture and the creeds of the ancient Church, the Reformation involved a Christological correction of the doctrine of the Church, rejecting the medieval view of the Church as a dualist mystical body and hierarchical institution and instead affirming the Church as the body of Christ on earth, formed by God's Word and Spirit.[106] Torrance notes that while the Lutheran Church considers order to be *adiaphora*—and therefore not doctrinally determined—and the Anglican Church views order as part of the historic tradition of the Church but not necessarily a matter of the faith, for the Reformed Church, Church order is a matter *de fide*.[107]

This is an appropriate point at which to mention Torrance's work *Kingdom and Church* comparing the eschatology of three Reformed theologians, that of Martin Luther, which Torrance deems an "eschatology of faith"; that of Martin Bucer,[108] which he deems an "eschatology of love"; and the eschatology of John Calvin, which he deems an "eschatology of hope." Torrance interacts with the doctrine of the Church as it is developed by each of these theologians, although there is a much closer correlation between his own ecclesiology and Bucer's and Calvin's work than that of Luther. Bucer's ecclesiology emphasized "the life of the Church in terms of a communion of love having its source in the activity of the divine love both in creation and in redemption," which is formed as humans are reconciled to God through Christ, made able to participate again in the divine love,[109] and thus are empowered to live out the communion of love among humanity.[110] Bucer stresses love more than Calvin, which we have seen is a key element of Torrance's focus on *koinōnia*, but Calvin's eschatology and ecclesiology are both more Christocentric than Bucer's.[111]

There are numerous points where Torrance's evaluation of Calvin's work reveals the strong connection between Torrance's and Calvin's ecclesiology. Calvin's central motif of union with Christ and our sharing in his new humanity is applied to the Church as the body of Christ, growing up in him throughout time.[112] Through faith we "participate in the motion of Christ's resurrection and ascension"[113] and look forward in hope to the advent of Christ. Torrance notes that election and eschatology, "pre-destination and post-destination," are twin doctrines for Calvin.[114] It is between these two that "the whole life of the Church on earth is to be understood."[115] The ascension is key. for Christ is already enthroned even though "He has not yet erected before the eyes of men that throne from which His divine majesty will be far more fully displayed than it now is at the last day."[116] In Christ all is already renewed, but this must be transferred to the Church that is his body by virtue of its union with Him.[117] Calvin views the Church as a structure already completed but reaching forward to the advent of Christ,[118] so we must think of the old age and new age as overlapping.[119] The parallels with Torrance's ecclesiology are unmistakable.

There are other similar points between Torrance and Calvin that we may briefly note here. Calvin views the Old Testament "Church" as the prelude to the New Testament Church, paralleling Torrance's three-stage ecclesiology,[120] and the Church experiences tension because of its existence in the overlap of the ages.[121] The sacraments are seen by Calvin as for the time between and as the way that Christ gives Himself to us within the limitations of space and time—involving both nearness (union with Christ) and separation (eschatological distance).[122] In addition, Calvin describes order as "essentially ambiguous"[123] for its structures now will pass away at the return of Christ so that in the here and now, it acts as "scaffolding"[124]—language that Torrance directly uses, as we saw earlier in this chapter. And finally, Calvin emphasizes that the Church should be engaged in ecumenical activity.[125]

ORDER IN THE TIME BETWEEN

At the start of this chapter, we introduced the metaphor of scaffolding, suggesting that the forms the Church uses in the course of its obedience to Christ are given for the time between the two advents of Christ and will be removed when the building is completed at Christ's second advent. Over against the disorder and chaos caused by sin, the Church is the place where men and women are genuinely able to meet with God and so it is vital that the order, or the visible life of the Church, reflects the true nature of the Church as we have explored in our discussion of *koinōnia.* Although the Church exists in space and time and has historical and finite expression, its real grounding is found in its ontological relation to Christ and the Holy Trinity. Torrance observes,

> As united to Christ in his incarnate reality the Church constitutes the sanctified community within which we may draw near to the Father, through the Son and

> in the Spirit and share in the eternal life, light and love of God himself. That was surely the primary truth embedded in the mind and worship of the Catholic Church in the fourth century, and was rightly given precedence over all questions of external form, organisation and structure. If it was, as they believed, the empirical Church that had been incorporated into Christ as his Body, then the real structure of the Church was lodged in Christ himself, and had to be lived out in space and time through union and communion with the risen, exalted and advent Lord whose kingdom will have no end.[126]

Structural and juridical forms should not stifle the Church's mission for although the Church is sent into history, it is "sent not to be fettered by the limitations and patterns of history"[127] but rather "to use the patterns and forms of the law of this age in the service of its new life in the risen and ascended Lord."[128] In thinking about its patterns and forms, the Church needs to ensure that these temporary structures are subject to its true nature, the creaturely *koinōnia* that is constituted by participation in the triune *koinōnia*. Torrance describes Church order as a "luminous sign" within the world that, when subordinated to Christ's real presence, manifests the true being of the Church as the body of Christ as far as this can be within history.[129] Church order is a matter of faith. Even though it uses these temporal forms, the Church must never become institutionalized in a way that prevents it from serving the Gospel.[130]

Since order is to support rather than stifle the Church in its mission, Torrance argues that the Church is to be ordered according to the love of God that we share in through our participation in the divine *koinōnia*. The Church's order and ministry are dynamic, not static, since its "faith is always proleptic, looking forward to a fullness which has not yet been manifest."[131] Living within the limitations of this age, the Church "must make use of *schēmata* without being schematised to them,"[132] instead having "an ordering correlative to the law of love in the Holy Spirit."[133]

We have seen that the love of God is constitutive for the Church. There is no other reason for God acting in creation and redemption besides God's own sovereign decision made in God's freedom. It is this divine love that lies behind any visible ordering or structure in the Church for

> behind and beyond the rites and the gifts there breaks in God's love which is to be lived out in the power of the One Spirit. All of the historical patterns of the Church's life will pass away but love will not pass away. That love is already given to the Church in its communion with Christ and as such its manifestation in the ordering of the Church on earth is an expression of the coming Kingdom.[134]

Recalling our discussion in chapter 4 of the Church as the body of Christ, since Christ is the head and the Church is merely the body, the Church's role is to point to God rather than to engage in self-promotion or become absorbed in its own existence.[135] The Lord has established the Church as the place on earth where humans may meet with the love of God and so it is vital that its visible life reflects its true being as a community composed of those who have been drawn into the union and communion of the Trinity through the work of the Spirit and Son.

Returning to the sense of disorder as *anomia*, the chaos caused by separation from and rebellion against God, Torrance emphasizes that it is exclusively through union with Christ that the Church is redeemed from disorder, not "by external obedience and conformity but by inner and outer sharing in his life."[136] The idea of participation is key for Torrance, which can be seen in his comment that "the order of the Church's ministry is the ordering of its life and work through participation in the obedience of Christ"[137] regardless of whether "that order be an ordering of its daily life, daily worship, daily fellowship, or daily mission."[138]

Structure and order should be understood in terms of participation and *koinōnia* in order to prevent Church order from becoming about external requirements and structures. There is a definite order given to the Church, a "mutual ordering of the Church in love," that takes place through the Spirit who makes us able to participate in the *koinōnia* of divine love that is the triune being of God and therefore able to live out the love of God. This divine ordering is one where "the Church serves Christ, is obedient to the Spirit, and engages in the mutual edification of love."[139] Torrance concludes that this love is "the very *esse* of the Church given to it through union with Christ" that "manifests itself in the Church in the form of self-denial, suffering and service"[140] for in the Church, "everything must be subordinate to love, in which each serves the other and is subject to the other."[141] Torrance comments further,

> It is the Spirit who is the law of the Church's ordered life; not the Spirit as a new law of nature, not the Spirit as the soul of the Church, not the Spirit as a new immanent norm in the development of the Church through history, but the Spirit who gives the Church to share in the obedience of Christ the head of the body and who is other than the Church, its Lord and King, but who in economic condescension has come to be obedient to the Father from within the Church, that the Church may share in an obedience not its own, and in an order that is new to it, indeed against its own nature; an order from beyond the Church's own being but in which it is given to participate by the Spirit.[142]

THE MINISTRY OF THE CHURCH AND THE MINISTRY OF CHRIST

Torrance argues that the validity of the Church's ministry is entirely dependent on Christ's presence in the Church's proclamation of the Gospel for

> the church is the bodily and historical form of Christ's existence on earth through which he lets his word be heard, so that as the church bears witness to him and proclaims the gospel of salvation in his name, he himself through the Spirit is immediately present validating that word as his own and communicating himself to people through it.[143]

The Church's ministry in the time between is a genuine participation in Christ's ongoing ministry as seen through Torrance's approach to the concept of *kerygma*, or proclamation. The New Testament *kerygma* has the incarnation of Jesus Christ at its very heart.[144] because the incarnation involved Jesus "declaring that what he proclaimed was *actually being fulfilled as current reality in and through his proclamation of it*."[145] This is only understood when one reads the historical and theological elements of the Gospel accounts in tandem. Jesus is described to us in the Gospels not as a mere historical character but rather "the whole account of Jesus Christ is illuminated, shaped and permeated with the glory and revelation that break out clearly in the resurrection."[146]

We see the pattern of *kerygma* most clearly in Jesus' own disclosure of his identity, which took place in a veiled fashion through his miracles and teaching before being explicitly revealed to the disciples by the Spirit.[147] Jesus taught about the nature of the kingdom of God and did miracles that demonstrated the power of the kingdom of God, and his incarnation heralded the arrival of the kingdom of God. His preaching and his miracles point to his divine identity. The parables confront humans with the Word of God and are then worked out on the Cross in such a way that they are "inserted as a reality into our history and life."[148] Because the eternal Word is not merely speech but also power and act, it must be communicated "in saving acts, in miraculous signs."[149] The parables and miracles of Jesus' historical ministry point to the crucifixion and resurrection where Word and Act are combined in the most intimate way.[150] This helps us grasp the way that although all that Jesus taught and did during his life pointed to his divine identity, it was only in the light of the resurrection that his acts were revealed to also be acts of God at work among humankind.[151]

The pattern of the Church's *kerygma* is found in the apostolic witness. The apostles journeyed with Jesus Christ, heard his words, saw his deeds, and were given understanding about the true meaning of the parables. They were called by Jesus to be "specially authorised and competent witnesses and proclaimers of the kingdom."[152] Torrance argues that their ministry after Jesus' ascension was an extension of Jesus' own *kerygma*. What is important here is not the actual act of evangelism but rather the way in which Jesus himself is present through the Spirit in the apostles' proclamation of the Gospel. This is why the witness of the apostles is so vital. As the hinge between Christ's own revelation and the embodying of that revelation in the written Scriptures, their teaching continued to repose on Christ's own *kerygmatic* presence. The apostles' proclamation is understood to be Christ's own self-proclamation,[153] which is the basis of all *kerygma* for the Church through the ages.

Torrance defines *kerygma* for the Church as "objective, sacramental preaching with an eschatological result such that the original event (Christ crucified) becomes event all over again in the hearer."[154] Just as the Word was "made flesh" in the incarnation, through *kerygmatic* proclamation the same Word is "made flesh" in the ongoing life of the Church. Torrance further describes *kerygma* as "in the fullest sense the sacramental action of the Church,"[155] for the living Word fills the witness of the Church so that it is able to refer to the Triune God in a way that transcends its own creaturely limitations. The sacramental action of the Church is to reveal the mystery of the kingdom,[156] but the mystery of the kingdom is the person of Christ. Christ himself is present when the Word is declared as both "its material content and its active agent, for in and through the Church's witness to him he proclaims himself and is present and active for our salvation."[157] This is why the New Testament clearly links *kerygma* and *baptisma*: "for they [share] the same semantic reference to the saving reality of Christ and his Gospel."[158]

Although Torrance's language around *kerygma* is predominantly Christocentric, this is simply related to the way in which the incarnation is central to the ontological bond formed between Christ and the Church. The proclamation of the Gospel by the Church is intrinsically trinitarian for while Christ is its content, the proclamation takes place through the Holy Spirit in a way that has a tangible effect within space and time, and it is actualized among humanity. *Kerygma* is thus

> the proclamation of the Christ-event, but such proclamation that by the Holy Spirit it becomes the actualization of that event among men. It is such proclamation that in and through it the living Christ continues to do and to teach what He had already begun before and after the crucifixion. *Kerygma* is the Word of the Kingdom that cannot be conveyed in mere speech, but is used by God to intervene Himself in the human situation as He who once and for all has wrought out His final act in the death and resurrection of Jesus Christ, so that through *kerygma* the Church is continually being called out of history to become the very Body of Christ, and by the communion of His Holy Spirit is given to taste the powers of the age to come and to stand already on the side of the resurrection.[159]

We may conclude with Torrance that the difference between the ministry of Christ and the Church is that the Church is "a ministry of redeemed sinners, whereas his ministry is that of the redeemer."[160] The Church does not save for Jesus has already accomplished that once and for all in his own person. The Church can only point to the One who saves.[161] Torrance explains,

> The Church participates in Christ's ministry by *serving* Him who is Prophet, Priest, and King. The ministry of the Church is related to the ministry of Christ in such a way that in and through the ministry of the Church it is always Christ Himself who is at work, nourishing, sustaining, ordering, and governing His Church on earth . . . Throughout the whole prophetic, priestly, and kingly ministry of the Church, it is Christ Himself who presides as Prophet, Priest and King, but He summons the Church to engage in *His* ministry by witness (*marturia*), by stewardship (*oikonomia*), and by service (*diakonia*).[162]

This is why it is so important, as Deddo notes, that our union with Christ is not merely moral, psychological, volitional, or telic but is a real union through which we are invited into real participation in Christ's ministry.[163] While Christ is absent in body yet present through the Spirit, the Church is called to proclaim the Word. It takes on the role of a servant and points away from itself to Christ, embracing the call to suffering that results from the proclamation of the Word of God,[164] for in the kingdom of God, "humility and service displace competition and achievement."[165]

THE CHURCH "IN VIA"

A Witness to the Divine Communion

We need to think further about how the concept of the "time between" shapes Torrance's understanding of the order and ministry of the Church. It is certainly not that Christ has left the Church to fend for itself for the doctrine of the Holy Trinity tells us that the incarnate, ascended Christ is "historically absent and actually present."[166] His physical body is absent, yet he is present through the Spirit.[167] This creates an "eschatological pause" between Christ's two advents that determines the way in which the Church is to engage in its mission.

The relationship between the Church and time is highly important because the Church is bound up in space and time. On one hand, the Church exists in "horizontal time," time that is marked by the consequences of sin. However, Jesus lived within our time and has redeemed the Church from "its guilt and irreversibility, its decay and corruption," through his new humanity,[168] and so on the other hand, the Church is oriented to "vertical time" in which it shares in the new humanity of Christ through the Spirit. The Church is both temporal and eternal, limited by the historical existence of this world and bound by fallen time, and yet through the Spirit it participates in redeemed time that has been sanctified through its union with Christ. Given that these two times overlap, Torrance's eschatology does not anticipate an act of God that brings an end to the current age but rather involves an ongoing sense of how the eternal acts within the temporal. The two times overlap for all of God's acts are both teleological and eschatological. They are enacted within time and they gather up time in order to serve the final outworking of the divine purpose.[169] While it is ultimately oriented to redeemed time, the Church continues its mission within fallen time so that Torrance describes this time as a period when the Church must walk by faith and not by sight. We are separated from seeing God clearly by both our senses and by time.

> In the here and now relation to Christ, what stands between us is the *veil of sense*, so that although we communicate with him immediately through the Spirit, he is mediated to us in our sense experience only through the sacramental elements. In the relation between the present and future, what stands in between us is the *veil of time*, so that although we communicate with him immediately through the Spirit, he is mediated to us only through temporal and spatial acts of sacramental communion with us in the Church until he comes.[170]

Since the Church has immediate communion in the Spirit with the risen and ascended Christ, in this "eschatological pause" there will always be a sense of imminence and urgency as if the final advent is about to break in.[171] However, this veiling is a vital component of understanding the Church's order and ministry since it is this veiling that creates the "time between revelation and decision, time between decision and act, time between present and future, time for the gospel."[172] The eschatological pause has been given to the Church primarily for Gospel proclamation as a time that God has allowed in God's grace so that the world has time to repent.[173] The Church is a witness, anticipating the second advent of Christ, in keeping with the nature of the "new time" of the resurrected Christ to which it is oriented[174] even in this period of history "where it has time to work, and time to obey him . . . time to exist and carry out its mission."[175]

Just as God is always gathering people into communion with himself, so too the Church is called to live out its historical life in such a way that people are drawn to join this communion. The Church is to proclaim this incredible truth to all people, bearing witness in both its word and its life. In doing so, Christ's love is "poured out upon them by the Spirit, breaking down all barriers, healing all divisions, and gathering them together as one universal flock to meet the coming of the great shepherd, the one Lord and saviour of all."[176]

The Distinctiveness of the Church in Relation to the World

Torrance was emphatic that the Church must maintain its distinctiveness in relation to the world. We can see this in one of his earliest publications from 1942, "The Church in the World." Torrance argues that the Church must retain its distinct nature for it has both a unique message and a unique function that cannot be merged with any form of social order. However, despite its distinct message and function, the Church requires a worldly form and "must look to her methods and to her organization, for she must have some outward form through which she can translate her message to society."[177]

Torrance viewed the state of the Church halfway through the twentieth century with dismay. We see this in his disappointment that "the Church has identified Christianity with Christendom," exemplified by the belief that good behavior makes one a Christian so that "a Christian life is hardly distinguishable from good citizenship or public-spiritedness, or philanthropy, or humanitarianism."[178] We also see it in his accusation that the supernatural nature of the kingdom of God had been reduced to a generic idea of civil life. The Church "has become so much a part of ordinary society that she finds herself unable to raise society,"[179] while on the other hand, the Church as an institution has become identified with the status quo so that rather than pioneering and forging new ways, "many look to the Church for a defence of the old order of things, social and political."[180]

Given this state of affairs, Torrance argues that the body of Christ "must be prepared for a thorough overhaul of her whole shape and form, for a radical alteration in her organizations and methods."[181] The first half of the twentieth century was a time of immense change. Torrance argued that the "tempo of the times" required the Church to make drastic changes—not simply to keep up, but to leap ahead.[182] Torrance's challenge to the Church is clear, asking it to regain a sense of its calling to be the "leaven" in the loaf since "it is not the Church's business to be the bulwark of the old order; rather, it is her business to throw the whole into ferment and upheaval."[183] The very nature of the Church, looking toward and longing for the new creation, means that it "cannot but be fundamentally destructive and revolutionary over against the 'fashion of this world.'"[184] Because the Church's ultimate existence is grounded in God and not in itself as an earthly institution, the Church "has no right to identify herself with the social order here or with any political system, far less with the 'status quo.'"[185] The very nature of the Christian Church is that it is "always on the move, always campaigning, always militant, aggressive, disruptive, revolutionary."[186] The Church must maintain its distinctive nature and character and recognize its inherent separation from the norms of society and, indeed, the world.

Furthermore, the Church must refuse to become merged in ordinary social life in order to show "that there is a world of difference between being Christian and just being nice and gentlemanly."[187] Although it is good for the Church to engage in serving the world through social activity, by itself this will never solve the problem of evil, which can flourish just as well under a good order as under an evil order. There is thus for Torrance an immovable discrepancy between the body of Christ and any form of political, social, or economic order.[188] The nature of the "time between" is that while the Church—if alive and with a right focus on the Gospel—can continue to witness in a way that supports the new order, that new order must not be associated with the Church or else the Church will lose its ability to curb that order if it becomes evil.[189] The Church must let its voice be heard "wherever there is evil in the industrial or the economic order, in the political or international sphere, or in the social fabric of ordinary life,"[190] but it is clear that Torrance views this as secondary to the Church's primary task of proclaiming the Gospel.

Similar themes are also found in Torrance's preaching from the World War II era. In his sermon series on Revelation published as *The Apocalypse Today*, Torrance notes the temptation to create a "so-called Christian civilization without Jesus Christ."[191] While there is no innate harm in collective human efforts, we must be careful not to idolize community or society and elevate it over the worship of God such as takes place in communism and totalitarianism. Torrance continues by stating that "when the Church begins to stress community and social cohesion . . . it is a sign that she is losing her true grip upon the living God and is binding herself together in a collective magnitude in order to make up for internal spiritual bankruptcy."[192] To worship the Christian community as an independent entity rather than as a community sustained by its communion with God is to engage in idolatry—a temptation that the Church must avoid.

OUR RESPONSE TO GOD IN CHRIST

We have considered the mediatorial role of Christ who both ministers the things of God to humans and represents humans to God. Christ is our representative and our substitute. He is our representative in that he represents our response to the Father, and he is the substitute who stands in our place. By itself neither concept is salvific, but when held together, they help us to understand the saving significance of the incarnation.[193] This is an appropriate place for us to consider the aspects of Christian life to which this applies. In *The Mediation of Christ*, Torrance spells out the significance of Christ's vicarious humanity in five areas: faith, conversion, worship, the sacraments, and evangelism. A brief synopsis of this discussion will help us see how

Torrance sees Christ's standing "in our place" as being worked out in the context of the Christian life.

Torrance argues against the idea that "faith" is something we possess independently, instead affirming that it is only as our weak faith is encircled by God's faithfulness that we can be truly faithful. In the Old Testament, God held Israel to covenant faithfulness through His own unswerving faithfulness. In the New Testament, Jesus "acts in our place and in our stead from within the depths of our unfaithfulness and provides us freely with a faithfulness in which we may share."[194] As we are yoked to Jesus, He shares our burden of placing our trust in God by allowing us to share in his vicarious faithfulness.[195]

The same applies to conversion, where we must allow Jesus to stand in for us in answering to God. We share in Jesus' vicarious repentance for he lays hold of us in the depths of our sinful enmity to God and bears God's judgment in our place, resulting in our regeneration—*paligenesia*.[196] Although this contradicts our contemporary notion that repentance and conversion are individual decisions, for Torrance, "our new birth, our regeneration, our conversion, are what has taken place in Jesus Christ himself" so that we share in his vicarious conversion.[197]

Faith and conversion could be considered rather more individualistic aspects of the Christian life; however, Torrance also affirms that corporate elements of the Church's life only take place through Christ's vicarious humanity. In his incarnate life, Jesus "embodied in himself in a vicarious form the response of human beings to God, so that all their worship and prayer to God henceforth become grounded and centred in him."[198] We cannot approach God with any sense of our own innate worthiness; we can only approach in the name of Jesus Christ alone, in whom our worship, prayer, and offerings to God are taken up and presented to God. We recall here our invitation to pray the Lord's Prayer in, through, and with Jesus Christ.[199]

We will attend to the sacraments in more detail in chapter 6, but here we may briefly note Torrance's description of the sacraments as "divinely provided, dominically appointed ways of response and obedience of a radically vicarious kind."[200] Baptism and the Eucharist direct us away from ourselves to Christ and are actions to which we can add nothing. Although we are commanded to participate in them, "they are nevertheless not sacraments of what we do but of what Christ Jesus has done in our place and on our behalf."[201]

Finally, Torrance notes that in evangelism we must proclaim the central mediatorial role of Christ who demands that we renounce ourselves, take up our cross, and follow him. Torrance argues that when the Gospel is proclaimed as being dependent on an individual human decision "for Christ," then we are preaching a Gospel of conditional rather than unconditional grace. Instead, we must preach the Gospel in such a way that the vicarious humanity of Jesus is affirmed, where to repent and believe is to trust in the sufficiency of what God in Christ has done rather than continuing to ask whether our faith is adequate enough to save us.[202]

There is an additional aspect of Church order that we must cover here, which is the role of catechism. Torrance argues that catechisms set forth doctrine in such a way that it becomes seed that bears fruit in the next generations of the Church, keeping the Church consistent in its apostolic foundation and protected from the vagaries of changing contexts. Torrance also comments that catechisms should be set forth "as far as possible in the universal language of the Church, and apart from the particular characteristics of any one Church and age,"[203] and yet should remain open to continued testing for faithfulness to the apostolic *kerygma* and *didache*.[204]

CONCLUSION

Our discussion of Church order has established that for Torrance, the nature of Church order must derive from the ultimate ground of the Church, which is the Triune God. The Church must be ever reforming because it needs to continually evaluate the characteristics of its ongoing life in space and time with reference to this source. Because the Church, existing between the two advents of Christ, has both a real union with Christ and yet lives awaiting the fullness of its redemption, it has no independent ministry of its own but instead participates in the ministry of Christ through the Spirit. It is to be ordered according to the love of God, which is given to the Church through the gifts of the Spirit, it is operative in the mode of servanthood, and thus it reaches towards the *telos* of the kingdom.[205]

NOTES

1. To see how Torrance develops the concept of order and disorder in relation to theology and natural science, see Thomas F. Torrance, *Divine and Contingent Order* (Edinburgh: T&T Clark, 1998), 85–139; Thomas F. Torrance, *The Christian Frame of Mind* (Eugene, OR: Wipf and Stock, 1989), 17–34; and Thomas F. Torrance, "The Ought and the Is: Moral Law and Natural Law," *Insight: A Journal of the Faculty of Austin Seminary* (Spring 1994): 49–59.

2. Thomas F. Torrance, *Conflict and Agreement in the Church: The Ministry and Sacraments of the Gospel* (Eugene, OR: Wipf and Stock, 1996), 13.

3. Thomas F. Torrance, *Gospel, Church and Ministry*, edited by Jock Stein, vol. 1 (Eugene, OR: Pickwick Publications, 2012), 99.

4. Eric G. Flett, *Persons, Powers, and Pluralities: Toward a Trinitarian Theology of Culture* (Cambridge: James Clarke, 2012), 111.

5. Thomas F. Torrance, *Reality and Evangelical Theology: The Realism of Christian Revelation* (Eugene, OR: Wipf and Stock, 2003), 9.

6. Thomas F. Torrance, *Royal Priesthood* (Edinburgh: Oliver and Boyd, 1955), 71. Geordie Ziegler refers to these as the "active ordering" and the "actual order" of the Church

(*Trinitarian Grace and Participation: An Entry into the Theological Thought of Thomas F. Torrance* [Minneapolis, MN: Fortress Press, 2017], 190–94, 201–4).

7. Torrance, *Gospel, Church and Ministry*, 97.

8. Ibid., 98; Torrance, *Royal Priesthood*, 82.

9. Torrance, *Royal Priesthood*, 67.

10. Ibid., 68.

11. Flett, *Persons, Powers, and Pluralities*, 84–115.

12. Torrance, *Royal Priesthood*, 70.

13. Thomas F. Torrance, *Conflict and Agreement in the Church: Order and Disorder* (Eugene, OR: Wipf and Stock, 1996), 135.

14. Torrance, *Conflict and Agreement in the Church: The Ministry and Sacraments of the Gospel*, 13.

15. Thomas F. Torrance, *Incarnation: The Person and Life of Christ*, ed. Robert T. Walker, 172 (Downers Grove, IL: InterVarsity Press, 2008).

16. Thomas F. Torrance, *Atonement: The Person and Work of Christ*, ed. Robert T. Walker, 356 (Downers Grove, IL: InterVarsity Academic Press, 2009).

17. Thomas F. Torrance, *The Trinitarian Faith* (Edinburgh: T&T Clark, 1993), 286.

18. Ibid.

19. Torrance, *Atonement*, 356.

20. Thomas F. Torrance, *The Trinitarian Faith* (Edinburgh: T&T Clark, 1993), 257.

21. Torrance, *Atonement*, 357.

22. Ibid., 156–60. We will discuss the nature of the Last Supper and the way it is transformed from mere memorial to an act of participation in chapter 6.

23. Thomas F. Torrance, *Theology in Reconstruction* (Grand Rapids, MI: Eerdmans, 1965), 203.

24. See Thomas F. Torrance, *The Christian Doctrine of God: One Being Three Persons* (Edinburgh: T&T Clark, 1996), 44, referring to the Synoptic Gospels.

25. Torrance, *The Trinitarian Faith*, 286. Torrance talks about the "twelve" and places great emphasis on the significance of this number for the 12 apostles represent the 12 tribes of Israel. See also Torrance, *Incarnation*, 15–16; and Torrance, *Conflict and Agreement in the Church: Order and Disorder*, 27.

26. Torrance, *Theology in Reconstruction*, 135.

27. Torrance, *Incarnation*, 22.

28. Torrance, *Theology in Reconstruction*, 203.

29. Torrance, *Atonement*, 352.

30. Torrance, *Incarnation*, 16.

31. Torrance, *Atonement*, 342.

32. Ibid., 349–58.

33. Thomas F. Torrance, *Space, Time and Incarnation* (Edinburgh: T&T Clark, 1997), 1–3.

34. Torrance, *Theology in Reconstruction*, 43.

35. Torrance, *Reality and Evangelical Theology*, 92–93.

36. Torrance, *Conflict and Agreement in the Church: Order and Disorder*, 31.

37. Ibid., 32. The laying on of hands was the sign of one being set apart for such roles, but it was not seen as a sacramental action.

38. Torrance, *The Trinitarian Faith*, 254.

39. Thomas F. Torrance, "The Deposit of Faith," *Scottish Journal of Theology* 36, no. 1 (1983): 2.

40. Torrance, *The Trinitarian Faith*, 286.

41. Ibid., 289.

42. Ibid., 286.

43. Torrance, "The Deposit of Faith," 12.

44. Ibid., 6.

45. Torrance, *The Trinitarian Faith*, 44.

46. Ibid., 259.

47. Torrance, "The Deposit of Faith," 5–6.

48. Torrance, *The Trinitarian Faith*, 33.

49. Ibid., 32.
50. Ibid., 260.
51. Torrance, "The Deposit of Faith," 7. Writing in 1941, Torrance notes that the Apostles Creed "was never a conclusion, but always a confession"—a phrase that he argues is demonstrative of the kind of theological thinking needed in the Church. See Thomas F. Torrance, "We Need a Decisive Theology Before We Can Restate the Creed," *British Weekly*, May 15, 1941.
52. Torrance, *The Trinitarian Faith*, 46.
53. Ibid., 14.
54. Torrance, "The Deposit of Faith," 16.
55. Ibid., 14.
56. Torrance, *The Trinitarian Faith*, 46.
57. Ibid.
58. Ibid., 288.
59. Ibid.
60. Ibid., 289.
61. Torrance, "The Deposit of Faith," 15.
62. Ibid., 15–16.
63. Ibid., 12–13.
64. Thomas F. Torrance, *Theology in Reconciliation* (Eugene, OR: Wipf and Stock, 1996), 31.
65. Ibid., 33.
66. Ibid., 36.
67. Ibid., 19.
68. Ibid., 27.
69. Ibid., 33.
70. Thomas F. Torrance, *The School of Faith* (London: James Clarke, 1959), xlv.
71. Torrance, *Theology in Reconciliation*, 31.
72. Thomas F. Torrance, "The Orthodox Church in Great Britain," in *Texts and Studies* (London: Thyateira House, 1983), 253.
73. Torrance, *Conflict and Agreement in the Church: The Ministry and Sacraments of the Gospel*, 7.
74. Torrance, *Theology in Reconciliation*, 34.
75. Ibid., 34–35.
76. Thomas F. Torrance, "Trinity Sunday Sermon on Acts 2:41–47," *Ekklesiastikos Pharos* 52 (1970): 191–99, 193–94.
77. Thomas F. Torrance, "Review of F. C. Schmitt (ed.), *S. Anselmi Opera Omnia*," *Scottish Journal of Theology* 9, no. 1 (1956): 89.
78. Torrance, *The School of Faith*, xlv.
79. Thomas F. Torrance, "Karl Barth and the Latin Heresy," *Scottish Journal of Theology* 39, no. 4 (November 1986): 469. A critical Roman Catholic response to this article, while remaining appreciative of Torrance, is Douglas Farrow, "T. F. Torrance and the Latin Heresy," *First Things* 238 (December 2013): 25–31.
80. Torrance, *The School of Faith*, xlv.
81. Thomas F. Torrance, *Kingdom and Church* (Eugene, OR: Wipf and Stock), 2–3.
82. Torrance, *Theology in Reconciliation*, 37.
83. Ibid., 38.
84. Ibid., 36.
85. Thomas F. Torrance, "Our Witness through Doctrine," in *Proceedings of the 17th General Council of the Alliance of Reformed Churches Throughout the World Holding the Presbyterian Order* (Geneva: World Presbyterian Alliance, 1954), 133–45.

137; Thomas F. Torrance, "Anglican-Presbyterian Conversations," *Presbyterian Record* (July–August 1957): 19.

86. Torrance, *Theology in Reconciliation*, 37.
87. Thomas F. Torrance, "History and Reformation," *Scottish Journal of Theology* 4 (1951): 282.

88. Torrance, *Conflict and Agreement in the Church: The Ministry and Sacraments of the Gospel*, 7.
89. Torrance, *Theology in Reconciliation*, 99.
90. Ibid.
91. Torrance, *The School of Faith*, l.
92. Torrance, *The School of Faith*, lv.
93. Ibid., li–lii.
94. Torrance, *Gospel, Church and Ministry*, 238. Torrance attributes this to Barth in Andrew Walker, *Different Gospels* (London: Hodder & Stoughton), 48.
95. Ibid.
96. Thomas F. Torrance, *The Doctrine of Grace in the Apostolic Fathers* (Eugene, OR: Wipf and Stock, 1996), 21.
97. Torrance, *The School of Faith*, xlvii. Torrance also attributes the difference in theology to different ways of thinking: Reformed theologians placed far more emphasis on hearing the Word of God than medieval theologians did.
98. Ibid., l–lii.
99. Torrance, *Theology in Reconciliation*, 100.
100. Thomas F. Torrance, "A New Reformation?" *London Holborn and Quarterly Review* 189 (1964): 279–80.
101. Ibid., 281.
102. Torrance, "The Orthodox Church in Great Britain," 254.
103. Thomas F. Torrance, *Christianity Divided: Protestant and Roman Catholic Theological Issues* (New York: Sheed and Ward, 1962), 286–95.
104. For a fuller discussion of objective and subjective justification, see Thomas F. Torrance, "Justification: Its Radical Nature and Place in Reformed Doctrine and Life," *Scottish Journal of Theology* 13, no. 3 (August 1960): 225–46.
105. See also Thomas F. Torrance, *God and Rationality* (Oxford: Oxford University Press, 2000), 56–86, in which Torrance notes the challenge of justification: it is "easy because it is so utterly free, and therefore so cheap in the sense that it is quite without price or condition; but it is so difficult because its absolute freeness devalues the moral and religious currency which we have minted at such cost out of our own self-understanding" (71).
106. Thomas F. Torrance, "What Is the Reformed Church?" *Biblical Theology* 9 (1959): 51–54.
107. Ibid., 55.
108. Spelled by Torrance *Martin Butzer*; we have adopted the more popular English spelling here.
109. Thomas F. Torrance, *Kingdom and Church* (Eugene, OR: Wipf and Stock, 1996), 74–75.
110. Ibid., 81.
111. Ibid., 89. See Torrance, *The School of Faith*, lix–lxv, for the shape that the Christological correction of Reformed theology took.
112. Torrance, *Kingdom and Church*, 94–95, 100–4.
113. Ibid., 103, quoting Calvin's *Commentary on Hebrews* (6.1).
114. Ibid., 105.
115. Ibid., 108.
116. Ibid., 109, quoting Calvin's *Commentary on Matthew* (25.31).
117. Ibid., 116.
118. Ibid., 109.
119. Ibid., 118.
120. Ibid., 117.
121. Ibid., 121
122. Ibid., 126–31.
123. Ibid., 136.
124. Ibid., 138.
125. Ibid., 164.
126. Torrance, *The Trinitarian Faith*, 275.

127. Torrance, *Royal Priesthood*, 71.
128. Torrance, *Gospel, Church and Ministry*, 98.
129. Torrance, *Royal Priesthood*, 82.
130. Thomas F. Torrance, "Review of *The Realm of Redemption: Studies in the Doctrine of the Nature of the Church in Contemporary Protestant Theology*. By J. Robert Nelson," *Scottish Journal of Theology* 6, no. 3 (September 1953): 323; and Thomas F. Torrance, "Why I'd Turn the Kirk Upside Down," *The Scotsman*, May 17, 1977.
131. Torrance, *Conflict and Agreement in the Church: Order and Disorder*, 61.
132. Torrance, *Royal Priesthood*, 99.
133. Ibid., 100.
134. Ibid., 65.
135. Torrance, *Atonement*, 379.
136. Torrance, *Gospel, Church and Ministry*, 97.
137. Torrance, *Conflict and Agreement in the Church: Order and Disorder*, 93.
138. Torrance, *Gospel, Church and Ministry*, 96.
139. Torrance, *Royal Priesthood*, 67.
140. Ibid., 66.
141. Ibid., 67.
142. Torrance, *Gospel, Church and Ministry*, 97.
143. Torrance, *Atonement*, 279.
144. Ibid., 13.
145. Torrance, *Incarnation*, 20.
146. Torrance, *Atonement*, 13.
147. Ibid., 19–20.
148. Torrance, *Conflict and Agreement in the Church: The Ministry and Sacraments of the Gospel*, 157.
149. Ibid.
150. Ibid., 158.
151. Torrance, *Incarnation*, 161–62.
152. Ibid., 23.
153. Ibid., 24–25.
154. Torrance, *Conflict and Agreement in the Church: The Ministry and Sacraments of the Gospel*, 72.
155. Torrance, *Conflict and Agreement in the Church: Order and Disorder*, 209.
156. Torrance, *Conflict and Agreement in the Church: The Ministry and Sacraments of the Gospel*, 158–59.
157. Torrance, *Theology in Reconciliation*, 83.
158. Torrance, *The Trinitarian Faith*, 294.
159. Torrance, *Conflict and Agreement in the Church: The Ministry and Sacraments of the Gospel*, 158.
160. Torrance, *Atonement*, 357.
161. Torrance, *Conflict and Agreement in the Church: Order and Disorder*, 251.
162. Torrance, *Royal Priesthood*, 37–38.
163. Gary W. Deddo, "The Christian Life and Our Participation in Christ's Continuing Ministry," in *An Introduction to Torrance Theology: Discovering the Incarnate Saviour*, ed. Gerrit Scott Dawson, 139, 143–48 (London: T&T Clark, 2007).
164. Torrance, *Royal Priesthood*, 61; and Thomas F. Torrance, *The Apocalypse Today* (London: James Clarke, 1960), 79–87.
165. Torrance, *The Doctrine of Grace in the Apostolic Fathers*, 24.
166. Torrance, *Atonement*, 293.
167. Torrance, *Royal Priesthood*, 45.
168. Torrance, *Gospel, Church and Ministry*, 101.
169. Torrance, *Atonement*, 308.
170. Ibid., 310. I do not believe Torrance intends to suggest through the use of sacramental language here that an individual can only meet with Jesus through the sacramental rites of the

Church but rather is emphasizing that in the time between the two advents of Christ, Christ is veiled from our sight.

171. Ibid., 304.
172. Torrance, *Gospel, Church and Ministry*, 102.
173. Torrance, *Atonement*, 304.
174. Torrance, *Royal Priesthood*, 50–51.
175. Torrance, *Gospel, Church and Ministry*, 102.
176. Torrance, *Atonement*, 343.
177. Torrance, *Gospel, Church and Ministry*, 75.
178. Ibid.
179. Ibid., 76.
180. Ibid.
181. Ibid., 80.
182. Ibid.
183. Ibid., 76.
184. Ibid., 77.
185. Ibid., 79.
186. Ibid. See also Torrance's reflection on the way that Jesus rejected every institutional system based on power and instead correlated the Church with the kingdom of God, "giving it an open eschatological dimension which builds into it a meta-institutional and meta-canonical orientation making it quite unlike anything else on earth" (Torrance, *Theology in Reconciliation*, 40).
187. Torrance, *Gospel, Church and Ministry*, 78. See also Torrance, *God and Rationality*, 117–19; and Torrance, *Theology in Reconciliation*, 271–75, in particular the discussion about the need for the Church to be emancipated from "built-in obsolescence."
188. This is illustrated in Torrance's sermon on Revelation 14, "The Triumph of the Gospel" in Torrance, *The Apocalypse Today*, 111–22.
189. Torrance, *Gospel, Church and Ministry*, 82.
190. Ibid., 81.
191. Torrance, *The Apocalypse Today*, 109.
192. Ibid., 145.
193. Thomas F. Torrance, *The Mediation of Christ* (Edinburgh: T&T Clark 1992), 80–81.
194. Ibid., 82.
195. Ibid., 84. On the understanding of faith as grounded in God's faithfulness in Christ, see Thomas F. Torrance, "One Aspect of the Biblical Conception of Faith," *Expository Times* 86 (1957): 111–14.
196. Ibid., 85.
197. Ibid., 86.
198. Ibid., 87.
199. Ibid., 88–89.
200. Ibid., 89.
201. Ibid., 90.
202. Ibid., 92–95.
203. Torrance, *The School of Faith*, xi. In the following passages, Torrance demonstrates a marked preference for the Reformation catechisms over those of the Westminster assembly, arguing that they are more universal, more Christological, less rationalistic, and do a better job of focusing upon the primary work of Christ rather than the response of humanity.
204. Ibid., xii.
205. Torrance, *Royal Priesthood*, 66.

Chapter Six

The Notes and Marks of the Church

Building on chapter 5 where we saw that Church order is intrinsically related to the *koinōnia* of the Church, we may now proceed to consider the notes of the Church. The essential being and nature of the Church is defined in the Nicene Creed as being one, holy, catholic, and apostolic. Understanding the characteristics of the Church in this way will help us to situate the marks of the Church—the Word, the sacraments, and the ministry—and their functional role in the life of the Church. While both notes and marks are related to the central motif of *koinōnia*, the notes have to do with the essential nature of the Church while the marks have a temporary function and are concerned with how believers participate in the union and communion of the Trinity in the time between Christ's two advents.

THE NOTES OF THE CHURCH

Although the Church is ultimately grounded in the being and work of the Triune God, the Church *in via* must contend with the limitations of its existence in space and time as it looks forward to the second advent of Christ and the fullness of its redemption.

One way in which we may distinguish Torrance's different ways of thinking about the Church's life is to identify the difference in his thought between the notes of the Church and the marks of the Church. Torrance uses these terms in his own way since what he describes as notes or attributes or predicates are more commonly referred to as the marks of the Church. (His use will be retained throughout.) For Torrance, the four notes of the Church are the four essential ecclesial attributes defined by the Nicene Creed, which are "first of all attributes of Christ himself, but attributes in which the church shares through its union and communion with him."[1] Unity, holiness, catholicity, and apostolicity "do not denote independent qualities inhering in the church, but are affirmations of the nature of the church as it participates in Jesus Christ and are strictly discernible only to faith."[2] This reflects the trend that we identified in patristic theology where organization and structure were not paramount in the development of "a definite ecclesiology"[3] but the nature of the Church as it derived from the being of God was central.

These four notes are distinct from what Torrance refers to as the marks of the Church. The marks, in keeping with Reformed theology, are visible elements of the Church's life, such as the "word of God purely preached, the sacraments of the gospel rightly administered, and godly discipline," which "indicate where the true church is to be found; they do not define it or describe it but point to it."[4] The notes describe the true being of the Church, while the marks describe the temporal life of the Church. We will thus initially explore the oneness, holiness, catholicity, and apostolicity of the Church, focusing on how these four notes fill out our understanding of the relationship between the Triune God, who is transcendent over all space and time, and the Church, which lives within space and time. Because they are first and foremost attributes of the Triune God, they derive from the being of God to shape the being of the Church.

Oneness

For Torrance, the Church's oneness is derived from the Trinity as a "holy fellowship of love" that reflects the community of love that God is. The church's unity is an earthly counterpart to the unity of the three persons of the Trinity.[5] Central to the oneness of the Church is its ontological relationship to Christ for through his incarnational atonement, humanity is united to him and formed into one new body. Through union with Christ, the Church participates in the communion of the Trinity. Its unity does not arise from the similarity of its members but from their shared participation in the fellowship of the Holy Trinity. This means that the Church in every manifestation throughout space and time is "intrinsically and essentially one" since it exists wherever Christ and the Spirit are active.[6]

To illustrate the oneness of the Church, we may turn to the account of the Spirit being poured out in Acts 2. Torrance describes the Holy Spirit as "the principle of multiplicity as well as unity, but he is the principle of unity in the heart and wealth of all multiplicity."[7] Despite the diversity of nations represented in Jerusalem on the Day of Pentecost, the Spirit was poured out regardless of language, gender, nationality, or socioeconomic background, unifying the multitude of Jewish believers from all over the world. This is clearly intended as the antithesis to the separation of the nations that took place at Babel in Genesis 11—where sin divides, the Spirit reconciles and reunites.[8]

Furthermore, there is an ahistorical aspect to the oneness of the Church that Torrance brings out in his diachronic approach to ecclesiology, emphasizing that even though the Church has existed in three different stages, there is only ever one Church. It is the same God who is at work in both the Old and New Testament, speaking through the Old Testament prophets to Israel, dwelling among us in Christ, and continuing to speak through the New Testament apostles to the Church. Many of the Church Fathers—including Cyril of Jerusalem, Irenaeus, and Epiphanius—use this point of continuity to emphasize the unity of the Church. Although it has existed in different forms in different stages of history, it is nonetheless gathered up as one in Christ.[9] The Church has an earthly and historical form but also has an eschatological form that is yet to be fully revealed.[10]

The oneness of the Church thus encompasses both the visible Church and the invisible Church, or to use alternative terms, the Church militant and the Church triumphant. The empirical Church, the Body of Christ, is in view in the Nicene Creed and traces its existence back to the "sovereign self-giving of God in his Spirit, who through his Word calls the Church into being and by his own breath makes it alive with the very life of God."[11] Nevertheless, we must acknowledge that even though oneness is an essential attribute of the Church, the historical life of the Church rarely reflects this, as seen in the competition between different church denominations. Torrance is realistic about this state of affairs but passes negative judgment upon it, observing that for the Church to allow "the divisions of the world to penetrate back into its life, is to live in disagreement with its own existence, to call in question its reconciliation, and to act a lie against the atonement."[12] Jesus Christ, the head, has only one body.

Holiness

Just as the oneness of the Church derives from its participation in the communion of the Holy Trinity, the holiness of the Church also originates from the way in which the Church is "drawn into the holiness of God himself, into the fellowship of the Holy Trinity, partaking of that fellowship through the Holy Spirit."[13] Holiness as an essential attribute of the Church does not derive from the purity or morality of the Church's human members; rather, it is the presence of the holy God that hallows the Church.[14] Holiness is given to the Church from its head, Christ, and is not something "achieved" by the members of the Church.[15] We must recall Christ's assumption of our fallen humanity in order to sanctify and heal it; through union with Christ, we are both justified and made holy as individuals. This holiness is extended to the Church as a whole because of our participation in the divine *koinōnia*. In this sense, holiness is an essential attribute of the being of the Church and a fully realized reality.

However, we must also reckon with the fact that just as the historical life of the Church doesn't demonstrate oneness, so too the life of the Church misses the standard of holiness. On one hand, the Church is "called out of the world and separated from secular society for fellowship with God."[16] It is not a society or community like any other for it has been "set apart as a spiritual house and a royal priesthood to offer spiritual sacrifices acceptable to God through Jesus Christ."[17] On the other hand, the Church also stands in solidarity with the sinful world and is in need of constant sanctification and healing.[18] As the body of the crucified Christ, the Church must continually submit itself to the judgment of the Cross since "this side of the final judgment, the Church in history is ever found to be in the wrong, and must ever be put in the right"[19] for "until Christ comes again the church constantly needs the cleansing of Christ and the fire of divine judgment."[20]

God "seeks and establishes fellowship with his human creatures, coming into their midst always as the Lord whose awful presence among them opposes and judges their impurity and sin, yet in such a way that he does not annihilate them but gathers them to himself within the embrace of his covenant mercies and grace."[21] As the Spirit comes among the Church, the Church is both judged and justified,[22] for the Spirit causes God's holiness "to bear upon [the Church] in conviction and judgment of its unrighteousness."[23] This fits with our earlier identification that Torrance considers the Church particularly a work of the Holy Spirit. Even though the historical life of the Church does not demonstrate this essential attribute of holiness, the Church is still essentially holy because it is sustained by the Holy Spirit. While individual members of the Church should aim to live a holy life, holiness as a measure of morality is not the goal; instead, individuals should aim to live out of their personal union with Christ in such a way that "their personal holiness, and all the qualities of the divine life and love found in their lives, are the fruits of the Holy Spirit."[24]

Catholicity

Following oneness and holiness, we come to the Church's catholicity, which Torrance defines as "its participation in the immensity of God, in the plenitude and fullness of the divine life in Christ, and in the universality of the Holy Spirit. It is the counterpart in the life of the church in space and time to the whole fullness of God."[25] While the simplest definition of catholicity is "universality," there is a particular theological understanding of catholicity that is intensified by the prior attributes of the Church, oneness and holiness. As Torrance explains, "to be catholic the Church must be one and holy, for unity and holiness interpenetrate each other in the essential nature of the Church as the Body of which Christ is the organising Head, and which through the indwelling of the Holy Spirit is united to the one and only God, the Holy Trinity."[26] The Church is catholic when viewed through the unifying lens of its common faith in the Trinity.[27] However, Torrance also notes the difference in the understanding of catholicity between East and West, which derives from a different understanding of the relationship of the Church to the Holy Spirit. Torrance suggests that the Western Church has traditionally viewed itself as possessing the Spirit and as able to dispense the Spirit. In contrast to this, the Eastern Church has viewed itself as possessed *by* the Spirit and thus able to reach out beyond its own bounds *in the power of* the Spirit.[28]

Developing his own understanding of catholicity, Torrance insists that it has to do with the Church's "identity, continuity, and universality"[29] for through union with Christ, "the Church is itself the fullness of him who fills all things."[30]

> [Catholicity] refers to the intensive wholeness and fullness of the Church in Christ, to the coordination of the Church, everywhere, in every place, and throughout all space and time, with the wholeness of Christ himself. The catholic Church does not live out of itself but out of Christ; nor does it derive inspiration from its own spirit but only from the one Spirit of the living God. It does not act in its own name and authority but only in the name and authority of the Father, Son and Holy Spirit. But throughout all its life the intensive oneness or wholeness of the Church in Christ unfolds as under the imperative of the Holy Spirit it seeks to be obedient to its commission to proclaim the Gospel to all mankind.[31]

This evokes thoughts of growth and outreach since the analogy of the Church as the body of Christ must be unconstrained by biological limitations. Torrance argues that we must think of the "body of Christ" as an expanding ingathering where "the Body (*soma*) presses out in expansion toward a fullness (*pleroma*) in the love of God in all its height and depth and length and breadth which more and more gathers into itself men and women from the ends of the earth."[32] This movement from "the intensive concretion of the new humanity in Christ to its extensive universalisation in the fullness of Christ who fills the whole creation"[33] is the mission of the Church for

> Jesus Christ has sent His Church out among the nations to be a fellowship of reconciliation . . . ready to bring to men the healing of the Cross, and to live out in their midst the reconciled life drawing them into its own fellowship of peace with God and with all men.[34]

We will consider more fully in chapter 7 the way that the mission of the Church interacts with its nature as a community of reconciliation. For now we note that as the catholic Church, the Church embraces both this age and the age to come so that what it is here and now reaches out to the *eschaton* through the Spirit. The universal range of the Church is why catholicity is intrinsically related to ecumenicity.[35]

Finally, there are two complementary aspects of catholicity that Torrance identifies that are useful for our discussion. The first is the "catholicity of extension," referring to the Church's essentially missionary nature as it participates in the movement of God's love that flows through Christ and the Spirit to the world, breaking down all barriers and boundaries so all may be reconciled to God.[36] In the context of the early Church, to affirm the catholic nature of the Church was in direct contrast to gnostic teaching, which denied the universal range of the atonement.[37] To be catholic in this sense is to be "faithful to the apostolic tradition in believing that Jesus Christ the incarnate Son of God died and rose again for all people irrespective of who they are."[38] The second aspect is that of "catholicity of depth," which is an understanding that the wholeness of the body of Christ is supreme to the individual members. "Catholic means that Christians are first members of Christ and therefore of the body of Christ the Church, and as such and only as such are they individual Christians in their own sphere and duty and private existence."[39] This is in keeping with Torrance's emphasis that it is on the basis of our participation in the divine *koinōnia* that we experience creaturely *koinōnia* with one another.

Apostolicity

Given that the catholic Church is "to be understood as embracing all dimensions of the people of God and their existence throughout space and time,"[40] it becomes apparent just how closely catholicity and apostolicity are related. The Church's apostolicity specifically has "to do with the continuing *identity* of the Church as the authentic Body of Christ in space and time."[41] The apostolicity of the Church rests on its unchanging foundation. Since the Triune God does not change, so also "the Church of Christ is one and the same today with what it was in its apostolic foundation."[42] The apostolic Church is the Church that seeks continuity with the words and deeds of Christ, as recorded through the apostolic tradition.[43] Apostolicity is consequently a criterion that bears on the oneness, holiness, and catholicity of the Church for each of these repose on the "continuity of the one holy catholic Church with Christ who through the apostles founded the church on himself."[44]

We have already examined the role of the apostolate as the hinge between Christ's self-witness and the witness to Christ recorded in Scripture. The apostolic Church does not depart from this original apostolic foundation, which was established because Christ caused the whole fact of his person, word, and life to be unfolded through the apostolic mind and embodied in the apostolic mission. Therefore, when we speak of apostolicity, we are referring "to the character and imprint of its distinctive apostolic origin, and to the nature of the Church as continuously embodying the apostolic witness and testimony in its life and mission, for it is through faithful transmission of the preaching and teaching of the apostles that the Church is itself constantly renewed and reconstituted as Christ's Church."[45] As an example of "adding" to the apostolic foundation, Torrance accuses the Roman Catholic Church of calling its apostolicity into question by its mid-twentieth-century announcement of the dogma of Mary's physical assumption into heaven.[46]

Apostolic succession primarily has to do with "succession in the unity of knowing and being, of word and deed, of message and ministry."[47] It is only on the basis of this primary sense of apostolic succession that we may speak of the secondary sense of apostolic succession, which is how the Word is "extended and mediated to a corporeal world by such physical, historical events as the Bible, Preaching, Sacraments, the physical society of the members of the Church, the historical communication and edification, and all that entails from age to age."[48] Consequently, ministerial succession is not to be thought of as anything other than a sign because "the historical succession of ecclesiastical representatives is not identical with the real succession of the corporate participation of the Church in the ministry of Christ, and can only point to it and signify it, important and indeed essential as that succession on the plane of history is."[49]

Summarizing Comments on the Notes of the Church

This discussion of what it means to affirm one, holy, catholic, and apostolic Church is useful in helping us grasp Torrance's interpretation of Nicene ecclesiology in more detail. Each of these four notes is derived from the being of the Triune God and on this basis has to do with the essential being of the Church. This can be correlated with the two aspects of order that we identified in Torrance's work, the order that comes from the historical life of the Church and the order that derives from its new being in Jesus Christ. Torrance refuses to separate these into any dualistic doctrine of the Church; instead he defines the Church with ultimate reference to the Triune God while simultaneously acknowledging that the historical period in which the Church exists between Christ's two advents will necessarily involve a constant struggle between what the Church essentially should be and how this is actually lived out. Molnar supports this with his observation that because Torrance grounds his ecclesiology in the Trinity, he rejects any idea that the true Church exists as "some mystical reality behind or above time, space and history; for that would undercut the realities of the incarnation and the atonement" while also rejecting "any reduction of the church to its historical form of existence; for that would imply the legalistic view that ignores our justification by faith."[50] Marks are the ways that God is at work among his people.

THE WORD

We now turn our attention from the notes of the Church to the marks of the Church, those visible elements of its life identified by Torrance. Purves comments that if "'practical theology' is something like 'a theology concerned with action,' then the theology of T. F. Torrance is most assuredly, as theology of the God who acts, practical theology."[51]

Torrance suggests that since the Word and sacraments "span the whole life and mission of the Church in the last times," it is in their light that we should "articulate our understanding of the ministry of the Church, of its order, and of the nature of its priesthood functioning through that order."[52] We will accordingly begin with the preaching of the Word, follow with the ministry of the sacraments, and then consider the priesthood, keeping in mind Torrance's definition of these marks as indicators that shape the life of the Church in the time between the two advents and that point to the presence of the true Church. They are temporal, intended to sustain the life of the Church, and will pass away at Christ's return.

The Word in the Life of the Church

In beginning with the Word, our concern is the role of the Word in the life of the Church, particularly through preaching. Earlier we noted Torrance's emphasis on interpreting the Scriptures "in depth," penetrating their literary surface to the dynamic objectivity of the Father, Son, and Holy Spirit. God himself is the reality to which the Scriptures witness for despite the rich diversity within Scripture, "they are found to have a deep underlying unity in Jesus Christ the incarnate and risen Lord, who is the dynamic center and the objective focus of their creative integration."[53] Since the Scriptures are "grounded and structured through the incarnation in the very Logos who inheres eternally in the Being of God and are the vehicles of his address to mankind . . . we must learn to trace back their objective reference beyond what is written to their source in the infinite depth of Truth in the Being of God."[54] The starting place of the doctrine of the Word is therefore the eternal Word who became incarnate, the person of Jesus Christ in the full, unbroken union of his divine nature and his human nature, who is in command of his Church.[55] We are thus reckoning with "both the eternal Word of God transcendent in history, and also the Word which in the Church of Jesus Christ has assumed historical form."[56]

While the Word and Truth remain transcendent to the form that they take in space and time, the very nature of the incarnation as a historical and personal event means that this revelation must be able to be communicated and received afresh in each generation of the Church,[57] following on from the unique role of the apostles. The church is a community of reciprocity that serves as the social coefficient of theological knowledge.[58] The Word of God can only be correctly heard and interpreted in the ecclesial context of worship and fellowship for

> it is only as we allow ourselves, within the fellowship of faith and through constant meditation on the Holy Scriptures, to come under the creative impact of God's self-revelation that we may acquire the disciplined spiritual perception or insight which enables us to discriminate between our conceptions of the Truth and the Truth itself. This is not a gift which we can acquire and operate for ourselves alone but one which we may have only as we share it with others in common listening to God's Word and in common adoration and worship of God through the Son and in the one Spirit.[59]

The Word and the Preacher

The preaching of the Word is not simply about communication of ideas and concepts but involves the whole event of reconciliation.[60] In order to learn how this takes place, we must turn to the role of the preacher. Torrance's autobiographical material has much insight to offer us. We have already noted his recollection that the ability to visit people in their homes and read Scripture with them allowed him to preach on Sundays in a much deeper and more personal way than he would have been able to otherwise.[61] We may also reference Torrance's ministerial contribution to the monthly parish newsletter at Beechgrove in November 1948. In the transcription of a message that he had preached on the texts of Jeremiah 7:2 and 2 Corinthians 5:20, Torrance describes the preacher as an "ambassador" who declares God's Word to the people gathered. The preacher is responsible for proclaiming the Gospel in faithfulness to the Word of God rather than pandering to the congregation and saying what it wants to hear. Torrance then describes his dramatic role as a preacher:

> As I prepared to come into the House of God, I donned black robes, to blot myself out as it were, so as not to attract attention to myself, but to be in the hand of God, solely the servant of His Word, the voice of one crying the Word of God. Moreover, before I came into the pulpit this morning I was preceded by the Bible. It is because the Bible is here that I stand, black-robed, behind it, to be a voice that God may use to make this Book speak aloud so that all may hear. My duty here is entirely one subordinated to the Word. My sole business as preacher is to translate the Bible into the language of the day, to expound God's Word, so that it lives and speaks as a contemporary word relevant to our human situation. Of course, it is really the Holy Spirit who animates the Word of the Bible and makes it the living contemporaneous Word of God speaking to us here and now; but that is done through the preacher as an interpreter sent by God to bring the Word out of the historical situation into the living present.[62]

The preacher must direct men and women toward God for the ministry of preaching is always subordinate to the Word of God and the voice to be heard is not that of the preacher but of the Lord Jesus. Torrance insists on the preacher bringing his or her congregation "face-to-face with God in Jesus Christ, for it is only God in Jesus Christ who can forgive and heal—only God in Jesus Christ who can reveal the ultimate truth to us about himself."[63] Although the preacher is to translate and make plain the relevance of the Bible to the congregation, his or her words have no power except as the Spirit illuminates them. The supreme example of this is found in the ministry of John the Baptist, who pointed away from himself to Christ and then faded into the background as his disciples recognized that Christ was the Messiah.[64] The weight falls entirely on what God does through the preaching of the Word rather than on the role of any individual who preaches. Human words are taken up by the Spirit who gives them utterance as the living Word.[65]

A similar perspective is expressed in another unpublished document written by Torrance, titled "Theology and the Church":

> Preaching is the great Sacrament of the Word in which certainly more is done than said, for it is the Presence of Christ that makes it a sacrament, but in which the speaking of the Word has a place of supreme importance, for without it there would be no sacrament at all, and no Presence of Christ to listening ears and believing hearts. Thus in preaching the Church believes there takes place a supreme spiritual act in which the whole of the Church's worship and obedience is centred. It is the preacher's task to give utterance to the Oracles of God, to proclaim the Word of the Cross, in which the living Christ comes Himself and acts. The preaching of the Cross, says St. Paul, may appear foolishness to the world but it is the very power of God; it is the re-enaction of the Word of the Cross in saving power. The Preacher himself cannot make it so; it is the Holy Spirit who reproduces through his speaking this living Word. The preacher is but the earthen vessel of the Holy Ghost.[66]

This way of thinking also informs the role of the hearer. Since the proclamation of the Word reveals a "living God who creatively interacts with man in the world and makes himself known to him,"[67] we are called to submit our minds to the "self-evidencing Reality of God" for faith is simply assent to the divine reality that exists objectively beyond the human individual.[68] Unless the transcendent authority of the Triune God over Scripture, the Church, and doctrine is recognized and our own inadequacy and deficiency acknowledged, we cannot hear the Word of God and submit to its demands.[69]

In his desire to emphasize the utter humility of the preacher, Torrance claims that a preacher should be "ashamed when he is praised, for applause tells him that he has preached in vain: he has drawn attention to himself, and has failed to point men away from himself to the Lamb of God."[70] However, this comment is unnecessarily harsh. It assumes that those who congratulate the preacher only do so because their "ears have been tickled," whereas it is possible to be genuinely excited by what is preached and to respond to the preacher and recognize them as a conduit of God's Word. Torrance would have been unlikely to take offence at a response of gratitude recognizing that through the preacher, God's Word had been heard and responded to.

The best published example of the breadth of Torrance's preaching is his set of published sermons *When Christ Comes and Comes Again*.[71] These sermons were gathered not as "a book about preaching but a book presenting some of the material that should be preached."[72] In the first section, "The Advent of the Redeemer," Torrance focused on the events of Christ's life, including the incarnation, the crucifixion, the resurrection, and the anticipation of the Second Advent. In the second section, "The Word of the Gospel," Torrance preached on core tenets of the Gospel, including John the Baptist and his proclamation of Christ as the Messiah; the need for humans to be born again and to take refuge in Christ; the healing work of God that takes place both in supernatural and in natural miracles such as the sacraments; and the need to be familiar with the voice of the Good Shepherd. In the third section, "The Foundation of the Church," Torrance deals with the nature of the Church, addressing how the Church is constituted by Christ's presence; the way that the kingdom is advanced by holy suffering; the fact that the Triune God invites us to approach him and cleanses us through the work of the Son's life; and the need for the fellowship of the Church to continually be cleansed and sanctified. In the fourth section, "The Faithfulness of God," Torrance considers the unswerving steadfastness of God, the patience and mediation of Jesus, and the nature of the Trinity as a Trinity of love. This brief synopsis allows us to see how theologically exhaustive Torrance considered preaching needed to be.

THE SACRAMENTS

Torrance's sacramentology is undoubtedly shaped by the Church existing in the "time between" the old age and the new age. Although the Church is a new creation risen with Christ in the new age of the resurrection, it still wears the body of sin, death, and the humiliation of old age. The sacraments are how the Church is enabled to participate in the union and communion of the Holy Trinity in the current time of history since their temporal nature signals that they will not be needed in the *eschaton*.

It is appropriate to place the sacraments after the discussion of the Word for they cannot be separated from the Word in the context of the Church's life. "The Word is itself the all-inclusive Sacrament of the Word made flesh which through the Spirit begets the Church as Body in sacramental union with Christ. It is because the Word is given this nature that through the Spirit it sacramentalises the Sacraments."[73] Expressed in another way by Torrance, "it is because Christ comes to us as the Word and gives us His real presence through the Word and so unites us to Himself that Word and Sacrament belong inseparably together. Both lose their significance and efficacy when separated."[74] As we will see, it is the *incarnate Christ* who is the true sacrament; in him, there is no separate act of God and act of humanity but rather the combination of these, which Torrance refers to the third dimension of the union of God and humanity in Christ. It is Christ's "new humanity risen from the dead and eternally in union with God, which is the *substance* or the *matter* of the Sacraments."[75]

What Are Sacraments?

The term "sacrament" does not appear in the New Testament, which simply refers to baptism and the Lord's Supper as two regular events that took place among the early Christian community. The New Testament uses interchangeable language when describing them, showing that "Baptism and Eucharist are just as parallel, and just as one, as *in Christ* and *Christ in us*."[76]

Although our consideration of the sacraments must be grounded in what the New Testament tells us about their celebration in the early Church, it is helpful to examine the language that Torrance uses. While theologians traditionally have used the terms *res* (reality) and *signum* (sign), Torrance dislikes the static connotations of these terms. He instead insists that "sign" must have a dynamic sense for in this case "sign is essentially event, the worldly form which the Christ-event assumes in action, the point at which Revelation embodies itself actively in history."[77] Rather than *res* and *signum*, Torrance prefers the terms "mystery" and "seal" since they make it clear that the sacramental relation "can no more be explained positively and put into precise rational terms than the hypostatic union which is stated by the Church only in negatives."[78]

The Latin term *sacramentum* is a translation of the Greek *mystērion*, parallel to the Roman *mysterium*. In describing the sacraments as mysteries, we remember Torrance's emphasis that the primary mystery that the New Testament refers to is "the incomprehensible union of God and man in one Person," Jesus Christ.[79] Consequently, the sacraments are only mysteries in a secondary or derivative sense. They do not merely point to Christ but are also means of his presence so that as a sign, each sacrament "represents only in the concrete act of re-presenting."[80] Torrance prefers not to engage in detailed metaphysical speculation about the sacraments, which necessarily includes the rejection of debates on matters such as how the Eucharist contains the real presence of Christ.[81] Instead, he chooses to describe the relationship between the sacraments and reality—the sign and the thing signified—as an analogical relationship, which once again involves both identity and difference.

Each sacrament is "analogous to the thing signified, and corresponds appropriately to its nature," pointing "to what Christ has done and does for us."[82] Torrance recommends that we think of each sacrament as "a sign with a meaning" in which, according to Christ's promise and command, the outward sign and inward reality are indivisible.[83] This way of describing the sacraments is different from the Augustinian tradition that views them as "outward and visible signs of inward and invisible grace"[84] and is why Torrance maintains that the elements—whether water, bread, or wine—are instrumental, and not just symbolic.[85] Consequently the sacraments are not just "confirming ordinances" but "converting ordinances."[86]

When we view the sacraments in this way, we come to understand (using Hunsinger's language) that the perfect tense of salvation has been accomplished and perfectly realized in Christ, while through his vicarious humanity and the union that we have with him through the Spirit that objective salvation is subjectively realized in us.[87] The sacraments are miracles—not of the type where a natural event takes place in a supernatural form such as miracles of healing, but of the type where a supernatural event takes place in a natural form. It is the sacramental miracle that Torrance believes is the "greater kind of miracle."[88]

Merely participating in the rites of the sacraments is not salvific for they must be filled with the Spirit. The Church does not control the efficacy of the sacraments.[89] Instead, truly belonging to the Church comes from participation in Christ and the Spirit and is revealed by the lived-out obedience of true belief. Torrance writes, "Participation in the Sacraments is not in itself a guarantee of salvation, for along with sacramental communion there must go the whole building up and ordering of the Body in the love of Christ."[90]

The Sacraments and Koinōnia

The sacramental relation for Torrance is intrinsically tied to the *koinōnia*-motif of his trinitarian ecclesiology. It is in Christ that the horizontal and vertical dimensions of the divine *koinōnia* meet, and so it is from Christ that the sacraments derive. They are pledges of our participation in the union and communion of the Triune God. As we participate in the secondary mystery of the sacraments, we actually participate in the primary mystery of union with Christ through the Holy Spirit.

> The primary *mysterium* or *sacramentum* is Jesus Christ himself, the incarnate reality of the Son of God who has incorporated himself into our humanity and assimilated the people of God into himself as his own Body, so that the sacraments have to be understood as concerned with our *koinonia* or participa-

> tion in the mystery of Christ and his Church through the *koinonia* or communion of the Holy Spirit.[91]

Placing this discussion of the sacraments within our wider discussion of *koinōnia* helps us understand how Torrance views the sacraments as more than symbols. As signs that are pledges of our full participation in the *koinōnia* of the Triune God, the sacraments "point beyond to a fullness which, as signs, in the conditions of our fallen world, they cannot altogether contain."[92] They are eschatological mysteries because our union with Christ is only partly revealed here and now but will be fully realized in the future. Through participation in the sacraments, one receives Christ's pledge of their future and fully realized participation in the *telos* of all creation.[93] The emphasis is not so much on "the future of the reality but the future of its full manifestation, so that the eschatological tension involved in the sacraments is the tension between the time of a present but hidden reality and the time of the same reality revealed in the *parousia*."[94]

In order to better understand *how* the sacraments relate to our participation in the divine *koinōnia*, we need to revisit Torrance's incarnational understanding of the atonement. Just as our union with Christ is correlative to the hypostatic union in that it is a real union but different since it involves asymmetry because God remains transcendent and free even as he enters into a bond of irreversible love with humanity,[95] so too the administration of the sacraments also involves a union between divine and human action. In the sacraments, the significance of the rite is not found in the human action but rather in the divine event that stands behind the human rite and impinges upon us—in other words, with the whole atoning work of Christ.[96] Our own human response can only be offered to God in Christ.

Although the language that we are using here is Christocentric, the reader should recall that Torrance's Christology involves understanding Christ in the light of both his *internal* relations to the Father and Spirit and the *external* matrix of historical relations through which his ministry had a specific context. On one hand, the sacraments have their "ultimate ground in the Incarnation and in the vicarious obedience of Jesus Christ"[97] and in abstraction from these historical events are merely empty rituals. On the other hand, the sacraments cannot be separated from the triune reality without losing the mystery of their "infinite recession in the Word that is in the bosom of God and is God."[98]

Torrance also explains the relationship between the sacraments and *koinōnia* with reference to the traditional Reformed emphasis on the covenant of grace. The inward form of the covenant is our union with Christ through the communion of the Spirit, leading to our participation in the fellowship of the Holy Trinity. The outward form of the covenant is the sacraments, described as "signs which mark out the sphere of God's self-revelation and self-giving to His people, and the seals of His real presence and of His faithfulness in fulfilling in them all His promises."[99] The centrality of the Trinity is key to both the inner and outer forms for as Torrance writes,

> *the whole substance* of this Covenant of Grace in its outer and in its inner form is *Jesus Christ Himself*, so that it is in accordance with the Person and Work of Christ, His Nature and His Mission, that the whole life and faith of the people of God in the economy of the New Covenant is to be understood. The New Covenant is in the Body and Blood of *Christ*, the Communion of the Spirit is Communion in the mystery of *Christ*, and the people of God, in its covenanted communion in Christ through the Spirit, is the Body of *Christ*. Everything is directed towards *Christ* and in and through Him to the union and communion of Father, Son and Holy Ghost.[100]

This way of speaking of the sacraments as related to our participation in the union and communion of the Trinity emphasizes that we cannot consider the sacramental rites in themselves but only in relation to the reality that they signify, which is the union of God and humanity in Christ and our own union with Christ. This can be explained by the metaphor of looking through a window: we look at what lies beyond the window rather than at the pane of glass itself. The only time we notice the glass is if it somehow obscures our vision.[101] In the same way, we are to look "through" the sacramental rites and to understand them "not in relation to what we do but in relation to what God in Christ has done and will do for us."[102] Their ultimate reality recedes into the mystery of the Trinity.

We may also incorporate here our previous discussion about the two dimensions of *koinōnia*. On one hand, the Church exists in its vertical dimension, already fully participating in the new creation, justified and holy as it shares in Christ's self-sanctification.[103] On the other hand, the Church exists in its horizontal dimension as a pilgrim people. It is composed of sinful men and women awaiting the day of their redemption, currently subject to the limitations and frustrations of fallen time.[104] These two elements of the Church's nature are inseparable and in Torrance's thought illustrate why "it is most important to hold Baptism and the Lord's Supper closely together; if they are allowed to fall apart, the essential relation between the finished work and the future consummation tends to be radically misunderstood."[105] Torrance explains further,

> Whereas Baptism is all-inclusive and final, the Eucharist is the continual renewal of that incorporation in time. The Eucharist cannot be understood except within the significance of Baptism, although the once-and-for-all significance of Baptism bears upon history only through the Eucharist. We must say, therefore, that strictly speaking there is only one sacrament, and that Baptism and Eucharist belong to this indivisible whole. It is the sacrament of the *Word*

> *made flesh*, of the *Christ-event*, which includes the life, teaching, death, and resurrection of Jesus Christ. It is the same Word which sacramentally becomes flesh in both Baptism and the Eucharist, and it is in that action of the Word becoming flesh that they have their underlying and indivisible unity.[106]

The Two-fold Nature of the Church and the Two Sacraments

At this point, we must also incorporate Torrance's eschatology into our discussion of the sacraments. Thinking of the Church as embodying a reality that fully exists in the present but is not yet fully unveiled means that the Church involves "sort of a hypostatic union between the eternal and the temporal in the form of new time."[107] The sacraments demonstrate this "union between the Church in history and the new creation as an abiding union here and now even in the heart of the world's estrangement."[108] Until the day when Christ comes again, "the sacraments have to do with the breaking of the Christ-event into time here and now, and with our participation in the new creation."[109]

Even though Christ has withdrawn himself from our sight, the sacraments are the "miraculous and active signs" through which the mystery of the union between Christ and the Church are embodied in space and time.[110] The sacraments are therefore the "concrete form" of the Church's "communion with Christ through the Spirit."[111] The water, bread, and wine are "visible, tangible and corruptible elements of this world" while simultaneously being signs of the new order that is veiled from our sight but that we participate in through the Holy Spirit.[112] The sacraments are how Christ "nourishes, sustains, orders and governs his people" within history.[113] One day they will become obsolete for at the *parousia*, when Christ is fully unveiled, the sacraments will pass away, as will faith and hope, and "*agape-love* only will abide as the eternal being of the new humanity in righteousness and truth."[114]

Torrance further expounds on the relationship between the sacraments with reference to the relationship between incarnation and atonement, suggesting,

> If Incarnation and atonement are to be understood in terms of each other, the same is true of Baptism and Eucharist in terms of one living, saving operation of reconciliation and unification. But if Incarnation and atonement are to be distinguished as dual moments in one movement, similarly Baptism and Eucharist enshrine a corresponding duality. Both Sacraments belong to the fullness of time and have to do with the whole Christ clothed with the Gospel of reconciliation and resurrection, but in Baptism we have particularly to do with the objective and perfected event, and in the Eucharist we have to do particularly with participation in that completed reality in the conditions of time within which the Church engages in the mission of the Cross.[115]

If we continue to work with baptism as the unrepeatable sacrament of justification and the Eucharist as the regularly repeated sacrament of sanctification, then we see that together these sacraments give expression to the ontological and the eschatological relation that the Church has to Jesus Christ.[116] Baptism is the sign that Christ has already made the Church his body so that in him it is presented to the Father as pure and spotless, while the Eucharist is given for the constant renewal of the "body of sinners waiting for the redemption of the body of sin and death, living in the midst of estrangement and the dividedness of mankind,"[117] and is a means for the Church's unity to be preserved and visibly manifested.[118]

The Sacrament of Baptism and the "Once-for-All" Nature of the Church's Incorporation

The New Testament authors creatively reinterpret Old Testament concepts and rituals in the light of Christ because "the reality in Christ is not bound by the ancient shadow or image; that was only a signitive pointer to the reality and now that the reality has arrived it interprets itself."[119] In the Old Testament, circumcision was the sign of the covenant; in the New Testament, baptism is the sign of the new covenant.[120]

Torrance argues that Jewish baptism developed as a rite of repentance, symbolic cleansing, and conversion.[121] This understanding shaped John's baptism with its messianic anticipation,[122] which in turn was transformed through Jesus' baptism. By submitting to John's baptism, Jesus transformed it by becoming its focus.[123] On this basis, our understanding of the sacrament of baptism is based upon Jesus' own baptism where he "identified himself with sinners in obedience to the Father's will that he should make righteousness available for 'the many.'"[124] In creedal terms, Christ's vicarious baptism was the ground of one baptism for the forgiveness of sins.[125] It was a public declaration of his mission as our representative and substitute, for all the mighty acts of his life are part of the same saving event.[126] As a result,

> we look *through* the rite of baptism in water, administered according to the dominical institution in the Triune Name of God, *back* to the corporate baptism of the Church at Pentecost which stands behind the baptism of every individual, and *through* that baptism in the Spirit *back* to the one vicarious baptism with which Christ was baptised and hold it in steady focus as the primary fact which gives baptism its meaning.[127]

This helps us understand why Torrance is not concerned with the baptismal rite in and of itself but with the reality behind the rite, "the event that stands behind it and that impinges upon us through it."[128] Jesus' baptism is vicarious and substitutionary, reaching its fullness at the Cross, while the disciples' baptism is one of "repentance and renewal" that comes to its fullness at

Pentecost.[129] In the same way, Jesus Christ is baptized "actively and vicariously as Redeemer" while the Church is baptized "passively and receptively as the redeemed Community."[130]

This can be illustrated by Torrance's contrast of the New Testament term *baptisma* with the more common Greek term *baptismos*. *Baptismos* referred to a generic and repeatable rite of cleansing, while *baptisma* seems to have been coined as a unique Christian term referring to the unique saving event of Christ's baptism.[131] While "ritual and ethical acts have their proper place,"[132] the use of *baptisma* rather than *baptismos* emphasizes the saving act of God as the actual content of baptism in place of the ritual act, which is not in itself efficacious.[133] This is why it is appropriate to say that "we are baptized" for baptism is "administered *to* us in the Name of the Triune God, and our part is only to receive it, for we cannot add anything to Christ's finished work."[134] Baptism is a "realisation or actualisation in us of what has already happened to us in him."[135] This is also why baptism is "once and for all and cannot be repeated" for "repetition would be tantamount to crucifying the Son of God afresh."[136]

When we baptize in the name of the Trinity, we are reminded of the concrete event of Jesus' baptism where the distinct triune persons are clearly seen—the Son is baptized, the Father speaks, and the Spirit is manifested as a dove.[137] The early Church considered this "the public proclamation of his divine Sonship"[138] as opposed to the adoption of a human to be the Son of God. This also illustrates that "the Church has imprinted upon it through holy baptism the seal and character of the Holy Trinity, and as such it is to be honoured and revered."[139] We are not simply baptized in the name of Christ but in the name of the Father, Son, and Holy Spirit. Being baptized into the name of all three persons also signals our invitation to participate in the *koinōnia* of the Triune God. Baptism is not simply about identification with Christ's death but with the whole triune work. It is "the sacrament of initiation into that communion and of participation in the relation of the Son to the Father,"[140] so Christ's life is "a reality in which we come to participate, not just a model to which we are conformed."[141] Torrance summarizes,

> We do not baptise ourselves but are baptised in the Name of the Father and of the Son and of the Holy Spirit. On the ground of what Christ has done for us and in accordance with his promise, we are presented before God as subjects of his saving activity, and are initiated into a mutual relation between the act of the Spirit and the response of faith. Faith arises as the gift of the Spirit, while it is through faith that we may continue to receive the Spirit, and it is in the Spirit that God continues to act creatively upon us, uniting us to Christ so that his atoning reconciliation bears fruit in us, and lifting us up to share in the very life and love of God, in the communion of the Father, the Son and the Holy Spirit.[142]

This also shows that baptism is essentially corporate for it can only take place in and through the Church. It may be a new experience for individuals, but it is not a "new baptism." Baptism is a covenant both of "the one and the many,"[143] for "the Baptism of the individual, child or adult, is not a new Baptism, but an initiation into and a sharing in the One Baptism common to Christ and His Church."[144] As the Church obeys Christ's command to baptize in water, "others are added to the Church that they may share in what has already taken place for them."[145]

Since the locus of baptism is found in Christ's obedience and not in our obedience, Torrance argues that infant-baptism does not present a difficulty for "it is then seen to be the clearest form of the proclamation of the Gospel and of a Gospel which covenants us to a life of obedience to the Father."[146] Infant baptism is a sign of the way God deals with us, bringing us new life and continual growth through the Holy Spirit.[147] Torrance reads Acts 2:14–19 and the promise made to those gathered, "to you and your children," as referring to the children of those who were present that very day rather than only to future generations. Just as Gentiles were now included in the promise of access to the Father through Christ and the Spirit, so were children, regardless of age.[148]

Gathering up our discussion of trinitarian baptism, we conclude that it is a sacrament of what God has *already done* in Jesus Christ, "in whom he has bound himself to us and bound us to himself, before ever we could respond to him,"[149] but it is also a sacrament of what God *continues to do* by his Spirit in uniting us to Christ so that Christ's faithfulness and his obedience become the ground of our own faith.[150] In this way we participate in the saving benefits of union with Christ that flow from belonging to the community of God's people for

> the remission of sins, the resurrection of the dead, and the life of the world to come, belong together to the very core of that mystery, for they are the saving benefits that flow from union with Christ through one baptism and one Spirit, and are enjoyed in one Body. They are not benefits that we may have outside of Christ but only in Christ, and so they may not be experienced in separation from one another for they cohere indivisibly in him. Nor may they be enjoyed in the experience of separated individuals, but only as individuals share together in the one baptism of Christ and his Spirit. People are certainly baptised one by one, yet only in such a way that they are made members of the one Body of Christ, share in his benefits as a whole, and share in them together with all other members of Christ's Body.[151]

Finally, the eschatological element means that the full unveiling of our participation in the divine *koinōnia* awaits the *eschaton*. Our participation in the fellowship of the Trinity is both present and future—the Church's incorporation into Christ is secure, but this is a reality that is not yet fully revealed in space and time. Torrance concludes, "The really significant event in Baptism is a hidden event; it recedes from sight in the ascension of Christ and waits to be revealed fully at the last day."[152]

The Eucharist and the Continual Renewal of the Church's Participation in Christ

While baptism has to do with the completeness of the Church's incorporation into Christ, the Eucharist illuminates our understanding of the Church as a "pilgrim people," sinners awaiting the full realization of their redemption. Of the two sacraments, the Eucharist is particularly shaped by the eschatological pause between the two advents of Christ because it is given for the continual renewal of the Church.[153] If we think of baptism as signaling that we are permanently united to Christ and enabled to participate through the Spirit in the *koinōnia* of the Trinity, then the Eucharist is to be thought of as showing that we simultaneously require that union to be renewed afresh each day. This is why Torrance describes the Eucharist as "the Sacrament of our continual participation in Christ," or alternatively, the "Sacrament of Sanctification."[154] God has not left his Church alone to grieve at the foot of the Cross, or looking up into heaven after the ascension, but instead has provided the Eucharist "for the renewal and maintenance of its life and faith"[155] and as a "foretaste of the Kingdom of God."[156]

There are a number of Jewish traditions that influence the eucharistic tradition, particularly the Passover meal.[157] When reading the Gospel accounts of the Last Supper, we must also consider how the "resurrection inevitably modified the character of the meal,"[158] giving a whole new dimension to the disciples' participation in the Last Supper.[159] As the disciples stood on the other side of the Cross and reflected on Christ's suffering,[160] they realized that the Last Supper had been designed for their remembrance, as "a sacramental counterpart to His atoning death."[161] If there had been no resurrection, the meal would have remained a somber memorial, but on the basis of the resurrection, it became a celebration of God's salvific work in Jesus Christ. The Eucharist draws from Jesus' actions at the Last Supper but is distinct from it because it not only recalls the historical pre-crucifixion meal but also celebrates the resurrection. It is "a historical action in remembrance of Christ, after the fashion of the Last Supper, and a Messianic Meal with the risen Lord, joined together in one."[162]

The Eucharist is interpreted in light of the wider life and ministry of Jesus, particularly his miracles of feeding large crowds, his teaching and parables with eschatological overtones, and his provocative actions in eating with those excluded from table fellowship.[163] Torrance pays special attention to Jesus' behavior at meals, noting that "these distinctly Messianic acts of Jesus at meals, especially in the light of His teaching about the divine constraint put upon the outcasts to come in and fill the house and partake of the Great Supper, are very important."[164] The Lord's Supper was not an eschatological meal exclusively reserved for holy people but rather the celebration of the One who had come to the "poor and the outcast, the weary and the heavy laden, the publicans and sinners" in order to nourish them with eternal life.[165]

We must also consider the practice of the Church as recorded in Acts, the instructions of Paul to the Church in Corinth, the teaching of the Epistle to the Hebrews, and the allusions to the Eucharist in the Book of Revelation.[166] These all create the biblical context from which the theology and practice of the Eucharist is drawn, based upon the whole Christ-event, including "His Incarnation, obedient life, His Self-sacrifice for us on the Cross, His Self-offering to the Father in His ascension on our behalf and His eternal advocacy of us or intercession on our behalf."[167] This is why the New Testament teaching on the Eucharist becomes skewed when the emphasis falls on the rite because the rite is interpreted either as a repetition of Christ's sacrifice or is thought "to only have a moral meaning evoked by its symbolism in the response of the participants."[168] Instead, Torrance describes the Eucharist as "essentially a prayer and hymn of thanksgiving, dramatic prayer acted out in the broken bread and poured-out wine."[169] The words of Christ himself, referring to his body broken, and blood shed on behalf of humanity, shows that "the stress should be laid upon the taking and eating and drinking, that is, in communicating in the body and blood of Christ."[170] The divine action that is the real content of the Eucharist is pictured by the physical actions of the minister.[171] However, we should maintain reverence in our exploration of how the sacramental union takes place through the Eucharist for as the consecrated elements are eaten, "there is enacted a *true and substantial union*, an ontological union, between Christ and His Church."[172] The only union of a closer nature is that between the persons of the Trinity. This is why Torrance argues that the Eucharist is such an important event in the time between Christ's two advents.

> It is in the Eucharist, then, that the Church really becomes the Church, both as the ontological and eschatological reality and as the extension into history of the visible sacramental fact which is the Church's existence on earth. It is both the filling of the Church with its divine mystery, and the manifestation of that mystery within history without its ceasing to be mystery.[173]

The eucharistic presence of Christ is anticipatory and limited for although he is really present "under the veil of bread and wine," his power, majesty, and glory are not fully revealed in order to give the Church time to fulfill God's will before the second advent.[174] In the tension between the new creation and a "world which continues in estrangement and alienation,"[175] the Lord's Supper "is given to teach us that while we are complete in Christ, yet we are engaged in a battle with the contradictions and divisions that mark the empirical history of our fallen world."[176] Torrance reminds us this is why we pray, "Your kingdom come, your will be done on earth as in heaven" at every eucharistic celebration.[177]

It follows that the Eucharist is given to the Church for the time between the two advents, when it exists both in its eternal reality as the Church triumphant and within time as the Church repentant. In the Eucharist, the Church communicates in the real presence of Christ but also receives his judgment on the passing forms and fashions of the world.[178] We may understand this better by relating the Eucharist to the idea of the eschatological pause. The Eucharist is given to the Church "as a sacramental measure for operation between the ascension of Christ and His coming again; an institution that very clearly reveals that our Lord contemplated a long period of waiting before He returned, a long period in which the Church would have time to grow and develop in union and communion with Him."[179]

Having described baptism as our participation in the whole Christ-event, Torrance elsewhere describes the Eucharist as having "sacramental significance as communion . . . as continual participation and renewing in this complete event."[180] This is efficacious only as "by the act of the eternal Spirit the believing Church is given to step over the eschatological boundary, and to partake of the divine nature."[181] In the Eucharist, we see that the new creation is constantly breaking into this world to enable the Church's "continual participation and renewal in that complete event throughout all the contradictions and abstractions of fallen time."[182] It is therefore not an act of memorial, or a rite of mystical repetition; instead, through our participation in the Eucharist, we partake of Christ, participate in Him, and therefore become conformed to him[183] as the Spirit brings us to our true *telos* of participation in the *koinōnia* of the Triune God.[184]

Torrance also describes the Eucharist as "the sacrament in which we receive wholeness into our earthly tensions,"[185] which reposes on the living, growing unity of baptismal incorporation into Christ. It is not "merely a cognitive sacrament, but an effective sacrament through which Baptismal unity is ever being inserted anew into the flesh and blood of our broken and divided humanity."[186] However, while the Church is already perfected through union with Christ, it lives within fallen space and time and is therefore "unable to realize that perfection in its wholeness here and now."[187] This raises obvious difficulties for the question of ecumenical intercommunion because "it is precisely in Holy Communion that we have to do with the centrality of Christ and His atonement directed to the faith and order of the Church."[188] Torrance observes,

> The Church that partakes of Holy Communion seeks to be renewed in it as a fellowship of reconciliation, but for that very reason it must be prepared to act

> out that which it receives at the Holy Table, and to live the reconciled life refusing to allow the sinful divisions of the world to have any place in its own life. The Church that nourishes its life on earth by feeding upon the Body and Blood of Christ must live out in its own bodily existence the union and communion in which it participates in Christ. Holy Communion by its own innermost nature and by its whole intention and purpose requires the Church to work hard to eliminate its division, to resolve to seek reconciliation with all from whom it is estranged. It is just because unity is God-given that the Church cannot throw it down in the dust or allow it to be trampled upon but must cultivate it as a holy gift and of the very essence of its salvation in Christ.[189]

The Eucharist is "the Sacrament of the communion in the Body of Christ and is therefore rightly celebrated with the whole Body of the Church in heaven and earth."[190] This is why working toward intercommunion was so important to Torrance. At the Lord's Supper, the *koinōnia* of the Church is made manifest, enshrining "not only the mutual relations in love of the members of Christ's Body but a two-way relationship between the spiritual and the physical, the invisible and the visible."[191]

The Liturgy

There is one final element to be included in our discussion of the sacraments: the role of liturgy. Torrance encouraged study of the history and theology of the liturgy in order to understand how it is related to the Gospel, arguing that the liturgical patterns "point beyond themselves to participation in the divinely-provided approach of God to man in which He lifts man up to share with him in His own divine life and love."[192] Vital to our understanding of liturgy is the vicarious humanity of Christ. We must be careful not to emphasize the majesty of Christ in such a way that we lose sight of his humanity, lest we misconstrue worship as something that we can offer on our own.[193] When liturgy is detached from the humanity of Christ, there is a risk of it becoming psychologically, rather than theologically, motivated.[194] Liturgy is offered to God through union with Christ.

Torrance also highlights the close relationship between liturgy and eschatology. We recall that apocalypse has to do with the fact that the kingdom of God is already fully realized but is veiled behind the forms of sinful human history. Eschatology thus has to do with the tension between the old order and new order that we experience between the ascension and return of Christ. Although it may seem as if the Church suffers without hope or purpose, the apocalypse unveils the truth that Christ reigns over all history and over the life of the Church.[195] Paradoxically, "this unveiling can be described only in the language and forms and symbols of this present age."[196] But when we reach the point where this language fails, and we must look beyond the present age to the *eschaton*, "eschatology makes use of the language of liturgy."[197]

Continuing this analogy, Torrance states that the earthly eucharistic liturgy is an echo of the heavenly liturgy. Using a musical analogy, he describes it as "counterpoint, not the *canto firmo*."[198] Although we cannot know the perfected new song that is sung by those who have been redeemed, the Church's imperfect liturgy is taken up through Christ and the Spirit—hence the central moment of the *sursum corda*—to sacramentally anticipate the full glory of the marriage supper of the Lamb and the day when all humanity will be brought into the fellowship of the Church.[199] Torrance concludes,

> True Christian liturgy is not only open toward heaven, leaving room for the Advent presence of the risen Christ, but is open to the whole world of men, in prayer for their salvation, and to the whole of creation in prayer for its renewal.[200]

THE DOCTRINE OF THE MINISTRY

We come now to the final mark of the Church identified by Torrance, the ministry of the priesthood.

Jesus Christ, the True Priest

As with our discussion of the Word and sacraments, the doctrine of the ministry must be derived from Jesus Christ who is the eternal high priest. This is not only about the ordination of some to Word and sacrament but must also include the corporate priesthood of the whole body of Christ.

In the Old Testament, the priesthood functioned within the covenantal relationship as a divinely instituted response to God's redemptive actions. Priests mediated God's words and witnessed to his revealed will.[201] Torrance suggests that all priestly action was "essentially witness . . . God is not acted upon by means of priestly sacrifice. Priestly action rests upon God's Self-revelation in His Word and answers as cultic sign and action to the thing signified."[202]

When we come to the New Testament, we see that Jesus Christ "insists on the subordination of priesthood and priestly function to God's sovereign initiative and royal grace."[203] Because Jesus is both fully God and fully human, both aspects of priesthood have been fulfilled in him. Jesus is both priest and victim, offer and offering. God in Christ did what we could not do for ourselves and "offered on our behalf a human obedience, a human response, a human witness and a human amen, so that in Him our human answer to God in life, worship, and prayer is already completed."[204] Any offering we could make is displaced and set aside by Christ's priestly offering. In his ascension, Christ eternally offers himself before the Father through the Spirit, interceding for us and "presenting us in Himself," and as the corresponding movement from the Father toward us, Jesus is our continuing assurance of divine peace and love.[205]

There is a distinction to be made between the priesthood of the whole Church and the specific ordination of some. Torrance separates these into sacramental categories where the priesthood of the whole Church derives from baptism and the particular priesthood derives from the eucharistic fellowship.[206]

The Priesthood of the Whole Church

Baptism is the sacrament of the "general or corporate priesthood," which is the sacrament of our once and for all incorporation into Christ. "All who are baptised into Christ are baptised into the Royal Priesthood, so that it is baptismal incorporation that gives us the rock foundation for a doctrine of order."[207] Torrance is cautious about the term "priesthood of all believers" because he feels that it conveys a "ruinous individualism."[208]

The Church's participation in Christ's ministry is corporate but the relationship of Christ's ministry and the Church's ministry is not to be thought of as "the less to the greater" or the "part to the whole." As we discussed earlier, Christ's ministry is unique and the Church participates in his ministry in a way appropriate to its creatureliness.[209] The ascended Christ is king, priest, and prophet, and from his ascended heavenly session, through the Spirit "the Church is sent out into history in the name of Christ, to *serve* Him."[210] Power or "the power of order" is given to Christ and devolved to those he calls to act in his name.[211] The Church's corporate priesthood is modeled on Christ's servanthood because the only identification in ministry between Christ and the Church is identification "on the ground of His servant-ministry on the Cross."[212] The Church must take up its Cross but does not die or suffer on behalf of the world in a substitutionary capacity; rather, the Church is called to identify with the guilt of the world and to stand in solidarity with sinners in prayer, intercession, sympathy, and compassion.[213]

The Church bears witness to Christ's servanthood in its own life, modeled after the relationship of a disciple to his master, or a servant to his lord, or the apostles to Christ.[214] In the time between it does not yet wear a crown of glory but a crown of thorns like Christ's so that through its "suffering witness" on earth—as it allows itself to be "broken in its own body and to shed its own blood for Christ's sake and the Gospel's," and as it is "inwardly and outwardly shaped by His servant-obedience unto the death of the Cross," becoming "ready to be made of no reputation"—it will come to a point where "it is ready to participate in Christ's own ministry."[215] Even while it must embrace the limitations of creaturely existence, the Church is proleptically participating in Christ's eschatological exaltation.

The Ordination of Some to Word and Sacrament

Torrance also notes some believers are to be set aside for the "special ministry" of teaching, preaching, and administering the sacraments. This is a ministry that continues in faithfulness and in dependence on the apostolic tradition and can never be separated from the apostolic revelation lest it become what Torrance terms "a "fundamentalism" in regard to the ministerial institution, parallel to "fundamentalism" in regard to the letter of the Scripture."[216] This "special institutional priesthood" is a gift of the Lord to the Church in the time between, like the Eucharist, for "the corporate priesthood of the whole Church endures on into the new creation, transformed in the likeness and glory of Christ, but the corporate episcopate will pass away."[217]

Torrance is against a hierarchical understanding of the ordained priesthood for since earthly priesthood is analogical to Christ's heavenly priesthood, introducing a notion of hierarchy or monarchy into the priesthood "isolates the episcopate from the Body and makes the Body hang upon a self-perpetuating and self-sufficient institution."[218] Since Christ's priesthood is the *hypodeigma* (pattern) upon which the priesthood of the Church is to be modeled,[219] Torrance explains that

> through the Spirit there is a direct relation of participation, but in form and order the relation is indirect. The priesthood of the Church is not a transcription in the conditions of this passing age of the heavenly Priesthood of Christ. No transubstantiation or fusion between the two is involved. The relation is truly sacramental and eschatological.[220]

The priesthood is ordered by the Eucharist so that the central moment of the rite of ordination is not actually found in the laying on of hands but rather when the one being ordained celebrates the Eucharist for "it is as *Christ fills the hands* of the presbyter with the bread and wine that his ordination is properly realised and validated."[221] A doctrine of ordination must be developed in this context where the *episcopos* "presides over the fellowship of the Church by exercising the ministry of Word and Sacrament but in such a manner that he is to be accounted a steward (*oikonomos*) of the mysteries of God and an able minister (*hupēretēs*) of the Spirit."[222] Those ordained to the particular priesthood of the Church "receive their commission or orders not from the Church but for it for their commission has its sole right in the gift given by Christ and in offering the gifts given by Christ in Word and Sacrament."[223]

Torrance offers a threefold understanding of the corporate episcopate. The foundation is the priesthood of the whole body through baptism, and within this corporate priesthood, each is to minister to each other. We see this in the Eucharist where "spiritually and theologically every one is a deacon at the Lord's Table,"[224] for their members minister to each other and are dependent upon one another. The second level is a modification of the all-inclusive priesthood that serves the body in Word and Sacrament. The *charisma* of the deacon within the ordained priesthood is "to prompt and shape the response of the congregation in life and worship,"[225] while the *charisma* of the presbyter "is to minister the Word and Sacraments and to shepherd the flock."[226] Finally, the episcopate is given "not as a higher priesthood but as a special gift for the oversight of the priesthood."[227] Since the priesthood is ordered by the Eucharist, this means that a bishop has no more sacramental authority than a priest. We may thus think of the deacon as the *leitourgos* who leads the congregation in worship, the priest or presbyter as the *shepherd* who feeds the flock through Word and Sacrament, and the bishop as the *watchman* who looks after the priesthood.[228]

Roles of priestly service in the Church are for "edification and not for destruction" for those who operate in them are "nothing more than servants of Christ, and, at the same time, servants of the people in Christ."[229] Their work is not efficacious because of their effort or merit but rather because Christ has called them and equips them with his Spirit: "men are ordained only in the sense that He gives them to share in His Priesthood."[230]

Elders or Deacons?

The Reformed Church instituted the office of elder in the sixteenth century out of a conviction that laypeople not ordained to Word and Sacrament should take part in the moral and judicial government of the Church. Initially elders were elected on a yearly basis, although an Act of the General Assembly in 1582 saw elders now "appointed, admitted and commissioned for life."[231] Issues arose over terminology, with the Westminster Assembly rejecting the term "presbyter" for the elder, but this term continued in common parlance, with a division between teaching presbyters and ruling elders.[232] However, Torrance notes that there is "no clear evidence in the New Testament for what we call 'elders,' let alone the theory that there are two kinds of presbyter."[233] Presbyterians are unique in how they interpret the biblical texts that they claim justify the office of elder, so elders can only turn to Presbyterian tradition and not Scripture for understanding their calling.[234]

However, Torrance proposes that a constructive approach would be to recognize that there are biblical grounds for the kind of ministry exercised by the Presbyterian eldership. Alongside the ordination of some to Word and Sacrament, there should be "others who are 'ordained' to a complementary ministry within the congregational life and activity of God's people."[235] If ministers are charged with ministering the Word and sacraments to the people, Torrance sees elders as also associated with the Eucharist, fulfilling a corresponding movement "from the people toward God."[236] Elders are not consecrated to administer the Word and sacraments but "are to be regarded among those who have been solemnly set apart and sanctified for holy office within the corporate priesthood of the Church."[237] The nature and function of the Presbyterian eldership is similar to the biblical description of deacons, whose role was to assist in serving communicants at the Lord's Supper, to take Communion to the house churches, and to distribute goods and alms brought as an offering to the poor.[238] Torrance thus suggests that "what we call 'elders' are really 'elder-deacons'"[239] and calls the Church of Scotland to subordinate its own tradition to Scripture. Such a return to Scripture would deepen the complementary nature of the "*presbyteral* ministry of the Word and Sacrament and the *diaconal* ministry of shared obedience to Christ," embracing a fuller sense of *diakonia* as service.[240]

Women in Ministry

While it was not until 1966 that the General Assembly of the Church of Scotland allowed women to be elected as elders in full equality to men,[241] Torrance reacts strongly against the idea that women may not be ordained. He quotes Paul's argument from Galatians 3 ("There is no longer Jew or Greek, slave or free, or male or female") as the basis for his position that "in Christ there is no intrinsic reason or *theological* ground for the exclusion of women, any more than of Greeks or Gentiles, from the holy ministry, for the old divisions in the fallen world have been overcome in Christ and in his body the Church."[242]

We cannot argue that the incarnation was dependent on the masculinity of Christ but should rather consider his assumption of human nature as being on behalf of both male and female.[243] Torrance insists that the incarnation heals any inequality or division between male and female. Despite the predominantly masculine language that he uses to describe the Trinity, particularly Father and Son, Torrance argues that when we use human language to speak of the divine being, it is important to beware of any anthropomorphic tendency. Even though we use gender-associated words in theological language, "sex belongs only to creatures and may not be read back into the being of God as Father."[244] The maleness of Christ may not be used a a justification to limit ordination to men.

CONCLUSION

This chapter has examined the notes of the Church and the marks of the Church in between the two advents of Christ. While the notes of the Church have to do with its essential being, derived from the Triune God, and while the marks of the Church are temporally instituted for the Church as it exists between the two advents of Christ, each of them, and indeed order as a whole, is ultimately grounded beyond the spatiotemporal limitations of history through the hypostatic union of Christ in the triune being of God himself. Thus the Word, the sacraments, and the ministry are gifts to the Church to enable its participation in the union and communion of the Trinity in the time between Christ's ascension and *parousia*.

NOTES

1. Thomas F. Torrance, *Atonement: The Person and Work of Christ*, ed. Robert T. Walker, 381 (Downers Grove, IL: InterVarsity Academic Press, 2009).
2. Ibid., 380.
3. Torrance, Thomas F. Torrance, *The Trinitarian Faith* (Edinburgh: T&T Clark, 1993), 255.
4. Torrance, *Atonement*, 380–81.
5. Ibid., 381.
6. Torrance, *The Trinitarian Faith*, 279.
7. Torrance, *Atonement*, 383.
8. Ibid.
9. Torrance, *The Trinitarian Faith*, 280.
10. Torrance, *Atonement*, 384.
11. Torrance, *The Trinitarian Faith*, 279.
12. Torrance, *Atonement*, 382.
13. Ibid., 385.
14. Ibid.
15. Ibid., 387.
16. Torrance, *The Trinitarian Faith*, 280.
17. Ibid., 282.
18. Torrance, *Atonement*, 373.
19. Thomas F. Torrrance, "Review of *The Realm of Redemption: Studies in the Doctrine of the Nature of the Church in Contemporary Protestant Theology*. By J. Robert Nelson" *Scottish Journal of Theology* 6, no. 3 (September 1953): 322.
20. Torrance, *Atonement*, 388.
21. Torrance, *The Trinitarian Faith*, 281.
22. Ibid., 282.
23. Ibid.
24. Torrance, *Atonement*, 387.
25. Ibid., 389. The term "catholic" seems to have been a nickname given by the Gnostics to those who believed in the universal scope of Christ's redemptive work. See Thomas F. Torrance, *Theology in Reconciliation* (Eugene, OR: Wipf and Stock, 1996), 16.
26. Torrance, *The Trinitarian Faith*, 283.
27. Torrance, *Atonement*, 392.
28. Thomas F. Torrance, "Trinity Sunday Sermon on Acts 2:41–47," *Ekklesiastikos Pharos* 52 (1970): 194–95.
29. Torrance, *Atonement*, 389.
30. Torrance, *The Trinitarian Faith*, 285.
31. Ibid.
32. Thomas F. Torrance, "What Is the Church?" *Ecumenical Review* 11, no. 1 (October 1958): 17. See also Thomas F. Torrance, *Royal Priesthood* (Edinburgh: Oliver and Boyd, 1955), 23–42. Torrance explains the *intensive* growth that takes place within the body of Christ, and the *extensive* growth as the body reaches out geographically.
33. Torrance, *Theology in Reconciliation*, 21.

34. Torrance, "What Is the Church?" 17. See also Torrance, *Theology in Reconciliation*, 20–23.
35. Torrance, *Theology in Reconciliation*, 15–16.
36. Torrance, *Atonement*, 391–92.
37. Ibid., 389.
38. Torrance, *The Trinitarian Faith*, 284.
39. Torrance, *Atonement*, 391.
40. Torrance, *The Trinitarian Faith*, 283.
41. Ibid., 287.
42. Ibid.
43. Torrance, *Atonement*, 393.
44. Ibid.
45. Torrance, *The Trinitarian Faith*, 287.
46. Thomas F. Torrance, "Review of Edmund Schlink (ed.), *Evangelisches Gutachten zur Dogmatisierung der leiblichen Himmelfahrt Mariens*," *Scottish Journal of Theology* 4 (1951): 91–96.
47. Torrance, *Royal Priesthood*, 69.
48. Ibid., 70.
49. Ibid., 41.
50. Paul Molnar, *Thomas F. Torrance: Theologian of the Trinity* (Farnham, UK: Ashgate, 2009), 269.
51. Andrew Purves, *Exploring Christology and Atonement: Conversations with John McLeod Campbell, H. R. Mackintosh and T. F. Torrance* (Downers Grove, IL: InterVarsity Press, 2015), 250.
52. Torrance, *Royal Priesthood*, 63.
53. Thomas F. Torrance, *Reality and Evangelical Theology: The Realism of Christian Revelation* (Eugene, OR: Wipf and Stock, 2003), 106.
54. Torrance, *Reality and Evangelical Theology*, 109.
55. Torrance, "Review of the Realm of Redemption," 323.
56. Thomas F. Torrance, "History and Reformation," *Scottish Journal of Theology* 4 (1951): 285.
57. Thomas F. Torrance, *The School of Faith* (London: James Clarke, 1959), lxvi–xlvii.
58. Thomas F. Torrance, "The Word of God and the Response of Man," *Bijdragen: Tijdschrift voor Filosofie en Theologie* 30, no. 2 (1969): 178.
59. Torrance, *Reality and Evangelical Theology*, 120. See also Torrance's specific comments about the role of the Word in the life of the Anglican Church in Thomas F. Torrance, "The Mission of Anglicanism," in *Anglican Self-Criticism*, ed. D. M. Paton, 206–7 (London: SCM Press, 1958).
60. Torrance, *The School of Faith*, xxiii; Thomas F. Torrance, *The Christian Doctrine of God: One Being Three Persons* (Edinburgh: T&T Clark, 1996), 88–91.
61. Thomas F. Torrance, *Preaching Christ Today: The Gospel and Scientific Thinking* (Grand Rapids, MI: Eerdmans, 1994), 55.
62. Thomas F. Torrance, "Minister's Notes," November 1948 (Box 20: Beechgrove Church Publications, Thomas F. Torrance Special Collection, Princeton Theological Seminary), 2–3.
63. Torrance, *Preaching Christ Today*, 56.
64. Torrance, "Minister's Notes," November 1948, 2–3.
65. Thomas F. Torrance, "Review of *The Oracles of God: An Introduction to the Preaching of John Calvin*. By T. H. L. Parker. Lutterworth Press. 12s. 6d.," *Scottish Journal of Theology* 1, no. 2 (1948): 213.
66. Thomas F. Torrance, "Theology and the Church" (Box 22: Theology and the Church, Thomas F. Torrance Special Collection, Princeton Theological Seminary), 14.
67. Torrance, *Reality and Evangelical Theology*, 98.
68. Ibid., 99–100.
69. Ibid., 19.
70. Torrance, "Minister's Notes," 2–3.

71. Thomas F. Torrance, *When Christ Comes and Comes Again* (Eugene, OR: Wipf and Stock, 1996).

72. Ibid., 8.

73. Torrance, *Royal Priesthood*, 75.

74. Ibid., 76.

75. Thomas F. Torrance, "The Place of the Humanity of Christ in the Sacramental Life of the Church," *Church Service Society Annual* 26 (1956): 3.

76. Thomas F. Torrance, *Conflict and Agreement in the Church: The Ministry and Sacraments of the Gospel* (Eugene, OR: Wipf and Stock, 1996), 156.

77. Ibid., 161.

78. Ibid., 142. Torrance is following Calvin in his preference for *mysterium* over *res*.

79. Ibid., 141.

80. Ibid., 140.

81. Torrance, *Theology in Reconciliation*, 122–25; and Torrance, *Conflict and Agreement in the Church: The Ministry and Sacraments of the Gospel*, 137. As an example of this kind of thinking that Torrance prefers to avoid, he notes that the interplay between "Platonic dualism and Aristotelian phenomenalism" caused the eucharistic rite to be viewed as containing a hidden mystery. In its crudest form, the Roman Mass was seen as a "repeated sacrificial immolation of Christ" so that the priests had "sacerdotal control" over the eucharistic elements. The Roman Church was thus forced into "highly artificial explanations as to how the body and blood of Christ are really present through the bread and wine which are circumscribed in their place on the altar or in the mouth without being confined to them, while they are *contained* in the whole host and each part of the host and in a thousand hosts at the same time," leading to the doctrine of transubstantiation, while priests were seen as mediators who built a bridge between God and humanity through re-enacting Christ's sacrifice by presiding over the eucharistic Mass.

82. Torrance, *Conflict and Agreement in the Church: The Ministry and Sacraments of the Gospel*, 141.

83. Ibid.

84. Torrance, *Theology in Reconciliation*, 127.

85. George Hunsinger, "The Dimension of Depth: Thomas F. Torrance on the Sacraments of Baptism and the Lord's Supper," *Scottish Journal of Theology* 54, no. 2 (May 2001): 169.

86. Thomas F. Torrance, *The Mediation of Christ* (Edinburgh: T&T Clark, 1992), 97. See also Ziegler's discussion of the sacraments within the context of his argument that grace is the key to Torrance's theology in Ziegler, *Trinitarian Grace and Participation*, 209–40.

87. Hunsinger, "The Dimension of Depth," 161.

88. Thomas F. Torrance, *Space, Time and Resurrection* (London: T&T Clark, 2000), 150.

89. Thomas F. Torrance, *Conflict and Agreement in the Church: Order and Disorder* (Eugene, OR: Wipf and Stock, 1996), 18.

90. Torrance, *Royal Priesthood*, 64.

91. Torrance, *Theology in Reconciliation*, 82.

92. Torrance, *Conflict and Agreement in the Church: The Ministry and Sacraments of the Gospel*, 161.

93. Torrance, *Atonement*, 297.

94. Torrance, *Conflict and Agreement in the Church: The Ministry and Sacraments of the Gospel*, 163.

95. Thomas F. Torrance, "The Place and Function of Reason in Christian Theology," *Evangelical Quarterly* 14 (1942): 38–41.

96. Torrance, *Theology in Reconciliation*, 83.

97. Ibid., 82.

98. Torrance, *Conflict and Agreement in the Church: The Ministry and Sacraments of the Gospel*, 164.

99. Torrance, *The School of Faith*, lvi.

100. Ibid., lvi–lvii.

101. Torrance, *Conflict and Agreement in the Church: The Ministry and Sacraments of the Gospel*, 110–11.

102. Ibid., 127.
103. Torrance, "What Is the Church?" 12.
104. Ibid.
105. Torrance, *Conflict and Agreement in the Church: The Ministry and Sacraments of the Gospel*, 146.
106. Ibid., 156.
107. Torrance, *Atonement*, 410.
108. Torrance, *Conflict and Agreement in the Church: The Ministry and Sacraments of the Gospel*, 163.
109. Ibid., 162.
110. Ibid.
111. Torrance, *Atonement*, 305.
112. Ibid., 306.
113. Ibid., 279.
114. Ibid., 136.
115. Torrance, *Conflict and Agreement in the Church: Order and Disorder*, 258.
116. Torrance, *Atonement*, 307–8.
117. Torrance, *Conflict and Agreement in the Church: Order and Disorder*, 259–60. See also Torrance, *Royal Priesthood*, 84.
118. Torrance, *Royal Priesthood*, 64.
119. Torrance, *Conflict and Agreement in the Church: The Ministry and Sacraments of the Gospel*, 95. For some helpful unfolding of what Torrance means by something being sacramentally signitive, see his comments on the way in which early church art communicated theology in Thomas F. Torrance, "History and Reformation," *Scottish Journal of Theology* 4 (1951): 279–91.
120. Torrance, *Conflict and Agreement in the Church: Order and Disorder*, 122.
121. Thomas F. Torrance, "Proselyte Baptism," *New Testament Studies* 1, no. 2 (November 1954): 150–51. Torrance references circumcision, baptism, and sacrifice as the three signs required for Gentile proselytes who wished to join the people of faith. Judaic baptism unto conversion was a once-and-for-all action unlike the repeated Jewish practice of ritual cleansing.
122. Torrance, *Conflict and Agreement in the Church: The Ministry and Sacraments of the Gospel*, 108.
123. Torrance, *Atonement*, 307.
124. Torrance, *Theology in Reconciliation*, 85.
125. Torrance, *The Trinitarian Faith*, 293.
126. Torrance, *Conflict and Agreement in the Church: The Ministry and Sacraments of the Gospel*, 113.
127. Torrance, *Theology in Reconciliation*, 88.
128. Ibid., 83.
129. Torrance, *Conflict and Agreement in the Church: The Ministry and Sacraments of the Gospel*, 165.
130. Torrance, *Theology in Reconciliation*, 87.
131. Torrance, *Conflict and Agreement in the Church: The Ministry and Sacraments of the Gospel*, 110–11; Torrance, *The Trinitarian Faith*, 293–94; and Torrance, *Theology in Reconciliation*, 95–100. When dualistic tendencies infiltrate a doctrine of baptism, then *baptisma* becomes divorced from *baptismos* and significance is given to the rite rather than to the reality. This can create error in a number of different directions, which Torrance identifies on one hand as Tertullian's emphasis on the subjective aspect of faith when he lays the stress and responsibility upon the individual's actions in baptism, or at the other end of the spectrum, Augustine's view of the sacraments as containing and therefore conveying grace. This is an apt place to also note Torrance's criticism of Karl Barth over the later development of his doctrine of baptism. See W. Travis McMaken, "Actualism, Dualism, and Onto-Relations: Interrogating Criticism of Barth's Doctrine of Baptism," *Participatio* 6 (2016): 1–31.
132. Torrance, *Theology in Reconciliation*, 83.

133. Ibid., 127. We must therefore be very cautious of speaking of either faith or baptism as salvific in itself. While the New Testament does so occasionally, we may only do so "with the greatest reserve."
134. Torrance, *Theology in Reconciliation*, 88.
135. Ibid., 89.
136. Torrance, *The Trinitarian Faith*, 295.
137. Ibid., 193.
138. Torrance, *Theology in Reconciliation*, 85.
139. Torrance, *The Trinitarian Faith*, 253.
140. Torrance, *Conflict and Agreement: Ministry and Sacraments*, 123.
141. Hunsinger, "The Dimension of Depth," 162.
142. Torrance, *Theology in Reconciliation*, 103.
143. Torrance, *Conflict and Agreement in the Church: The Ministry and Sacraments of the Gospel*, 120–21.
144. Ibid., 115.
145. Ibid.
146. Ibid., 125.
147. Ibid., 129.
148. Thomas F. Torrance, "The Bible's Guidance on Baptism," *Life and Work* (September 1982): 17.
149. Torrance, *Theology in Reconciliation*, 103.
150. Ibid.
151. Torrance, *The Trinitarian Faith*, 297–98.
152. Torrance, *Conflict and Agreement in the Church: The Ministry and Sacraments of the Gospel*, 167. Readers are also directed to Torrance's involvement with the Special Commission on Baptism between 1953 and 1963. The published minutes reflect a significant investment of time from Torrance. He was not alone on the committee, but he certainly exercised his influence. See T. F. Torrance and the Special Commission on Baptism, *Interim Reports, and Reports* (General Assembly of the Church of Scotland, 1955–1963).
153. Torrance, "What Is the Church?" 12.
154. Torrance, *Space, Time and Resurrection*, 150.
155. Torrance, *Conflict and Agreement in the Church: The Ministry and Sacraments of the Gospel*, 167.
156. Thomas F. Torrance, *The Apocalypse Today* (London: James Clarke, 1960), 179.
157. Torrance, *Conflict and Agreement in the Church: The Ministry and Sacraments of the Gospel*, 134–35.
158. Ibid., 136.
159. Ibid.
160. Ibid., 170.
161. Ibid., 168.
162. Ibid., 136.
163. Ibid., 135.
164. Ibid.
165. Ibid., 169.
166. Ibid., 136–37.
167. Ibid., 144.
168. Torrance, *Theology in Reconciliation*, 108.
169. Torrance, *Conflict and Agreement in the Church: The Ministry and Sacraments of the Gospel*, 148.
170. Ibid., 185.
171. A somewhat obscure but quite illuminating article is Thomas F. Torrance, "Comments on Eucharistic Practice in the Church of Scotland Today," *Church Service Society Record* 5 (Summer 1983): 17–18.
172. Torrance, *Conflict and Agreement in the Church: The Ministry and Sacraments of the Gospel*, 188.
173. Ibid., 189.

174. Ibid., 139.
175. Torrance, *Conflict and Agreement in the Church: Order and Disorder*, 258.
176. Ibid., 259.
177. Torrance, *Conflict and Agreement in the Church: The Ministry and Sacraments of the Gospel*, 139.
178. Torrance, *Conflict and Agreement in the Church: Order and Disorder*, 52.
179. Torrance, *Conflict and Agreement in the Church: The Ministry and Sacraments of the Gospel*, 146.
180. Torrance, *Conflict and Agreement in the Church: Order and Disorder*, 217.
181. Torrance, *Conflict and Agreement in the Church: The Ministry and Sacraments of the Gospel*, 187–88.
182. Torrance, *Atonement*, 413.
183. Torrance, *Conflict and Agreement in the Church: The Ministry and Sacraments of the Gospel*, 139.
184. Torrance, *The Trinitarian Faith*, 229.
185. Torrance, *Conflict and Agreement in the Church: Order and Disorder*, 199
186. Ibid., 261.
187. Torrance, *Conflict and Agreement in the Church: The Ministry and Sacraments of the Gospel*, 172.
188. Torrance, *Conflict and Agreement in the Church: Order and Disorder*, 123.
189. Ibid., 118–19.
190. Torrance, *Conflict and Agreement in the Church: The Ministry and Sacraments of the Gospel*, 151.
191. Ibid.
192. Thomas F. Torrance, "Review of Joachim Beckmann, *Quellen zur Geschichte des Christlichen Gottesdienstes*," *Scottish Journal of Theology* 12, no. 1 (1959): 109.
193. Torrance, *Theology in Reconciliation*, 287–89.
194. See also Torrance's excellent chapter "The Mind of Christ in Worship: The Problem of Apollinarianism in the Liturgy," in *Theology in Reconciliation*, 139–214.
195. Thomas F. Torrance, "Liturgy and Apocalypse," *Church Service Society Annual* 24 (1953): 5.
196. Ibid., 7.
197. Ibid., 5.
198. Ibid., 14.
199. Ibid., 14–15.
200. Ibid., 16.
201. Torrance, *Royal Priesthood*, 3–7. Torrance notes that the tension between priest and prophet throughout the Old Testament represents an effort to separate the sacrificial priesthood from the mediation of the Word.
202. Ibid., 3.
203. Ibid., 8.
204. Ibid., 14.
205. Ibid., 15.
206. Ibid., 82.
207. Ibid., 74.
208. Ibid., 35n1.
209. Ibid., 36.
210. Ibid., 86.
211. Thomas F. Torrance, "The Eldership in the Reformed Church," *Scottish Journal of Theology* 37, no. 4 (November 1984): 511.
212. Torrance, *Royal Priesthood*, 83; Torrance, *Theology in Reconciliation*, 101; and Torrance, *The School of Faith*, lvii–lviii. Torrance illustrates different ways of thinking about the relation between Christ and the Church through the doctrine of *Totus Christus*. While the Roman Church saw this as referring to the whole *corpus mysticum*, the Church in heaven and on earth that embraces Christ, "gives birth" to him, and mediates him to each generation, the Reformed Church saw it to refer to Christ alone who refuses to be without his Church and

therefore takes it into union and communion with Him. The Roman Church viewed the Church as having an actual role in the continuing salvific work of Christ while the Reformed Church emphasized that the Church does not participate in the act of redemption.

213. Torrance, "What Is the Church?" 19.
214. Torrance, *Royal Priesthood*, 84.
215. Ibid., 86–87.
216. Thomas F. Torrance, "What Is the Reformed Church?" *Biblical Theology* 9 (1959): 61.
217. Torrance, *Royal Priesthood*, 97.
218. Ibid., 92.
219. Ibid., 95.
220. Ibid., 97.
221. Ibid., 81.
222. Ibid., 77.
223. Ibid., 41.
224. Ibid., 100.
225. Ibid., 102. In the Reformed Church, this is traditionally the role filled by an elder.
226. Ibid.
227. Ibid., 99.
228. Ibid., 102–3.
229. Ibid., 91, quoting Calvin, *Institutes*, 4.8.1.
230. Ibid., 81.
231. Torrance, "The Eldership in the Reformed Church," 503.
232. Ibid., 507–8.
233. Ibid., 508.
234. Ibid., 509.
235. Ibid. Torrance puts "ordained" in quotation marks because the traditional sense of ordination involved "the power of order," which is not part of the office of an elder. Elders are not to operate in "authority" but rather in "charity," not offering "the service of the Word" but "the service of response to the Word."
236. Ibid., 510.
237. Ibid., 514.
238. Ibid., 511–12.
239. Ibid., 512.
240. Ibid., 518. See also observations about the role of politics and bishops in Torrance, "What Is the Reformed Church?" 56–58.
241. Thomas F. Torrance, *Gospel, Church and Ministry*, ed. Jock Stein, 148 (Eugene, OR: Pickwick Publications, 2012). Published as a chapter in *Gospel, Church and Ministry*, this article that was originally published in *Touchstone Magazine* provoked a response from Patrick Reardon, who took issue with Torrance's theological and historical findings. Interestingly, given Torrance's strong Orthodox connections, Reardon wrote from an Eastern Orthodox perspective. A correspondence between the two was published in another issue. See Thomas F. Torrance, "The Ministry of Women: An Argument for the Ordination of Women," *Touchstone Magazine* (Fall 1992), www.touchstonemag.com/archives/article.php?id=05-04-005-f#at; Patrick Henry Reardon, "Women Priests: History & Theology—A Response to Thomas F. Torrance," *Touchstone Magazine* (Winter 1993), www.touchstonemag.com/archives/article.php?id=06-01-022-f#at; and Thomas F. Torrance and Patrick Henry Reardon, "On the Ordination of Women: A Correspondence between Thomas F. Torrance and Patrick Henry Reardon," *Touchstone Magazine* (Spring 1993), www.touchstonemag.com/archives/article.php?id=06-02-005.
242. Torrance, *Gospel, Church and Ministry*, 206.
243. Ibid., 208.
244. Ibid., 212.

Chapter Seven

Reconciliation, Ecumenism, and Missions

Torrance viewed his theological work as a task done in service of the Church's mission. We will draw together the various strands of his ecclesiology by considering its practical outcomes, considering his involvement in the ecumenical movement as well as his calling as an ordained minister in the Church of Scotland. Torrance's influence in spearheading an Orthodox-Reformed dialogue on the Holy Trinity with a view to reaching theological agreement also serves as an excellent illustration of the fruitfulness of his theological endeavors in ecclesiology. All of these practical examples draw on Torrance's insistence that the Church cannot be a reconciling community, nor can it proclaim the gospel of reconciliation, unless first there is reconciliation within the Church.

TORRANCE'S INVOLVEMENT IN THE ECUMENICAL MOVEMENT

During the 1950s and 1960s, Torrance participated in a bilateral dialogue between the Church of England and the Church of Scotland, attended various World Council of Church conferences, and served on the Faith and Order Commission.[1] McGrath observes that this period was the "high-water mark of the ecumenical movement" but suggests that even though Torrance attended a number of official events, his main contribution "lay not so much in his personal participation in the bilateral conversations of the time, but in his rigorous exploration of the fundamental theological principles which he considered to be the necessary basis of such dialogue."[2] Much of his theological work has been gathered in Torrance's published volumes *Theology in Recon-*

ciliation; *Theology in Reconstruction*; and the two volumes of *Conflict and Agreement in the Church*.

A Brief History of the Ecumenical Movement

Torrance identifies a number of historical issues that contributed to the lack of Church unity. The earliest disagreement was over whether Christianity should remain a Jewish sect, continuing to promote its distinction and exclusivity, or embrace inclusivity and the proclamation of the Gospel to all humanity. The Jerusalem Council (Acts 15) affirmed that the Gospel had been preached to the Jews first so although the Church reached out to the ends of the earth, it could never do so independent of its historical and spiritual Jewish foundation.[3] Unfortunately, events led to a Jewish-Gentile schism, which Torrance argues "constitutes the deepest ecumenical problem for the whole Christian Church."[4]

The second issue was a later development of this Jewish-Gentile split because detaching Christianity from its Jewish roots allowed the Church to adapt itself too easily "to the socio-legal framework of empire."[5] Not only did this involve dualistic aspects of culture, but as the Church experienced rapid growth in the bifurcated Graeco-Roman world, it could not help but become entangled with the philosophy of that world. Although the Fathers did much work to reconstruct the Christian worldview, Hellenistic philosophical dualism remained latent and eventually lead to the Western Church's hierarchical structure and its synthesis of spiritual and temporal power.[6]

On the other hand, the Reformation had an ambivalent impact upon the realized catholicity of the Church. In a positive sense, the Reformers re-embraced the centrality of the Church as the body of Christ and a community of believers, but the Reformation also gave rise to an ever-increasing number of Church splits. Protestant Churches still entrench themselves in a separatist fashion over matters of doctrine and practice.[7] The Reformation failed to overcome the "deep tension between theological catholicity and institutional universality"[8] that Torrance attributes to sociopolitical, theological, and scientific factors.[9]

This is when we come to the twentieth-century ecumenical movement. Torrance viewed the modern ecumenical movement as continuing the Reformers' intent to seek the biblical and theological renewal of the one Church.[10] In one of his clearest articles on the ecumenical movement, "We Are Learning Together," he parallels the Reformation, the Evangelical Revival, and the ecumenical movement, describing the latter as "a continuation of the other movements . . . and the blending of them together . . . a great revival not so much after the pattern of D. L. Moody or John Wesley as after the pattern of the Reformers like Luther and Calvin and Knox."[11] Although positive progress has been made in recent decades, especially with Vatican II and the release of documents such as *Lumen Gentium*,[12] there is still a long way to go to reach a "unity of the faith." Nevertheless, Torrance considered the ecumenical movement "the most distinctive feature of twentieth-century Christianity."[13] He had great hopes for the future of the ecumenical movement and was realistic about the danger of its obsolescence.[14] but believed that if the Church retained the missional outlook that was such a strong impetus in the ecumenical movement, this danger could be avoided.[15]

Torrance's Contribution to Ecumenical Theology

Torrance saw a strong connection between the catholicity of the Church and its ecumenicity. From its original Greek usage referring to "world community" or "inhabited earth," the term *oikoumene* took on a "distinctively Christian and theological slant in reference to the all-embracing people of God, the universal Church, which is the somatic correlate in space and time to the Kingdom of Christ which shall have no end."[16] Grounded in the incarnation through Christ who reconciles all things in and through himself, catholicity and ecumenicity both refer to the "inner wholeness or essential universality" of the Church "even when there is no extensive world-wide manifestation of universality," anticipating the *eschaton*.[17] Torrance consequently viewed the ecumenical movement as an imperative. Although not yet realized, it functions as a vision of what the Church will become at the *eschaton* as the universal people of God.[18]

The overall shape of Torrance's participation in the ecumenical context emerges in his response to Karl Barth's suggestion that the Amsterdam 1948 World Council of Churches Conference should adopt the method of examining theological agreements to discover what disagreements were contained and then examining those disagreements in order to reveal their concealed agreements. Barth posited that this approach would have the effect of demonstrating that "disagreements were but differences within a total unity."[19] However, after the Faith and Order Conference that Torrance attended at Lund in 1952—he served on the commission from 1952 to 1962—he noted that while this approach helped to expose the differences between Churches so that they could be talked about, the continuing comparison of different traditions actually cemented those differences in place, preventing confessional unity.

Torrance suggested that rather than engaging in simplistic comparison of differing theological traditions, "what was wanted was a theological method whereby we could think together our one faith in the one Christ, beginning with the very centre, with Christ Himself, and proceeding on this Christological basis seek to think through our differences in regard to Church, Worship and Sacrament."[20] Despite the Christocentric focus of this statement, what

Torrance is calling for is simply a return to the doctrine of God for it is only as every doctrine is thought of in relation to the others that churches "will reach back to the most ultimate truths and put to a Christian test even their doctrine of God."[21] This is consistent with Torrance's approach to the theological task. The object of inquiry—the Triune God—remains subject, dictating both the method and content of theological knowledge.

On the basis of the Church's relation to Jesus Christ, which is what Torrance refers to as its "ontological unity," it is also given a "dynamic unity," a unity in its mission.[22] The Church is sent into the world to bring the healing power of God to those who are alienated from God and estranged from each other.[23] However, while Torrance is content to speak of the Church as "called to continue the mission of Christ," he steadfastly insists that this must not be understood as "prolonging His atonement or continuing His redeeming work."[24] The Church's mission is not something that it undertakes independently because this mission flows from the redemptive work of God. It is only as God is actively present in the Church's *kerygmatic* proclamation that the witness of the Church has any divine validity. Expressing this another way, Torrance remarks that "by taking its rise from God's mighty acts in reconciling the world to himself in Christ, the Church is constituted 'a community of the reconciled,' and in being sent by Christ into the world to proclaim what God has done in him, the Church is constituted a reconciling as well as a reconciled community."[25]

Consequently, Torrance appreciates the description of the Church as a "fellowship of reconciliation" for through the Church's participation in the vertical dimension of *koinōnia* it is formed by God as "a communion of love, a fellowship of reconciliation, a community of the redeemed."[26] To belong to the Church is to participate in the *koinōnia* that derives from its eternal counterpart in the *koinōnia* of the Holy Trinity. As the Church gathers, it points to the One who has called it. Whatever terms we choose to use, whether "mission," "witness," or "proclamation," these are tasks of the whole community of reconciliation and not just of a few isolated individuals. Torrance explains this with the suggestion that the marriage relationship is an act of witness, developing a parallel between the union of man and woman in Christ and the reconciliation of God and humanity.[27]

Torrance further notes that the New Testament has much more to say about our corporate gathering and witness than our individual witness, a point creatively described when he insists that there is no such thing as a "Robinson Crusoe" Christian.[28] As Christians are joined in union to Christ, they become "a witness to the Truth in a profound sense because he is in the Truth and the Truth is in him. He has a relation to the Truth which Paul calls 'communion' (*koinōnia*) and which John calls 'abiding' (*menein*)."[29] Our witness is not ours alone but is witness offered on the basis of being reconciled to God and others. Reconciliation is much more than the restoration of a holy relation between God and human because "the eternal communion of love in God overflows through Jesus Christ into our union with God and gathers us up to dwell with God and in God."[30] The end goal of reconciliation is not only atonement but our participation in the life and light of the Father, Son, and Spirit.[31]

THE THEOLOGICAL NECESSITY OF RECONCILIATION

One of Torrance's most fundamental convictions about his calling as a theologian is that the task of theology must be shaped by the Church's existence as a reconciling community. The importance of this concept is apparent in the foreword to *Theology in Reconciliation*, which begins with the statement "Any theology which is faithful to the Church of Jesus Christ within which it takes place cannot but be a theology of reconciliation, for reconciliation belongs to the essential nature and mission of the Church in the world."[32] As a Reformed theologian, Torrance also argues that since theology is "the dialogue of the one Covenant people with God . . . a theology that is not essentially ecumenical is a contradiction in terms."[33] Furthermore, a theology that is not concerned with the proclamation of the Gospel will not be ecumenical for only through "actual engagement in the mission of the Gospel can we produce, as a *parergon*, a doctrine of the Church in which our differences are lost sight of because they are destroyed from behind by a masterful faith in the Saviour of men."[34] Theology must be directed toward equipping the Church to witness to the divine work of reconciliation and to "find ways of overcoming disunity within the Church as part of its service to reconciliation in the world, but also to come to grips with the divisive forms of thought and life in human society wherever the Church is planted and takes root."[35]

With a strong missionary heritage influencing his sense of theological vocation, Torrance was aware of the need for unity in the mission field to avoid Church politics hindering the proclamation of the Gospel. Torrance recalls that although his Presbyterian father did not agree with his mother's support for Anglican bishops, "he was by no means a narrow-minded Presbyterian for his outlook had been considerably widened on the mission field, as well as in College, through association and friendship with members of other Churches."[36] Torrance's father also attended the Conference on Evangelism in Edinburgh in 1910, which is considered the start of the modern ecumenical movement. These formative influences make it unsurprising that Torrance insists on the close relationship between ecumenism and evangelism and the need for internal reconciliation in the Church. Torrance further credits his own involvement in the ecumenical movement with exposing his "Presbyterian spectacles" and bringing his "bigoted prejudices" into the light.[37]

The Sinful State of the Church's Division

The life of the Church should point to the end of all things when we will see God face to face and should anticipate as best it can the new creation when there will be no division or discord.[38] For this reason we can understand why the current state of disunity within the body of Christ is so serious. The world does not see one Church that bears witness to the Triune God but rather multiple Churches that are separated from each other and even competing with one another. God's work of reconciliation is complete, but the Church is divided, "acting a lie" against its proclamation of God's work of reconciliation.

Since the consequence of sin is the rupture of relationship between God and humanity, the Church can only bear imperfect witness to reconciliation in its own life. Even though Christ's work of reconciliation is already complete while awaiting its full revelation in the *eschaton*, the Church is unable to live this out completely here and now. However, division comes from more than just sin and is also the result of contextual challenges. Torrance holds that the Church has laid itself open to "relativism, secularism, and syncretism"[39] in a way that has led it to exhibit the same "fragmentation and pluralism" that are characteristic of modern secular culture.[40] In part this is the consequence of the timing of the Reformation. Because Europe was dividing into clearly demarcated nation-states, the movement for reform resulted in many nationalistic and doctrinally divided churches.[41] The division of the Church also arises from the assimilation of Christianity to frameworks of thought that are incompatible with the Gospel, which is the primary cause of the majority of the theological and ecclesiological divisions that exist today. Influenced by "a world fraught with deep divisions in its social and cultural existence, profound inter-national and inter-racial cleavages, sharp political and ideological confrontations," the Church continues to wrestle with disunity.[42]

Identifying these causes of division allows us to grasp Torrance's perspective that churches do not really differ in "their essential relation to Christ" but rather in the way that the Christian faith has been expressed and communicated in "divergent cultural traditions."[43] This is why understanding the historical development of theology is vital. As Torrance notes, "certain theological conceptions, even of a basic kind, were thrown up in the process of historical development clothed in forms that were conditioned by a particular culture, but which are now in need of clarification."[44] The unfortunate reality is that Church order and structures often represent the "fossilization of traditions that have grown up by practice and procedure, and have become so hardened in self-justification that even the word of God can hardly crack them open."[45]

Torrance argues that to reject any other part of the Church because they disagree with your own perspective "not only manifests the divisive spirit of the sect, but implies both a Pelagian doctrine of sin and a doctrine of God which is unbiblical, while Catholicity itself is impugned."[46] The only way forward is, as it so often is for Torrance, one of repentant rethinking. It is "in the saving work of Christ as well as in His Person that we must look for the oneness which God bestows upon us, and which alone can solve our theological and ecclesiastical divisions, for in the heart of those divisions there is sin, and not least the sin of refusal to acknowledge it."[47] This is where Torrance applies the kataphysic method to evaluate ecumenicity. Since in Torrance's scientific approach, the doctrine of the Trinity dictates the questions that we ask about ecclesiology, then we are better able to clarify which essentials unite us and which dividing doctrines are less essential. This takes place as

> the basic and central concepts are thrust forward more and more into their commanding position, close to the heart of the faith, as manifestations of its very substance, while other concepts, important and necessary as they may be, fall towards peripheral significance, and some actually fall away altogether after having fulfilled their transitory functions.[48]

Torrance's Response to Division: The Centrality of the Trinity

Torrance's stance is that re-centralizing the Trinity would allow for the simplification of doctrine by making it clearer which concepts are part of the "inner core" of theology and which only have "temporal or peripheral significance,"[49] with the result that the Church would regain "an ecumenical significance which it has not had since the seventh century."[50] Ecumenical encounter is a gift that allows us to reflect upon how our own reading of Scripture and our theological positions have been conditioned by the Church tradition in which we have participated,[51] but it is hard for the Church as an institution to engage in this self-reflexive, critical process because "by its nature it embodies, and carries over from the past into the present, a vast development of tradition."[52] Nevertheless, doctrines must be critiqued in the light of how faithful they are to the triune revelation of God in the light of the shared ecumenical foundation that Orthodox, Roman Catholic, and Protestant churches all have in common in the Apostles' and Nicene Creed.[53]

Torrance offers explicit suggestions to each of the three major branches of the Church. He suggests that the Orthodox should resist taking an immovable stance within the Athanasian-Cappadocian tradition but instead should embrace the Athanasian-Cyrilline axis, which would allow healing between the autocephalous Orthodox divisions. Roman Catholics should embrace the Greek patristic understanding of the doctrine of the Trinity and Christ's vicarious humanity, which would allow them to overcome the difficulties of dualism in the life of the Church.[54] Protestants should look beyond the pluralism of society and the fragmentation that this has imported into the Church to the wholeness of the Church that is grounded in Christ, thus escaping cultural relativism and a dualistic Christology. Finally, each of these churches must return to the central doctrine of the Trinity as the only true ground for unity among the body of Christ.[55]

The potential danger for the ecumenical movement is that we focus so much on the historical shape of the Church and the contemporary challenges of division that we forget that while the Church exists within the finite and concrete conditions of space and time, it is sustained by the Triune God who exists outside space and time. This is the danger that has faced the modern ecumenical movement since its inception.[56] Looking to the Trinity first safeguards ecumenical dialogue from wrongly veering into anthropocentric concerns while keeping the "obligation of unity"[57] before us. Churches must listen to each other and "think out every doctrine into every other doctrine" so that they may be enabled to "get behind the secondary questions which are the immediate causes of our divisions."[58] This issues a distinct challenge to the body of Christ to free itself from having adopted so many of the "forms and fashions" of the world that it is "too committed to the world and too compromised with it to be able to deliver the revolutionary Word of the Gospel with conviction and power."[59] Even though the Church is divided, there is a fullness of reconciliation that will be manifest at the *eschaton*. The full unity of the Church is conditioned by the *parousia*; unity will not be reached within fallen time, but it must be our vision nonetheless.

Eucharistic Thinking

This trinitarian basis for unity is further developed by Torrance in his encouragement for the Church to embrace a form of ecumenism he calls "eucharistic thinking." Because sacramental thinking "entails an entirely different conception of validity from worldly or historical validity,"[60] eucharistic thinking is "not that primarily in which we offer of our own traditions and efforts toward a common pool, but an ever-new and thankful *receiving together* of the Body of Christ."[61] While Torrance does consider the Church's oneness in terms of its baptismal unity,[62] he develops a much fuller argument for the unity of the Church deriving from the nature of the Eucharist. Just as each individual receives a fragment of one loaf, so "in the receiving of this one sacrifice and its unity into our multiplicity healing is given for our divisions."[63] Just as fragments of a loaf that were originally one, no single historical tradition may claim that it has correctly received and interpreted the whole of divine revelation. No temporal structure or form may be said to belong to the *esse* of the Church for there is no warrant for insisting that these will endure into the new creation.[64] The Church is both under judgment and risen with Jesus Christ—it can only live this out by refusing to conform to the patterns of this world and constantly being renewed by the resurrection in the power of the Spirit.[65]

Torrance also offers repeated comment on the need for healing the schism between Jew and Gentile, observing that "Jews and Christians must come together in the Messiah, if the world is to be reconciled" but acknowledging that we cannot encourage reconciliation between Jew and Gentile if all the Jews see is the rivalry between different Christian groups.[66] Torrance warns against trying to change Jewish people into Gentile Christians, instead acknowledging that we must not impose Western religious culture on their faith.[67] Torrance also suggests that just as God was present during the Holocaust, it is in this way that Christians must explain the Cross to the Jewish people for "unless they can relate God to their suffering, there will be no way for Jews to find reconciliation with the Arabs or other peoples."[68]

Two further brief comments from Torrance are worth mentioning here. First, since the Church tends not to take Paul's teaching about the importance of the root (Israel) over the branches (the Church) seriously, we deny that "Jerusalem"—by which Torrance means Israel—is the true center of the Church. It is on this basis that Torrance argues that the issue of geographical primacy for the Church—a historical sticking point for relationships between Roman Catholics and Orthodox—is "a false problem that arises only when the Church loses its real centre in its relation to Israel."[69] Second, if Protestant and Orthodox churches were to think out more deeply the doctrine of the Virgin Mary—recognizing that Mary is the chosen representative of Israel who bears the Messiah—and should do so without detaching her from her Jewish context, then we might find a way forward that avoids furthering the Jewish-Christian schism and also avoids Roman Catholic dogmas such as Mary's assumption into heaven.[70]

TORRANCE'S INVOLVEMENT IN THE CHURCH OF SCOTLAND

We now move from Torrance's theology of reconciliation as it informs his ecumenical involvement to Torrance's service as an ordained minister. Torrance is clearly a Reformed theologian, although Habets notes that he brings his own "catholic, broad and generous" interpretation to the Reformed tradition.[71] Torrance served as an ordained minister in the Church of Scotland throughout his life and retained a special interest in the history of Scottish theology.[72] He saw the need for critical reinterpretation of the history of his own denomination, repeatedly emphasizing that because the Reformed Church is only subject to the Word and not to its own tradition, it must avoid exalting "the Reformed tradition to a place of irreformability like that of Roman tradition."[73] He often exhorts the Reformed church to be ever-reforming. It is not surprising that Torrance, as an academic theologian, also issued challenges throughout his career for an increase in theological faithfulness to the Church of Scotland, which is in keeping with our observations about the tenor of his involvement in the ecumenical movement.[74]

Moderator of the Church of Scotland

McGrath thinks it "perhaps inevitable" that Torrance became Moderator of the Church of Scotland in 1976–1977. We noted in our introductory material the conversation between Hugh Ross Mackintosh and Robert Wilder in which Mackintosh predicted that one day Torrance would be Moderator of the Church of Scotland. Despite the one-year limit of the position, which is intended to limit the influence of any one individual, Torrance did what he could to inject serious theological reflection into the life and thought of the Church.[75] During his moderatorship, Torrance made a particular point of visiting the four Scottish universities that trained clergy for ordained ministry in the Church of Scotland as well as undertaking a number of international trips, including a visit to the Ecumenical Patriarch of the Orthodox Church to initiate the theological dialogue between Orthodox and Reformed that will be explored in the final section of this chapter.

To help us understand the approach of Torrance to this appointment, we may examine some of the sermons that he delivered in his capacity as moderator. One example is his inaugural address in 1976. Responding to the rise of what he described as "militant 'theologies of liberation' which have assimilated the prophetic passion of Jewish messianism, and the revolutionary nature and impetus of the Christian message, to Marxist theology," Torrance reflected that this combination of Christianity and Marxism had no real future for it would not correspond to humanity's demands for an open, free society or their deep spiritual hunger.[76] Noting that the Church was in a "deep spiritual crisis," Torrance argued against simply changing the outward forms of Church life, suggesting that "tinkering about with the institutional structures of the Kirk will only affect superficial patterns of religious behaviour."[77] He insisted that the only way to genuinely answer the human needs that the Church was not currently meeting was to place the staggering reality of the incarnation at the center of ecclesial life once more.[78]

In another example, preaching to the 1977 general assembly at the end of his time as moderator with Colossians 1:13 as his text, Torrance reflected that he had "tried to call the Church and Nation to put Christ and his Gospel of reconciliation in the centre, so that from that centre we may take our bearings and shape the course of our mission in his Kingdom."[79] This sermon integrated many of his key themes, including the vicarious humanity and divine identity of Christ and the bond between Christ and the Church where the Church is "inwardly and organically so bound up with Christ that the Church is his expression in our world of time and history."[80] Torrance spoke forthrightly to his Presbyterian colleagues, asking,

> Are we ready to set Christ and his Gospel so entirely in the centre of everything in the Kirk, that all other questions such as differences between the Church of Scotland and the Methodist Church, or between Presbyterians and Episcopalians, are regarded as subordinate and peripheral, in comparison? Or sharper still: Is the Church of Scotland more concerned with the transcendent glory of Christ or with the glory of the national Kirk? Is the Kirk to be primarily an expression of Scottish nature and culture, or Presbyterian tradition, or is it truly and above all *the expression of Jesus Christ as his Body*?[81]

This sermon expresses a theme consistent in Torrance's wider body of work; he called on all churches, including his own, to place Christ at the center and to subordinate all things to Christ. No church, including the Church of Scotland, should allow its national or doctrinal identity to have primacy over the proclamation of the Gospel.[82]

The "Urgent Call to the Kirk"

Along with his focus on reconciliation between churches, Torrance also emphasized that the local life of the Church should stress the centrality of Christ. This is particularly evident in a document that Torrance coauthored titled the "Urgent Call to the Kirk," which was prompted by the discouraging situation of decline in the Church of Scotland as identified by a widespread drop in attendance. The "Urgent Call" challenged the current state of the Church, arguing that among other things that

> erosion of fundamental belief has sapped [the Church's] inner confidence, discarding of great Christian convictions has bereft it of vision and curtailed its mission, detachment of preaching from the control of biblical Revelation has undermined its authority as the Church of Christ, neglecting in teaching the truth of the Gospel has allowed the general membership to become seriously ignorant of the Christian Faith.[83]

Although the document had four primary signatories, the tone and language are distinctively Torrancian. Recognizing this, R. D. Kernohan, editor of the Scottish Presbyterian monthly *Life and Work*, commented that "it read like a censored theological dispatch from Professor Tom Torrance. The other three . . . seemed to have toned it down without changing the style."[84] The document called "upon the Kirk to commit itself afresh to Jesus Christ and his Gospel and to carry out an evangelical rebuilding of its faith, life and mission, "[85] emphasizing relational evangelism rather than institutional schemes for growth. Every congregation needed to prioritize missions and evangelism. The vision was for each presbytery to develop missional strategies appropriate to its own context so that mission would become a regular and vital part of each parish's activity. Alongside this, the writers of the "Urgent Call" hoped that there would be a recommitment to the holy calling of ministry along with an increased commitment to regular pastoral visitation, not just for the sick but for pastoral evangelism.[86] "Urgent Call" concluded,

> This call for a repentant return of the Church of Scotland to Christ clothed with his Gospel is unashamedly evangelical and theological, for the grave crisis facing the Church is essentially spiritual. Only through spiritual and evangelical renewal will the Church of Scotland meet the compelling claims of Christ upon it to carry the Gospel to the millions in our own land who have not been gathered into the fold of Christ but who are desperately hungry for the bread of life.[87]

The "Urgent Call to the Kirk" was presented to the 1983 general assembly, who commended it to the consideration of local presbyteries.[88] While the moderator that year, Dr. J. Fraser McLuskey, appreciated the "note of realism" sounded by the "Urgent Call,"[89] it proved to be a polemic document as evident in some of the correspondence that Torrance subsequently received. Although Torrance sent out a letter to those who had signed the "Urgent Call" early on, stating that he considered its reception at the general assembly a success and urging everyone to do all they could to keep things moving in their own churches and presbyteries, not everyone felt the same way. One minister's response is fairly typical. Writing directly to Torrance, he said, "I had hoped that the 'Call' would bring out some sense of vision and purpose; instead I found only an evasion of responsibility and a trivialising of issues . . . There was no sense of a Church girding itself for mission, only a hope that we can keep the show going for a bit longer."[90] Another minister, reporting on a meeting to discuss the "Urgent Call" at the local level, wrote, "All present were very happy with the sentiments of the Call itself, and would not wish in any way to be disassociated from it. But there are some misgivings regarding the practical course of action which might flow from it."[91]

While some individuals were wholeheartedly supportive, others were wary despite agreeing with the concerns expressed about the state of the Church of Scotland. Some took umbrage with the presumption of declaring that the Church of Scotland was in such dire straits, noting that there was no affirmation of those parishes that were doing a good job and not experiencing decline, while others welcomed the "Urgent Call" and its discussion. Still others considered the challenge to return to the Gospel simplistic and argued that the "Urgent Call" needed to have a stronger note of social justice, while others disliked the statement that there had been "an erosion of fundamental belief," arguing that this statement had the potential to introduce still more division into the Church. There was also frustration among those who had been involved in previous calls for renewal who felt that their message and methods had not been taken seriously.

Life and Work is a less biased and therefore helpful tool in evaluating the response of the wider Church of Scotland to the "Urgent Call." Two issues (November 1983 and to a lesser extent March 1984) dedicated a significant amount of print to a response. The editorial comment of the November 1983 issue suggested that for the Church of Scotland, it was "not a time for recrimination but for general and constructive repentance. There is no need to hunt down heretics but a very real need for leadership and mutual encouragement in the faith"[92]—a comment that Torrance endorsed in his March 1984 article "The Tide has Turned."[93] However, although Torrance had commented ten months after the 1983 general assembly that he was encouraged by the progress that had taken place, the "Urgent Call" failed to gain significant long-term traction, as suggested by Torrance's comment five years later that the "Urgent Call" had been "shrugged off" by most committees and presbyteries.[94] The "Urgent Call" is an example of Torrance's commitment to a strong theological underpinning for local Church life and clearly reveals "commitment to the spiritual renewal of the Church and his passion for Christ,"[95] but it was unsuccessful in provoking widespread change within the Church of Scotland.

Life and Work: The Crises of the Church

Another example of Torrance's involvement in the Church of Scotland is seen in his articles intended for laypeople. An excellent exemplar of Torrance's dismissal of the Church's search for relevance, and his disgust at the way the diminished centrality of Christ had affected the life of the Church, can be found in a series of three articles published in *Life and Work* in 1990. The series was titled "The Real Crises." In the first article, "The Kirk's Crisis of Faith," Torrance argues that because of the Church's obsession with being relevant, little attention is paid to the actual content of the Gospel, with Christianity "reduced to being not much more than the sentimental religious froth of a popular socialism."[96] Torrance repeats, as he has elsewhere, that at the Council of Nicea and during the Reformation, it was the deity of Christ that was at stake, but he adds in this article that this is the same struggle that the Church is confronted with today, for "the more the distinctive doctrines of divine revelation are set aside in the obsession of the Church to be socially relevant, the more the Church disappears into secular society."[97]

In his second article, "The Crisis of Morality," Torrance suggests that the moral decline of society is caused by the same issue of Christ's displacement and through a "strange hesitation to apply the truths of Christ and his Gospel directly to the moral and social problems of the age."[98] The Church has divorced moral law from theological truth, with the result that morality is no longer grounded in creation and redemption but in the ethic of human well-being. This has led to a prioritization of utilitarian values, with the result that "the institutional Church keeps coming between the people and Jesus Christ"[99] because rather than the Gospel being trusted as a transformer of human culture and society, the Church has become enslaved to political ideals.

Although the first two articles refer primarily to the doctrine of the incarnation, Torrance draws out the significance of the doctrine of the Trinity for ecclesiology in his third article, "The Crisis of Community." Arguing on the basis of the first two articles that the Church must take radical steps to regain its distinctiveness, he presents the need to recognize the significant divergence between a political society that relies on legislative compulsion and a Christian community that is formed through participating in the divine *koinōnia* of the Holy Trinity. It is not that the Church should be thought of as standing "against" the world but rather that in the radical call of Jesus Christ to take up our crosses and follow him, conformity to the Risen One is likely to result in conflict with the status quo.

Torrance further points out that "any decentralising of the doctrines of the Incarnation and the Trinity in the life and faith of the Church leads to the crisis of community and the depersonalisation of society that we experience today."[100] He then goes on to tie community and mission together:

> The crisis of community is a crisis of mission. The Church is not sent into the world to exist as a comfortable community, but as a community embodying the mission of God's reconciling love to all mankind. Since Jesus Christ is the propitiation not for our sins only but for the sins of the whole world, missionary activity that proclaims Christ as the one Mediator between God and man, does not arise from any arrogance in the Church . . . The very existence of the Christian community and its missionary proclamation of Christ as the Saviour of the world belong inseparably together. Where there is no mission, there is no community, for the community arises and continues to spread in being sent by Christ to carry the Gospel into the uttermost parts of the earth in evangelical transformation of human life and society. Where there is no engagement in that mission the community severs itself from the very reason and purpose for its existence, and plunges into crisis.[101]

Elsewhere, Torrance utilizes the same comparison of society and community, suggesting that the Church "is the medium by which society is transmuted into community. Indeed, the Church as such is precisely the new community in the heart of our human society."[102] Such a transformation is inherently disruptive for "the Church, if it really undertakes to become what it is intended to be, a new community, will inevitably disrupt the society in which it lives."[103] Torrance suggests that the Church is both like salt, as a preservative, and like bread yeast, bringing change. The Church is simultaneously the most radical and the most conservative force in society. It is only as the Church disregards the status quo, and the forms and fashions of the world, that the Gospel will be preached and the Church truly live out its calling as a new community.[104] Once again the centrality of the Church's ontological relation to Christ is vital. Transformation is not only for the people of God but rather "society may at last be transmuted into a community of love" because of the pervasive, redemptive work of God.[105]

Frustration with Church Structures

Torrance was also frustrated with the way in which the centralization of Church administration had impeded local parishes and presbyteries. Torrance viewed the general assembly and its committees as a top-heavy structure, suggesting that responsibility for evangelism and finances in particular should be handed back to local presbyteries (a proposal also made in the "Urgent Call to the Kirk").[106] He published an article titled "A Right-About Turn for the Kirk" in Scotland that directly criticized the general assembly and also published a version in the United States in which he refrained from commenting on specific national features and widened the scope of his criticism, calling for the "devolution of responsibility from central administration to life at the parish and presbytery level."[107]

Chief among his concerns was the Church of Scotland's process of Union and Readjustment, that is, uniting some parishes and closing others. Torrance felt that while some adjustment was necessary to respond to the population shifts that had taken place, the closure of parishes had far exceeded any expansion. He commented quite harshly in 1981, "It is now abundantly clear that Union and Readjustment has been strangling the Kirk . . . It is probably to U. and R. alone that one could put down the sad decline in membership."[108]

TORRANCE'S INVOLVEMENT IN THE ORTHODOX-REFORMED DIALOGUE

After retirement in 1979, Torrance continued to be very active in ministry. McGrath suggests that Torrance's "most important ecumenical activity" took place after his retirement from New College in 1979. It was then that the dialogue between the Orthodox Church and the World Alliance of Reformed Churches on the Holy Trinity took place.[109] This was a theological dialogue at the inter-Church level that illustrates for us Torrance's hope that the doctrine of the Trinity could lead to genuine ecumenical accord.

The bilateral dialogue was initiated on the basis of personal relationships and a "deep theological rapport" that Torrance had established through his prior involvement with Orthodox theologians in ecumenical contexts, particularly Archbishop Methodius of Aksum.[110] Formal contact between the Patriarchate of Alexandria and the Church of Scotland began in 1970, with Torrance being ordained a lay Protopresbyter of the Greek Orthodox Church in 1973.[111] The dialogue was first proposed in 1977, and it concluded in 1992 with a statement summarizing the accord that a group of Orthodox and Reformed theologians had reached on the doctrine of the Holy Trinity. The papers from the dialogue were edited by Torrance and published as *Theological Dialogue between Orthodox and Reformed Churches*.[112]

Torrance's appreciation for the Orthodox Church is obvious.[113] Orthodox theologian Matthew Baker observes that Torrance is one of "a very small category of Western theologians of his time engaged in a deep and significant dialogue not only with the ancient Fathers of the East, but likewise with contemporary Orthodox theologians."[114] While Orthodox-Reformed dialogue had existed since the 1960s, Torrance felt strongly that this dialogue had a "rather different objective" from these other conversations.[115] When he made his first international visit as moderator to the Middle East in 1977, Torrance carried with him a letter written by Professor Jan M. Lochman on behalf of the World Alliance of Reformed Churches formally suggesting that exploration begin toward establishing a theological dialogue between the Orthodox Church and the World Alliance of Reformed Churches.[116] This letter was presented to His Holiness Dimitrios I, the Ecumenical Patriarch, and discussed by Torrance with other heads of the Greek Orthodox Church during his trip, who received the suggestion positively.[117] The proposal was for "formal theological consultations," recognising the shared "'theological axis' of Athanasian/Cyrilline theology" that had influenced both Greek Orthodox and Reformed theological history.[118] This was an outworking of Torrance's view that the Church must undertake historical studies and ecumenical studies together in order to fully understand the Church's historical development.[119]

Theologians from both churches would enter into "fruitful exchange" since a dialogue that began with the Holy Trinity would be significant "for the whole Church Catholic and Evangelical in East and West."[120] This would allow the dialogue to "cut behind" the disagreements of East and West and clear the ground for fuller agreement on other doctrinal issues.

The dialogue began with a five-day consultation in July 1979 in Istanbul that focused on "method and the underlying assumptions that gave rise to divergence in doctrinal formulation and in the structure of the ministry."[121] The only paper published from this initial gathering was Torrance's "Memoranda on Orthodox/Reformed Relations,"[122] in which he acknowledges the existence of "contextual division" between the Orthodox and Reformed Churches. Torrance observes that while the Reformed Churches had arisen "through the exigencies of history and changing cultures,"[123] developing in a "different cultural and historical milieu"[124] than the Orthodox Churches, both were nonetheless committed to the unity of the Church.

Torrance also points out that while the Reformed Churches had been influenced by the Western-Augustinian tradition in some areas, including the doctrine of grace, sacramentology, and understanding of the Church, it had followed Calvin's Eastern orientation in the doctrines of the Trinity, Christology, soteriology, and eschatology.[125] Torrance uses this to highlight that the Reformed Church shares the Orthodox conviction that "sharing in the worship of the Father, which Christ himself is, is the heart of the Church's Eucharistic worship and communion, and that it is from that centre that the life and activity of the Church on earth are nourished and directed."[126] While the Reformed understanding of apostolic faith and apostolic practice had resulted in significant differences in "ethos, practice and order" from the Orthodox Church, it was clear that there was a deep agreement on the necessity of the Holy Trinity for shaping all doctrine.

Torrance proposed that discussion should begin with the Trinity, followed by the doctrines of the Son and the Spirit and then the Eucharist.[127] He felt that the Athanasian-Cyrilline approach was the best one to take, particularly given its deep grasp of the vicarious humanity of Christ, which was vital to Torrance's own approach. Torrance hoped that this would allow the dialogue to "cut behind the difference between East and West over the '*Filioque*' clause,"[128] although Dragas notes that the *filioque* issue was never actually discussed in the dialogue.[129] Torrance notes that rather than the Antiochene teaching, which tended to be ebionite, or the docetic tendencies of Alexandrian theology, this "middle stream" of Christology ran from Irenaeus to Athanasius and to Cyril and became the foundation for orthodox Christology.[130] By drawing on this middle stream, the dialogue managed to avoid the potential dualisms of the Antiochene/Alexandrian schools and Chalcedonian/non-Chalcedonian theology.[131]

This links to Torrance's approach to the ecumenical movement and his call for a theology of reconciliation. He felt that reaching agreement in foundational doctrines would cause the emergence of "a common basis for agreement on the questions of authority in the Church and in the formulation and development of Christian doctrine," an agreement that would be significant not only to Orthodox and Reformed but also for the wider division between the Eastern and Western Churches and the Roman Catholic and Evangelical Churches.[132] Torrance believed that the denominational particularity of the Orthodox-Reformed dialogue would result in something of much wider ecumenical significance, although this did not happen.

The second consultation took place in February 1981 in Geneva, recognizing that the conversation was still "of an interim preparatory nature."[133] Participants from both sides emphasized the centrality of the Triune God, stating that while agreement could be reached on issues such as communion in the Church, the process must begin "not from the doctrine of the Church and the authority of its ministry but from a centre deep in the doctrine of the Holy Trinity." Only when agreement was reached there could the implications for other doctrines be thought out.[134] On this basis, the third consultation in Chambésy in March 1983 focused on the "trinitarian foundation and character of the Faith and of Authority in the Church," centered around the Nicene-Constantinopolitan Creed,[135] for which Torrance prepared a similarly named paper in which he explored the idea of ecclesial authority from a trinitarian perspective, focusing on Church Fathers such as Athanasius, Cyril, and Nazianzen.[136] It was agreed during this final discussion that "a deep consensus among the participants had emerged" on the basis of which Torrance prepared a summary draft that would be used to orient the anticipated official dialogue of the future.[137] This was published as the chapter "Agreed Understanding of the Theological Development and Eventual Direction of Orthodox/Reformed Conversations Leading to Dialogue."[138]

At the end of these three consultations, each delegation returned to their governing body to seek permission to move forward, the Greek Orthodox to the fourteen autocephalous Orthodox Churches,[139] and the Reformed to the World Association of Reformed Churches, representing 143 autonomous denominations comprised of some 60 million Church members.[140] The first three consultations were viewed as preparatory consultations, while the second series of dialogues was of a more formal nature since it was officially approved and attended by mandated representatives.

The official theme for the fourth, fifth, and sixth consultations was "The Doctrine of the Holy Trinity on the Basis of the Niceno-Constantinopolitan Creed."[141] The first official consultation took place at Leuenberg, Switzerland, March 7–11, 1988. Both sides presented historical overviews of their own Church traditions, although the main body of discussion focused on differences in the understanding of the Trinity as expressed in the Nicene-Constantinopolitan Creed. Ecclesiological considerations were mentioned as necessary, but it was decided that these would be the subject of a later conversation. It also seems that there was some concern from the Orthodox about the Reformed using the dialogue as an opportunity for doctrinal proselytizing because Torrance notes that there was common agreement that this should not take place![142] Torrance presented a paper on the Triunity of God in which he systematically traced the development of thought from Athanasius to Basil, the Gregories and Didymus, Epiphanius and the Council of Constantinople and then evaluated their influence on the development of the doctrine of the Trinity within the Church's theology and worship.[143]

On the basis of the agreement reached in Switzerland, Dragas and Torrance drafted a "Working Document on the Holy Trinity,"[144] which was presented to the delegates of the next consultation at the Moscow Patriarchate in October 1990. The process of writing this document was described as "interesting" by Dragas, who felt that Torrance's tendency was to allow his perspective to dominate, thus watering down the Orthodox position. In particular, Dragas identified the way that Torrance pitted the "Athanasian-Cyrilline approach" against the "Orthodox-Cappadocian deviation" as an issue, given that the Orthodox do not interpret the Fathers in this way.[145] Along with papers on the biblical and patristic doctrine of the Trinity and consideration of the Trinity in the Church's worship, the "Working Paper on the Holy Trinity" was revised and affirmed as "Agreed Statement on the Holy Trinity." It needed some minor linguistic adaptations, which were undertaken by a smaller group of delegates at Chambésy, Geneva, in 1991, however, this brought to light further issues needing clarification so that the final form of the statement was reached at the third official consultation near Zurich in March 1992.

The statement should be read in tandem with two other documents. The first of these is "Historical Agreement by Reformed and Orthodox on the Doctrine of the Holy Trinity,"[146] in which Torrance identifies the most significant features of the consensus. These include the insistence that "one being, three persons" must be understood in a personal way; the agreement that the monarchy refers to the whole Godhead so that there is no subordination in the Trinity and that this then shapes the understanding that the Spirit proceeds from the shared *ousia* of Father, Son, and Spirit; and finally, the offering of an ecumenical approach that does not move from the one to the three (as in the West) or from the three to the one (as in the East).

The second supporting document is titled "Significant Features: A Common Reflection on the Agreed Statement."[147] This document identifies three particular aspects of the statement as important. First, the limitations of human language for describing divine realities are acknowledged. The need to think in a spiritual way when considering spiritual realities is stressed, particularly when using terms like *ousia* and *hypostasis* for they were not to be thought of in their ordinary sense but only as they pointed beyond themselves to the content of divine revelation.[148] Second is the understanding of the monarchy that the *Agreed Statement* proposes, which understands monarchy as belonging to the whole Godhead and the Being of the Father rather than the Person of the Father. This is particularly important regarding the schism over the *filioque* given that "the doctrine of the Monarchy that is not limited to one Person, and the doctrine of the *perichoresis* of the three Divine Persons, or their reciprocal containing of one another, when taken together, may help towards a fuller understanding of the Mission of the Holy Spirit from the Father and gift of the Holy Spirit by the Son."[149] This approach avoids any sense that the Spirit proceeds from two *archai*, or causes, which was what the Eastern Church had felt the need to avoid historically. The third point related to this second point, which was the anticipated ecumenical significance of the "Agreed Statement" and which acknowledged that the statement followed neither Latin theology, which moves from the Oneness of God to the three persons, nor Greek theology, which moves from the three persons to the oneness of God, but rather "cuts across mistaken polarised views" as a statement "on the Triunity of God as Trinity in Unity and Unity in Trinity."[150]

Also helpful for understanding Torrance's own perspective on the "Agreed Statement" is "Commentary on the Agreed Statement." Dragas notes that this commentary "was pretty much all a work of Tom but was respectfully received by the full commission,"[151] which may be why it was not included in *Theological Dialogue between Orthodox and Reformed Churches* but published in another of Torrance's books, *Trinitarian Perspectives.*[152] In this final commentary, Torrance highlights certain aspects of the "Agreed Statement" that largely line up with his own perspective, including God's self-revelation as triune; the way in which theological terms must be used; the mutuality of the eternal relations between the persons; the way in which we must think about the order of the persons; the mutual indwelling and shared monarchy of the three persons; and the way in which we are to understand "one being" and "three persons" to bear upon each other.

It is difficult to fully evaluate the contemporary significance of this dialogue and the official statements released. However, it is notable that contemporary Orthodox scholars like Matthew Baker consider other Torrancian works, such as *Divine Meaning*, as having more significance for Orthodox theologians than the Reformed-Orthodox dialogue. This judgment is on the basis that *Agreed Statement on the Holy Trinity* "has received neither official acceptance by the holy synods of the autocephalous Orthodox Churches nor a wide reception by Orthodox theologians"[153] despite being jointly issued by the representative Orthodox and Reformed theologians who took part in the dialogue.

While, as Baker notes, the Reformed-Orthodox dialogue has not had much lasting impact, it is an area of Torrance's theological output that still offers significant potential for the Church. Dragas's comment that "it was a general and balanced agreement on initial points, which was not accepted as if it clarified all problems or questions" helps us to contextualize the significance of this particular dialogue. The statements released should not be regarded as all-encompassing documents but as offering a foundation from which further dialogue may proceed.

CONCLUSION

This chapter has sought to fill out Torrance's view that ecumenism and evangelism are intertwined, exploring his theological stance on the ecumenical movement and how this is related to his view of the Church's mission. It has done so by further exploring the notion of the Church as those reconciled to Christ who then participate in Christ's work of reconciliation, which in turn requires reconciliation within the body of Christ. We have also paid particular attention to Torrance's involvement in the ecumenical movement as well as his call for reform within the Church of Scotland. While the doctrine of the Holy Trinity is not always directly in view, this chapter has drawn on the theological work of the previous chapters to draw out both the explicit and implicit implications of the doctrine of the Trinity within Torrance's ecclesiology when it is applied.

NOTES

1. Torrance also offered reflection on other bilateral dialogues. For examples, see Thomas F. Torrance, "Anglican-Methodist Reconciliation," *British Weekly*, February 28, 1963.
2. Alister McGrath, *Christian Theology: An Introduction*, 5th ed. (Oxford: Wiley-Blackwell, 2011), 94–95.
3. Thomas F. Torrance, *Theology in Reconciliation* (Eugene, OR: Wipf and Stock, 1996), 24–27.
4. Ibid., 27.
5. Ibid.
6. Ibid., 27–34.
7. Ibid., 39.
8. Ibid., 41.
9. Ibid., 42–44.
10. Ibid., 41.
11. Thomas F. Torrance, "We Are Learning Together: The Ecumenical Movement, Another Great Movement of the Gospel," *Life and Work* (August 1954): 197.
12. Torrance, *Theology in Reconciliation*, 39, 58–67. Torrance views *Lumen Gentium* as moving closer to a position that is more like his own ecclesiology.
13. Ibid., 15.
14. Ibid., 70–81.
15. Thomas F. Torrance, *Conflict and Agreement in the Church: Order and Disorder* (Eugene, OR: Wipf and Stock, 1996), 198.
16. Torrance, *Theology in Reconciliation*, 16.
17. Ibid., 17.
18. Ibid., 20.
19. Torrance, *Conflict and Agreement in the Church: Order and Disorder*, 202.
20. Ibid., 228. See also Thomas F. Torrance, "Anglican-Presbyterian Conversations" *Presbyterian Record* (July–August 1957): 19, 36–37 in which Torrance describes a shift needed in ecumenical dialogue, focusing on the need to set any discussion upon the basis of having our being "in Christ."
21. Ibid., 200.
22. Torrance, *Theology in Reconciliation*, 22–23.
23. Thomas F. Torrance, "What Is the Church?" *Ecumenical Review* 11, no. 1 (October 1958): 17.
24. Torrance, *Conflict and Agreement in the Church: Order and Disorder*, 12.
25. Torrance, *Theology in Reconciliation*, 7.
26. Torrance, "What Is the Church?" 9.
27. Thomas F. Torrance, *The Christian Doctrine of Marriage* (Edinburgh: Handsel Press, 1984), 3–15. See also Thomas F. Torrance, "A Comment on the New Morality," *Salt and Light Periodical* 2, no. 1 (Spring 1964): 17–20 in which Torrance argues against the idea that the Christian vision of marriage can change to suit a change in ethics.

28. Thomas F. Torrance, "Answer to God," *Biblical Theology* 2, no. 1 (1951): 10.

29. Thomas F. Torrance, *Conflict and Agreement in the Church: The Ministry and Sacraments of the Gospel* (Eugene, OR: Wipf and Stock, 1996), 71.

30. Thomas F. Torrance, *The Mediation of Christ* (Edinburgh: T&T Clark, 1992), 64.

31. Ibid., 66.

32. Torrance, *Theology in Reconciliation*, 7.

33. Thomas F. Torrance, *The School of Faith* (London: James Clarke, 1959), lxviii.

34. Torrance, *Conflict and Agreement in the Church: Order and Disorder*, 19.

35. Torrance, *Theology in Reconciliation*, 7.

36. Thomas F. Torrance, "Itinerarium Mentis in Deum" (Box 10: Itinerarium Mentis in Deum. Thomas F. Torrance Manuscript Collection, Princeton Theological Seminary), 3.

37. Thomas F. Torrance, "Thomas Ayton's 'The Original Constitution of the Christian Church,'" in *Reformation and Revolution: Essays Presented to the Very Reverend Principal Emeritus Hugh Watt on the Sixtieth Anniversary of His Ordination*, ed. Duncan Shaw, 274–75 (Edinburgh: Saint Andrew Press, 1967).

38. Torrance, "What Is the Church?" 20.

39. Thomas F. Torrance, *Gospel, Church and Ministry*, ed. Jock Stein, 1:241 (Eugene, OR: Pickwick Publications, 2012).

40. Thomas F. Torrance, *Reality and Scientific Theology*, 2nd ed. (Eugene, OR: Wipf and Stock, 2001), 150–51.

41. Thomas F. Torrance, "A New Reformation?" *London Holborn and Quarterly Review* 189 (1964): 292. Torrance comments that "the Protestant Church tended to become a servant of public opinion, an expression of the national and cultural consciousness of the people."

42. Torrance, *Theology in Reconciliation*, 22.

43. Ibid., 8.

44. Thomas F. Torrance, *Transformation and Convergence in the Frame of Knowledge: Explorations in the Interrelations of Scientific and Theological Enterprise* (Eugene, OR: Wipf and Stock, 1998), 326.

45. Thomas F. Torrance, *Theology in Reconstruction* (Grand Rapids, MI: Eerdmans, 1965), 165.

46. Thomas F. Torrance, "Review of *The Realm of Redemption: Studies in the Doctrine of the Nature of the Church in Contemporary Protestant Theology*, by J. Robert Nelson," *Scottish Journal of Theology* 6, no. 3 (September 1953): 324.

47. Torrance, *Conflict and Agreement in the Church: Order and Disorder*, 13.

48. Torrance, *Transformation and Convergence in the Frame of Knowledge*, 327. Torrance explores at the length the contribution that scientific method can make to the ecumenical movement in Thomas F. Torrance, *God and Rationality* (Oxford: Oxford University Press, 2000), 112–34.

49. Torrance, *Transformation and Convergence in the Frame of Knowledge*, 282. See also Torrance, *Reality and Scientific Theology*, 154.

50. Torrance, *Transformation and Convergence in the Frame of Knowledge*, 283.

51. Torrance, *Conflict and Agreement in the Church: Order and Disorder*, 8.

52. Torrance, *Transformation and Convergence in the Frame of Knowledge*, 328.

53. Torrance, *Theology in Reconciliation*, 8–9.

54. Ibid., 10. See also Thomas F. Torrance, "Ecumenism and Rome," *Scottish Journal of Theology* 37 (1984): 59–64 in which Torrance suggests specific changes that the Roman Catholic Church needed to undertake in order to move forward in ecumenical dialogue.

55. Torrance, *Theology in Reconciliation*, 10, 13. Torrance further argues that we need unified thinking not only in terms of denominational divisions but also in ethnic and geographic divisions.

56. Torrance identifies two potential errors that might occur: (1) The weakening of Christology so that Christ is set to the side and the significance of the incarnation is reduced; instead, inwardness of spirit is promoted, as is true of much Protestantism; and (2) Allowing the Church to obscure Christ, which is most obvious where the Church is seen as an extension of the incarnation or where the Church focuses on itself more than Christ. Both these errors, whether Roman Catholic or Protestant, lead to the same result: the centrality of Jesus Christ is lost, and

the Trinity no longer is in focus, displaced instead by humanity or abstract principles. The ecumenical movement must constantly be wary of both these extremes. See Torrance, *Conflict and Agreement in the Church: Order and Disorder*, 12–16.

57. Thomas F. Torrance, "Changed Outlook of Christians: The 'Obligation' of Unity," *Scotsman*, January 29, 1964.

58. Torrance, *Conflict and Agreement in the Church: Order and Disorder*, 200.

59. Ibid., 223.

60. Ibid., 199.

61. Ibid., 197.

62. Thomas F. Torrance, "The Way of Reunion," *Christian Century* 71 (1954): 204–5.

63. Torrance, *Conflict and Agreement in the Church: Order and Disorder*, 197.

64. Ibid., 205.

65. Ibid., 63.

66. Torrance, *The Mediation of Christ*, 46.

67. See Torrance's comments in Thomas F. Torrance, "God, Destiny and Suffering," *The Healing Hand, Journal of the Edinburgh Medical Missionary Society* (Summer/Autumn 1977): 15.

68. Ibid., 13.

69. Thomas F. Torrance, "Review of Bernard Lambert, *Le Problème Oecumenique*," *Scottish Journal of Theology* 16, no. 1 (1963): 104.

70. Thomas F. Torrance, "The Orthodox Church in Great Britain," *Participatio* 4 (2013): 258–59.

71. Myk Habets, *Theology in Transposition: A Constructive Appraisal of T. F. Torrance* (Minneapolis, MN: Fortress Press, 2013), 19.

72. Thomas F. Torrance, *Scottish Theology: From John Knox to John Mcleod Campbell* (Edinburgh: T&T Clark, 1996).

73. Thomas F. Torrance, "What Is the Reformed Church?" *Biblical Theology* 9 (1959): 60. See also Torrance, *The School of Faith*, lxix–cxxvi; and Torrance, "Thomas Ayton's 'The Original Constitution of the Christian Church.'"

74. Thomas F. Torrance, "What Is 'The Substance of the Faith'?" *Life and Work* (November 1982): 16–17.

75. Alister McGrath, *T. F. Torrance: An Intellectual Biography* (Edinburgh: T&T Clark, 1999), 101.

76. Thomas F. Torrance, "The Transforming Power of Jesus Christ," *Life and Work* 32, no. 7 (July 1976): 8.

77. Ibid., 9.

78. Torrance, "We Are Learning Together," 8.

79. Thomas F. Torrance, "The Pre-eminence of Jesus Christ," *Expository Times* 89, no. 2 (1977): 54.

80. Ibid.

81. Ibid., 54–55. This was not a new theme for Torrance but one that he had raised over a decade earlier (Thomas F. Torrance, "Put First Things First: Queries to Assembly on Church Union," *Scotsman*, May 27 1966). He addresses the historical developments that led the Reformed Church to embrace rigid tradition rather than the constant reformation of the Spirit in a more academic article, Thomas F. Torrance, "History and Reformation," *Scottish Journal of Theology* 4 (1951): 286–91. It is helpful to note that Torrance aims this sort of comment not only at the Reformed Church for he asks a very similar question of the Anglican Church. See Thomas F. Torrance, "The Mission of Anglicanism," in *Anglican Self-Criticism*, ed. D. M. Paton, 194–208 (London: SCM Press, 1958).

82. In an earlier article published at the end of the war, Torrance called on the Church to put the Cross back at the head of the theological task, removing every false Christian ideology. The power of the Cross is not the story of a good man laying down his life for his friends but rather God *himself* on the Cross, which alters the whole situation—including our much-cherished doctrinal affirmations! See Thomas F. Torrance, "In Hoc Signo Vinces," *Presbyter* 3, no. 1 (1945): 13–20.

83. Torrance, "Urgent Call to the Kirk." Similar themes can be found in other articles published by Torrance, including Thomas F. Torrance, "A Serious Call for a Return to a Devout and Holy Life," *Life and Work* (July 1979): 14–15.

84. R. D. Kernohan, "Analysis of a Diagnosis," *Life and Work* (November 1983): 14.

85. Torrance, "Urgent Call to the Kirk."

86. Thomas F. Torrance, "Summary of the Urgent Call to the Kirk" (Box 96: Urgent Call to the Kirk—Description of, instructions, May 1983, Thomas F. Torrance Manuscript Collection, Princeton Theological Seminary).

87. Torrance, "Urgent Call to the Kirk."

88. Torrance, "Summary of the Urgent Call to the Kirk."

89. J. Fraser McLuskey, "From the Assembly to Skye—Via Dublin and Atlanta," *Life and Work* (October 1983): 14.

90. Quotes taken from various letters (Box 96: "Correspondence from Churches and Church Organisations June–July 1983," Thomas F. Torrance Special Collection, Princeton Theological Seminary).

91. Ibid.

92. R. D. Kernohan, "Editorial Comment," *Life and Work* (November 1983): 5.

93. Thomas F. Torrance, "The Tide Has Turned," *Life and Work* (March 1984): 15.

94. Thomas F. Torrance, "Where Is the Church of Scotland Going?" *Life and Work* (May 1989): 26.

95. Elmer M. Colyer, *How to Read T. F. Torrance: Understanding His Trinitarian and Scientific Theology* (Downers Grove, IL: InterVarsity Press, 2001), 28.

96. Thomas F. Torrance, "The Kirk's Crisis of Faith," *Life and Work* (October 1990): 15. This is not a new point—Torrance observed in 1950 that any evangelistic technique that forgets that the Gospel has already been made relevant to humanity through Jesus Christ will not be effective in Gospel proclamation. See Thomas F. Torrance, "A Study in New Testament Communication," *Scottish Journal of Theology* 3, no. 3 (1950): 298–313 (also published in Torrance, *Conflict and Agreement in the Church: The Ministry and Sacraments of the Gospel*).

97. Torrance, "The Kirk's Crisis of Faith," 16. Although somewhat tangential, Torrance's comments elsewhere help us grasp the seriousness with which he made comments such as this. Torrance urges the Church not to be scared into translating Christianity into acceptable contemporary language and social involvement but instead "to follow the example of the Greek Fathers in undertaking the courageous, revolutionary task of a Christian reconstruction of the foundations of culture: nothing less is worthy of the Christian Gospel." See Torrance, *Theology in Reconciliation*, 271.

98. Thomas F. Torrance, "The Crisis of Morality," *Life and Work* (November 1990): 15. Torrance also argues that we must beware the danger of moral inversion: the replacement of deep evangelical conviction by a sense of "consciously meritorious involvement in socio-political issues." He sees this as a sign of the soul atrophying so that people search for meaning externally. See Torrance, *Theology in Reconciliation*, 276–78.

99. Torrance, "The Crisis of Morality," 16.

100. Thomas F. Torrance, "The Crisis of Community," *Life and Work* (December 1990): 17.

101. Ibid.

102. Thomas F. Torrance, "Answer to God," *Biblical Theology* 2, no. 1 (1951): 13.

103. Ibid., 14.

104. Ibid.

105. Torrance, *The Mediation of Christ*, 72.

106. Thomas F. Torrance, "A Right-About-Turn for the Kirk," *Presbyterian Record* 105, no. 10 (November 1981): 32.

107. Thomas F. Torrance, "Putting First Things First," *Presbyterian Survey* (1981): 12.

108. Torrance, "A Right-About-Turn for the Kirk," 31.

109. McGrath, *T. F. Torrance*, 102.

110. Thomas F. Torrance, ed., *Theological Dialogue between Orthodox and Reformed* Churches (Edinburgh: Scottish Academic Press, 1985), 1:x.

111. Interestingly, 1973 was the Year of St. Athanasius, which Torrance celebrated in Addis Ababa with Archbishop Methodios of Aksum. See Matthew Baker, "Interview with Protopres-

byter George Dion. Dragas Regarding T. F. Torrance," *Participatio* 4 (2013): 37 for reflection on how unusual this honor was.

112. The first three consultations of a preparatory nature are in the first volume, while the next three of a more formal nature are documented in the second volume, Thomas F. Torrance, ed., *Theological Dialogue between Orthodox and Reformed Churches* (Edinburgh: Scottish Academic Press, 1993).

113. Torrance, "God, Destiny and Suffering," 8–15. In this particular example, Torrance highlights his appreciation for the Orthodox Church's faithful witness and "tenacious adherence to Christianity" in the face of persecution in the Holy Land, their faith and commitment to hold properties in trust for the future proclamation of the Gospel during this persecution, and their modern reemergence as a missionary force.

114. Matthew Baker, "Introduction," *Participatio* 4 (2013): 3.

115. Torrance, *Theological Dialogue between Orthodox and Reformed Churches*, 1:ix–x. Torrance notes that contacts formed during the early ecumenical movement were key to this, beginning with the World Missionary Conference (Edinburgh 1910) and progressing with the first Faith and Order Conferences (Lausanne 1927 and Edinburgh 1937). It was at the first World Council of Churches meeting (Amsterdam 1948) and the third Faith and Order Conference (Lund 1952) that serious dialogue began to take place. Torrance notes his own involvement in the Lund Commission on Christ and His Church, in which Professor Chrysotomos Konstantinides—the Metropolitan of Myra—also participated.

116. For the full text of the letter see Torrance, *Theological Dialogue between Orthodox and Reformed Churches*, 1:xi–xiv. The observation in Baker, "Introduction," 4 is also useful, noting how unusual it was for Torrance to begin his international visits as moderator by traveling to meet Eastern Orthodox patriarchs rather than to visit another Reformed community.

117. Baker, "Interview with Protopresbyter George Dion. Dragas," 39–40. Dragas relates that prior to the official proposal being made to His Holiness, Torrance asked Dragas to read over and revise Torrance's initial memorandum. When Dragas found significant difficulties from the Orthodox perspective within the document, Torrance asked Dragas to rewrite it as if he were a Reformed theologian requesting dialogue with the Orthodox. Torrance then revised that document further himself and presented both his original and the revised version to Patriarch Dimitrios!

118. Torrance, *Theological Dialogue between Orthodox and Reformed Churches*, 1:x.

119. Torrance, *The School of Faith*, lxviii. Torrance states that this call for ecumenical conversation and consideration applies to Evangelical and Catholic churches, Western and Eastern churches, and Jews and Christians.

120. Torrance, *Theological Dialogue between Orthodox and Reformed Churches*, 1:xv.

121. Ibid., xxi.

122. Ibid., 3–18.

123. Ibid., 3.

124. Ibid., 5.

125. Ibid., 3–18. See also Robert J. Stamps, *The Sacrament of the Word Made Flesh: The Eucharistic Theology of Thomas F. Torrance* (Edinburgh: Rutherford House, 2007), 239–65.

126. Torrance, *Theological Dialogue between Orthodox and Reformed Churches*, 1:6. See also Torrance's contrast of Protestant and Orthodox worship in Thomas F. Torrance, "Trinity Sunday Sermon on Acts 2:41–47," *Ekklesiastikos Pharos* 52 (1970): 196–9 where he notes that Protestant worship tends to be about expressing ourselves before God and is therefore shaped by contextual patterns and habits, but if worship is truly about participating in something transcendent to ourselves—as the Orthodox believe—then "it is in and through worship that we can transcend our differences and be united with one another."

127. Torrance, *Theological Dialogue between Orthodox and Reformed Churches*, 1:10.

128. Ibid., 11.

129. Baker, "Interview with Protopresbyter George Dion. Dragas," 42.

130. Thomas F. Torrance, *Incarnation: The Person and Life of Christ*, ed. Robert T. Walker, 198 (Downers Grove, IL: InterVarsity Press, 2008).

131. Torrance, *Theological Dialogue between Orthodox and Reformed Churches*, 1:11.

132. Ibid., 12.

133. Ibid., xxii.
134. Ibid., xxiv.
135. Ibid.
136. Ibid., 79–120.
137. Ibid., xxvi.
138. Ibid., 157–58.
139. Ibid., xxvii.
140. Ibid., xiii.
141. Torrance, *Theological Dialogue between Orthodox and Reformed Churches*, 2:x.
142. Ibid., xiii.
143. Ibid., 3–37.
144. Ibid., xiii–xix contains the draft text of this document.
145. Baker, "Interview with Protopresbyter George Dion. Dragas," 39–42. We will not return to this issue at length here as comment was already offered when we considered Torrance's reading of the Fathers, particularly the Cappadocians, as exemplified by the contrast between Torrance and Zizioulas.
146. Thomas F. Torrance, "Historical Agreement by Reformed and Orthodox on the Doctrine of the Holy Trinity," in Thomas F. Torrance, *Trinitarian Perspectives: Toward Doctrinal Agreement* (Edinburgh: T&T Clark, 1994), 110–14.
147. Torrance, *Trinitarian Perspectives*, 123–26; and Torrance, *Theological Dialogue between Orthodox and Reformed Churches*, 2:229–32.
148. Torrance, *Theological Dialogue between Orthodox and Reformed Churches*, 2:230.
149. Ibid., 231.
150. Ibid., 232.
151. Baker, "Interview with Protopresbyter George Dion. Dragas," 42–43.
152. Torrance, *Trinitarian Perspectives*, 127–43.
153. Baker, "Introduction," 6–7.

Chapter Eight

Theological Dialogues

Bringing Torrance into dialogue with other theologians who connect the doctrine of the Trinity and the doctrine of the Church enables us to locate Torrance in a broader theological conversation. What follows is not intended as a definitive or comprehensive engagement but rather as a series of representative dialogues. We will draw first on the work of Kathryn Tanner, an American theologian who also engaged with Karl Barth. She is sympathetic to but not uncritical of Barth's legacy and is theologically similar to Torrance. Greater divergence is found in our second and third dialogue partners, Jürgen Moltmann and John Zizioulas, whose use of social trinitarianism results in greater dissonance with Torrance than is found in Tanner's work.

KATHRYN TANNER

While Kathryn Tanner draws explicitly upon Torrance, she does not simply replicate his theology. They share many core premises but Tanner develops in detail some theological elements that Torrance only deals with perfunctorily. Neither her brief systematic theology, *Christ, Humanity and the Trinity*, nor its sequel, *Christ the Key*, pay sustained attention to ecclesiology, but the key relationship between the doctrine of the Trinity and the life of the people of God is present.[1] Pauw describes Tanner as having an "incipient ecclesiology."[2] In what follows, we will explore Tanner's take on humanity's union with God in Christ and the consequences of this for the shape of human life in terms of both humanity's relationship to God and humanity's relationships with each other before acknowledging Tanner's critique of social trinitarianism.

God as Gift-Giver: Increasing Unity with God

The common theme throughout Tanner's work is the idea of God as gift-giver: "God as the giver of all good gifts, their fount, luminous source, fecund treasury, and store house."[3] She focuses on *how* God gives gifts to humanity and the way that humans are made "ministers of divine beneficence" called to witness to God's goodness.[4] Tanner places this in a historical framework where throughout history God has increasingly brought the world into closer unity within himself. God is able to gift the world with the abundant fullness of his Triune life "only to the extent the world is united by God to Godself over the course of the world's time."[5]

There are significant parallels between Tanner's work and Torrance's three-phase diachronic ecclesiology. Torrance's first phase is the "preparatory form before the Incarnation"[6] and the whole story of Israel as a covenanted people. Tanner also draws upon the covenant between God and Israel but highlights that in this historical period, God's gifts are external to God rather than the communication of his own divine being.[7] Even though God gives *himself* as gift to Israel, "unlike trinitarian relations, these covenant relations are still, however, relations at a distance."[8]

The second phase of the Church in Torrance's account begins when the Church is given new form through Jesus Christ, who "gathered up and reconstructed the one people of God in himself, and poured out his Spirit upon broken and divided humanity."[9] The incarnation is the key transitory event for Torrance and Tanner. Tanner comments that the incarnation is how God removes the distance inherent in humanity's relation with God because in Jesus, God undertakes to "relate to us in a less external way than God does in covenant relations with us."[10] God (the Word) unites himself to what is not God (through Jesus' assumption of humanity) in such a way that what is not God (humanity) is made God's own (because it is united to God fully in the hypostatic union). Humanity and divinity are united in Christ in such a way that God can fully give the gift of himself to that which is not God.[11] In the present age, the "overlap of the ages," this is only imperfectly realized.

It is important that Tanner views the God-world relationship as fundamentally asymmetrical: while God freely gives the world all that he has to give, that which is not God cannot receive this in its fullness for "creatures are not of the same essence or substance as God and therefore the Persons of the Trinity cannot communicate to creatures what they communicate to one another."[12] This is why the incarnation is unique. Jesus is the perfect embodiment of God's goodness in the world and "lives out in a fully human form the mode of relationship among Father, Son and Spirit in the Trinity"[13] in a way that we cannot because of our sin and our temporality. It is only through Christ that we are incorporated into the life of the Trinity—specifically, in the place of the second person of the Trinity.

The third phase of the Church according to Torrance is the "final and eternal form when Christ comes again to judge and renew his creation."[14] The *telos* of history cannot be hurried along by humanity's efforts but must wait for the *parousia* of Christ. Tanner also notes that in the current time "a gap exists between the results of world processes and the world's consummation, a gap to be bridged by a God with the power to reverse those results."[15] However, for Tanner, "the central claim of eschatology must not refer to what happens at the end"[16] because what is really important is the character of our new relationship to God, described as eternal life.[17]

Tanner's Doctrine of God

There are many similarities in how both theologians draw on history to describe the relation of God to humanity. This leads us to Tanner's doctrine of God, which starts with the stance that the incarnation uniquely enables us to know the Triune God. She explicitly cites Torrance's influence when making the point that

> the whole of who God is for us as creator and redeemer, which in its varied complexity might simply overwhelm and mystify us, is found in concentrated compass in Christ. Christ in this way provides, we shall see, a clue to the pattern or structure that organizes the whole even while God's ways remain ultimately beyond our grasp.[18]

In support of her point here, Tanner cites *Theology in Reconciliation* where Torrance highlights Athanasius's emphasis that theology must proceed from the starting point of God's "economic condescension to us in Jesus Christ."[19] She also cites from *Divine Meaning* where Torrance draws on Irenaeus's discussion of *anakephalaiosis*, his understanding of Christ's recapitulation in the descent and ascent of the incarnation.[20] Tanner herself frequently draws on the Fathers, although she notes that *Christ the Key* is "highly eclectic in its use of the history of Christian thought . . . [intending] to show the fruitfulness of a kind of internalizing of the history of Christian thought for its creative redeployment."[21]

While Torrance makes use of the doctrine of *perichoresis* as a regulative principle for his doctrine of the Trinity, Tanner rarely refers to *perichoresis* and only really does so in order to critique social trinitarianism's use of the concept. She notes that in a "politically progressive trinitarian" approach, *perichoresis* has to carry a heavy load that has not been shown to be compatible with an emphasis on the economic subordination of the Son;[22] *perichoresis* is sometimes little more than a projection of what the theologian already thinks perfect mutuality and relationality should look like[23] and is at risk of being reduced to a "way of being" that humans can replicate, despite their finitude.[24] She makes no significant mention of *koinōnia* and commits little energy toward explaining the notion of a human community that derives from the Triune communion.

Despite these differences, the parallels still bear fruitful comparison. Both Tanner and Torrance use the language of a twofold movement: descent as the Son and the Spirit are sent into a sinful world for the sake of humanity's reconciliation to God, and ascent as the Son and Spirit accomplish their mission and return to the Father. Tanner holds that the Son and Spirit are intertwined in the "mission of redemption that they undertake from the Father,"[25] echoing Torrance's view of their mutual mediation.

At the heart of this dual movement is the vicarious humanity of Christ. We hear the influence of Torrance in Tanner's observation that "each aspect of Jesus' life and death, moreover, is purified, healed and elevated over the course of time, in a process that involves conflict and struggle with the sinful conditions of its existence."[26] Tanner believes that "the connection between incarnation and atonement disrupts 'external forensic and juridical' accounts of the atonement" and also highlights Torrance's influence on this aspect of her work by commenting that he emphasizes this argument more strongly than she does.[27] The incarnation has a central role for Tanner's theology as the means of humanity's union with God through union with Christ as empowered by the Holy Spirit.

Tanner also notes that baptism and the Eucharist offer us a way to understand the dual movement of descent and ascent. In baptism we are made one with Christ before we ever demonstrate that unity in our lives, just as Christ chooses us before we ever choose him. The Eucharist "repeats in miniature the whole movement of ascent and descent, going to the Father and receiving from him, through Christ in the power of the Spirit."[28] In contrast to this, Torrance doesn't associate baptism and the Eucharist with descent and ascent, instead describing baptism as a one-time sacrament through which we are incorporated into Christ once and for all and the Eucharist as a gift for the continual renewal of the Church in the time between the two advents. Tanner critiques Torrance here, suggesting that along with Josef Jungman, he tends to "associate assent to the Father so exclusively with the humanity of Jesus that they overlook return as part of a divine trinitarian movement as well."[29] Tanner's critique is overstated because Torrance is very careful to emphasize the hypostatic union and to develop a doctrine of mutual coinherence and the mutual mediation of the Son and the Spirit in the economy.

Torrance maintains the traditional pattern of the movement of descent as *from* the Father, *through* the Son, and *in* the Spirit, and the movement of ascent as *in* the Spirit, *through* the Son, *to* the Father.[30] He views these prepositions and their specific order as describing how "the distinctive mode of operation by each of the three divine Persons is maintained"[31] within the indivisible Triune unity. Tanner is markedly less concerned about maintaining the specific economic order of the persons, arguing that "because they both come out and return together [from the Father], either Son or Spirit can be viewed as the hinge of the whole movement, at the end, so to speak, of the coming out and return."[32] Thus Tanner argues that we can describe the pattern of descent and ascent as either F>sp>S>sp>F (with an emphasis on the Son), or F>s>SP>s>F (with an emphasis on the Spirit), because it is both at once."[33] However, despite Torrance's insistence on maintaining the traditional economic pattern in comparison with Tanner's fluidity in discussing the economic order, the difference is a matter of language rather than content.

Humanity's Participation in the Trinity

In order to maintain the fundamental asymmetry between the divine and the human, Tanner proposes that God must give us something that we cannot independently possess.[34] This is what takes place in Christ, who is "more than a paradigm . . . He has become for us the very means" of our participation in the Triune life.[35] Tanner defines participation as "sharing in something that one is not,"[36] recognizing the difference between the way that Jesus participates in the divine life and the ways that created humans participate in the divine life. Jesus is the image of God in a unique way since he shares fully in the divine nature. By contrast, humans can image God in either a weak sense—that is, simply the fact that we derive our life and being from God—or a strong sense, where God gifts to us that which is not ours by nature.[37]

It is the latter sense that Tanner draws on for Christians. In this "strong sense of participation," our lives take on a trinitarian shape not because of who we are intrinsically but only as we remain in continuous connection to the Word. As Tanner reflects, "if we image the relations among members of the trinity, we do not do so in and of ourselves, because, for example, the relations among our own creative capacities imitate those of the persons of the trinity. We image them instead by way of an actual close attachment to them."[38] In other words, the incarnation does not change God's being by assimilating our humanity into the divine nature. God remains transcendently God. Through the hypostatic union, humanity's relationship to God is changed but only if we remain in dependent fellowship with God. To return to the language of descent and ascent, Christ descends into our humanity and becomes one of us and one with us. In this way, humanity is unified with Christ through the Spirit, and thus in his corresponding movement of ascent, we are brought to God in Christ, which makes us increasingly able to receive God's good gifts. Tanner subsequently explains the way that God is not changed but humanity is changed through union with God when she writes,

> In the language of the ancient Church, God is not going anywhere when God becomes human; we are being brought to God, assumed into the divine trinitarian life. God is doing what God is always doing, attempting to give all that God is to what is not God.[39]

Although Tanner suggests that we are "assumed into the divine trinitarian life," this is awkward wording that belies her wider theological stance and suggests blurring the absolute distinction between God and humanity, which is not her intent. It is helpful to instead hold in the forefront of our thought Tanner's perspective that there is an asymmetry to the hypostatic union so that God is "free to enter into intimate community with us, without loss to the divine nature, without sacrificing the difference between God and us."[40] God does not become less God, and becoming fully human does not make us God. Tanner directly draws on Torrance to make this point in her own work, citing his statement that "because the presence of God is creative, instead of excluding or overwhelming what is human, it posits it, upholds, and renews it."[41] The Triune God does not "make itself over in a human image of community" but rather "makes over human life in the trinity's image by way of our entrance into its own life through Christ."[42]

Tanner's Ecclesiology

We come now to consider the relationship between the Trinity and Tanner's incipient ecclesiology. Tanner acknowledges that Father, Son, and Holy Spirit are unified in action, albeit in their different modes of being—she uses Barth's terminology here unlike Torrance who speaks of the three Triune persons who are constituted by their relations with each other—and then asks what this means for our relations with each other. How are humans to live as a result of our connection to the life of the Trinity? The following quote helpfully introduces us to some of the major ecclesiological points that Tanner believes are implied by our assumption into the Trinity through our union with Jesus Christ.

> We are united with one another, we form a community, the church, as we are united in Christ through the power of the Spirit. This is to be a universal community in that the whole world is at least prospectively united with Christ in and through the triune God's saving intentions for the whole world that has always been the object of God's gift-giving, from the beginning. We are brought together in this community without overriding the particularities of our persons; we are united with one another as what we are and remain in our differences. Thus, the Holy Spirit unites us in Christ even as the Holy Spirit encourages the uniqueness of our persons by a diversity of gifts of the Spirit.[43]

This is as close as Tanner comes in either *Jesus, Humanity and the Trinity* or *Christ the Key* to developing a formal doctrine of the Church. We can quite clearly identify some similarities with Torrance here. They both hold that humankind is formed into the Church only as each person is united to Christ through the Spirit so that the ground of our union with each other is our union with God. They also both hold that the scope of redemption is the whole *cosmos*. Finally, they also both note the unity and diversity of the Church; even though there are significant differences between humans, the Spirit brings us into unity while retaining our diversity.

Tanner dislikes the approach of modeling human relations directly on trinitarian relations, but this does not mean that she has nothing to say about what the life of the Christian community should look like. She contends that "we are to be for one another as God the Father is for us through Christ in the power of the Spirit"[44] because "human community is to reflect the structure of God's own relations with us."[45] However, Tanner stops short here of arguing for a direct correlation between trinitarian relations and human relations; she is uncomfortable with the way that some theologians have applied the social model of the Trinity to the doctrine of the Church, particularly given that most proponents of social trinitarianism tend to be more concerned with political rather than distinctly ecclesiological outcomes.

In *Jesus, Humanity and the Trinity*, Tanner argues that social trinitarianism downplays the difference between divine trinitarian relations and finite human social relations. Tanner is emphatic that we need to respect "the creature's finite boundedness."[46] Furthermore, this approach loses a realistic sense of the capacities of human relations by trying to force them into trinitarian modes since humans are only capable of experiencing fellowship with God as an external form of relationship rather than sharing coinherently in God's being.

Tanner offers a more extended critique in her chapters "Trinitarian Life" and "Politics" in *Christ the Key*, where she negatively assesses attempts to use the doctrine of the Trinity to "establish how human societies should be organized" and as an "indicator of the proper relationship between individual and society."[47] Tanner is adamant that "figuring out the socio-political lessons of the trinity is a fraught task,"[48] not least because of the varied interpretations that can be derived from the doctrine of the Trinity. The chief problem in basing human relationships on the Trinity is that there are essential differences between God and humanity. Tanner identifies three specific challenges that arise when drawing on the doctrine of the Trinity to describe what human relationships should look like.

The first challenge is the limitations of our knowledge of the Trinity. "What we are puzzled about—the proper character of human society—is explicated with reference to what is surely only more obscure—the character of the divine community."[49] This is where Tanner's critique of the way in which social trinitarianism uses the concept of *perichoresis* may be situated.

The second challenge is that much of the content of the doctrine of the Trinity simply cannot have a direct application to humanity because of the "essential finitude of human beings."[50] This particularly applies to the form of relationality that exists between the Triune persons and the different forms of relationality between humans. When one divine person acts, all the divine persons act. However, humans are never this closely intertwined with other humans.[51] As Tanner notes, human finitude "seems to require the policing of boundaries between themselves and others that breaks off relationships."[52]

Finally, the third challenge Tanner observes is that the trinitarian persons can give and receive without cost. But for humans, giving and receiving involves loss and gain. "Direct translation of the trinity into a social program is problematic because, unlike the peaceful and perfectly loving mutuality of the trinity, human society is full of suffering, conflict, and sin."[53] At its worst, trinitarian community is presented to humanity as a fanciful ideal, and humanity is simply left "with no clue as to how we might get to it."[54]

Of these three challenges, it is the absolute separation between divinity and humanity that presents the most significant challenge to applying the model of the Trinity to human life. This is easily answered by Tanner because it is Jesus Christ who is the solution. Humans are not called to *imitate* the Triune relations but to *participate* in them,[55] which we can only do through the Son, the second person of the Trinity. This is why Tanner argues that Christology is more helpful than the doctrine of the Trinity for making observations about the proper character of human relationships.[56] All humans are incorporated into the Trinity at the same point: through the Son. This Christocentric approach, which leads us into the Trinity, does not require us to find ways around the irreconcilable differences between God and humanity because humanity and divinity are joined in Christ. This is a "strong form" of participation in the life of the Trinity: "humans do not attain the heights of trinitarian relations by reproducing them in and of themselves . . . but by being taken up into them as the very creatures they are."[57] Humankind can only share in trinitarian relations by way of our union with Christ—and can only do so imperfectly "because of our finitude and our sin."[58]

The Nature and Mission of the Church

In Tanner's opinion, Jesus' relations to the Father and Spirit do not show us what relationships among humans should be; they show us how to relate to the Triune God as created humans.[59] "The trinity itself enters our world in Christ to show us how human relations are to be reformed in its image."[60] The question that concerns us in this final section is the nature of the Christian community and how it participates in the redemptive mission of God while it awaits the *eschaton*. We may commence our inquiry here by noting

Tanner's insistence that while there is an analogy between the Trinity and the nature of the Church, this is not an exclusive analogy; we might derive the same understanding of the kingdom of God from any other number of doctrines. She insists that the *principles of the kingdom* are more important than *which doctrine they are derived from.*[61] As God communicates his gifts to us, "we, in short, are sanctified and serve the ends of trinitarian love. Human beings become in this way the administrative center of cosmic-wide service."[62] God does not need anything from us but the world does, which is why our union with Christ and the Spirit results in an "active fellowship or partnership with the Father."[63] Through union with Jesus Christ, our lives come to be incorporated "within the workings *ad extra* of the Trinity."[64] Participation in the Triune life of God is not simply about adoration, but rather,

> eternal life means a community of life with God in Christ, a community of action in which we are taken up into Christ's own action for the world. As Jesus does the life-giving work of the Spirit, we, in virtue of our union with Christ, are to do the same. Eternal life turns attention, then, not just to the benefits we are to receive through Christ—our being healed, purified, elevated by Christ in the power of the Spirit—but to our active participation in Christ's own mission.[65]

Tanner is insistent that Christians are empowered by Jesus' own ministry to be ministers of "divine beneficence" to each other.[66] The Eucharist provides us with a model for ministry in which the minister "distribut[es] outwards, to others, the gifts of the Father that have become ours in and through the Son by the power of the Holy Spirit."[67] We must receive from God before we can share God's good gifts to others. Tanner does not differentiate between the Son and Spirit here, arguing that humans are sent "from the Father to become the image of the Son in the world by way of the power of the Spirit, or from the Father to live a Spirit-filled life with Christ in his mission from the world."[68] Whichever way we describe this, "the Christian experience of service to God's mission for the world . . . assumes a properly trinitarian shape."[69] This is very similar to Torrance's view of the mission of the Church as participation through the Spirit in the ongoing work of the Triune God. When the Spirit is at work through us, Tanner suggests that our acts attain an extrospective shape so that we should live "eccentrically"—looking beyond ourselves and paying attention "to what is being done by God for us."[70] The mission of God involves

> bringing in the kingdom or new community that accords with Jesus' own healing, reconciling, and life-giving relations with others. . . . Jesus' relations with Father and Spirit make his whole life one of worshipful, praise-filled, faithful service to the Father's mission of bringing in the kingdom; that is to be

> the character of our lives too, both in and out of church, as we come to share Jesus' life.[71]

Concluding Reflections

There are several key similarities for Tanner and Torrance, and the most fundamental of these are Christological. They both insist that we only know God through the incarnation and understand atonement as taking place through Christ's vicarious humanity. Placing these two theologians side by side helps us appreciate the subtleties of their work in a more nuanced fashion. The main point on which Tanner and Torrance diverge is in the scope of their account of the Trinity-Church relationship. Although she and Torrance both draw on the Fathers, Tanner draws her trinitarian theology primarily from the Gospel narratives and how they describe the relationship between Father, Son, and Spirit. She does less work to ground the doctrine of the Church in the doctrine of the Trinity than we find in Torrance, which is related to her wariness of social trinitarianism and the ways in which it can be manipulated—for example, to support divergent political visions. She reacts critically to the suggestion that the Christian community should be modeled after the social relationships within the Trinity, which is why she makes little use of *perichoresis* and *koinōnia* as regulative ecclesiological motifs, whereas they are central for Torrance. Instead of focusing on these technical theological terms, Tanner instead focuses on the idea of God as gift-giver who brings humanity into union with himself in order to be able to give them good gifts, including participation in the union of the Holy Trinity. This language does not conflict with, but rather complements, Torrance's trinitarian ecclesiology.

JÜRGEN MOLTMANN

Just as much of Torrance's theology is related to his experience in being raised in the mission field, leading in parish ministry and serving as a wartime chaplain, Jürgen Moltmann acknowledges that his theology also stems from his wartime experience.[72] Captured and held as a prisoner of war for almost three years, Moltmann turned to God in a POW camp and began his theological journey. His experience of death in the war, acknowledgement of the German peoples' guilt, and recognition of "the inner perils of utter resignation behind barbed wire" became the foundations of his eschatological and liberation theology.[73] This led to the consistent themes in his theological oeuvre of "God as the power of hope and of God's presence in suffering."[74] For Moltmann, suffering intrinsically shapes one's theology because "it is in suffering that the whole human question about God arises."[75]

Moltmann's Focus on Eschatology

The Christocentric doctrine of the Trinity is constitutive for Torrance's approach to the theological task. However, it is not the Trinity but a Christocentric eschatology that is constitutive of Moltmann's approach to theology. This is particularly exemplified in his first trilogy. Moltmann notes in the introduction to the reprint of *Theology of Hope* that he had "tried to see *the whole of theology in a single focus*,"[76] combining "eschatological redemption and historical liberation in a single coherent perspective of the future."[77] For Moltmann, eschatology is not simply to do with the "last days" since

> Christian faith lives from the raising of the crucified Christ, and strains after the promises of the universal future of Christ . . . Hence eschatology cannot really be only a part of Christian doctrine. Rather, the eschatological outlook is characteristic of all Christian proclamation, of every Christian existence and of the whole Church.[78]

Christians draw upon the promises of God as their "sure foundation" for the longed-for future. This eschatological hope should shape the present, which is why liberation and freedom, and promise and hope, are such persistent elements of Moltmann's theology. Moltmann emphasizes that the Christian understanding of salvation is not to be limited to individual reconciliation with God but must also involve "the eschatological *hope of justice*, the *humanizing* of man, the *socializing* of humanity, *peace* for all creation."[79] Although the eschatological element is also present in Torrance's work, it is worked out differently: Torrance focuses more on the people of God and the new creation than on God's liberating justice for humanity.

Moltmann's Doctrine of God

As we turn to Moltmann's doctrine of God, it is necessary to keep these themes of promise and hope, and eschatology and liberation, in mind. Moltmann undertakes an extensive criticism of Christian monotheism[80] and rejects the Western ideas of "God as Supreme Substance" and "God as Absolute Subject."[81] Like Torrance, he argues that in order to properly understand the tri-unity of God, "we must dispense with both the concept of the one substance and the concept of the identical substance" and focus upon *perichoresis*.[82] This is in keeping with Moltmann's reaction against moral and monotheistic interpretations of the New Testament. Instead, Moltmann begins with the historical life of Jesus as narrated in Scripture and moves from that toward a doctrine of the Trinity,[83] highlighting the way in which the New Testament proclaims "in narrative the relationships of the Father, the Son and the Spirit, which are relationships of fellowship and are open to the world."[84]

Moltmann refers to *koinōnia* and *perichoresis* as key concepts for his doctrine of the Trinity but does not construct his theology around them. The doctrine of *perichoresis* is used to explain that the three persons are not three different individuals nor are they three modes of being of the one God; they are the coinherent Triune persons.[85] Hunsinger makes the helpful observation that instead of attempting to hold God's oneness and God's threeness equally, Moltmann sets them against each other.[86] Furthermore, Moltmann offers a critique of the word "persons," believing that describing the three Triune persons as persons, hypostases, or "modes of being" suggests "that they are homogenous and equal [and] blurs the specific differences."[87] He therefore proposes that we should apply different words to each of the three persons in order to avoid modalism and asserts that "no summing-up, generic terms must be used at all in the doctrine of the Trinity. For in the life of the immanent Trinity everything is unique . . . we can only really tell, relate, but not sum up."[88] Aside from the confusion that would result from such a move, Moltmann does not emphasize the way in which the language of "person" emphasizes the personal nature of the knowledge of God, which is a key contribution that "person" makes to Torrance's doctrine of the Trinity.[89]

Moltmann is cautious around the idea of subordinationism, noting that "if we talk about an order of origin within the Trinity, we must underline its uniqueness and its incomparability when contrasted with any order of origin which is thought of cosmologically."[90] As a related comment on the *filioque*, Moltmann argues that a change in the creedal text will not heal the East-West schism, instead suggesting that we must instead discover a shared solution to the issue of the Son and Spirit's relationship.[91] Moltmann's suggestion is that humans should talk about "the Holy Spirit who proceeds from the Father of the Son."[92] He argues that the Father is not called Father "because he is the Sole Cause and because all things are dependent on him"[93] but because he is *always and only* the Father of the Son. This is in keeping with Moltmann's emphasis on the mutuality and equality of the Triune persons. However, Moltmann also offers his own take on relations of origin within the Trinity, suggesting that each person is a focal point for the unity in the Trinity in their own way: "The Father forms the 'monarchial' unity of the Trinity," the perichoretic unity of the three persons is "concentrated round *the eternal Son*," and the "uniting mutuality and community proceeds from *the Holy Spirit*."[94] Although Moltmann claims that this approach aligns with the perichoretic unity of the Trinity, Torrance would question whether this truly communicates the full equality and mutual coinherence of the persons. For Torrance, a form of the doctrine of appropriation can only function at the economic or evangelical level of the Holy Trinity and not at the theological or immanent level of God's ontological being *in se*, as it seems to for Moltmann.

The Mutual, Reciprocal Relationship between God and the World

The element of Christ's incarnate life that Moltmann focuses on is the Cross, in keeping with his focus on God's presence as a form of hope in suffering. Moltmann further argues that the Cross stands at the center of the Trinity, and he illustrates this by referring to Rublev's icon of the Trinity. "Just as the chalice stands at the centre of the table round which the three Persons are sitting, so the cross of the Son stands from eternity in the centre of the Trinity."[95] Bauckham helps us grasp the significance of the Cross for Moltmann, commenting that it led to Moltmann's development of the "trinitarian history" of God: "God experiences a history with the world in which he both affects and is affected by the world, and which is also the history of his own trinitarian relationships as a community of divine Persons who include the world within their love."[96] It is through the Cross that God's openness to the world is made clearest. Moltmann argues that the Cross involves not just the incarnate Son but also the Father and the Spirit and that suffering, therefore, is not external to God but affects God's very being.

Moltmann's position here reveals both agreement and disagreement with Torrance. In positive terms, Torrance appreciates Moltmann's insight that the whole Trinity is involved in the Cross, although he notes that Moltmann's "somewhat tritheistic understanding of the unity, rather than the oneness, of the Father, the Son and the Holy Spirit, in spite of what he intends, damages this insight."[97] Torrance also cites Moltmann when he notes that in the Cross we are "led to distinguish between Christ the Son of God and God the Father, while at the same time we think of Christ and worship him as our Lord and God."[98] In support of this point, Torrance notes Moltmann's comment that it is through Christ's death and his experience of godforsakenness "that our understanding is opened to the Trinity."[99] The crucifixion only makes sense because God is Triune: the incarnate Son is crucified, both in differentiation from the Father and Spirit, but still remains in "unbroken oneness with the Father and the Spirit in being and activity."[100]

However, the disagreement between Torrance and Moltmann emerges with Moltmann's insistence that the God-world relation must be *reciprocal* because it is *living*. Moltmann states this in axiomatic fashion: "What God means for the world was expressed in the doctrine of the *opera trinitatis ad extra*. But this doctrine was incapable of expressing what the world means for God."[101] In other words, Moltmann is positing that God is in some way *dependent* upon the world, leading to his observation that the world

> puts its impress on God too, through its reactions, its aberrations and its own initiatives. It certainly does not do so in the same way; but that it does so in its *own* way there can be no doubt at all. If God is love, then he does not merely emanate, flow out of himself; he also expects and needs love.[102]

Moltmann also blurs the absolute distinction between God and creation, suggesting that creation is "a part of the eternal love affair" of the Trinity.[103] As Hunsinger explains, Moltmann's "claim is simply that the world was created to satisfy God's needs . . . The fatal move here, of course, is the idea that God's love requires something external, that it is not self-sufficient."[104] Bauckham describes this as Moltmann's form of panentheism, which for Moltmann is "a way of expressing an intimate relationship between God and his creation, which does justice both to the divine immanence in creation and to the divine transcendence beyond creation."[105] However, for Moltmann this is not an indiscriminate assimilation of the world into God. As Bauckham comments, "panentheism in Moltmann's understanding is a movement towards the goal of the future in which 'God *will* be all in all.'"[106]

In comparison, Torrance explicitly rejects classical panentheism[107] and Moltmann's particular form of panentheism with his insistence that there is "no necessary relation between God and the world which he has freely created, for God does not need the world to be God."[108] If Moltmann were to make use of Torrance's stratified structure of reality, he would still ascribe primacy to the top-down model where the tertiary level governs the lower levels but would argue for a stronger reciprocal movement from the basic level to the tertiary level than Torrance does in his use of this model. Moltmann holds that for the relationship between God and the world to be truly mutual, God must change *in his inner being*.

Consequently, Moltmann affirms Rahner's thesis but chooses to "surrender the traditional distinction between the immanent and the economic Trinity"[109] because of his view that the relationship between God and the world is one of mutuality—although not fully reciprocal mutuality—because God's inner life is affected by God's outward actions in history. McDougall observes here that Moltmann "reformulates Rahner's axiom by emphasizing the identity between the loving relationships of the trinitarian persons with the world and the essence of the divine life."[110] We see this expounded further in Moltmann's explanation of God's freedom, which is not the type of sovereignty where "freedom means lordship, power and possession."[111] Instead God's freedom "is his vulnerable love, his openness, the encountering kindness through which he suffers the human beings he loves and becomes their advocate."[112] In comparison, for Torrance God's freedom is his freedom to become human in Christ and to impart himself to us through the Spirit, all without ceasing to be the transcendent God who is free because he needs nothing.[113] The understanding of God's freedom that Moltmann promulgates here is not the absolute freedom of God *in se*. Moltmann ends up suggesting that because God's freedom is found in relationship to others, the God-world relation is necessary for God to be God.

Relating the Doctrine of the Trinity to the Doctrine of the Church

While Moltmann recognizes many valid ways to develop a theory of the Church, whether from experience, sociologically, historically, or in religious comparison, he argues that the theological doctrine of the church must take seriously its claim to be "the church of Christ . . . [that] does everything in the name of the triune God."[114] Moltmann also shows the same independent focus on Christology, and on the Spirit, in relation to ecclesiology,[115] but we must make the same move of viewing his Christology and pneumatology as part of trinitarian doctrine as we did for Torrance.

To understand how Moltmann explores the Trinity-Church relation, we begin with his own vision, "to understand the triune God as the God who *is* community, who calls community into life and who invites men and women into sociality with him" for it is only on this basis that "the community of Christ is permitted to see itself as an earthly reflection of the divine Triunity."[116] Moltmann rejects the psychological doctrine of the Trinity and develops a social doctrine that is based on salvation history.[117] While Moltmann agrees with Torrance that the fellowship of God's people is related to the divine *perichoresis* since "the history of God's trinitarian relationships of fellowship corresponds to the eternal perichoresis of the Trinity,"[118] his focus falls much more on the egalitarian nature of the Christian community. *Perichoresis* necessarily entails rejecting the notion of a hierarchical trinitarian monarchy; instead, "the perichoretic at-oneness of the triune God corresponds to the experience of the community of Christ, the community which the Spirit unites through respect, affection and love."[119]

The liberationist themes of Moltmann's theology are also evident when he describes the nature of the Christian community, insisting that "the glory of the triune God is reflected, not in the crowns of kings and the triumphs of victors, but in the face of the crucified Jesus, and in the faces of the oppressed whose brother he became. He is the one visible image of the invisible God."[120]

> It is not the monarchy of a ruler that corresponds to the triune God; it is the community of men and women, without privileges and without subjugation. The three divine Persons have everything in common, except for their personal characteristics. So the Trinity corresponds to a community in which people are defined through their relations with one another and in their significance for one another, not in opposition to one another, in terms of power and possession.[121]

Moltmann often argues that the Church needs to reform "from a religious institution that looks after people into a congregational or community church in the midst of the people, through the people and with the people."[122] He further suggests that the Church's vision must be for "free decision in faith, voluntary sociality, mutual recognition and acceptance of one another and a common effort for justice and peace in this violent society of ours."[123] It is in response to this that Karen Kilby raises a significant critique of Moltmann's social trinitarianism based on the issue of projection. Kilby argues that since social trinitarians begin with the three persons, they then must describe how the three are bound together into oneness. In order to define *perichoresis*, Kilby argues, they take the best of the things that bind humans together, whether love, mutuality, or empathy, and project a perfected version into God's being.[124] She suggests that in Moltmann's social doctrine of the Trinity, "much of the detail is derived from either the individual author's or the larger society's latest ideas of how human beings should live in community . . . Social theories of the Trinity often project our ideal onto God."[125] As we saw earlier, Tanner agrees with Kilby's critique. Speaking specifically of using social trinitarianism as a source for political insight, Tanner notes that when a theologian bases their understanding of trinitarian terminology on their understanding of humans and society, "the account of the trinity loses its critical edge on political questions and begins simply to reflect the theologian's prior political views."[126]

The Nature of the Church

We have indicated Torrance's view of the four essential ecclesial attributes as attributes of Christ that the Church shares on the basis of its union with him.[127] Moltmann agrees that these statements about the Church are "integrated components of the confession of the triune God, and cannot be detached from [their creedal] context."[128] Moltmann continues to observe that these are not characteristics that belong to the Church but are instead *received* from Christ through the Spirit.[129]

The difference between Torrance's and Moltmann's takes on the notes of the Church is in the ways that these attributes are applied. Torrance argues that because they have to do with the essential being of the Church, the current period of the Church's life involves tension between what the Church essentially is and the flawed forms of the Church's visible life. Moltmann also recognizes this tension in a way shaped by his emphasis on the historical realization of eschatology in the form of liberation. He describes the four notes of the Church as *statements of hope*, which point to the eschatological and messianic fulfillment of God's promises, and *statements of action*, which the Church ought to seek.[130] He highlights the implications of how the Church is to be known in the world under the headings of unity in freedom, catholicity and partisanship, holiness in poverty, and the apostolate in suffering.[131]

This all elucidates Moltmann's stance that for the Church to understand itself, it must find its bearings within the trinitarian history of God. "Without an understanding of the particular church in the framework of the universal history of God's dealings with the world, ecclesiology remains abstract and the church's self-understanding blind."[132] The Church participates in God's dealings with the world and so gains knowledge of its place.[133] The trinitarian history has to do with the "gathering, uniting and glorifying of the world in God and of God in the world,"[134] in the light of which Moltmann contends that the Church "is not in itself the salvation of the world, so that the 'churchifying' of the world would mean the latter's salvation."[135] Instead, the Church *serves* "and is like an arrow sent out into the world to point to the future."[136] The Church is called to eschatological witness that can only be understood within the *missio dei*. "The goal is not the glorification of the church but the glorification of the Father through the Son in the Holy Spirit"[137]—a comment mirrored by Torrance's insistence that the Church takes on the role of a servant, pointing to Christ.

Particular Aspects of the Church's Visible Life

Moltmann views the Church as representing the "eschatological exodus." The Church is not to escape society but rather is to embody the "beginning of liberation of the whole of enslaved creation for its consummation in glory."[138] Moltmann considers that the forms of the Church's "fellowship and public functions, and the shape of its order and ministries, are not merely externals and inessentials; they are no less important than the word and the sacraments,"[139] giving more theological significance to these elements than Torrance does. In practical terms, although the Church lives in the tension between the claims of Christ and society, Moltmann holds that it must not "adopt its social order from the way in which the society it lives is run . . . for it has to correspond to its Lord and to represent new life for society."[140] Consequently, while the Church will reflect its particular environment, it must not passively accept the societal imprint for Moltmann argues that church order is "part of the church's living witness" and must be geared toward the new creation.[141] Here we may think again of Torrance's admonition that the Church has "no right to identify itself with the social order here or with any political system."[142]

Moltmann and Torrance both emphasize the necessity of order in the Church and agree that this true order must be derived from the Church's ontological relation to the Triune God. Where Torrance focuses on the Word as preaching in the life of the Church, Moltmann focuses upon the broader framework of Gospel proclamation. Moltmann suggests that we cannot limit this to public preaching but rather should include any activity that tells the story of God, proclaiming his promise of liberation.[143] The Gospel has to do with the eschatological liberation of all things, and so through the Spirit this light is thrown back onto history, which gives rise to a "messianic fellowship," a community that Moltmann claims "narrates the story of Christ, and its own story with that story, because its own existence, fellowship and activity springs from that story of liberation."[144] Moltmann stands at odds here with Torrance. For Torrance, the Church derives from the God who liberates and sets his people free through the work of Christ and the Spirit and not from the story of liberation as Moltmann holds.

Torrance embraces the traditional forms of the Church, and much of his theology has to do with correct structure and working formally toward ecumenical rapprochement. By contrast, Moltmann argues that this "messianic fellowship" cannot embody any of the traditional forms of the Church, whether the exclusive voluntary fellowship, or the state church, or the public form of Christianity. It must be a community free from the prevailing social systems that instead seeks to proclaim liberation through "actions of hope in the fellowship of the poor, the sad, and those condemned to silence . . . The truth of the proclamation is recognizable from the freedom it creates."[145] This is a freedom that "realizes the possibilities of the messianic era" and offers the space to humanity to live a "life which takes on a messianic character."[146]

In sacramental terms, Torrance suggests that it is Jesus Christ who is the primary *mystērion* and that baptism and the Eucharist are only *mystērion* in a secondary sense. Moltmann argues that the terms *mystērion* and *sacramentum* refer not to baptism or the Lord's Supper but to "the divine eschatological secret,"[147] and unlike Torrance, he rejects a solely Christological understanding of *mystērion*, arguing that the *mystērion* in its New Testament sense "spreads beyond Christology and flows into pneumatology, ecclesiology and the eschatology of world history."[148] Consequently, Moltmann calls for a trinitarian understanding of *mystērion* that emphasizes the Spirit as an eschatological gift in history, pointing to the new creation.[149] Proclamation, the sacraments, and the charismatic gifts of the Spirit are to be understood as "the 'signs and wonders'" of the history of the Spirit who creates salvation and brings about the new creation and who through Christ unites us with the Father and glorifies him."[150]

When it comes to dealing with the two sacraments, however, Moltmann and Torrance are surprisingly similar in the way that they describe the relation between baptism and the Lord's Supper (which is Moltmann's preferred term for the Eucharist). Torrance notes that both baptism and the Eucharist "have to do with the whole Christ clothed with the Gospel of reconciliation and resurrection," but he specifies that baptism has to do with the objective and complete event while the Eucharist has to do with humanity's ongoing participation in that event.[151] Moltmann, for his part, affirms their inseparability, describing baptism as a sign of grace, the "eschatological *sign of starting out*," and the Eucharist as a sign of hope, the "eschatological *sign of being on the way*."[152]

Moltmann observes that the primary form of ministry in the Church is that which is given to all members of the community, who are corporately a prophetic, priestly, and kingly people.[153] Although the traditional justification of ministry was one God, one Christ, one bishop, and one Church, Moltmann argues that this "unified hierarchy reflects a clerical monotheism which corresponded to contemporary 'political monotheism,' but which is a contradiction of the trinitarian understanding of God and his people."[154] When the trinitarian understanding that Moltmann espouses is allowed to govern ecclesiology, then the essential tasks of the community are *kerygma*, *koinōnia*, and *diakonia*—proclamation, fellowship, and service.[155] Even where one person may be called to a particular task, they are neither higher, nor lower, than the rest of the charismatic community. Moltmann acknowledges here the preeminence of baptism; ordination does "not confer any higher dignity than baptism," instead symbolizing the special call of a particular individual.[156]

This results in a different doctrine of the ministry than Torrance's. While Torrance affirms that baptism is the sacrament of the corporate priesthood, he argues that there is a distinction between the priesthood of the whole Church and the specific ordination of some who are set apart for teaching, preaching, and administering the sacraments. Torrance is careful to emphasize that these roles of authority are for "edification and not for destruction" because those who operate in them are "nothing more than servants of Christ, and, at the same time, servants of the people in Christ."[157] Nevertheless, Moltmann pays significantly more attention than Torrance to the concrete ways in which members of the Church must engage in witness that is not simply proclamation of what God has done in Christ but is instead active affirmation of the difference that this makes for humankind.[158]

Israel

While Israel is not a predominant element of the Church's visible life, it is worth noting because both Moltmann and Torrance relate the salvation of Israel to eschatology and the way in which the Church is to participate in God's redemptive work. Moltmann agrees with Torrance that Israel is "Christianity's original, enduring and final partner in history."[159] He also rejects replacement theology, stating clearly that "the church is not the organization that succeeds Israel in salvation history. It does not take Israel's place."[160] In eschatological terms, Moltmann comments upon the enduring theological specificity of Israel, which is particularly accentuated by their modern possession of the land,[161] and he posits that the *parousia* will not take place without Christians and Jews being in fellowship with one another because "the still unfulfilled promises of the Old Testament must be transplanted into the soil of the new."[162] This is in keeping with Torrance's call for the schism between Jewish and Gentile people to be healed in Christ because it hinders the proclamation of the Gospel.[163] Moltmann and Torrance both have an eschatological perspective on the corporate salvation of Israel. Moltmann holds that when Israel comes to faith in Christ it will be "the external sign of the transition from messianic world mission to the messianic kingdom"[164]—a view paralleled by Torrance in his comment that to expect the *parousia* means that one must also actively hope for the conversion of the Jews.[165]

Concluding Reflections

Moltmann and Torrance both develop a trinitarian ecclesiology but diverge in the different aspects that they emphasize. They have different theological methodologies: Torrance begins with divine revelation as recorded in Scripture and draws on the Fathers' doctrine of the Trinity to develop his doctrine of God, while Moltmann draws on the biblical narrative but develops his doctrine of God in alignment with his eschatological and liberationist concerns. This results in different expressions of the relationship between God and the Church. Torrance is concerned with the ontological relation between the Triune God and the Church and argues that the fellowship of the Church is correlated with but absolutely distinct from the Triune fellowship. Moltmann argues that the history of the Trinity shows that God is open to the world. The relationship between God and the world is not one of utter distinction because God needs the world and God can be affected by the world. In the final evaluation, Torrance's approach avoids the danger of remaking God in our own image as one who has needs external to his own being, but Moltmann does more to highlight the importance of the Church bearing practical witness to the hope and promise of the Gospel.

JOHN ZIZIOULAS

Our final dialogue partner is John Zizioulas. As one of the most influential Orthodox theologians of the twentieth century, he is particularly well regarded by non-Orthodox theologians, leading Rowan Williams to suggest that Zizioulas may be "the most widely read Orthodox theologian in the Western milieu."[166] Zizioulas makes a significant contribution to Orthodox theology by recontextualizing the patristic writings for the Orthodox Church, especially in the areas of anthropology, ontology, and ecclesiology, and bringing these insights into ecumenical dialogue.

The relationship between Torrance and Zizioulas is not easy to define. On one hand, Torrance was instrumental in Zizioulas's introduction to the English-speaking world, and Zizioulas spent three years as Torrance's teaching assistant at the University of Edinburgh. On the other hand, while there was relatively little written interaction between them, there is a tacit debate between Torrance and Zizioulas that "runs as a sub-current throughout their respective writings on the Trinity, personhood, and nature."[167] The exchange between them largely centers on their different readings of the Cappadocian Fathers, illuminating the variances in their approaches to trinitarian ecclesiology. We will begin by comparing their doctrines of God, identifying similarities and differences, and then turning to their ecclesiology.

By way of introduction, where Moltmann's central theological concern was eschatology with its corresponding themes of promise and hope, Douglas Knight suggests that Zizioulas's central theological concern is

> human freedom and the relation of freedom and others. Freedom is not restricted, but enabled, by our relationships with other persons, Zizioulas argues, for the community in which God includes us is the place in which our personal identity and freedom come into being. God is intrinsically communion and free, and his communion and freedom he shares with us.[168]

This quote signals that for Zizioulas, freedom is not simply the arbitrary freedom to do whatever one wants without considering the consequences for others. Instead, freedom is to be free of restricting necessity and is also intrinsically connected with relationality. God's being is communion, and as he brings us into that communion, we are made free for relationship with others while retaining our own unique specificity. It is the twin themes of communion and otherness that are intrinsic to personhood and therefore to a trinitarian ecclesiology in Zizioulas's account.

Zizioulas's Doctrine of God

Del Colle contends that "neither Zizioulas nor Torrance consider themselves innovators"[169] when it comes to the doctrine of God. They both draw on the Fathers as their primary source and agree that the focus of the patristic period was on the doctrine of God with barely any doctrinal development regarding the Church. However, both Zizioulas and Torrance can't help but communicate their own perspectives in their adoption of the Fathers. In *Being as Communion*, Zizioulas uses their language, concepts, and arguments in order to develop his own understanding of correct Orthodox theology. This is paralleled by our earlier observation that Torrance's claim to let the Fathers speak for themselves in *The Trinitarian Faith* is somewhat inefficacious. Nevertheless, Zizioulas was "one of the most prominent stars" of the 1960s "'neo-patristic' synthesis . . . a movement responsible for the rediscovery of the patristic notion of the person in Orthodox theology."[170]

Their shared use of the Fathers leads to a shared commitment that God's being is communion. Zizioulas is adamant that to speak of God is to speak of communion for "the being of God is a relational being: without the concept of communion it would not be possible to speak of the being of God."[171] He expounds further that to speak of God's "substance" is to speak of "communion." "The Holy Trinity is a *primordial* ontological concept and not a notion which is added to the divine substance or rather which follows it."[172] Torrance would have no difficulty with these general claims, stating explicitly, "Being and Communion are one and the same."[173]

The next similarity is that Torrance and Zizioulas both emphasize the absolute distinction between God and creation. Zizioulas affirms that "between God and the world there is total ontological otherness: God's being is uncreated, while that of the world is created, that is, contingent."[174] The distinction between God and his creation is a consistent theme in Torrance's work as is the contingency, or dependence, of creation.[175]

Another similarity is that Torrance and Zizioulas both argue that the only way to truly overcome the divide between God and the world is through the incarnation of Jesus Christ, who unites God and humanity in himself. Zizioulas describes the God-world relation as hypostatic—it is only in and through the Son that the absolute distinction is bridged.[176] Zizioulas explains this as an "ontology of love understood in a personal way" through which God and the world "can be united without losing their otherness."[177] Torrance also affirms that it is only through Christ as the unique mediator that humans are united to God and able to participate in the communion of the Trinity.

This leads us to the final similarity between Torrance and Zizioulas, which is the inseparability of the economic work of the Son and the Spirit. Zizioulas notes that this has traditionally been a weakness of Orthodox theology so that the question of how to bring pneumatology and Christology into a "full and organic synthesis" is "one of the most important questions facing Orthodox theology in our time."[178] He concludes that the question of doctrinal priority remains a *theologoumenon*: "as long as the essential *content* of both Christology and Pneumatology is present, the synthesis is there in its fullness."[179] Zizioulas comments that only the Son becomes incarnate and enters history, while the Spirit remains discarnate and is in many ways beyond history so that "when [the Spirit] acts in history he does so in order to bring into history the last days."[180] We also see this affirmation of the mutual work of the Son and Spirit in Torrance's material. Torrance observes that the Son becomes incarnate to form an *objective* union with us in history, and then in the eschatological pause that is created by the Son's ascension, the Spirit is at work *subjectively* actualizing humanity's union with Christ.[181]

We turn now to the differences that emerge, first in methodology, and then in content. In methodological terms, Torrance argues that the Nicene Creed formalized what the Fathers "had to say about God" and arose "in compulsive response to the objective self-revelation of God."[182] Torrance appeals in an almost romantic fashion to the "distinctive *mind* or *phronēma* of the Catholic Church" and suggests that this mind was what the Fathers appealed to, "in forming theological judgments and making conciliar decisions."[183] In contrast to Torrance, Zizioulas's argument for the methodology behind the development of the doctrine of the Trinity is noticeably more grounded in the experience of the Christian community. Zizioulas maintains that it was the "ecclesial experience of the Fathers" in the Eucharist that led to the affirmation of God's being as communion.[184] Since "the being of God could only be known through personal relationships and personal love," this understanding of the divine ontology "came out of the eucharistic experience of the Church."[185]

However, the difference in content is far more significant. The most notable divergence has to do with their conflicting interpretations of the Cappadocian Fathers about how the relationships between the Triune persons are to be understood. The issue is not over the understanding of personhood—both theologians maintain that the concept of "person" developed in accordance with the doctrine of the Trinity.[186] The issue instead is whether some form of causality is present in the relationships between the Triune persons. To understand this, we must briefly trace Zizioulas's train of thought as to *how* the patristic writers developed the concept of person because this will help us understand why he explains the relationships between the Triune persons in the way that he does.

According to Zizioulas, ancient Greek thought was shaped by the concept of ontological monism where the being of God and the being of the world existed in unbreakable unity.[187] To be a person was to have something added to one's being: the vocabulary of *prosōpon* was associated with the idea of wearing a mask in the theatre,[188] while *hypostasis* meant one's nature or substance. A similar tendency existed in Roman thought where the idea of *persona* was not a reference to the being of the person but rather to one's varying relational roles. "*Persona* is the role which one plays in one's social or legal relationships, the moral or 'legal' person which either collectively or individually has nothing to do with the *ontology* of the person."[189] This understanding of personhood was obviously untenable with the Church's ability to say that "God is Father, Son and Spirit without ceasing to be *one* God."[190]

Zizioulas argues that a revolution in thought had to take place in what was understood by personhood. Two new presuppositions were needed: "a radical change in cosmology which would free the world and man from ontological necessity" and "an ontological view of man which would unite the person with the *being* of man, with his permanent and enduring existence, with his genuine and absolute identity."[191] The Greek Fathers were uniquely positioned to do this, drawing on the biblical outlook of Christianity for the first presupposition and on the Greek interest in ontology for the second.[192] As a result of this change in thought, *hypostasis* became associated with "person." For Zizioulas, personhood has to do with one's being and includes freedom, uniqueness, and relationality. This is what separates the "person" from simply being an "individual."[193]

This is all rather oblique but becomes clearer when we return to the concept of communion. Zizioulas argues that in order for the concept of communion to be "personal" and not simply another way of talking about an abstract "substance," communion must derive from a *hypostasis*. He proposes that

> just like "substance," "communion" does not exist by itself: it is the *Father* who is the cause of it. This thesis of the Cappadocians that introduced the concept of "cause" into the being of God assumed an incalculable importance. For it meant that the ultimate ontological category which makes something really *be*, is neither an impersonal and incommunicable "substance," nor a structure of communion existing by itself or imposed by necessity, but rather the *person*.[194]

Zizioulas further argues that God demonstrates his ontological freedom precisely by "the way in which He transcends and abolishes the ontological necessity of the substance by being God as *Father*, that is, as He who 'begets' the Son and 'brings forth' the Spirit."[195] Zizioulas ascribes preeminence to the notion of *hypostases* within trinitarian doctrine—so much so that Wilks suggests that personhood rather than ontology is the primary concern of Zizioulas's trinitarian writings.[196] Zizioulas thus holds that the *hypostasis* is the cause of the Triune communion; for the Triune communion to be personal, it must come from a distinct, concrete hypostasis and result in distinct, concrete hypostases.[197] Also commenting upon this element of Zizioulas's work, Melissaris notes that "a consistent theological notion of personhood demands that ultimacy be given not to an abstract, impersonal principle, such as relatedness, but to a personal first cause of the existent."[198]

Zizioulas's claim that the Father is the "'cause' both of the generation of the Son and of the procession of the Spirit"[199] is where Torrance most obviously takes issue with Zizioulas's work. Torrance argues instead that the Son and Spirit proceed from the shared *ousia* of the Godhead, which results in an understanding of the divine *monarchia* being grounded in the whole Godhead and not simply in the person of the Father. Torrance attributes to "being" what Zizioulas attributes to the "persons";[200] he insists that "if one is to speak of the generation of the Son and the procession of the Spirit from the *Person* of the Father this is not to be equated with the *causation of their being*, but only with the *mode* of their enhypostatic differentiation within the one intrinsically personal Being of the Godhead."[201]

This is a point of vital importance for Torrance. Attributing the divine *monarchia* to the perichoretic union of the three persons allows Torrance to insist that each triune person is wholly God and they each experience complete mutual coinherence with the other two persons of the Trinity. On this basis, Torrance continues, we can affirm with both East and West that the Spirit proceeds "from the Father and the Son" and "from the Father through the Son." The Spirit proceeds from the whole Godhead, which refutes any notion of causality or of superiority and inferiority within the Trinity.

Furthermore, because each of the persons is whole of a whole, we must not speak of causal relationships when considering the immanent Trinity. Del Colle explains that for Torrance, Zizioulas's perspective that the *hypostasis* of the Father is the cause of the Son and Spirit is "inevitably subordinationist" for "no matter how one describes it a distinction is being drawn between underived and derived deity, between superiority and inferiority in degrees of deity."[202] As Molnar also observes, for Torrance, "*any* claim that the Father is the *cause* of the Son and the Spirit has to involve an element of subordinationism and to that extent a negation of the *homoousion* of the three persons."[203]

Zizioulas responds with the argument that Torrance's understanding of *perichoresis*, which necessarily entails rejecting causal relationships within the Trinity, makes the Cappadocian Fathers "look logically inconsistent, as they teach both causality and coinherence in divine being."[204] This critique is helpful because it brings to light what is really at stake in the debate between Torrance and Zizioulas, namely, their differing interpretation of the Cappadocian Fathers.[205] While this is a much more extensive issue than we have time to engage with here, we may use Radcliff's summary that the scholarly debate came to be less about the Cappadocians vs. Athanasius, or about Cappadocian vs. Cappadocian, and instead became more about Torrance vs. Zizioulas.[206] It is useful for us to simply highlight their differing conclusions as summarized by del Colle: "Torrance develops an ontology of God's triune Being; Zizioulas, an ontology of divine personhood."[207]

Zizioulas's Doctrine of the Church

We come now to explore the way that Zizioulas's doctrine of God shapes his ecclesiology. He confesses the importance of thinking rightly about God, commenting that since the Church "must herself be an image of the way in which God exists . . . the Church must have a right faith, a correct vision with respect to the being of God."[208] Zizioulas draws a "straight line" from the Trinity to the Church, while Torrance is much more nuanced about the relationship between the Triune communion and the correlative creaturely communion that is the Church. Behr critiques Zizioulas, noting that the problem of "juxtaposing the Trinity *and* the Church . . . communion ecclesiology sees the Church as parallel to the 'immanent Trinity' . . . This results in a horizontal notion of communion, or perhaps better parallel 'communions,' without being clear about how the two intersect."[209] As we have seen, Torrance is careful to explain that the two dimensions of *koinōnia* are uniquely related through the person of Jesus Christ, thus avoiding Behr's point of critique.

Zizioulas argues that "salvation is identified with the realization of personhood in man,"[210] which only takes place in the Church. Humans must be translated from the "hypostasis of biological existence" into a new "ecclesial hypostasis." This is what takes place in "baptism as new birth . . . Baptism leads to a new mode of existence, to a regeneration . . . and consequently to a new 'hypostasis.'"[211] In order for human persons to be free from ontological necessity and thus made true persons, one's hypostasis must be constituted by "an ontological reality which does not suffer from createdness."[212] This is an *eschatological* reality for humanity, and so Zizioulas argues that even while humans may realize their "ecclesial hypostasis" now, we still need a third ontological category, that of a "sacramental or eucharistic hypostasis,"[213] that embraces the eschatological element of one's new personhood.

This idea of the ecclesial hypostasis leads to the different ways in which Torrance and Zizioulas understand the Church as the body of Christ. Torrance argues that this is the most apt analogy for the Church because on the basis of Christ's assumption of humanity, the Church is comprised of all those who are united to him through the Spirit. Zizioulas demonstrates a different understanding of the Church as the body of Christ. He develops this in reference to the inseparability of Christology and pneumatology, insisting that Christ is a "pneumatological being, born and existing in the *koinonia* of the Spirit." Consequently, Zizioulas argues that "we must stop thinking of Christ in individualistic terms and understand Him as a 'corporate person,' an inclusive being."[214] Expressing this another way, he states that "the Church becomes Christ Himself in human existence, but also every member of the Church becomes Christ and Church."[215] Zizioulas's language here risks eradicating the distinction between Christ and the Church.

Torrance disavows the notion that Christ is only a person in relation to the Church, arguing that while we may say "Christ is the Church . . . that proposition cannot be reversed, so as to make Christ the predicate of the Church."[216] From a Torrancian perspective, Zizioulas risks minimizing the absolute uniqueness, supremacy, and sufficiency of Jesus Christ.

The One and the Many

Zizioulas declares that since Christians "believe in a God who is in His very being *koinonia*," then "ecclesiology must be based on Trinitarian theology if it is to be an ecclesiology of communion."[217] This is common to both Torrance and Zizioulas and does not require any further explanation. In this final section, instead of exploring the forms and structure of the Church as we did in our previous comparisons, we will instead address the issue of the "one and the many" as it is illuminative of a key principle for Zizioulas.

Zizioulas emphasizes the way in which the Orthodox church argues for the importance of the local church, holding that there is no dichotomy between the local church and the universal Church.[218] From his perspective, Roman Catholicism gives precedence to the one Church, while Protestantism gives precedence to the local community. Instead, Zizioulas calls for a "middle way" in ecclesiology: "the 'many' must have a constitutive and not a derivative role in the Church's being; local and universal must somehow coincide."[219]

Zizioulas continues, "There is one Church, as there is one God. But the expression of this one Church is the communion of the many local Churches. Communion and oneness coincide in ecclesiology."[220] Each local church is made a full Church through the Holy Spirit and must not become "submissive" to a "universal Church structure."[221] The Orthodox Church works this out through the synodal system and the ministry of primacy.[222] This is why the ministry of *episkopé*, or the bishop, is so important. Orthodox synodality requires every province to have one ordained head who cannot be replaced by a form of collective ministry and yet also requires the "one" to be in relation to the "many." In short, "the multiplicity is not to be subjected to the oneness; it is constitutive of the oneness."[223]

Zizioulas holds that regardless of contextual circumstances, neither the baptismal structure nor the eucharistic structure of the Church can be changed. Consequently, Zizioulas argues that churches should try to recognize each other as "ecclesial communities" since God calls us from our divided state toward such an "existential *rapprochement*."[224] More specifically, Zizioulas draws on *koinōnia* to support his vision for Church unity, suggesting that it can

> help us to overcome traditional dichotomies between the institutional and the charismatic, the local and the universal, conciliatory and primacy. This concept, if it is used creatively in ecclesiology, would destroy all legalistic and pyramidical views of ministry, authority and structure in the Church, which hinder progress towards unity.[225]

Torrance appreciated Zizioulas's efforts toward ecumenism and also called for an ecumenicity that is grounded in our shared unity through *koinōnia* with the Holy Spirit. Torrance and Zizioulas both called for a Christological and pneumatological approach rather than one based on those elements of the Church's visible life that divide us.

CONCLUDING REFLECTIONS

Both Torrance and Zizioulas are proponents of communion ecclesiology, drawing on the theme of *koinōnia* in their respective bodies of work. Our most robust discussion had to do with Zizioulas's understanding of the triune persons and his insistence that in order for *ousia* to be personal, it must derive from a unique *hypostasis*. This is the basis for his argument that the triune communion is grounded in the person of the Father, in differentiation from the Son and Spirit. We then noted Torrance's strong reaction against Zizioulas's view of the Triune communion. Torrance argues that to say that the Son and Spirit derive from the *hypostasis* of the Father introduces causality into the immanent Trinity, which negates the *homoousion* of the three persons.

This led to our major criticism of Zizioulas in relation to Torrance. In referring to the Church as an image of God's existence, Zizioulas draws a much more direct line from the being of God to the being of the Church. This is outworked in a number of ways, but we highlighted in particular how Zizioulas understands what it is to describe the Church as the "body of Christ." Where Torrance views this as a metaphor that involves union with Christ despite humanity's unlikeness to and difference from him, Zizioulas eradicates the distinction between Christ and the Church by arguing that because of the joint work of the Son and the Spirit, on one hand, the Church becomes Christ, and on the other hand, every member of the Church becomes Christ. Where Torrance is exceedingly careful to maintain the uniqueness of Christ even though it is in Christ that the vertical and horizontal dimensions of the Church meet, Zizioulas blurs the lines with his view of the relationship between God's being and the being of the Church.

NOTES

1. Kathryn Tanner, *Christ the Key* (Cambridge: Cambridge University Press, 2010), vii, notes that *Christ the Key* takes the "heart of the theological vision" presented in *Jesus, Humanity and the Trinity* and applies it in a less systematic fashion to "otherwise tired theological topics."
2. Amy Plantinga Pauw, "Ecclesiological Reflections on Kathryn Tanner's *Jesus, Humanity* and the Trinity," *Scottish Journal of Theology* 57, no. 2 (2004): 221.
3. Kathryn Tanner, *Jesus, Humanity and the Trinity: A Brief Systematic Theology* (Edinburgh: T&T Clark, 1991), 1.
4. Ibid., 89.
5. Ibid., 2.
6. Thomas F. Torrance, *Theology in Reconstruction* (Grand Rapids, MI: Eerdmans, 1965), 193.
7. Tanner, *Jesus, Humanity and the Trinity*, 42–43.
8. Ibid., 45.
9. Torrance, *Theology in Reconstruction*, 193.
10. Tanner, *Jesus, Humanity and the Trinity*, 46.
11. Ibid., 47.
12. Ibid., 42.
13. Ibid., 19.
14. Torrance, *Theology in Reconstruction*, 193.
15. Tanner, *Jesus, Humanity and the Trinity*, 99.
16. Ibid., 104.

17. Ibid., 109.
18. Tanner, *Christ the Key*, viii.
19. Thomas F. Torrance, *Theology in Reconciliation* (Eugene, OR: Wipf and Stock, 1996), 260.
20. Thomas F. Torrance, *Divine Meaning: Studies in Patristic Hermeneutics* (Edinburgh: T&T Clark, 1995), 121–23.
21. Tanner, *Christ the Key*, ix.
22. Ibid., 218.
23. Ibid., 223.
24. Ibid., 231.
25. Ibid., 172.
26. Tanner, *Jesus, Humanity and the Trinity*, 27.
27. Ibid., 29.
28. Tanner, *Christ the Key*, 200.
29. Ibid., 200n97.
30. Thomas F. Torrance, *The Christian Doctrine of God: One Being Three Persons* (Edinburgh: T&T Clark, 1996), 196.
31. Ibid.
32. Tanner, *Christ the Key*, 195.
33. Ibid., 195.
34. Ibid., 7–8.
35. Ibid., 14. Tanner also notes that Jesus "does not just *have* the divine image within himself through participation but *is* it, and therefore his humanity can neither exhibit the divine image in an imperfect way nor lose it" (35).
36. Ibid., 7.
37. Ibid., 8–17.
38. Ibid., 142–43.
39. Tanner, *Jesus, Humanity and the Trinity*, 15.
40. Ibid., 11.
41. Tanner, *Christ the Key*, 297, citing Torrance, *Theology in Reconciliation*, 155.
42. Ibid., 235.
43. Tanner, *Jesus, Humanity and the Trinity*, 83.
44. Ibid., 79.
45. Ibid., 81.
46. Ibid., 81–82.
47. Tanner, *Christ the Key*, 207.
48. Ibid.
49. Ibid., 222.
50. Ibid., 224.
51. Ibid., 224–26.
52. Ibid., 227.
53. Ibid., 228.
54. Ibid., 229.
55. Ibid.
56. Ibid., 208.
57. Ibid., 236. Tanner's lengthy discourse on the difference between weak and strong forms of participation in the Triune life is found in *Christ the Key*, 1–57.
58. Ibid., 245.
59. Ibid., 243.
60. Ibid., 234.
61. Ibid., 242.
62. Tanner, *Jesus, Humanity and the Trinity*, 61.
63. Ibid., 70.
64. Ibid., 67.
65. Ibid., 121.
66. Ibid., 79.

67. Ibid., 80.
68. Tanner, *Christ the Key*, 205.
69. Ibid., 206.
70. Tanner, *Jesus, Humanity and the Trinity*, 73.
71. Tanner, *Christ the Key*, 240–41.
72. Jürgen Moltmann, *Experiences in Theology*, trans. Margaret Kohl (London: SCM Press, 2000), xviii.
73. Ibid., 4.
74. Richard Bauckham, "Jürgen Moltmann" in *The Modern Theologians*, ed. David Ford, 147 (Malden, MA: Blackwell, 2005).
75. Jürgen Moltmann, *The Trinity and the Kingdom*, trans. Margaret Kohl (Minneapolis, MN: Fortress, Press, 1993), 47.
76. Jürgen Moltmann, *Theology of Hope*, trans. James W. Leitch (Minneapolis, MN: Fortress Press, 1993), 11.
77. Ibid., 10–11.
78. Ibid., 16.
79. Ibid., 329.
80. Moltmann, *The Trinity and the Kingdom*, 129–48.
81. See Moltmann's description and critique in Moltmann, *The Trinity and the Kingdom*, 10–19.
82. Ibid., 150. Moltmann uses this term in a pejorative sense.
83. Ibid., 19.
84. Ibid., 64.
85. Ibid., 175.
86. George Hunsinger, "*The Trinity and the Kingdom*, by Jürgen Moltmann," *The Thomist* 47, no. 1 (January 1983): 131.
87. Moltmann, *The Trinity and the Kingdom*, 189.
88. Ibid., 190.
89. Readers should recall our earlier discussions of the influence that Michael Polanyi's work had on Torrance in this regard.
90. Moltmann, *The Trinity and the Kingdom*, 166.
91. Ibid., 182.
92. Ibid., 185.
93. Ibid., 183.
94. Ibid., 178.
95. Ibid., xvi.
96. Bauckham, "Jürgen Moltmann," 149.
97. Torrance, *The Christian Doctrine of God*, 247n39.
98. Ibid., 54.
99. Ibid., 54n81.
100. Ibid., 247.
101. Moltmann, *The Trinity and the Kingdom*, 98.
102. Ibid., 99.
103. Ibid., 59.
104. Hunsinger, "*The Trinity and the Kingdom*," 135.
105. Richard Bauckham, *The Theology of Jürgen Moltmann* (New York: T&T Clark, 1995), 243.
106. Ibid., 244.
107. Torrance, *The Christian Doctrine of God*, 239.
108. Ibid., 207. Torrance also states that God "does not need relation to us to be what he is as the living acting God" (4).
109. Moltmann, *The Trinity and the Kingdom*, 160.
110. Joy Ann McDougall, "The Return of Trinitarian Praxis? Moltmann on the Trinity and the Christian Life," *Journal of Religion* 83, no. 2 (April 2003): 183.
111. Moltmann, *The Trinity and the Kingdom*, 56.
112. Ibid.

113. Torrance, *The Christian Doctrine of God*, 152–53.
114. Jürgen Moltmann, *The Church in the Power of the Spirit*, trans. Margaret Kohl (Minneapolis, MN: Fortress Press, 1993), 5.
115. Ibid., 6.
116. Ibid., xv.
117. Moltmann, *The Trinity and the Kingdom*, 157.
118. Ibid.
119. Ibid., 157–58.
120. Ibid., 197–98.
121. Ibid., 198.
122. Moltmann, *The Church in the Power of the Spirit*, xiii.
123. Ibid., xiv.
124. Karen Kilby, "Perichoresis and Projection: Problems with Social Doctrines of the Trinity," *New Blackfriars* 81, no. 956 (October 2000): 441.
125. Ibid.
126. Tanner, *Christ the Key*, 223, citing Kilby, "Perichoresis and Projection," 442.
127. Thomas F. Torrance, *Atonement: The Person and Work of Christ*, ed. Robert T. Walker, 380 (Downers Grove, IL: InterVarsity Academic Press, 2009).
128. Moltmann, *The Church in the Power of the Spirit*, 337.
129. Ibid., 338.
130. Ibid., 339–40.
131. Ibid., 342–61.
132. Ibid., 51. Moltmann explains that we need integrative thinking, which understands events within history and experience as part of a whole life.
133. Ibid., 53.
134. Ibid., 60.
135. Moltmann, *Theology of Hope*, 328.
136. Ibid.
137. Moltmann, *The Church in the Power of the Spirit*, 11.
138. Ibid., 83.
139. Ibid., 290.
140. Ibid., 106.
141. Ibid., 292.
142. Thomas F. Torrance, *Gospel, Church and Ministry*, ed. Jock Stein, 179 (Eugene, OR: Pickwick Publications, 2012).
143. Moltmann, *The Church in the Power of the Spirit*, 206.
144. Ibid., 225.
145. Ibid., 225–26.
146. Ibid., 225.
147. Ibid., 202.
148. Ibid., 204.
149. Ibid., 205.
150. Ibid., 206.
151. Torrance, *Conflict and Agreement: Conflict and Disorder*, 258.
152. Moltmann, *Church in the Power of the Spirit*, 243.
153. Ibid., 300; see extended discussion in Moltmann, *The Trinity and the Kingdom*, 191–202.
154. Ibid., 305.
155. Ibid., 307.
156. Ibid., 314.
157. Thomas F. Torrance, *Royal Priesthood* (Edinburgh: Oliver and Boyd, 1955), 91.
158. Moltmann, *The Church in the Power of the Spirit*, 150–96.
159. Ibid., 135.
160. Ibid., 148.
161. Ibid., 137–44. Moltmann notes that the modern state of Israel is "a foretoken, but an ambiguous one" (149).

162. Ibid., 138.
163. Thomas F. Torrance, *The Mediation of Christ* (Edinburgh: T&T Clark, 1992), 45–46.
164. Moltmann, *The Church in the Power of the Spirit*, 139.
165. Thomas F. Torrance, *Conflict and Agreement in the Church: Order and Disorder* (Eugene, OR: Wipf and Stock, 1996), 285.
166. Rowan Williams, "Eastern Orthodox Theology" in *The Modern Theologians*, ed. David Ford, 584 (Malden, MA: Blackwell, 2005).
167. Matthew Baker, "Introduction," *Participatio* 4 (2013): 4.
168. Douglas H. Knight, "Introduction" in *The Theology of John Zizioulas: Personhood and the Church*, ed. Douglas H. Knight, 1 (New York: Routledge, 2016).
169. Ralph Del Colle, "'Person' and 'Being' in John Zizioulas' Trinitarian Theology: Conversations with Thomas Torrance and Thomas Aquinas," *Scottish Journal of Theology* 54, no. 1 (2001): 73.
170. Athanasios G. Melissaris, "The Challenge of Patristic Ontology in the Theology of Metropolitan John (Zizioulas) of Pergamon," *Greek Orthodox Theological Review* 44 (Spring 1999): 486.
171. John D. Zizioulas, *Being as Communion: Studies in Personhood and the Church* (New York: St. Vladimir's University Press, 1985), 17.
172. Ibid.
173. Torrance, *The Christian Doctrine of God*, 104.
174. John D. Zizioulas, *Communion and Otherness: Further Studies in Personhood and the Church* (London: T&T Clark, 2006), 17.
175. Thomas F. Torrance, *Divine and Contingent Order* (Edinburgh: T&T Clark, 1998), vi–vii. Torrance describes the universe as "contingent for it depends on God entirely for its origin and for what it continues to be in its existence and its order."
176. Zizioulas, *Communion and Otherness*, 30.
177. Ibid., 29.
178. Zizioulas, *Being as Communion*, 126.
179. Ibid., 129.
180. Ibid., 130.
181. Torrance, *Atonement*, 359.
182. Thomas F. Torrance, "The Deposit of Faith," *Scottish Journal of Theology* 36, no. 1 (1983): 7.
183. Torrance, *The Christian Doctrine of God*, ix. Readers may revisit the extended discussion of this element in chapter 3.
184. Zizioulas, *Being as Communion*, 16.
185. Ibid., 16–17.
186. In *The Christian Doctrine of God*, Torrance argues that the doctrine of the Trinity gave rise to the "new *concept of person*, unknown in human thought until then, according to which the relations between persons belong to what persons are" (102). Zizioulas echoes Torrance when he states that "the concept of the person with its absolute and ontological content was born historically from the endeavour of the Church to give ontological expression to its faith in the Triune God." See Zizioulas, *Being as Communion*, 16.
187. Zizioulas, *Being as Communion*, 16.
188. Ibid., 31.
189. Ibid., 34.
190. Ibid., 36.
191. Ibid., 35.
192. Ibid.
193. Ibid., 39.
194. Ibid., 18.
195. Ibid., 44.
196. John G. F. Wilks, "The Trinitarian Ontology of John Zizioulas," *Vox Evangelica* 25 (1995): 64.
197. Zizioulas, *Being as Communion*, 19.
198. Melissaris, "The Challenge of Patristic Ontology," 488.

199. Zizioulas, *Being as Communion*, 41.
200. Del Colle, "'Person' and 'Being,'" 78.
201. Torrance, *The Christian Doctrine of God*, 179.
202. Del Colle, "'Person' and 'Being,'" 76. See also Thomas F. Torrance, *The Trinitarian Faith* (Edinburgh: T&T Clark, 1993), 238.
203. Paul D. Molnar, "Theological Issues Involved in the *Filioque*," in *Ecumenical Perspectives on the Filioque for the Twenty-First Century*, ed. Myk Habets, 38 (London; New York: Bloomsbury, 2014).
204. Zizioulas, *Communion and Otherness*, 136.
205. While there are scholars who support either Zizioulas or Torrance, there are quite a number who observe that neither Zizioulas nor Torrance is wholly correct in his reading of the Cappadocians. For two examples, see Matthew Baker, "Interview with Protopresbyter George Dion. Dragas Regarding T. F. Torrance," *Participatio* 4 (2013): 44; and Nikolaos Asproulis, "T. F. Torrance, John Zizioulas, and the 'Cappadocian' Theology of Divine Monarchia: A Neo-Athanasian or Neo-Cappadocian Solution?" in *T. F. Torrance and Eastern Orthodoxy: Theology in Reconciliation* (Eugene, OR: Wipf & Stock, 2013).
206. See Jason Radcliff, *Thomas F. Torrance and the Church Fathers: A Reformed, Evangelical, and Ecumenical Reconstruction of the Patristic Tradition* (Eugene, OR: Pickwick Publications, 2014), 139 as part of a longer section on the Cappadocian distinction. Further readings on this debate and the interaction between Torrance and Zizioulas include Dick O. Eugenio, *Communion with the Triune God: The Trinitarian Soteriology of T. F. Torrance* (Eugene, OR: Pickwick Publications, 2014), 166–70; Colin Gunton, "Being and Person: T. F. Torrance's Doctrine of God," in *The Promise of Trinitarian Theology: Theologians in Dialogue with T. F. Torrance*, ed. Elmer M. Colyer, 129–34 (Lanham, MD: Rowman & Littlefield, 2001); Thomas F. Torrance, "Thomas Torrance Responds," in *The Promise of Trinitarian Theology: Theologians in Dialogue with T. F. Torrance*, ed. Elmer M. Colyer, 314–18 (Lanham, MD: Rowman & Littlefield, 2001); and Najeeb G. Awad, "Between Subordination and Koinonia: Toward a New Reading of the Cappadocian Theology," *Modern Theology* 23, no. 2 (April 2007): 181–204.
207. Del Colle, "'Person' and 'Being,'" 79.
208. Zizioulas, *Being as Communion*, 15–16.
209. John Behr, "The Trinitarian Being of the Church," *St Vladimir's Theological Quarterly* 48, no.1 (2003): 68.
210. Zizioulas, *Being as Communion*, 50.
211. Ibid., 53.
212. Ibid., 54.
213. Ibid., 50.
214. John Zizioulas, "The Church as Communion," *St Vladimir's Theological Quarterly* 38, no. 1 (1994): 6.
215. Zizioulas, *Being as Communion*, 58.
216. Thomas F. Torrance "What Is the Church?" *Ecumenical Review* 1[illegible], no. 1 (October 1958): 9.
217. Zizioulas, "The Church as Communion," 6.
218. Zizioulas, *Being as Communion*, 133.
219. Zizioulas, *Communion and Otherness*, 38.
220. Ibid., 135.
221. Zizioulas, "The Church as Communion," 10.
222. Ibid., 11–12.
223. Zizioulas, *Being as Communion*, 136.
224. Ibid., 246.
225. Zizioulas, "The Church as Communion," 16.

Chapter Nine

Moving Onward

SUMMARIZING THE PROJECT

We began this work by acknowledging that in order to answer practical questions about the visible life of the Church, one must first answer the question "What is the Church?" However, an even more basic step is first required, which is to identify and critique one's evaluation of how this question should best be answered. In this work, we have explained that in order to correctly answer the question "What is the Church?" we must begin with the doctrine of God rather than focusing on the Church as an institution. It is only by recognizing that the empirical Church has a transcendent foundation that we are properly able to answer questions about its visible life.

As a means of considering this question, we have unfolded the way in which Thomas Torrance views the historical actuality and empirical existence of the Church as intrinsically derived from the gathering of humanity into union and communion with the Triune God. Father, Son, and Holy Spirit are a rich, full communion of triune love, and the free outpouring of this love upon humanity, alongside the invitation to humanity to participate in the triune fellowship, is key to understanding the transcendent nature of the Church.

We established the foundations for our engagement with Torrance's trinitarian ecclesiology by acquainting ourselves with his biographical background and then turning our attention to the main characteristics of his approach to the theological task, including his missional emphasis and key characteristics of his scientific theology. We saw his preference for the kataphysic approach, his rejection of dualism, and the importance of theological knowledge being recognized as personal knowledge.

Next we dealt with the doctrine of the Trinity and the historical development of the Church. Torrance's weaving together of various historical and modern sources was demonstrated, and the point was firmly established that Torrance focuses upon the incarnation as the key to our knowledge of the Trinity because it is in and through Jesus Christ that the Triune God makes himself known to us within the objectivities of the created world. This was a key methodological clarification because we noted that even when Torrance uses solely Christological language, this is inseparable from his trinitarian theology. We also introduced theological terms like *ousia*, *hypostasis*, *perichoresis*, and *homoousion*.

At this stage, we introduced Torrance's stratified structure of theological knowledge and saw that while this model does not "create" or "systematize" theology, it clarifies that God the Trinity is not isolated and self-contained but a rich fullness of "being for others." We also saw how God has increasingly revealed himself throughout history—culminating with the complete revelation of God's trinitarian nature in the New Testament—in a way that parallels the development of the one people of God in three stages. Each stage has led toward the *telos* of history, the full participation of humans in the eternal love of the Triune God, and the actualization of this in space and time on earth.

The fifth chapter was where we integrated the discussion of the first half of the book. Incorporating our discussion of Torrance's scientific and dogmatic methodology, we focused on understanding *how* Torrance views the Triune God as the ultimate ground of the Church. Highlighting once again the doctrinal precedence of the Trinity in relation to ecclesiology, we acknowledged the consequent need to look "through" the external appearance of the Church, whether institution, community, or people, and to instead look at the divine foundation of the Church. We used Torrance's stratified structure of knowledge again, this time to clarify the inner structure of his thought about the Trinity-Church relationship. This emphasized *koinōnia* as a central motif in Torrance's ecclesiology. The Trinity *in se* is a rich communion of love. It is replete and needs nothing beyond itself. However, because God's being is also "being for others," God's love freely flows to humanity and creates a human community that is the creaturely correlate of the divine *koinōnia*. Torrance uses *koinōnia* language in two ways. He describes a "threefold communion" between the Trinity and the Church and also talks about the two dimensions of *koinōnia*. The Church is a community that is formed on the basis of our participation together in the life of the Trinity and thus becomes a "community of reciprocity" or the "social coefficient of theological knowledge," the place where God's love is poured out and is made known among humanity.

Having established the theological relationship between the doctrine of the Holy Trinity and the doctrine of the Church, we then turned to develop the implications of this relationship for the empirical life of the Church in between Christ's two advents. Torrance argues that the Church requires certain forms of order in the eschatological pause between Christ's two advents, which he describes with the metaphor of scaffolding that supports the structure of a building while the building is being built but is torn down and removed once the building is finished. In a similar way, the forms of order and structure are not essential to the true being of the Church but are necessary in the historical period when the Church lives in the "overlap of the ages." The Church is to be visibly ordered in a way that, even though it is temporal, witnesses to the triune love. In this way the life of the Church retains its essential character of participation in the triune fellowship even though that is only imperfectly realized here and now. The Church has no independent ministry of its own but instead is called to witness to what Christ has already done through his life, death, and resurrection; this witness is itself the ongoing work of Christ through the Spirit. We also noted the dangerous temptation for the Church to identify itself too closely with the world under the guise of making the Gospel relevant.

Having considered the theological framework of order, we then turned to the essential attributes of the Church—its oneness, holiness, catholicity, and apostolicity. These were identified as interrelated attributes of the Triune God that the Church shares in through its union and communion with Christ through the Spirit. Following this, specific elements of the Church's visible life were elucidated. We unpacked how Torrance describes these as indicators of the presence of the true Church. Word, sacrament, and ministry are all temporal forms given for the sustenance of the life of the Church in between the two advents of Christ, and they point to our participation in the triune *koinōnia* and have their ultimate ground in the mystery of Christ.

We next considered Torrance's view of the mission of the Church and his involvement in the ecumenical movement. We attended to his ministry in the Church of Scotland and involvement in ecumenical dialogue, investigating his suggestion that by grounding ecclesiology in the Trinity, we can relativize many of the issues that have caused division in the Church. By focusing on the Trinity as that which unites us, the Church can embrace the call to be a community of reconciliation and thus more effectively participate in Christ's reconciling mission.

Finally, we compared Torrance's work with representative samples of work from Kathryn Tanner, Jürgen Moltmann, and John Zizioulas, showing how each of these theologians develops the relationship between the doctrine of the Trinity and the doctrine of the Church and then bringing these divergent streams into dialogue with Torrance's trinitarian ecclesiology.

IMPLICATIONS AND POTENTIAL

Recognizing Torrance's Impact

It is clear that for Thomas F. Torrance, ecclesiology cannot be separated from the doctrine of the Trinity without negative consequences for the life of the Church and the fulfilment of its mission. This was not merely an academic consideration for Torrance; although most of Torrance's material is geared toward the theological academy, he undertook his theological calling in service to the Church and its mission. However, Torrance's work is surprisingly underappreciated in the wider theological academy. For example, Torrance is not mentioned in Stephen Holmes's *The Quest for the Trinity* in which Holmes explores the revival of trinitarian doctrine in the twentieth century. Being challenged on this, Holmes notes that his omission of Torrance is characteristic of the lack of mention of Torrance in the "story of Trinitarian renewal," which was the narrative Holmes had been taught at King's College. Holmes acknowledges, however, that he should have incorporated Torrance in his initial publication.[1]

The theology that we have explored can also can be used as a filter for critically constructive reflection on theological works of a less academically rigorous nature. In the twenty-first century there continues to be significant growth in the publication of books that deal with Church-related topics such as growth and leadership strategies, the increasing apathy of many contemporary cultures toward Christianity, and the search for a relevant Gospel. However, many of these books do not contain sustained theological reflection. By highlighting the importance of grounding the practical elements of a doctrine of the Church in the doctrine of God, our approach offers a "yardstick," as such, for the evaluation of the theology contained in works of a more popular nature.

Following on from the above point, Torrance's work also offers significant potential for engaging theologically with the rise in charismatic and Pentecostal churches in recent decades as has been demonstrated by Alexandra Radcliff in her recent book *The Claim of Humanity in Christ: Salvation and Sanctification in the Theology of T. F. and J. B. Torrance.*[2] While we have begun to move in this direction, seeking to develop a robustly theological understanding of the particular work of the Holy Spirit in relation to the life of the Church in the time between the two advents of Christ, further dialogue would be beneficial. Torrance comments that the resurgence of belief in the Spirit is a reaction against the Church's temptation to replace the power of the Spirit with worldly power. He suggests two things that we must keep in mind. The first has to do with the patristic formula "from the Father, through the Son, in the Spirit," which is parallel to the contemporary reappreciation that God is at work here and now, interacting with the world that he has made. While Torrance warns against the Pentecostal tendency to concentrate only upon the phenomenal acts of the Spirit in space and time, he posits, second, that by also reminding ourselves of the other side of the patristic formula, "in the Spirit, through the Son, and to the Father," we are reminded to lift our vision away from the phenomena of the Spirit to the mystery of the Triune God in his own being.[3] This is a helpful corrective to some of the untheological excesses of the charismatic movement.[4] At the same time, Torrance's position would also benefit from a reciprocal dialogue with contemporary Pentecostal theologians by becoming more open to experience that is reflected upon theologically. Habets suggests that Torrance's general rejection of anything he considers mysticism is because he adopts "a partial and inaccurate definition of mysticism, which leads him to an *a priori* exclusion of mystical elements."[5] This is also noted by Radcliff, who suggests that because Torrance emphasizes that humanity can both know and experience God, his scholarly theology would benefit from "a greater openness to and consideration of the mystical and experiential aspects of the Christian life."[6] This does not necessarily have to undermine Torrance's scientific theology where an object is known in accordance with its unique reality. We know God through being reconciled to him, an experience that deals with who we are essentially as human beings. While one's subjective individual experiences should not be allowed to dictate one's knowledge of God, this experiential aspect fits well with what Torrance describes as the basic level of the stratified structure of humanity's knowledge of God.

Finally, Torrance's stratified structure of knowledge as a theological "disclosure model" could be of significant use in teaching theological students how to evaluate different theological sources. Rather than teaching students to evaluate texts and traditions through a lens such as the "Wesleyan Quadrilateral," Torrance's stratified model offers a much better lens for theological interpretation. It does this by explicitly acknowledging the challenge of ensuring that our finite, human statements about God correlate as far as possible with the transcendent reality of the Trinity and by proposing a way forward that allows for the cross-referencing of our individual and corporate experience with the revelation of God in space and time and with the reality of God in his own being. On this basis, we are able to further think out the relationship between God and humanity and to critically evaluate our theology as a faithful—or unfaithful—response to the triune revelation. The task of theology is to serve the Church by seeking to clarify and test its speech and knowledge in relation to the Triune God but also to heed Torrance's call that the Church must be ever-reforming, willing to submit its own life to the judgment and mercy of Jesus Christ. This model offers a way for doing this.

Contribution to the Dialogue about Communion Ecclesiology and Church Unity

In defining communion ecclesiology, Doyle, a Roman Catholic theologian, appreciatively notes that communion ecclesiology

> represents an attempt to move beyond the merely juridical and institutional understandings by emphasising the mystical, sacramental, and historical dimensions of the Church. It focuses on relationships, whether among the persons of the Trinity, among human beings and God, among the members of the Communion of Saints, among members of a parish, or among the bishops dispersed throughout the world.[7]

In contrast to Doyle, a more critical, but simpler, view of communion ecclesiology is offered by Healy, who argues that

> communion ecclesiologies relate the primary reality of the church to the Trinity as such. The true identity or reality of the church lies in its participation in the inner-trinitarian *koinonia* or communion. That is, this participatory relation is at the same time the mode of our salvation, which is therefore realized in an ecclesial and communal form.[8]

According to both of these definitions, Torrance's ecclesiology fits within the wider definition of communion ecclesiology. Consequently, while Torrance's relating the doctrine of the Church to the doctrine of the Holy Trinity is not an original move, this work makes an important contribution to the ongoing dialogue within communion ecclesiology by opening up Torrance's work, highlighting the salient relationships that exist between the doctrine of the Trinity and his ecclesiology, and thus situating him as another voice in ongoing ecclesial conversation.

One further point may be noted here, although we must be careful not to give Torrance's work more weight than its due. Given the centrality of the *koinōnia* motif in Torrance's work, it is encouraging to see the way that this became a preeminent theme in the ecumenical movement later in the twentieth century. *Koinōnia* was selected as the theme of the Fifth World Conference on Faith and Order held in Santiago de Compostela in 1993. Throughout the conference, a number of different perspectives on *koinōnia* were offered, and different discussions were held on what this could mean for the life of the Church. There was a consistent hope expressed during the gathering that the theme of *koinōnia* would provide further opportunities for Church unity to flourish. This is the same understanding that we have identified in Torrance's ecclesiology: the being of the Church is not primarily an institution or an organization but rather a creaturely *koinōnia* that correlates in appropriate ways to the triune *koinōnia*, which leads to a substantial theological argument for the need for unity. Although there is no clear line of connection between Torrance's work and this development in the Faith and Order Commission, it signals ecumenical dialogue moving in a direction that Torrance would have celebrated.[9]

The other area of unity that is related to this is Torrance's perspective on the schism between Israel and the Church. Although Israel's geographical claim is contentious, Torrance emphasized in a joint statement after the Evanston meeting of the World Council of Churches that his concern for the Jewish people was "wholly biblical and is not to be confused with any political attitude towards the State of Israel."[10] At the same time, he acknowledges that because revelation takes spatiotemporal forms, we cannot detach Israel from its land without this resulting in an ethical abstract Judaism.[11] Although there are marked difficulties in the geo-political and religious debates over the modern nation-state of Israel, there is significant opportunity for positive interfaith dialogue to emerge between Jews and Christians given that the apostolic and prophetic foundation of the Church was laid in a Jewish context. Perhaps Torrance's perspective could offer a middle way that is neither the extreme of replacement theology on the one hand nor Zionism on the other hand but instead affirms the preparatory role that the Jewish people played in preparing for the Messiah—thus appreciating Torrance's belief that the spiritual people of Israel will yet experience future redemption given his eschatological position that "to expect Jesus Christ means to hope for the conversion of the Jewish people, and to love Him means to love the people of God's promise."[12] This would be a fitting response to Torrance's critique that the schism between Israel and the Christian Church is the most significant schism in the body of Christ and his observation that unless this schism is healed, and the proclamation of the Gospel is hindered.[13]

The Life of the Church

Despite the inherently academic nature of this work, the aim has been to honor Torrance's own sense of participating in the mission of God during his theological career and to avoid divorcing theology from the life of the Church. It is thus fitting to conclude with some reflections of a more pragmatic nature for while ecclesiology must be solidly grounded in the doctrine of God, it is of supreme relevance to the life of the Church.[14]

The simplest and yet most profound contribution of Torrance's trinitarian ecclesiology is the reminder to look beyond the external forms of Christian life and beyond the contextual debates about doctrine and to fix our eyes instead upon the God who calls the Church into being and sustains it in relationship with himself. This directly counteracts our contemporary tendency to focus upon the individual unit of the parish, or the congregation, and instead reminds believers that to belong to the Church is not primarily about belonging to one's congregation, or even to the one, holy, catholic, and apostolic Church, but is to belong first and foremost to the Triune God.

The fact that we are invited into the communion of the Holy Trinity also has profound implications for our relationships with other humans. Just as God's being has been shown to be "being for others," so too our lives should be characterized as "being for others." The only way in which the Church can do this is to follow Christ and for individuals to give their life in following the example of Christ's servant nature, spending their life "in the service of the love of God toward all."[15] Jesus Christ obediently embraced the way of the servant, even unto death, and through his life, the new order of creation is revealed. As we participate through the Spirit in Christ's obedient humanity, we are enabled to live out the gospel of reconciliation. In Christ all divisions and separation are overcome so that Torrance may state, "Participation in Christ carries with it participation in one another, and our common reconciliation with Christ carries with it reconciliation with one another."[16]

However, we often fail to demonstrate this reality in our common life, as is illustrated by the scandal of division within the Church. Jesus has made participation in the fellowship of the Trinity accessible to both Jew and Gentile, male and female, and has broken down every barrier that exists between them.[17] Yet the modern Church is not predominantly a unified community of those who have been reconciled to God because "fragmentation and pluralism in the Church reflect fragmentation and pluralism in our secular culture."[18] While, as we saw, there is a genuine need to adapt our communication of the Gospel to be relevant to specific languages and cultures, the Gospel itself is of unchanging relevance so that Torrance views devising new methods of evangelism as a somewhat pointless exercise![19] The true relevance of the Gospel is found in the way that the work of Christ is directed to humanity's deepest need since "in Jesus Christ the Truth of God has already been made relevant to man and his need, and therefore does not need to be made relevant by us."[20]

This has the follow-on consequence of reminding us that in an era when we are surrounded by predictions of the Church's decline, God is in control. It is not our job to "prop up" the Church but rather to work out our call to participate in God's mission in faithfulness. We must trust God not only for the sustenance of God's people but that he will bring the Church to the fullness of unity. This has significant potential to change our perspective on evangelism so that the focus is not on the numerical growth of our congregations. Instead the focus becomes celebrating the work that *God* is doing among us rather than boasting about the work that *we* have done for God.

While the things that separate Christians from each other should not be dismissed as irrelevant, whether at the level of individuals, communities, or denominations, the theological approach of focusing on the Triune God rather than on the Church as an institution calls us to recognize that these dividing issues are secondary to the fact that we are united through our participation in the fellowship of the Trinity.[21] Again, as Torrance writes,

> the primary constitutive facts, then, are the one faith and one baptism, coordinated to the activity of the one Spirit, the one Lord and the one Father. The true Church is marked by its unity and holiness, and by its fidelity to the Holy Trinity. One Church is to be understood strictly in that context of belief in the Holy Trinity.[22]

It is in this spirit that we conclude with the prayer offered by the Fifth World Conference on Faith and Order and that echoes so well Torrance's own vision for the life of the Church.

> O God, holy and eternal Trinity,
> We pray for your Church in all the world.
> Sanctify its life; renew its worship;
> Empower its witness; heal its divisions;
> Make visible its unity.
> Lead us, with all our brothers and sisters,
> Toward communion in faith, life, and witness
> So that, united together in one body by the one Spirit,
> We may together witness to the perfect unity
> Of your love.
> Amen.[23]

NOTES

1. Stephen R. Holmes, "Response: In Praise of Being Criticized," in *The Holy Trinity Revisited: Essays in Response to Stephen R. Holmes*, ed. Thomas A. Noble and Jason S. Sexton, 151–53 (Milton Keynes, UK: Paternoster, 2015). Holmes takes the opportunity here to briefly raise his concerns about Torrance's redefinition of historical terms and notes his concern that Torrance's use of terms like *homoousion* is not theologically robust. However, Holmes has acknowledged his lack of proficiency in Torrancian theology, and we should note that this comment is not made as an extended critique of Torrance but rather as part of a brief response that deals primarily with other theological points.
2. Alexandra S. Radcliff, *The Claim of Humanity in Christ: Salvation and Sanctification in the Theology of T. F. and J. B. Torrance* (Eugene, OR: Pickwick Publications, 2016).
3. Thomas F. Torrance, *Theology in Reconciliation* (Eugene, OR: Wipf and Stock, 1996), 289–93.
4. This observation is made by one who is deeply grateful to the Pentecostal Church and the charismatic movement but is also concerned to see it remain faithful to the self-revelation of God and aware of the whole tradition of the Church, not merely the Book of Acts.
5. Myk Habets, *Theology in Transposition: A Constructive Appraisal of T. F. Torrance* (Minneapolis, MN: Fortress Press, 2013), 141.
6. Radcliff, *The Claim of Humanity in Christ.*
7. Dennis M. Doyle, *Communion Ecclesiology* (Maryknoll, NY: Orbis Books, 2000), 12. Doyle's work focuses on Roman Catholic communion ecclesiology, but his definition is sufficiently broad. He notes particularly in regard to his own tradition that "Catholic theologians cannot interpret either Vatican II or communion ecclesiology apart from each other" (2).

8. Nicholas M. Healy, "Communion Ecclesiology: A Cautionary Note," *Pro Ecclesia* 4, no. 4 (1995): 442. See also Nicholas M. Healy, *Church, World and the Christian Life: Practical-Prophetic Ecclesiology* (Cambridge: Cambridge University Press, 2000), 6–8, 26–51.

9. For a full report of the proceedings, see Thomas F. Best and Günther Gassmann, eds., *On the Way to Fuller Koinonia: Official Report of the Fifth World Conference on Faith and Order* (Geneva: WCC Publications, 1994).

10. Thomas F. Torrance, *Conflict and Agreement in the Church: Order and Disorder* (Eugene, OR: Wipf and Stock, 1996), 284.

11. Thomas F. Torrance, *Mediation of Christ* (Edinburgh: T&T Clark, 1992), 16–17.

12. Torrance, *Conflict and Agreement in the Church: Order and Disorder*, 285.

13. Torrance, *The Mediation of Christ*, 45–46.

14. Gary D. Badcock, *The House Where God Lives: Renewing the Doctrine of the Church for Today* (Grand Rapids, MI: Eerdmans, 2009), 336.

15. Thomas F. Torrance, *Atonement: The Person and Work of Christ*, ed. Robert T. Walker, 375 (Downers Grove, IL: InterVarsity Academic Press, 2009).

16. Ibid.

17. See Thomas F. Torrance, *The Christian Doctrine of God: One Being Three Persons* (Edinburgh: T&T Clark, 1996), 68, referring to Ephesians 2:13–22.

18. Thomas F. Torrance, *Reality and Scientific Theology*, 2nd ed. (Eugene, OR: Wipf and Stock, 2001), 151.

19. Torrance, *Conflict and Agreement in the Church: Order and Disorder*, 223.

20. Thomas F. Torrance, *Theology in Reconstruction* (Grand Rapids, MI: Eerdmans, 1965), 26.

21. A short but helpful example of the way that this can be done at a more accessible level than we find in many of Torrance's works is Martyn Atkins, "What Is the Essence of the Church?" in *Mission-Shaped Questions: Defining Issues for Today's Church*, ed. Steven Croft, 16–28 (London: Church House Publishing, 2008). Atkins argues, in brief, that theology should be read through the lens of missiology and will produce ecclesiology.

22. See Thomas F. Torrance, *The Trinitarian Faith* (Edinburgh: T&T Clark, 1993), 263 where Torrance refers to Irenaeus's citation of Paul in Ephesians 4:4–6.

23. Best and Gassmann, *On the Way to Fuller Koinonia*, xii.

Bibliography

Asproulis, Nikolaos. "T. F. Torrance, John Zizioulas, and the 'Cappadocian' Theology of Divine Monarchia: A Neo-Athanasian or Neo-Cappadocian Solution?" In *T. F. Torrance and Eastern Orthodoxy: Theology in Reconciliation*. Edited by Matthew Baker and Todd Speidell, location 4158–905. Eugene, OR: Wipf and Stock, 2015.

Atkins, Martyn. "What Is the Essence of the Church?" In *Mission-Shaped Questions: Defining Issues for Today's Church*. Edited by Steven Croft, 16–28. London: Church House Publishing, 2008.

Awad, Najeeb G. "Between Subordination and Koinonia: Toward a New Reading of the Cappadocian Theology." *Modern Theology* 23, no. 2 (April 2007): 181–204.

Badcock, Gary D. *The House Where God Lives: Renewing the Doctrine of the Church for Today*. Grand Rapids, MI: Eerdmans, 2009.

Baker, Matthew. "Interview with Protopresbyter George Dion. Dragas Regarding T. F. Torrance." *Participatio* 4 (2013): 30–46.

———. "Introduction." *Participatio* 4 (2013): 3–7.

Barth, Karl. *Church Dogmatics* I/1, *The Doctrine of the Word of God*. 2nd edition. Translated by G. W. Bromiley. Edited by G. W. Bromiley and T. F. Torrance. Edinburgh: T&T Clark, 1956.

Bauckham, Richard. "Jürgen Moltmann." In *The Modern Theologians*. Edited by David Ford, 147–62. Malden, MA: Blackwell Publishing, 2005.

———. *The Theology of Jürgen Moltmann*. New York: T&T Clark, 1995.

Bauman, Michael. *Roundtable Conversations with European Theologians*. Grand Rapids, MI: Baker Book House, 1990.

Behr, John. "The Trinitarian Being of the Church." *St. Vladimir's Theological Quarterly* 48, no.1 (2003): 67–88.

Best, Thomas F., and Günther Gassmann, eds. *On the Way to Fuller Koinonia: Official Report of the Fifth World Conference on Faith and Order*. Geneva: WCC Publications, 1994.

Camerson, Daniel J. *Flesh and Blood: A Dogmatic Sketch Concerning the Fallen Nature View of Christ's Human Nature*. Eugene, OR: Wipf and Stock, 2016.

Colle, Ralph Del. "The Church." In *The Oxford Handbook of Systematic Theology*. Edited by Kathryn Tanner, John Webster, and Iain Torrance. New York: Oxford University Press, 2007.

———. "'Person' and 'Being' in John Zizioulas' Trinitarian Theology: Conversations with Thomas Torrance and Thomas Aquinas." *Scottish Journal of Theology* 54, no. 1 (2001): 70–86.

Colyer, Elmer M. *How to Read T. F. Torrance: Understanding His Trinitarian and Scientific Theology*. Downers Grove, IL: InterVarsity Press, 2001.

———. “The Incarnate Saviour: T. F. Torrance on the Atonement.” In *An Introduction to Torrance Theology: Discovering the Incarnate Saviour*. Edited by Gerrit Scott Dawson, 33–54. London: T&T Clark, 2007.

———. *The Nature of Doctrine in T. F. Torrance's Theology*. Eugene, OR: Wipf and Stock, 2001.

———. “Thomas F. Torrance on the Holy Spirit.” *Word and World* 23, no. 2 (Spring 2003): 162.

Deddo, Gary W. “The Christian Life and Our Participation in Christ's Continuing Ministry.” In *An Introduction to Torrance Theology: Discovering the Incarnate Saviour*. Edited by Gerrit Scott Dawson, 135–56. London: T&T Clark, 2007.

———. “The Holy Spirit in T. F. Torrance's Theology.” In *The Promise of Trinitarian Theology: Theologians in Dialogue with T. F. Torrance*. Edited by Elmer M. Colyer, 81–114. Lanham, MD: Rowman & Littlefield, 2001.

Doyle, Dennis M. *Communion Ecclesiology*. Maryknoll, NY: Orbis Books, 2000.

Emery, Gilles. *The Trinitarian Theology of Saint Thomas Aquinas*. Oxford: Oxford University Press, 2010.

Eugenio, Dick O. *Communion with the Triune God: The Trinitarian Soteriology of T. F. Torrance*. Eugene, OR: Pickwick Publications, 2014.

Farrow, Douglas. “T. F. Torrance and the Latin Heresy.” *First Things* 238 (December 2013): 25–31.

Flett, Eric G. *Persons, Powers, and Pluralities: Toward a Trinitarian Theology of Culture*. Cambridge: James Clarke, 2012.

Gray, Bryan J. “Towards Better Ways of Reading the Bible.” *Scottish Journal of Theology* 33, no. 4 (1980): 301–15.

Grenz, Stanley J., and Roger E. Olson. *20th-Century Theology: God and the World in a Transitional Age*. Downers Grove, IL: InterVarsity Press, 1992.

Gunton, Colin. “Being and Person: T. F. Torrance's Doctrine of God.” In *The Promise of Trinitarian Theology: Theologians in Dialogue with T. F. Torrance*. Edited by Elmer M. Colyer, 115–37. Lanham, MD: Rowman & Littlefield, 2001.

Habets, Myk. “The Doctrine of Election in Evangelical Calvinism: T. F. Torrance as a Case Study.” *Irish Theological Quarterly* 73 (2008): 334–54.

———. “How Creation Is Proleptically Conditioned by Redemption.” *Colloquium* 41 (2009): 3–21.

———. “Theological Interpretation of Scripture in Sermonic Mode: The Case of T. F. Torrance.” In *Ears That Hear: Explorations in Theological Interpretation of the Bible*. Edited by Joel B. Green and Tim Meadowcroft, 43–69. Sheffield, UK: Sheffield Phoenix Press, 2013.

———. *Theology in Transposition: A Constructive Appraisal of T. F. Torrance*. Minneapolis, MN: Fortress Press, 2013.

———. *Theosis in the Theology of Thomas Torrance*. Surrey, UK: Ashgate, 2009.

Hardy, Daniel W. “T. F. Torrance.” In *The Modern Theologians*. Edited by David F. Ford, 163–77. Malden, MA: Blackwell Publishing, 2005.

Healy, Nicholas M. *Church, World and the Christian Life: Practical-Prophetic Ecclesiology*. Cambridge: Cambridge University Press, 2000.

———. “Communion Ecclesiology: A Cautionary Note.” *Pro Ecclesia* 4, no. 4 (1995): 442–53.

Holmes, Stephen R. “Response: In Praise of Being Criticized.” In The Holy Trinity Revisited: Essays in Response to Stephen R. Holmes . Edited by Thomas A. Noble and Jason S. Sexton, 137–55. Milton Keynes, UK: Paternoster, 2015.

Hunsinger, George. “The Dimension of Depth: Thomas F. Torrance on the Sacraments of Baptism and the Lord's Supper.” *Scottish Journal of Theology* 54, no. 2 (May 2001): 155–76.

———. “The Trinity and the Kingdom. By Jürgen Moltmann.” *Thomist* 47, no. 1 (January 1983): 129–39.

Kelly, Douglas F. "The Realist Epistemology of Thomas F. Torrance." In *An Introduction to Torrance Theology: Discovering the Incarnate Saviour*. Edited by Gerrit Scott Dawson, 75–102. London: T&T Clark, 2007.

Kernohan, R. D. "Analysis of a Diagnosis." *Life and Work* (November 1983): 14–16.

———. "Editorial Comment." *Life and Work* (November 1983): 5.

Kettler, Christian D. *The Vicarious Humanity of Christ and the Reality of Salvation*. Eugene, OR: Wipf and Stock, 2011.

Kilby, Karen. "Perichoresis and Projection: Problems with Social Doctrines of the Trinity." *New Blackfriars* 81, no. 956 (October 2000): 432–45.

Knight, Douglas H. "Introduction." In *The Theology of John Zizioulas: Personhood and the Church*. Edited by Douglas H. Knight, 1–14. New York: Routledge, 2016

Lee, Kye Won. *Living in Union with Christ: The Practical Theology of Thomas F. Torrance*. New York: Peter Lang, 2003.

Luoma, Tapio. *Incarnation and Physics: Natural Science in the Theology of Thomas F. Torrance*. Oxford: Oxford University Press, 2002.

MacLean, Stanley S. *Resurrection, Apocalypse, and the Kingdom of Christ*. Princeton Theological Monograph Series. Eugene, OR: Pickwick Publications, 2012.

Marley, Alan G. *T. F. Torrance in a Nutshell*. Edited by Jock Stein. Edinburgh: Handsel Press, 1992.

McDougall, Joy Ann. "The Return of Trinitarian Praxis? Moltmann on the Trinity and the Christian Life." *Journal of Religion* 83 no. 2 (April 2003): 177–203.

McGrath, Alister. *Christian Theology: An Introduction*. 5th edition. Oxford: Wiley-Blackwell, 2011.

———. *T. F. Torrance: An Intellectual Biography*. Edinburgh: T&T Clark, 1999.

McIntosh, Adam. "The Contribution of Karl Barth's Doctrine of Appropriation to a Trinitarian Ecclesiology." In *Trinitarian Theology after Barth*. Edited by Myk Habets and Phillip Tolilday, 221–40. Eugene, OR: Pickwick Publications, 2011.

McLuskey, J. Fraser. "From the Assembly to Skye—Via Dublin and Atlanta." *Life and Work* (October 1983): 14–15.

McMaken, W. Travis. "The Impossibility of Natural Knowledge of God in T. F. Torrance's Reformulated Natural Theology." *International Journal of Systematic Theology* 12, no. 3 (July 2010): 319–40.

Melissaris, Athanasios G. "The Challenge of Patristic Ontology in the Theology of Metropolitan John (Zizioulas) of Pergamon." *Greek Orthodox Theological Review* 44 (Spring 1999): 467–90.

Molnar, Paul. *Faith, Freedom and the Spirit*. Downers Grove, IL: InterVarsity Press, 2015.

———. "Natural Theology Revisited: A Comparison of T. F. Torrance and Karl Barth." *Zeitschrift für dialektische Theologie* 21 (2005): 53–83.

———. "Theological Issues Involved in the *Filioque*." In *Ecumenical Perspectives on the Filioque for the Twenty-First Century*. Edited by Myk Habets, 20–39. New York: Bloomsbury, 2014.

———. *Thomas F. Torrance: Theologian of the Trinity*. Farnham, UK: Ashgate, 2009.

Moltmann, Jürgen. *The Church in the Power of the Spirit*. Translated by Margaret Kohl. Minneapolis, MN: Fortress, Press, 1993.

———. *Experiences in Theology*. Translated by Margaret Kohl. London: SCM Press, 2000.

———. *Theology of Hope*. Translated by James W. Leitch. Minneapolis, MN: Fortress Press, 1993.

———. *The Trinity and the Kingdom*. Translated by Margaret Kohl. Minneapolis, MN: Fortress, Press, 1993.

Morrison, Stephen D. *T. F. Torrance in Plain English*. Columbus, OH: Beloved Publishing, 2017.

Morton, Colin, and Chris Wigglesworth. "Response to 'Mission to the Jews.'" *Life and Work* (June 1989): 7.

Myers, Benjamin. "The Stratification of Knowledge in the Thought of T. F. Torrance." *Scottish Journal of Theology* 61, no. 1 (2008): 1–15.

Noble, T. A. *Holy Trinity: Holy People*. Eugene, OR: Cascade Books, 2013.

Pauw, Amy Plantinga. "Ecclesiological Reflections on Kathryn Tanner's Jesus, Humanity and the Trinity." *Scottish Journal of Theology* 57, no. 2 (2004): 221–27.

Peterson, Cheryl M. *Who Is the Church? Ecclesiology for the 21st Century*. Minneapolis, MN: Fortress Press, 2013.

Purves, Andrew. *Exploring Christology and Atonement: Conversations with John McLeod Campbell, H. R. Mackintosh and T. F. Torrance*. Downers Grove, IL: InterVarsity Press, 2015.

———. "Who Is the Incarnate Saviour of the World?" In *An Introduction to Torrance Theology: Discovering the Incarnate Saviour*. Edited by Gerrit Scott Dawson, 23–32. London: T& T Clark, 2007.

Radcliff, Alexandra S. *The Claim of Humanity in Christ: Salvation and Sanctification in the Theology of T. F. and J. B. Torrance*. Eugene, OR: Pickwick Publications, 2016.

Radcliff, Jason. "T. F. Torrance and the Patristic Consensus on the Doctrine of the Trinity." In *The Holy Trinity Revisited: Essays in Response to Stephen R. Holmes*. Edited by Thomas A. Noble and Jason S. Sexton, 68–81. Milton Keynes, UK: Paternoster, 2015.

———. "T. F. Torrance and Reformed-Orthodox Dialogue." In *T. F. Torrance and Eastern Orthodoxy: Theology in Reconciliation*. Edited by Matthew Baker and Todd Speidell, location 855–1332. Eugene, OR: Wipf and Stock, 2013.

———. *Thomas F. Torrance and the Church Fathers: A Reformed, Evangelical, and Ecumenical Reconstruction of the Patristic Tradition*. Eugene, OR: Pickwick Publications, 2014.

Randall, David J. "T. F. Torrance: Reflections of a Parish Minister." *Theology in Scotland* 16 (2009): 147–54.

Reardon, Patrick Henry. "Women Priests: History and Theology—A Response to Thomas F. Torrance." *Touchstone Magazine* (Winter 1993). www.touchstonemag.com/archives/article.php?id=06-01-022-f#at.

Reardon, Patrick Henry, and Thomas F. Torrance. "On the Ordination of Women: A Correspondence between Thomas F. Torrance and Patrick Henry Reardon." *Touchstone Magazine* (Spring 1993). www.touchstonemag.com/archives/article.php?id=06-02-005).

Sarisky, Darren. "T. F. Torrance on Biblical Interpretation." *International Journal of Systematic Theology* 11, no. 3 (July 2009): 332–46.

Sonderegger, Katherine. *Systematic Theology: Vol. 1, The Doctrine of God*. Minneapolis, MN: Fortress Press, 2015.

Special Commission on Baptism. *Interim Reports, and Reports*. General Assembly of the Church of Scotland, 1955–1963.

Stamps, Robert J. *The Sacrament of the Word Made Flesh: The Eucharistic Theology of Thomas F. Torrance*. Rutherford Studies in Contemporary Theology. Edinburgh: Rutherford House, 2007.

Stone, Bryan P. *A Reader in Ecclesiology*. Surrey, UK: Ashgate, 2012.

Tanner, Kathryn. *Christ the Key*. Cambridge: Cambridge University Press, 2010.

———. *Jesus, Humanity and the Trinity: A Brief Systematic Theology*. Edinburgh: T&T Clark, 1991.

"T. F. Torrance Society Website: Urgent Call to the Kirk." www.tftorrance.org/call-to-kirk.php.

Torrance, Alan. *Persons in Communion: Trinitarian Description and Human Participation*. Edinburgh: T&T Clark, 1996.

Torrance, David W. "Introduction: Discovering the Incarnate Saviour of the World." In *An Introduction to Torrance Theology: Discovering the Incarnate Saviour*. Edited by Gerrit Scott Dawson, 1–22. London: T&T Clark, 2007.

———. "The Mission of Christians and Jews." In *A Passion for Christ: The Vision That Ignites Ministry*. Edited by Gerrit Dawson and Jock Stein, 114–29. Eugene, OR: Wipf and Stock, 2010.

Torrance, Thomas F. "Aberdeen." Box 10: Aberdeen. Thomas F. Torrance Manuscript Collection, Princeton Theological Seminary.

———. "Anglican-Methodist Reconciliation." *British Weekly*. Feb 28, 1963.

———. "Anglican-Presbyterian Conversations." *Presbyterian Record* (July–August 1957): 19, 36–37.

———. "Answer to God." *Biblical Theology* 2, no. 1 (1951): 3–16.

———. "Answer to Prosch on Polanyi's Convictions about God, Letter to the Editor." *Tradition and Discovery* 14, no. 1 (1986–1987): 30.

———. "The Apocalypse Now 1: On the Book of Revelation." *Life and Work* (October 1988): 19–20.

———. "The Apocalypse Now 2: The Gospel Depends on the Cross." *Life and Work* (November 1988): 20–21.

———. "The Apocalypse Now 3: Babylon—Symbol of Worldly Power." *Life and Work* (December 1988): 16–17.

———. "The Apocalypse Now 4: The Voice of Jesus Breaks Through." *Life and Work* (January 1989): 19–20.

———. *The Apocalypse Today*. London: James Clarke, 1960.

———. "Athanasius: A Reassessment of His Theology." *Abba Salama* 5 (1974): 171–87.

———. *Atonement: The Person and Work of Christ*. Edited by Robert T. Walker. Downers Grove, IL: InterVarsity Academic Press, 2009.

———. "Auburn." Box 10: Auburn. Thomas F. Torrance Manuscript Collection, Princeton Theological Seminary.

———. "Being and Nature of the Church." Thomas F. Torrance Manuscript Collection, Princeton Theological Seminary.

———. "The Bible's Guidance on Baptism." *Life and Work* (September 198[illegible]): 16–17.

———. *Calvin's Doctrine of Man*. London: Lutterworth Press, 1949.

———. "Calvin on the Knowledge of God." *Christian Century* 81, no. 2[illegible] (May 27, 1965): 696–99.

———. "Changed Outlook of Christians: The 'Obligation' of Unity." *Scotsman*, January 29, 1964.

———. "The Christ Who Loves Us." In *A Passion for Christ: The Vision That Ignites Ministry*. Edited by Gerrit Dawson and Jock Stein, 9–20. Eugene, OR: Wipf and Stock, 2010.

———. *The Christian Doctrine of God: One Being Three Persons*. Edinburgh: T&T Clark, 1996.

———. *The Christian Doctrine of Marriage*. Edinburgh: Handsel Press, 198[illegible].

———. *The Christian Frame of Mind*. Eugene, OR: Wipf and Stock, 1989.

———. *Christian Theology and Scientific Culture*. Eugene, OR: Wipf and Stock, 1998.

———. "A Comment on the New Morality." *Salt and Light Periodical* 2, no. 1 (Spring 1964): 17–20.

———. *Conflict and Agreement in the Church: Order and Disorder*. Eugene, OR: Wipf and Stock, 1996.

———. *Conflict and Agreement in the Church: The Ministry and Sacraments of the Gospel*. Eugene, OR: Wipf and Stock, 1996.

———. "The Crisis of Community." *Life and Work* (December 1990): 16–17.

———. "The Crisis of Morality." *Life and Work* (November 1990): 14–15.

———. "The Deposit of Faith." *Scottish Journal of Theology* 36, no. 1 (1983): 1–28.

———. *Divine and Contingent Order*. Edinburgh: T&T Clark, 1998.

———. *Divine Meaning: Studies in Patristic Hermeneutics*. Edinburgh: T&T Clark, 1995.

———. "The Divine Vocation and Destiny of Israel in World History." In *The Witness of the Jews to God*. Edited by David W. Torrance, 85–104. Edinburgh: Handsel Press, 1982.

———. *The Doctrine of Grace in the Apostolic Fathers*. Eugene, OR: Wipf and Stock, 1996.

———. "The Doctrine of Grace in the Old Testament." *Scottish Journal of Theology* 1 (1948): 55–65.

———. *The Doctrine of Jesus Christ*. Eugene, OR: Wipf and Stock, 2002.

———. "The Eclipse of God." *Baptist Quarterly* 22 (October 1967): 194–214.

———. "Ecumenism and Rome." *Scottish Journal of Theology* 37 (1984): 59–64.

———. "The Eldership in the Reformed Church." *Scottish Journal of Theology* 37, no. 4 (November 1984): 503–18.

———. "The Framework of Belief." In *Belief in Science and in Christian Life: The Relevance of Michael Polanyi's Thought for Christian Faith and Life*. Edited by Thomas F. Torrance, 1–27. Eugene, OR: Wipf and Stock, 1998.

———. *God and Rationality*. Oxford: Oxford University Press, 2000.

———. "God, Destiny and Suffering." *The Healing Hand* (Summer/Autumn 1977): 8–15.

———. "The Goodness and Dignity of Man in the Christian Tradition." *Modern Theology* 4, no. 4 (July 1988): 309–22.

———. *Gospel, Church and Ministry*. Edited by Jock Stein. Volume 1. Thomas F. Torrance Collected Studies. Eugene, OR: Pickwick Publications, 2012.

———. *The Ground and Grammar of Theology*. Charlottesville: University Press of Virginia, 1980.

———. "History and Reformation." *Scottish Journal of Theology* 4 (1951): 279–91.

———. "Hugh Ross Mackintosh: Theologian of the Cross." *Scottish Bulletin of Evangelical Theology* 5, no. 2 (Autumn 1987):160–73.

———. "If I Were Starting Again." *New Pulpit Digest* (March/April 1997): 64.

———. "Immortality and Light." *Religious Studies* 17, no. 2 (1981): 147–61.

———. "The Importance of Fences in Religion." *British Weekly*, 1941.

———. *Incarnation: The Person and Life of Christ*. Edited by Robert T. Walker. Downers Grove, IL: InterVarsity Press, 2008.

———. "In Hoc Signo Vinces." *Presbyter* 3, no. 1 (1945): 13–20.

———. "Introduction." In *The Incarnation: Ecumenical Studies in the Nicene-Constantinopolitan Creed*. Edited by Thomas F. Torrance, xi–xxii. Edinburgh: Handsel Press, 1981.

———. "Israel: People of God—God, Destiny and Suffering." *Theological Renewal* 13 (October 1979): 2–14.

———. "Itinerarium Mentis in Deum." Box 10: Itinerarium Mentis in Deum. Thomas F. Torrance Manuscript Collection, Princeton Theological Seminary.

———. "Justification." In *Christianity Divided: Protestant and Roman Catholic Theological Issues*. New York: Sheed and Ward, 1962.

———. "Justification: Its Radical Nature and Place in Reformed Doctrine and Life." *Scottish Journal of Theology* 13, no. 3 (August 1960): 225–246.

———. *Karl Barth: An Introduction to His Early Theology, 1910–1931*. London: SCM Press, 1962.

———. "Karl Barth and Patristic Theology." In *Theology beyond Christendom: Essays on the Centenary of the Birth of Karl Barth*. Edited by John Thomson, 215–39. Allison Park, PA: Pickwick Publications, 1986.

———. "Karl Barth and the Latin Heresy." *Scottish Journal of Theology* 39, no. 4 (1986): 461–82.

———. "Kerygmatic Proclamation of the Gospel: The Demonstration of Apostolic Preaching of Irenaios of Lyons." *Greek Orthodox Theological Review* 37, nos. 1–2 (1992): 105–21.

———. *Kingdom and Church*. Eugene, OR: Wipf and Stock, 1996.

———. "The Kirk's Crisis of Faith." *Life and Work* (October 1990): 15–16.

———. "The Light of the World: A Sermon." *Reformed Journal* 38, no. 12 (December 1988): 9–12.

———. "Liturgy and Apocalypse." *Church Service Society Annual* 24 (1953): 1–18.

———. *The Mediation of Christ*. Edinburgh: T&T Clark, 1992.

———. "Michael Polanyi and the Christian Faith—A Personal Report." *Tradition and Discovery* 27, no. 2 (2000–2001): 26–32.

———. "Minister's Notes," November 1948. Box 20: Beechgrove Church Publications. Thomas F. Torrance Manuscript Collection, Princeton Theological Seminary.

———. "The Ministry of Women: An Argument for the Ordination of Women." *Touchstone Magazine* (Fall 1992). www.touchstonemag.com/archives/article.php?id=0 –4-005-f#at.

———. "The Mission of Anglicanism." In *Anglican Self-Criticism*. Edited by D. M. Paton, 194–208. London: SCM Press, 1958.

———. "My Boyhood in China, 1913–1927." Box 10: My Boyhood in China. Thomas F. Torrance Manuscript Collection, Princeton Theological Seminary.

———. "My Interaction with Karl Barth." In *How Karl Barth Changed My Mind*. Edited by Donald K. McKim. Grand Rapids, MI: Wm. B. Eerdmans, 1986.

———. "A New Reformation?" *London Holborn and Quarterly Review* 189 (1964): 275–94.

———. "A New Vision of Wholeness: An Interview of Thomas F. Torrance, Given to Mary Doyle Morgan." *Presbyterian Survey* (December 1980): 21–23.
———. "One Aspect of the Biblical Conception of Faith." *Expository Times* 86 (1957): 111–14.
———. "The Orthodox Church in Great Britain," in *Texts and Studies* (London: Thyateira House, 1983).
———. "Our Witness through Doctrine." In *Proceedings of the 17th General Council of the Alliance of Reformed Churches Throughout the World Holding the Presbyterian Order*, 133–45. Geneva: World Presbyterian Alliance, 1954.
———. "The Place and Function of Reason in Christian Theology." *Evangelical Quarterly* 14 (1942): 22–41.
———. "The Place of the Humanity of Christ in the Sacramental Life of the Church." *Church Service Society Annual* 26 (1956): 3–10.
———. *Preaching Christ Today: The Gospel and Scientific Thinking*. Grand Rapids, MI: Eerdmans, 1994.
———. "Predestination in Christ." *Evangelical Quarterly* 13 (1941): 108–41.
———. "The Pre-eminence of Jesus Christ." *Expository Times* 89, no. 2 (1977): 54–55.
———. "The Problem of Natural Theology in the Thought of Karl Barth." *Religious Studies* 6, no. 2 (Fall 1970): 121–35.
———. "Proselyte Baptism." *New Testament Studies* 1, no. 2 (November 1954): 150.
———. "Put First Things First: Queries to Assembly on Church Union." *Scotsman*, May 27, 1966.
———. *Reality and Evangelical Theology: The Realism of Christian Revelation*. Eugene, OR: Wipf and Stock, 2003.
———. *Reality and Scientific Theology*. 2nd edition. Eugene, OR: Wipf and Stock, 2001.
———. "Reconciliation in Christ and His Church." *Biblical Theology* 12 (1961): 26–35.
———. "Reformed Dogmatics Not Dogmaticism." *Theology* 70 (1967): 152–56.
———. "Review of Bernard Lambert, Le Problème Oecumenique." *Scottish Journal of Theology* 16, no. 1 (1963): 101–5.
———. "Review of C. R. B. Shapland (trans.), *The Letters of St Athanasius: Concerning the Holy Spirit*." *Scottish Journal of Theology* 5, no. 2 (June 1952): 205–8.
———. "Review of Edmund Schlink (ed.), *Evangelisches Gutachten zur Dogmatisierung der leiblichen Himmelfahrt Mariens*." *Scottish Journal of Theology* 4 (1951): 90–96.
———. "Review of F. C. Schmitt (ed.), *S. Anselmi Opera Omnia*." *Scottish Journal of Theology* 9, no. 1 (1956): 88–90.
———. "Review of Joachim Beckmann, *Quellen zur Geschichte des Christlichen Gottesdienstes*." *Scottish Journal of Theology* 12, no. 1 (1959): 108–09.
———. "Review of *The Oracles of God: An Introduction to the Preaching of John Calvin*. By T. H. L. Parker. Lutterworth Press. 12s. 6d." *Scottish Journal of Theology* 1, no. 2 (1948): 212–14.
———. "Review of *The Prophetic Faith of Our Fathers: The Historical Development of Prophetic Interpretation*. By Leroy Edwin Froom. Vols. I–III" *Scottish Journal of Theology* 6 (1953): 207–12.
———. "Review of *The Realm of Redemption: Studies in the Doctrine of the Nature of the Church in Contemporary Protestant Theology*. By J. Robert Nelson." *Scottish Journal of Theology* 6, no. 3 (September 1953): 320–25.
———. "A Right-About-Turn for the Kirk." *Presbyterian Record* 105, no. 10 (November 1981): 30–32.
———. *Royal Priesthood*. Edinburgh: Oliver and Boyd, 1955.
———. "Salvation Is of the Jews." *Evangelical Quarterly* 22 (1950): 164–73.
———. *The School of Faith*. London: James Clarke, 1959.
———. "Science, Theology, Unity." *Theology Today* 21 (1964): 149–54.
———. *Scottish Theology: From John Knox to John Mcleod Campbell*. Edinburgh: T&T Clark, 1996.
———. "A Serious Call for a Return to a Devout and Holy Life." *Life and Work* (July 1979): 14–15.

———. "A Sermon on the Trinity." *Biblical Theology* 6, no. 2 (1956): 40–44.

———. *Space, Time and Incarnation*. Edinburgh: T&T Clark, 1997.

———. *Space, Time and Resurrection*. London: T&T Clark, 2000.

———. "Student Years—Edinburgh to Basel, 1934–1938." Box 10: Student Years—Edinburgh to Basel. Thomas F. Torrance Manuscript Collection, Princeton Theological Seminary.

———. "A Study in New Testament Communication." *Scottish Journal of Theology* 3, no. 3 (1950): 298–313.

———. "Summary of the Urgent Call to the Kirk." Box 96: Urgent Call to the Kirk—Description of, instructions, May 1983. Thomas F. Torrance Manuscript Collection, Princeton Theological Seminary.

———. *Theological and Natural Science*. Eugene, OR: Wipf and Stock, 2002.

———. "Theological Realism." In *The Philosophical Frontiers of Christian Theology, Essays Presented to D. M. MacKinnon*. Edited by B. Hebbelethwaite and S. Sutherland. Cambridge: Cambridge University Press, 1982, 169–96.

———. *Theological Science*. Edinburgh: T&T Clark, 1996.

———. "Theology and the Church." Box 22: Theology and the Church. Thomas F. Torrance Manuscript Collection, Princeton Theological Seminary.

———. "Theology and the Common Man." *Life and Work: The Record of the Church of Scotland* (1940): 177–78.

———. *Theology in Reconciliation*. Eugene, OR: Wipf and Stock, 1996.

———. *Theology in Reconstruction*. Grand Rapids, MI: Eerdmans, 1965.

———. "Thomas Ayton's 'The Original Constitution of the Christian Church.'" In *Reformation and Revolution: Essays Presented to the Very Reverend Principal Emeritus Hugh Watt on the Sixtieth Anniversary of His Ordination*. Edited by Duncan Shaw. Edinburgh: Saint Andrew Press, 1967.

———. "Thomas Torrance Responds." In *The Promise of Trinitarian Theology: Theologians in Dialogue with T. F. Torrance*. Edited by Elmer M. Colyer, 303–40. Lanham, MD: Rowman & Littlefield, 2001.

———. "The Tide Has Turned." *Life and Work* (March 1984): 14–15.

———. "Tom Torrance's Reply on Israel." *Life and Work* (July 1989): 33–34.

———. *Transformation and Convergence in the Frame of Knowledge: Explorations in the Interrelations of Scientific and Theological Enterprise*. Eugene, OR: Wipf and Stock, 1998.

———. "The Transforming Power of Jesus Christ." *Life and Work* 32, no. 7 (July 1976): 8–10, 22.

———. *The Trinitarian Faith*. Edinburgh: T&T Clark, 1993.

———. *Trinitarian Perspectives: Toward Doctrinal Agreement*. Edinburgh: T&T Clark, 1994.

———. "Trinity Sunday Sermon on Acts 2:41–47." *Ekklesiastikos Pharos* 52 (1970): 191–99.

———. "Universalism or Election?" *Scottish Journal of Theology* 2, no. 3 (1949): 310–18.

———. "War Service." Box 10: War Service. Thomas F. Torrance Manuscript Collection, Princeton Theological Seminary.

———. "The Way of Reunion." *Christian Century* 71 (1954): 204–5.

———. "We Are Learning Together: The Ecumenical Movement, Another Great Movement of the Gospel." *Life and Work* (August 1954): 197–98.

———. "We Need a Decisive Theology before We Can Restate the Creed." *British Weekly*, May 15, 1941.

———. "What Is the Church?" *Ecumenical Review* 11, no. 1 (October 1958): 6–21.

———. "What Is the Reformed Church?" *Biblical Theology* 9 (1959): 51–62.

———. "What Is 'the Substance of the Faith'?" *Life and Work* (November 1982): 16–17.

———. *When Christ Comes and Comes Again*. Eugene, OR: Wipf and Stock, 1996.

———. "Where Is the Church of Scotland Going?" *Life and Work* (May 1989): 24–26.

———. "Why I'd Turn the Kirk Upside Down." *Scotsman*, May 17, 1977.

———. "The Word of God and the Nature of Man." In *Reformation Old and New: Festschrift for Karl Barth*. Edited by F. W. Camfield, 121–41. London: Lutterworth Press, 1947.

———. "The Word of God and the Response of Man." *Bijdragen: Tijdschrift voor filosofie en theologie* 30, no. 2 (1969): 172–83.

———, ed. *Theological Dialogue between Orthodox and Reformed Churches 1*. Volume 1. Edinburgh: Scottish Academic Press, 1985.

———, ed. *Theological Dialogue between Orthodox and Reformed Churches 2*. Volume 2. Edinburgh: Scottish Academic Press, 1993.

Various Authors, Correspondence from Churches. Box 96: Correspondence from Churches and Church Organisations June–July 1983. Thomas F. Torrance Special Collection, Princeton Theological Seminary.

Walker, Andrew. "Interview with Professor Thomas F. Torrance." In *Different Gospels*. London: Hodder and Stoughton, 1988.

Webster, John. "On Evangelical Ecclesiology." In *Confessing God: Essays in Christian Dogmatics II*, 153–93. New York: T&T Clark International, 2005.

———. "T. F. Torrance on Scripture." *Scottish Journal of Theology* 65, no. 1 (2012): 34–63.

———. *Thomas Forsyth Torrance, 1913–2007*. Volume 13. Biographical Memoirs of Fellows of the British Academy: British Academy, 2014.

———. *Word and Church*. Edinburgh: T&T Clark, 2001.

Wilks, John G. F. "The Trinitarian Ontology of John Zizioulas." *Vox Evangelica* 25 (1995): 63–88.

Williams, Rowan. "Eastern Orthodox Theology." In *The Modern Theologians*. Edited by David Ford, 572–88. Malden, MA: Blackwell, 2005.

Yeung, Jason Hing-Kau. *Being and Knowing: An Examination of T. F. Torrance's Christological Science*. Hong Kong: Alliance Bible Seminary, 1996.

Ziegler, Geordie. *Trinitarian Grace and Participation: An Entry into the Theological Thought of Thomas F. Torrance*. Minneapolis, MN: Fortress Press, 2017.

Zizioulas, John D. *Being as Communion: Studies in Personhood and the Church*. New York: St. Vladimir's University Press, 1985.

———. "The Church as Communion." *St. Vladimir's Theological Quarterly* 38, no. 1 (1994): 3–16.

———. *Communion and Otherness: Further Studies in Personhood and the Church*. London: T&T Clark, 2006.

Index

About the Author

Kate Tyler is interested in developing theology that serves the Church. She holds a bachelor of theology degree from Bishopdale College, a postgraduate diploma in theology from Laidlaw College, and a PhD in systematic theology from the University of Otago. Her studies focused on the ecclesiology of Thomas Torrance and what it has to say to the Church in the twenty-first century. Since receiving her PhD in 2016, she has been college director at Bishopdale College in Nelson, New Zealand. With significant diversity in her denominational history and a preference for simply being identified as a Jesus-follower, Kate and her husband Chris worship at All Saints Anglican Church.